THE COMPLETE ILLUSTRATED ENCYCLOPEDIA OF

SAINTS

THE COMPLETE ILLUSTRATED ENCYCLOPEDIA OF
SAINTS

AN AUTHORITATIVE VISUAL GUIDE TO THE LIVES AND WORKS OF OVER 500 SAINTS,
WITH EXPERT COMMENTARY AND OVER 500 BEAUTIFUL PAINTINGS, STATUES & ICONS

TESSA PAUL

CONSULTANT: FATHER RONALD CREIGHTON-JOBE

HERMES
HOUSE

CONTENTS

INTRODUCTION

What does it mean to be a saint? What individuals and groups have been conferred this honour? What characteristics single out an individual as deserving of sainthood, and by what process is a saint chosen and canonized? This book seeks to answer these questions and more, presenting an accurate explanation of the mysterious company of saints while largely avoiding the distraction of theological debates.

The work is divided into three sections. The first section, Sainthood, explores the importance of saints in the Roman Catholic Church and charts the progression of sainthood from the early Church to modern

Above Mosaic of martyrs in the Basilica Sant'Appolinare Nuovo, Ravenna, Italy (5th and 6th centuries).

Above left St Paraskeva (Byzantine icon, 15th century). Above centre Archangel Michael (Demetrius Matthiosi, 20th century). Above right St Menas (Palestinian icon, 17th century).

times. The second section, the Directory of Saints, tells the story of sainthood through the biographies of selected saints, listed in chronological order. Beautiful illustrations throughout show how these saints have been represented in art. The third section, the Gazetteer of Other Saints, deals briefly with a number of more obscure, interesting saints.

During the long and complex history of Christianity, sainthood has been invested with many different meanings. However, many characteristics of sainthood are agreed upon. Whether a saint devotes their life to God, or demonstrates their holiness in secular life, they must be a person of great faith and religious devotion. A saint can be born to grace, or a reformed character, but whatever path their life has traced, they must show certain characteristics that make them "heroic", such as piety, fortitude, humility and courage.

Saints, having been awarded a privileged place in heaven, are thought to be close to God and able to function as intermediaries between the human and the divine. This combines with the human achievements of the saints to make them exemplars of virtue that the faithful can turn to in times of need. The importance of saints for particular people, professions and countries is seen in the adoption of "patron" saints by these groups.

This book examines various aspects of sainthood – such as miracles, martyrdom and relics – and shows how they have changed in nature and importance throughout the ages. It describes the process of canonization and the diverse ways in which the qualities of sainthood have manifested themselves over time, from martyrdom to missionary work.

The response of believers to the company of saints is described and the official attitudes of both the Roman Catholic and the Orthodox Churches are examined. However, the focus here is on Roman Catholic saints and feast days, because the complex subject of Orthodox saints deserves its own study.

Modern readers may dismiss the extravagant legends of the early saints as untrue, but the number of new saints that have been created may also surprise those outside the Roman Catholic Church. However, even the sceptical must applaud the shining example of devotion and sacrifice made by the recently canonized.

The wide range of people who have achieved sainthood is fascinating, for this special company does not recognize wealth, social status or professional achievement, and thus the canon includes peasants, merchants and kings. The Directory of Saints is also interspersed with essays on special groups who have been accorded saintly status, such as the Holy Family, the Apostles and martyrs, taken to represent much larger groups whose tragic sacrifices have left no trace in the historical record.

The study of saints is fraught with difficulty; many saints have been forgotten over time, while thousands of names are obscure or entirely absent from the historical record. There are more than 4,000 saints in the Roman Catholic canon and the selection made here is not intended to be comprehensive or exclusive. Instead, the purpose of this work is to show that while all Christian saints are identical in their devotion to God, each one has their own talent and personality, and their own story of struggle.

Above The Wilton Diptych *(right wing) showing the Madonna and angels (French School, c.1395).*

SAINTHOOD

The company of saints is filled with souls from all walks of life. These former human beings have been granted the highest accolade that their fellow Christians can give in honour of their holiness and worldly achievements.

In this section, Sainthood, there is a clear explanation of the qualities a person must show before they are officially recognized as a saint. Many have devoted their lives to spreading the word of God, others have sacrificed their own well-being for the welfare of their fellow men, women and children. Believers choose candidates for sainthood from a spontaneous understanding of their superior qualities as humans, but the Church is more circumspect in granting this status.

Official and non-official attitudes within the Church are given a full history, and the religious beliefs surrounding saints are clearly described. Also covered is the alteration of custom and religious practice brought by the religious wars of the Reformation, a change that affected the regard in which saints are now held. Ritual expressions of faith, such as pilgrimages and the veneration of shrines and relics, are analysed in both historic and modern expressions. Feast days and the festivals that have developed around these occasions are discussed. The reasoning behind certain saints being selected as patrons of nations, professions and causes is explained. This is not a history of the Church, but a revelation of the role saints play in art and the prayers of the faithful.

Left Detail of Procession in St Mark's Square *(Gentile Bellini, c.1500).*

Top Twelfth Night Altarpiece *on wood. St Ursula and companions (left), the Adoration of the Kings (middle) and St Gereon with companions (right) (Stefan Lochner, c.1440).*

WHAT IS A SAINT?

A SAINT IS A DEAD INDIVIDUAL WHOSE EXCEPTIONAL HOLINESS CHRISTIANS BELIEVE HAS EARNED HIM OR HER A PLACE IN HEAVEN. THERE, SAINTS ACT AS CELESTIAL AGENTS. THE FAITHFUL MAY PRAY TO THEM AND BESEECH THEM TO CONVEY THEIR PRAYERS TO GOD.

Above Detail from the Communion of the Apostles, *a 15th-century fresco at Platanistasa in Cyprus.*

Saints are not gods, they are not worshipped. But they are believed to exist so close to God in heaven that they fulfil a key role as intermediaries for the Roman Catholic and Eastern Orthodox Churches.

Lacking the temerity to approach God directly, worshippers call upon these holy souls for assistance. In 1545, the defining Council of Trent stated that the saints, who "reign" with Christ, offer people's prayers to God to obtain his benefits.

A Christian mystic once described the feelings of all believers when he said, "We worship Christ, as the Son of God; as to the saints, we love them as the disciples and imitators of the Lord."

CULT FOLLOWING

From the earliest days of the Church, the cultus of veneration developed to include figures besides Jesus who were deemed to be holy. Their lives, which showed great piety and humility, served as inspiration to the inchoate community of believers.

On the day of their death, these holy individuals were believed to have been reborn into God's presence. Possessing this elevated status, the saints quickly developed cult followings. Their death was commemorated with a feast day at which time typically

Right From the early Renaissance, Madonna Enthroned with Saints *(Domenico Ghirlandaio, 1484).*

the faithful would gather at the saint's tomb. The bodily remains, or relics, were believed to possess power. Not only were saints in a privileged position to get prayers answered, they could also work fabulous miracles.

MARTYRS

The judgement of an individual's imitation of Christ in this early period of Christianity was concerned as much with the manner of their death as with the conduct of their life. A martyr – he who dies for the Christian faith – became an automatic choice for the company of saints. As the Church grew, especially

once the pope became the sole authority in conferring such status in the 2nd millennium, other factors became as important, if not more so, in determining a saint.

HEROIC VIRTUE

Those who did not die a martyr had to be shown by their cultus to have led a life of "heroic virtue", as it is defined by the Vatican. In Christian terms, this means they must have abandoned worldly interests. Whatever their station in life, whether prince or pauper, their devotion to faith in Jesus had to be manifest in their humility, charity and prayer.

As bureaucracy and suspicion played ever greater roles in the assessment process, so fewer saints were created. The late John Paul II did much to rationalize and clarify the procedure of canonization (literally, adding a name to the canon of saints).

SINNERS REDEEMED

Not all saints led virtuous lives from beginning to end. Some were formerly tyrants, thieves or prostitutes before they turned to Christ. Even St Paul once cheered the stoning of the martyr St Stephen. St Pelagia was a harlot.

But these lives inspire believers, who feel hope when they learn that anyone might be redeemed through devotion. Perhaps St Paul summed up the quality of sainthood best when he said, "I live, yet not I, but Christ liveth in me."

Right A panel showing Christ and the apostles at Pentecost (Georgian School, 12th century).

SAINTS IN OTHER FAITHS

Veneration of holy people, as messengers of the Almighty, has a place outside the Christian faith, too. Judaism refers to a category of holy figures known as Tzadikkim. In Islam, certain holy men, known as *Sufis*, are remembered with festivals. Thousands of Muslims in Pakistan, for example, commemorate the life and death of a 12th-century Sufi, Lal Shahbaz Qalandar, with sacred songs and dances performed by dervishes (followers of Sufism).

In Hinduism, *Sadhus*, or holy men, are considered to have reached saintly status while still alive. Likewise in Buddhism, *Arhats* are monks who are considered to have reached a state of nirvana.

Although there are some similarities in concept between the faiths, each has its own meaning. None are identical with that of Christian sainthood, which constitutes a unique doctrine of heavenly community.

Right Dancing dervishes from a Persian miniature (c.1650).

SAINTS IN THE EARLY CHURCH

THE FIRST CHRISTIANS WERE FORBIDDEN TO PRACTISE THEIR FAITH AND WERE CRUELLY PERSECUTED BY THE ROMANS. MANY EVEN DIED FOR THEIR BELIEFS. THESE MARTYRS WERE HONOURED AS SAINTS BY THEIR FELLOW BELIEVERS IN THE EARLY CHURCH.

There has never been any argument over the saintly status of the Holy Family, or the apostles and friends of Jesus on earth, but other saints have had slower recognition, or their status has been disputed. The earliest figures chosen for sainthood were usually those who died as martyrs.

Christianity was born in Palestine, a land that was then part of the Roman Empire. The Roman authorities who had condemned Jesus to death forbade any practice of his faith. Periodic state persecutions of Christians were merciless.

Whole communities who refused to abandon their faith were massacred, and some individuals suffered hideous torture. Some, dressed in rags with no weapon, were pitted against well-armed Roman gladiators, or fierce beasts. Thousands were murdered. While the names of many survive, we know few details beyond the date, and perhaps the place, of their death.

Records of these martyrs, the first Christians, can be read in the grave inscriptions found in the catacombs of Rome where the dead were laid to rest.

EARLIEST MARTYRS

The first martyr (protomartyr) known to us was murdered about five years after the death of Christ. St Stephen was carried to the outskirts of Jerusalem and stoned to death. As he fell to his knees, he cried out, "Lord, lay not this sin to their charge." Thus, in his dying, he showed his belief in

Below The martyrdom of St Erasmus as illustrated in the Golden Legend, *a 13th-century hagiography of saints written by Jacobus de Voragine.*

Above St Agnes, fellow virgins and singing angels in an altarpiece from the Upper Rhine (c.1460).

Jesus' message of love and forgiveness towards the wrongdoer. Many of the early martyrs showed a similar courage in their deaths. St Catherine of Alexandria endured the cruel spikes of a wheel. St Lucy refused to forsake her faith, even under torture, and was savagely beheaded.

It must be accepted that many legends grew up around the martyrs. For instance, although Lucy's tormentors had gouged out her eyes, it was said that she could fit them back into their sockets. Likewise, it was said that divine intervention broke Catherine's wheel, rescuing her from pain. Sebastian survived being tied to a column and shot through by a shower of arrows. And when Januarius was thrown to the lions, the beasts refused to attack him, instead laying quiescent at his feet. There are accounts of saints being thrown into vats of boiling oil and

emerging unscathed. Others who suffered a beheading were said to have merely replaced their heads.

BLESSED VIRGINS

Many of the earliest female saints were chosen not only for their status as martyrs, but also for their purity in imitation of the Blessed Virgin. The importance of virginity has always been a strong (but not essential) consideration in the sainthood of women. As late as the 15th century, when St Joan of Arc claimed this status, she was given humiliating physical inspections to test the truth of her words.

During the Roman persecutions, St Agnes, at the age of 14, consecrated her virginity to Christ. She refused marriage, and both her faith and innocence were put to the sword. St Irene, a young girl, was forced by the Romans to go naked into a brothel, but she radiated such purity that no man dared go near

her. She was martyred in AD 305. In the same century the most extravagant legend of proud virgins involves the British St Ursula and her 11,000 virgin companions. Forced to flee their homelands to avoid "violation" through marriage, they finally reached Germany. There they were martyred for their beliefs, yet they died joyously.

TRUTH IN LEGEND

Sceptics tend to dismiss these tales. But Christians honour them because they symbolize the superhuman courage and piety of the persecuted, and confirm that all suffering is eased by faith in Christ. As the novelist Sir Arthur Conan Doyle once said, "a legend however exaggerated upon fact is its own fact, witnessing belief." Although in many cases these stories are embellishments of a terrible reality, they still hold a certain truth for believers.

CATACOMBS OF ROME

Beneath the city of Rome lies a great labyrinth of caves and tunnels. Probably first used by pagans as burial grounds, the early Christians tunnelled into this underground world to lay their dead. Some of the catacombs had been dug out to form large halls with connecting chapels. Recesses were hollowed out to hold three or four bodies apiece. They were sealed with slabs of marble or tiles bearing inscriptions and motifs. The labyrinth was also used as a place of refuge to escape Roman persecutors. By the late 4th century AD, the catacombs were no longer burial vaults but pilgrimage sites, which are still visited today.

Above The interior of a catacomb in Rome dating from the 3rd century AD.

Left One of the 40 martyrs of Sebaste being killed in AD 320, during the Roman persecution of Christians under the rule of Emperor Licinius (Byzantine, 12th century).

DOCTORS OF THE CHURCH

LEADERS EMERGED FROM THE EARLY CHRISTIAN COMMUNITIES TO HELP DEVELOP THE STRUCTURE OF THE CHURCH. LEARNED WRITERS AND THINKERS AMONG THEM WHO MADE SIGNIFICANT CONTRIBUTIONS WERE CALLED "DOCTORS OF THE CHURCH".

A landmark change in the fortunes of the Church occurred early in the 4th century AD when Emperor Constantine I converted to Christianity. His edict permitting the worship of all faiths meant saints were no longer chosen primarily for their martyrdom. More important was the purity of a life dedicated to Christ. Some did so by renouncing the world, others played key roles in developing the Church for the benefit of the flock.

Scholarly writers and thinkers worked on formulating doctrine for the Church. Some helped develop new forms of prayer and

Above St Augustine of Hippo *(Piero della Francesca, 15th century).*

ritual. The greatest among these learned Christians were the early "Doctors of the Church", a term meaning great teachers. Unlike other saints who are championed by the people, the Church authorities alone decide who is worthy to receive this title.

GREAT TEACHERS

To be recognized as a Doctor, the saint must formulate a special doctrine. Alternatively, he or she may make a profound interpretation of the faith, as well as having a "remarkable holiness" of life.

St Jerome (c.AD 341–420), who started his life as a monk, translated the Bible from Greek into Latin. St Ambrose interpreted the significance of the sacraments, and

Left Detail of St Ambrose from the fresco Doctors of the Church *(Giotto di Bondone, 13th century).*

defended the authority vested in the office of the pope. St Gregory the Great (c.AD 540–604) was a successful missionary, notably directing the conversion of the English. St Augustine of Hippo's interpretation of Christ's message profoundly influenced Christian moral principles.

MODERN DECLARATIONS

Recognition as a Doctor of the Church could be a long process, sometimes taking centuries to complete. Sts Ambrose, Jerome, Augustine of Hippo and Gregory the Great all lived before the 8th century, but they were not declared Doctors until Pope Benedict XIV came to office in 1740.

The tradition of creating doctorships still continues today. St Theresa of Lisieux (1873–97) was declared a Doctor by John Paul II in 1997 for her simple but inspirational devotion. She is now one of the most popular of saints.

Above St Gregory in the Golden Legend *(Jacobus de Voragine, c.1370).*

DESERT FATHERS

Christ said, "If any man will follow me, let him deny himself, take up his cross and follow me" (Mark 8:34). In the first centuries of Christianity, there were believers who took these words as a direction to forsake all earthly pleasure. They followed the example of John the Baptist in hoping that hardship would wash away their sinful selves, and isolated themselves from society by living in deserts and other uninhabited places.

They led harsh lives, with little food. Legends say they were fed by ravens or wolves, and that water gushed from stony wastelands. The genuine humility and devotion shown by these ascetics attracted others, and soon groups of hermits chose to inhabit huts and caves close to each other.

From these loose communities, particularly those in Egypt, emerged teachers known as the "Desert Fathers". First among them was St Pachomius who lived alone on the banks of the Nile until other ascetics gathered around him. Some were so fanatical in their contempt for their own bodies they risked starvation and madness. To impose some constraints, Pachomius set up a community of 100 followers who committed to abide by his "Rules". To vows of chastity, poverty and obedience, he added orders of prayer and routine.

By his death, c.AD 346, Pachomius had founded ten monasteries, among the first such Christian institutions. Another popular Egyptian hermit of the 4th century, St Antony, also organized a monastic community. Over the centuries many other founders have established similar orders.

Above This 12th-century wall painting from Macedonia depicts St Antony, sometimes referred to as "the eremite" for his desert life.

EASTERN SAINTS

THE CHURCHES OF RUSSIA, EASTERN EUROPE AND THE MIDDLE
EAST DEVELOPED THEIR OWN THEOLOGY, VARYING FROM THAT OF
ROMAN CATHOLICISM. EASTERN SAINTS FORM A DISTINCT
COMPANY AND EVOKE A PARTICULAR KIND OF VENERATION.

The Eastern Church treats its
saints in a slightly different
way from that of Rome. Saints
are not approached primarily as a means of conveying
prayers to God, but rather to
bring the believer closer to
the reality of God. The
reason for this difference
lies in the Eastern Church's
separate development in
history from the West.

A formal schism between
Western and Eastern
Christians in 1054 led to
the formation of a branch of
Christendom known as the

Eastern Orthodox Church. The
two branches of Christianity had
different beliefs about the
dual nature of Christ, as
both man and God.

The Roman Catholic
and Orthodox Churches
both believe that Christ is
the Son of God who nev-
ertheless assumed human
form. The Orthodox inter-
prets this to mean humans
can attain the spiritual

*Left An icon of St Gregory
Palamas (Russian School,
19th century).*

*Above Mosaic detail in the apse of
the Basilica Eufrasiana in Porec,
Croatia (4th century). The work
draws the eye to focus on the Blessed
Virgin and the Christ child.*

qualities of God; the Roman
Church believes humans can only
strive for these qualities.

The Orthodox Church has not
altered its dogma or ritual since
the 8th century. So tradition is
paramount, and the saints form a
key part of their worship.

EARLY HOLY FIGURES

Pre-eminent among the Eastern
saints is the Blessed Virgin. But
everyone who is in heaven is a
saint for the Orthodox, including
pre-Christian Jews such as Moses.
Popular early saints, such as John,
Nicholas of Myra, George and
Christopher, are common to
both branches, but post-medieval
saints are not.

The Orthodox categorize their
saints according to type: prophets
(those who foretold the coming of

*Left Detail from a manuscript
showing St Sergius of Radonezh
overseeing the building of a church
(Andrei Rublev, 15th century).*

Jesus), the apostles, martyrs, Church Doctors (or Fathers), monastics (Desert Fathers) and the just (those who imitate Christ).

St John Chrysostom is highly honoured as a preacher and teacher. In AD 398, he was elected as archbishop of Constantinople (now Istanbul) and is recognized as a Doctor of the Church.

Another Doctor is St Basil the Great (c.AD 330–79) who laid down rules of organization for monastic life. His friend, St Gregory of Nazianzus, also ranks high among Orthodox saints.

BYZANTINE MYSTICS

St Gregory's spiritual theology was developed by Simeon the New Theologian (d.1022) to reach a high point in Byzantine mysticism. Another Gregory, of

Below The transfiguration of Christ in an Armenian manuscript (1362).

Sinai (d.1346), devised new methods of meditation that influenced Orthodox practice. Other saints include Sergius of Radonezh (c.1315–92), monastic founder beloved of the Russians.

Mount Athos in Greece has a tradition of saintliness. Here the monk St Gregory Palamas (d.1359) founded an ascetical order, Hesychasm. Controversially it claimed visions of God's "uncreated light", an idea later accepted.

WINDOWS INTO HEAVEN

The Eastern Orthodox Church regards images of the holy saints as "windows of perception". It is believed these images open a vista leading to God. By so doing, they convey the message of the gospels.

Images of saints often appear on icons and architectural mosaics, rarely as statues. Depictions are lavishly decorated, with details worked in gold. In following the traditional Byzantine style of art, these images reflect the conservative nature of the Orthodox Church.

The icons are portable, being painted on three folding panels, and are designed as objects of meditation. By creating "a window into heaven", their contemplation and prayer increases the spirituality of the believer, bringing them closer to a knowledge of God.

Whether in church or at home, the icon is positioned with reverence. It may be surrounded by candles or placed near a crucifix, creating the appearance of a small altar. But the icon is never an object of worship. It is a symbol and an aid to spiritual awareness.

CANONIZATION

As the Church grew, its communities revered more and more devout figures as saints. The need to control the creation of sainthood resulted in the establishment of a system of universal recognition in a canon of holy souls.

Although some living people are described as saints, to be a real saint, the person must be dead. Up until the 4th century AD, when Christianity was adopted as the official religion of the Roman Empire, the devout were made saints only if they had died for their faith, for example were martyrs.

In the early, unstructured Church, groups began to identify individuals who, in their life and particularly in their death, imitated Christ. Such a group, known even today as a "cult" or "cultus", acknowledged the saintly qualities of the individual at their death.

The cultus prepared a joyous burial at which the death was celebrated with the eucharist. The

Below Pope John Paul II canonized 120 Chinese martyrs in a ceremony held in St Peter's Square, Rome, on 1 October 2000.

earthly remains, or relics, of the saint were carefully wrapped in an effort to preserve them. Every anniversary of the death called for a reunion of followers, and this day came to be known as the saint's "feast day".

GROWTH OF CULTUSES

The proclamation of these devout members of local communities as saints was based on no established criteria in the early period. Vague ideas of holiness based on manner of life and death were frequently supported by claims of miracles and visions.

By the 4th century AD, local priests or bishops were being drawn into debate on the worthiness of these decisions. In some cases, for instance, there was suspicion that a person had committed suicide in the hope of being granted the glory of a martyr-

Above Pope Pius II canonizes St Catherine of Siena (Pinturicchio, 16th century).

saint. This was a particular problem among the desert hermits of North Africa. So priests began to assess the claims of the cultuses.

Bishops saw formal procedures of investigation as the best way to tackle the growth of false cultuses. Priests kept records of saints and the reasons for their sanctification.

PAPAL SAINTS ONLY

At last, in the 12th century, the right to confer, or "canonize", sainthood was reserved for the Holy See, the office of the pope.

The official implementation of this development was attributed to Pope Alexander III (1159–81), though recent scholarship prefers Innocent III (1199–1216). From the 13th century, papal commissions were ordered to investigate claims to sainthood. The cultuses continued to select an individual but the commission required evidence that the candidate had lived a life worthy of Christ. Any claims

to miracles were to be thoroughly investigated by the Church. These rules are followed to this day, although in 1983 Pope John Paul II streamlined the regulations, making them more precise.

MAKING A SAINT

Step One: The cultus makes its choice of saint, but the local bishop does not automatically accept it. For five years after the candidate's death, he conducts research into his or her virtues, or the circumstances of martyrdom. This allows time for a calm assessment of the candidate's life and death.

Then, the bishop's approval is submitted to the Congregation for the Causes of Saints, a panel made up of theologians and cardinals of the Church. If the panel

DECANONIZATION

The Holy See knows the early saints have poor records, if any, to support their status. But it generally accepts the situation.

However, the Holy See did decanonize St Barbara in 1969 and Simon of Trent in 1965 because they were purely legendary characters. St Brigid of Ireland was accused of being a pagan figure, and so she too was decanonized.

Official announcements are often ignored. Cultuses can remain attached to saints, despite formal abolishment. In recognition of this loyalty, the Church has allowed certain cultuses to venerate "their" saint, but has withdrawn universal recognition.

Some decanonized saints in history include: Barbara, Brigid of Ireland, Christopher, George, Philomena, Simon of Trent, Valentine and William of Norwich.

approves, the name is submitted to the pope who then declares the candidate "Venerable".

Step Two: Martyrs will be canonized by the pope, but the Venerable must now be supported by a written claim from the recipient of a purported miracle performed by the holy candidate.

This miracle must occur after the death of the candidate. The believer must avow that they prayed to the Venerable who then interceded with God in answer to that prayer. This is seen as proof that the dead one's spirit is close to God. The pope approves the beatification of the candidate, who

Above Detail from a fresco showing the canonization of St Francis by Pope Gregory IX (Giotto di Bondone, c.1295).

can now be venerated by his or her cultus as "Blessed". Mother Teresa of Calcutta is an example.

Step Three: The third and last step towards sainthood needs evidence of one more miracle. When the pope has this, he agrees to canonize the beatified who is then named a saint. This status identifies the person as one who lived and died in imitation of Christ, and is officially in heaven. He or she can be honoured by all.

MYSTERIES AND MIRACLES

LEGENDS OF MIRACLES AND EXTRAORDINARY BRAVERY ARE WELL-
KNOWN ATTRIBUTES OF THE SAINTS, BUT SOME WERE WITNESSED
MANIFESTING MYSTERIOUS POWERS AND PHYSICAL CHANGES THAT
DEFY SCIENTIFIC EXPLANATION.

Saints were so named because they led lives in imitation of Christ. It followed therefore that, like Jesus, they might be capable of performing miracles. The early saints were credited with having all sorts of supernatural powers. Evil spirits, disease, mortal ene- mies and wild animals were all claimed to be overcome. The per- ceived holiness of saints and their closeness to God led the faithful to believe that their prayers might be answered, and in miraculous fashion, too. Once a devout Christian had been declared a

Above St Denys is said to have carried his severed head to his burial place, as shown in this stained glass window in St Aignan Church, Chartres, France.

saint, their lives often became embellished with events of the miraculous, such as inexplicable cures or angelic assistance.

VOICES AND VISIONS
St Joan of Arc claimed she had heard the voices of three saints instructing her to save France. The mystic and writer St Hildegard of Bingen described heavenly visions she experienced during her life. Crowds of people in Milan heard a unearthly child's voice calling out repeatedly, "Ambrose for bishop." The divine message persuaded them to elect Ambrose, despite him being unbaptized.

Another account of a divine apparition involved St Isidore the farmer, a humble, browbeaten peasant. He was so tired and in

Left St Januarius visited in prison by Proculus and Sosius *(Francesco Solimena, c.1700).*

such pain from beatings he could not work, but two angels appeared and ploughed the fields for him.

St Clement was said to have experienced a vision of Jesus while suffering extreme thirst digging a quarry under Roman coercion. The vision which came in answer to the saint's prayers was accompanied by a spring of water gushing suddenly from the rocks.

HEALING

The more obvious imitation of Christ involves miraculous cures reminiscent of his ministry, such as healing disease. St Odile, for example, was said to have been born blind, but was given sight after her baptism. During her life, she restored the sight of others.

Saints' relics were believed to have the power to effect miraculous cures. Pilgrims travelled great distances to be in the presence of a saint's tomb, so that they might receive the healing power believed to reside within the corpse.

The relics of St Martin, for instance, were said to ooze curative oil and the faithful would flock to his tomb for a mere dab. Likewise, in the 7th century, oil was said to weep from the tomb of St John the Baptist and bore the odour of the honey upon which he had survived.

RESCUE

Miraculous cures save the body from physical peril. Closely associated in terms of salvation are the rescues of individuals or whole communities from evil, frequently in the shape of a human enemy.

A painting of Our Lady of Czestochowa, commonly referred to as the Black Madonna, became the focus of Polish nationalism in the 14th century. When the Hussites overran the monastery of Jasna Gora (Mount of Light) in 1430, the painting was said to resist all attempts to destroy it. Every subsequent siege failed and Our Lady of Czestochowa was officially named Queen of Poland.

In times of war, saints are invoked for their protection, especially in great peril. And when victory comes against all odds, guardian angels and patron saints often receive the credit.

The blood of St Januarius has been revered in Naples ever since 1631 when Mt Vesuvius erupted. Subsequent prayers to the saint are believed to have prevented any repetition of such a disaster. Every year the vial containing the blood is displayed. If it liquefies the year will be free from disaster.

THE STIGMATA

The appearance of wounds on the hands, feet and in the ribs, in imitation of those made by the nails that pinned Christ to the Cross, are a phenomenon known as the stigmata. St Francis of Assisi was the first Christian to manifest the marks, in 1224, which remained on his body for two years until his death. Since then, the Catholic Church has recognized 62 men and women as stigmatics. Listed below are the best-known sufferers, some saints, others Blessed.

St Angela of Foligno
Blessed Baptista Varani
Blessed Carlo of Sezze
St Catherine of Genoa
Blessed Catherine of
   Racconigi
St Catherine de' Ricci
St Catherine of Siena
St Clare of Montefalco
St Colette
St Francis of Assisi
St Frances of Rome
St Gertrude
St John of God
St Lidwina
Blessed Lucy of Narnia
St Lutgardis

St Margaret of Cortona
Blessed Margaret Mary
   Alacoque
Blessed Marie de l'Incarnation
Blessed Mary Anne of Jesus
St Mary Frances of the Five
   Wounds
St Mary Magdalene de' Pazzi
Blessed Osanna of Mantua
Padre Pio (St Pius of Pietrelcina)
St Rita of Cascia
St Veronica Giuliani

Right St Francis of Assisi receiving the stigmata on the mountain of La Verna in Italy (School of Bonaventura Berlinghieri, 13th century).

HOLY RELICS

WHETHER SKELETON OR MERE SCRAP OF CLOTHING, RELICS WERE BELIEVED TO REPRESENT A SAINT'S PRESENCE ON EARTH. FOR THE DEVOUT, THEIR POWER WAS SUCH THAT EVEN SIGHT OF THESE ARTEFACTS WAS SAID TO EFFECT MIRACULOUS CURES.

From the earliest period of Christianity, the bodily remains of saints were venerated. A custom developed in which the saint's relics were no longer buried or laid in catacombs, but placed beneath church altars.

Churches sheltering relics were perceived by St Augustine of Hippo to be "as tombs of mortal men, whose spirits live with God". To this day, in the Roman Catholic Church, altars upon which mass is celebrated must contain the relics of a saint, according to canon law.

Gradually, the term "relic" embraced lengths of bone, scraps of burial wrappings, jewellery. Indeed, it could mean any little thing that had once belonged to the saint. The Church accepted this development because in the 1st century AD in Ephesus, Turkey, tradition held that God had performed miracles through the handkerchiefs and aprons of St Paul. The sick believed they had been cured simply through their proximity to Paul's clothing.

The faithful believed that their prayers for forgiveness were more likely to be heard when uttered before relics or tombs. Other believers claimed the very sight of the relic summoned forth the saint who, through God, might perform miraculous cures of any ailment, from warts to infertility.

COLLECTORS' ITEMS

Holy sites were not limited to the saints' burial places but included any site where a relic was housed. Their bodily relics became valuable, some fetching large sums, and were often plundered

Above A reliquary of the hand of St Thomas Becket kept at Burgos Cathedral, Spain.

THE HOLY HOUSE

The story attached to the "Holy House" of Loreto in Italy indicates the crazed, but profound, attachment medieval Christians had for their greatest saints.

According to the extravagant legend, an angel lifted the house in Nazareth where Joseph and the Virgin Mary had once lived, and carried it away. The house landed in random places before finally coming to rest in Loreto. The event was precisely recorded as ending on 7 September 1295. So many pilgrims flocked to see this wondrous relic, coined the "Holy House", that the authorities constructed an imposing church on the site. It continues to attract visitors.

Right The Basilica (Holy House) of Loreto, Italy, is one of the most revered sites in the Christian world. It was built in 1469 to house what is believed to be the miraculously transported home of the Virgin Mary.

by clergy and believers who strove to build up collections. In the process relics were moved – "translated" – from one place to another. There could be a finger at one church, a shinbone elsewhere, while a third might claim to have a saint's sandal or cloak.

The faithful might ideally have wished to visit tombs, but a relic would serve just as well. It held the power of the saint. Even the churches of Jerusalem, whose significance rested on their association with the sites of Jesus' passion, boasted ownership of the relics of the True Cross upon which the Saviour had suffered crucifixion.

Every Christian pilgrim longed to visit the shrine of a saint, and many collected relics. The more precious items were kept in beautiful caskets, known as reliquaries, shaped like small tombs.

These containers were wrought in precious metals and adorned with jewels and enamelled images. Many are treasured to this day in Roman Catholic and Eastern Orthodox churches, although most are housed in museums across Europe and the USA.

STRANGE AND BIZARRE

Some of the more interesting relics include a small carving of St Foy (also known as St Faith), from the 9th century. The figure is covered in gold plate and, over the centuries, believers bedecked the surface with precious emeralds, pearls and amethysts. This martyr was just 12 years old when she died. In the back of the carving there is a cavity containing her tiny wrapped skull.

Pope Urban V had the head of St Cassian encased in an elaborate casket. But Charlemagne (Charles the Great AD 747–814), emperor

of the Holy Roman Empire, did better than that. He built a cathedral to house his huge collection of relics.

Among them, he claimed, were the cloth that once wrapped the decapitated head of John the Baptist, the tunic of the Virgin Mary, and swaddling cloths of the Infant Jesus. His collection of relics was displayed every seven years for a week in July. Vast crowds visited the church in Aachen, formerly Aix-la-Chapelle. The custom is still followed, revealing 200 relics every seventh year.

Right A reliquary of St Foy (also known as St Faith) made of gold and jewels, held in the church in Conques, France (9th century).

Above left This reliquary depicts the martyrdom of the Roman St Candidus. It is made of nutwood and covered in gold and silver (c.1165).

Above Reliquary of St Stephen with enamel work from Limoges (12th century).

MEDIEVAL PILGRIMAGE

A JOURNEY TO VISIT THE SACRED RELICS OF A SAINT WAS AN IMPORTANT ACT OF DEVOTION IN THE MIDDLE AGES. THE HEALING POWER BELIEVED TO RESIDE IN THEM, AND THE SPIRITUAL ENERGY ASSOCIATED WITH THEIR SHRINES, DREW HORDES OF PILGRIMS.

Early Christians believed it an important act of piety to pray at the places where the Saviour and his company of saints had lived and died. A pilgrimage involved hardship. It was a form of penance, a humble mission to offer prayers of contrition, and call on the saints to intercede with God. From as early as the 2nd century AD, records tell of Christians travelling great distances on foot to the Holy Land in order to visit Bethlehem and Jerusalem.

They would have had a hard job, for these sites in Palestine were lost after AD 132, when the Roman emperor Hadrian demolished Jerusalem and rebuilt the city with temples dedicated to

Roman gods. Only in AD 326, when Emperor Constantine I ordered Christian bishops to find the sites of Christ's passion, were shrines and churches built there.

One such site, the Holy Sepulchre, built by Constantine himself, stands to this day, albeit with some modification. The emperor's mother, St Helen, also a convert, founded churches in the Holy Land which drew yet more pilgrims.

HEART OF THE EMPIRE

Outside the Holy Land, the most significant destination was Rome. Here the tombs and relics of the Holy Martyrs, including Sts Peter and Paul, were located. In AD 326,

Above The chapel at Aachen Minster was built AD 788–805 for Emperor Charlemagne to house his huge collection of relics.

St Helen brought to the city a marble staircase taken from the judgement hall of Pontius Pilate in Jerusalem. Purported to be the very steps upon which Christ had trodden as he went to his trial, these Holy Stairs were installed in the church of St John Lateran, and are said to be stained with Christ's blood. To this day, pilgrims climb the 28 stairs on their knees.

ROADS THROUGH EUROPE

In England, thousands trekked to Canterbury to see the relics of St Thomas Becket, or made their way to Norfolk to pray before the holy shrine of Our Lady of Walsingham. Pilgrims took the Via Francigena, a popular route from Canterbury to Rome.

On the way was Paris, with Christ's crown of thorns, and Chartres, which held the holy tunic of the Virgin Mary. Pilgrims

Left An illustration from John Lydgate's The Troy Book and The Siege of Thebes, *shows pilgrims leaving Canterbury for London (1412–22).*

flocked to Tours, where the relics of St Martin were kept. And Cologne, in Germany, possessed the relics of the Magi, the three wise men who visited the stable to pay homage to the baby Jesus.

Once in Italy, pilgrims could glimpse the Holy Shroud of Jesus in Turin. And travelling on south-wards, they would throng the streets of Assisi where St Francis was buried. From all over Europe, devout Christians journeyed to Santiago de Compostela in Spain, where the relics of St James the Great lay in his tomb.

IMPACT OF REFORM

Pilgrimage had become so popular, even hysterical in its folksy enthusiam, that the whole activity invited disdain in some quarters. The bishop of Salisbury was moved to describe the veneration of relics as "abominable idolatry".

In 1517, the German priest Martin Luther introduced a radical idea. He argued Christians

NEW MARTYR SAINTS

A major consequence of the Reformation (1517–1648) was that new martyrs joined the company of saints. Hundreds of Welsh and English Roman Catholics were burnt, crushed between milling stones or beheaded by Protestants during the religious strife.

Some deaths were political in intent, and since then 200 have been named as martyrs. In 1970, Pope Paul VI found 40 to be worthy of canonization. They are known as the Forty Martyrs of England and Wales. Of these, 13 were priests, 20 monks and friars, and the remaining 7 consisted of lay men and women.

could approach God for forgiveness, without the intercession of the saints. So began the great division in the Church, the Reformation, which separated Christians into Roman Catholics and Protestants.

As Christendom became a battlefield, shrines were destroyed and relics burnt. In England, the shrine of St Thomas Becket was melted down to enrich the king's coffers, and the beautiful shrine in Walsingham violated.

Even Luther, the angry reformer, was distressed at such destruction wrought by the mobs. After these calamitous events, relics no longer gripped the reli-

Above The Church of the Holy Sepulchre in Jerusalem, c.AD *335, commemorates the tomb of Christ and is a special place of pilgrimage.*

gious mind. Pilgrimages, too, lost their worldly appeal and were not the major social events they were in the pre-Reformation period.

Instead, pilgrimages reverted to being the pious causes of penance they had once been. Modern believers still honour relics, even venerate them, especially on feast days. Some recently canonized saints, such as the Aztec peasant Juan Diego, command huge followings of pilgrims who come to witness their relics.

IMPORTANT FEAST DAYS

FEAST DAYS, TRADITIONALLY SET TO MARK THE DAY OF THE SAINT'S DEATH, ARE A CELEBRATION OF BIRTH INTO HEAVEN. CHURCHES CONDUCT SPECIAL MASSES, AS WELL AS PUBLIC EVENTS OUTDOORS. PROCESSIONS, MUSIC AND DANCE INVOLVE THE WHOLE COMMUNITY.

Roman Catholics and members of the Orthodox Churches venerate the saints' feast days in their liturgy. Important saints are celebrated on these days with special processions, particularly when the church houses their relics and images.

JANUARY
Gregory of Nazianzus, Basil the
  Great 2
Genevieve 3
Elizabeth Seton 4
Sava 14
Antony of Egypt 17
Sebastian 20
John the Almsgiver 23
Thomas Aquinas 28

FEBRUARY
Brigid of Ireland 1
Agatha 5

Below Russian priests celebrating the feast day of St Cyril and St Methodius, known as "apostles to the Slavs", in 2007.

Jerome Emiliani 8
Valentine, Cyril and
  Methodius 14
Martyrs of China 17

MARCH
David of Wales, Gregory of
  Nyssa 1
Katharine Drexel 3
Patrick, Joseph of Arimathea 17
Joseph (husband of Mary) 19
Cuthbert 20

APRIL
Isidore of Seville 4
John-Baptist de La Salle 7
Teresa of Los Andes 12
Bernadette of Lourdes 16
Anselm 21
George 23
Mark 25
Catherine of Siena 29

MAY
John 6
Pachomius (West) 9
Helen with Constantine (East) 21
Rita of Cascia 22

Above Thomas Aquinas being received into the Dominican order (German School, 16th century). His feast day is 28 January.

Madeleine Sophie Barat,
  Bede 25
Philip Neri, Augustine of
  Canterbury 26
Bernard of Montjoux 28
Joan of Arc 30

JUNE
Justin 1
Martyrs of Uganda 3
Boniface 5
Martha (East) 6
Columba of Iona 9
Antony of Padua 13
Thomas More 22
John the Baptist 24
Peter and Paul 29

JULY
Thomas 3
Athanasius the Aconite 5
Benedict 11
Mary Magdalene 22
Bridget of Sweden 23
Christopher, James the Great 25

Anne (West) 26
Martha (West) 29
Ignatius of Loyola 31

AUGUST
Jean-Baptiste Vianney 4
Fourteen Holy Helpers,
  Dominic 8
Edith Stein 9
Clare of Assisi 11
Maximilian Kolbe 14
Mary, the Blessed Virgin
  (Assumption) 15
Stephen of Hungary 16
Rose of Lima 23
Augustine of Hippo 28

SEPTEMBER
Gregory the Great 3
John Chrysostom (West) 13
Hildegard of Bingen 17
Matthew 21
Padre Pio 23
Sergius of Radonezh, Firmin 25
Wenceslas 28
Archangel Michael 29

Below The running of the bulls in Pamplona takes place on 7 July, the day the relics of St Fermin, a popular local saint, came to the town.

Above St Athanasius the Aconite, a Greek Father of the Church (print, 16th century). His feast day is 5 July.

OCTOBER
Theresa of Lisieux 1
Francis of Assisi 4
Denys of Paris, Martyrs of
  the Spanish Civil War 9
Edward the Confessor 13
Theresa of Ávila 15
Luke 18
Crispin and Crispinian 25
Simon, Jude 28

NOVEMBER
All Saints 1
All Souls 2
Malachy 3
Vincent Liem 7
Leo the Great (West) 10
Martin of Tours (West) 11
John Chrysostom (East) 13
Albert the Great 15
Elizabeth of Hungary 17
Cecilia 22
Alexander Nevski 23
Andrew 30

DECEMBER
Francis Xavier 3
Nicholas of Myra 6
Ambrose (West) 7
Eulalia of Mérida 10
Lucy 13
John of the Cross 14
Thomas 21
Stephen (West) 26
John 27
Holy Innocents (West) 28, (East) 9
Thomas Becket 29

Below The Feast of St Lucy (Carl Larsson, 20th century). On 13 December, the oldest girl in a Scandinavian family wears a crown of candles.

HEROES AND MARTYRS

REVERENCE FOR RELICS AND DEEP ATTACHMENT TO THE SAINTS DID NOT SIT WELL WITH ALL BELIEVERS. PROTESTANTS REGARDED THESE PASSIONS AS IDOLATRY, AN AFFRONT TO THE TRUE FAITH, AND THREW OUT THE SAINTS. YET THE IDEA OF HONOURING HEROES REMAINS.

Above A portrait of Martin Luther, the priest who started the Protestant movement (Lucas Cranach, the Elder, 1529). He is greatly honoured for his brave and radical reforms.

For more than a thousand years, Christendom guarded and reigned over Europe, Russia and Eastern Europe. The pope, his bishops, archbishops and clergy played a major role in economic and political life. The vast majority of the people recognized the authority of the Church. Even kings and queens, believed to be anointed by God to rule, formed an integral part of the system.

But by the 14th century, the Church was not the fervent, disciplined institution it once had been. Popes lived in splendour and

Below Protestant Martin Luther is shown here in triumph over Catholic Pope Leo X (woodcut, 1568).

priests were corruptible. The Reformation started as a call to return to the "purity" of early Christianity, and was not intended to create a major rift. However, great differences of opinion arose, and during the 15th and 16th centuries Christendom became a realm of war and disorder.

CRY FOR REFORM

Reformers insisted the individual was important to God and no person needed the intercession of saints or priests to reach him. They insisted that veneration of the saints was contrary to the teachings of the Bible. As a result, the Protestants, as reformers came to be known, refuted the need for

saints as intermediaries, and dismissed the rule that priests be ordained by the pope. In acts of rebellion against the Roman Church, Protestants in countries across northern Europe forbade all worship relating to saints: relics, shrines and pilgrimages

were all considered unnecessary and banned. Even images of the Blessed Virgin were prohibited.

EVENTS IN ENGLAND

However, the Church of England was born out of political need rather than religious fervour. Henry VIII (1491–1547) chafed under papal rule and rejected the authority of Rome.

A period of killings and torture of Roman Catholics under Henry was followed by a similar persecution of Protestants by Mary Tudor (1516–58). By the death of Elizabeth I in 1603, most English subjects had learnt to accept that their monarch, and not the pope, was the head of their Church. However, English Protestants did not reject all the practices of the Roman Church. Indeed, in the Preface to their new Book of Common Prayer, the English Church emphasized the continuation of "the main essentials".

Priests continued to be ordained (though not by the pope), and the saints were not abandoned. The English simply decided not to create any more. Their Church proclaimed that images, relics and the "invocation of the saints is a fond thing vainly invented…but rather repugnant to the Word of God".

CATHOLIC CUSTOMS

Despite this general antipathy towards sainthood, the English Church does acknowledge feast days for the Blessed Virgin and the apostles in the Book of Common Prayer. Obscure regional customs also hint at an English attachment to the old saints.

For instance, in Derbyshire, to avoid the charge of idolatry, it was rumoured that people would create temporary icons of the saints. It is thought that in former remote places, such as Buxton,

Eyam and Tideswell, the villagers dressed the village wells with intricate images of flowers that represented an apostle, a saint or the Blessed Virgin. These decorations appeared on the feast days.

The habit of honouring the most devout Christians in the community was hard to abandon, too. Consequently, in rejecting the title of saint, the Church of England chose instead to define such people as "Heroes and Martyrs". On 9 July 1998, Queen Elizabeth II, Supreme Head of the Church of England, accompanied by the highest priestly officer of her Church, the Archbishop of Canterbury, unveiled ten statues of 20th-century martyrs. The list was cross-denominational, and in fact none of the men and women so honoured were members of the Church of England.

20TH-CENTURY MARTYRS

Instead of saints, the Church of England recognized heroes and martyrs. Statues of ten heroes and martyrs were erected on the façade of Westminster Abbey in London.

Grand Duchess Elizabeth of Russia: Murdered in 1918 during the Russian Revolution.
Manche Masemola: Killed in 1928 by her parents in South Africa for converting to Christianity.
Maximilian Kolbe: Polish priest murdered in 1941 in a Nazi concentration camp.
Lucian Tapiedi: Peasant from Papua New Guinea murdered in 1942 by Japanese troops.
Dietrich Bonhoeffer: German pastor murdered in 1945 by the Nazis.
Janani Luwum: Teacher murdered in 1977 by Idi Amin in Uganda.
Esther John: Indian missionary martyred in 1960.
Dr Martin Luther King Jr: Civil rights campaigner assassinated in 1968 in the USA.
Wang Zhiming: Chinese pastor killed in 1973 by the government.
Archbishop Oscar Romero: Murdered in 1980 in San Salvador.

Above The martyrs' statues at Westminster Abbey: Martin Luther King Jr, Oscar Romero, Dietrich Bonhoeffer, Esther John and Lucian Tapiedi.

NEW WORLDS

EXPLORATIONS BEYOND EUROPE HELPED SPREAD THE CHRISTIAN FAITH TO THE AMERICAS, AFRICA, INDIA AND THE FAR EAST. MISSIONARIES AND THEIR CONVERTS FACED HARDSHIP, EVEN MARTYRDOM, AND INEVITABLY THE COMPANY OF SAINTS EXPANDED.

The apostles set a pattern of evangelism, making it a duty for Christians to spread the Gospel. Whether Roman Catholic, Eastern Orthodox or Protestant, churches have always treated this duty as a serious commitment.

The faith of these missionaries was tested during the widespread explorations of the Europeans in the 17th and 18th centuries. Adventurers and merchants first traded with, then colonized, far-flung lands, and Christian evangelists followed in their wake.

MISSIONARY MARTYRS
Modern secular opinion asserts that these missions forced their faith on people for mere political purpose or to exploit natural resources. This may be true of

Below A Catholic nun in Africa teaches children how to use knitting needles during the 1920s.

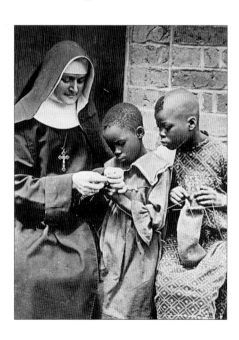

ambitious leaders, but thousands of lowly religious gave their lives to the service of the indigenous people of these lands. Frequently, the missionaries protected their flock from both colonial masters and local warlords.

In remote, uncharted parts of the world, nuns and monks from Ireland, France, Portugal and Spain suffered the same hardship as their flock. They also filled non-religious roles as nurses and educators. Many paid the ultimate price of martyrdom and were canonized for their faith.

St Francis Xavier was among the first to be venerated for his life as an evangelist beyond the bounds of old Christendom. He travelled through the Far East, spreading the gospel, and was martyred. As other Europeans followed his example through the Americas, Asia and Africa, so the company of saints expanded.

NATIVE CONVERTS
The legends of the saints were told to inspire converts and it mattered not that the Blessed Virgin was depicted with Chinese or Mexican features. With the infant in her arms, she became a universal symbol. Regardless of ethnic features, St Francis was recognized with his stigmata, and St Roch with the dog at his feet.

One of the earliest New World converts to inspire a cultus was Blessed Kateri Tekakwitha, a Native American who died in 1680 and was beatified in 1980. Similarly, a cultus developed after

Above A Chinese representation of The Nativity (Lu-Hang-Hien, 19th century).

the death of the Spanish Dominican St Joachim Royo, who died in China in 1748.

In Japan, Paul Miki and his companions, converts of St Francis Xavier, suffered relentless persecution before finally being tortured and crucified in 1597. Survivors venerated the blood-stained clothes of these 26 victims who were all canonized.

In Uganda, Charles Lwanga and his 21 companions, all under the age of 25, were burned alive for their faith in the 1880s. As they faced their horrific deaths, "their exemplary courage and cheerfulness were comparable with those of the early Christians". They were canonized in 1964.

The first native saint of the USA, Elizabeth Seton, died in 1821, and was canonized only in 1971 for her charity towards deprived children.

St Josephine Bakhita was taken into slavery in Africa, but found refuge in a convent in Italy. Her

Right Missionaries and their catechumens experience floodwater in Hindustan, north India, in 1910.

work as a nurse, together with her humility, attracted a cultus after she died in 1947. She was canonized in 2000.

MASS CANONIZATION

Pope John Paul II recognized the neglected martyrs of the New and Developing Worlds. Tireless in visiting Catholic communities and in reinforcing the Universal Church, the late pope created more than 480 new saints. Through this pope's concern for his global flock, victims of mass persecution have been sanctified. He canonized 117 martyrs of Vietnam, all of whom gave their lives between 1745 and 1862. The Martyrs of Mexico, 25 Christians killed between 1915 and 1937, were also made saints in 2000.

Furthermore, he initiated the process of sanctification of the estimated 6,832 priests and religious put to death during the Spanish Civil War (1936–39). By creating native sainthoods, the pope hoped to encourage the Church in those parts.

Above A painting of the Madonna on animal hide, made by Pueblo Indians in a traditional style (1675).

Left An armed ship carrying missionaries under the monogram of Jesus off the coast of New Granada, modern-day Colombia (artist unknown, 18th century).

MODERN PILGRIMS

THE MODERN ERA HAS SEEN A REVIVAL IN PILGRIMAGE AS A CHRISTIAN DUTY. NOT SINCE THE 16TH-CENTURY REFORMATION OF THE CHURCH HAVE SO MANY PILGRIMS UNDERTAKEN THE LONG JOURNEYS TO SHRINES FOR CURES, PENANCE AND PRAYER.

The pious duty of pilgrimage, although never abandoned by Roman Catholics, regained some of its former popularity during the Victorian era. The Ottoman Islamic hold on Palestine had weakened, and in 1855 a cross was borne through Jerusalem for the first time since the Crusades.

Pilgrims began visiting again the holy sites of Jerusalem, Bethlehem and Nazareth. By 1900, the traveller Gertrude Bell described a hostelry "packed with pilgrims tight as herrings sleeping in rows on the floor".

VISIONS OF MARY

Various extraordinary events have contributed to this latter-day increase in the popularity of saints. In 1876, more than 100,000 pilgrims attended the dedication of the church at Lourdes, in south-west France, where St Bernadette received a vision of the Virgin Mary. Three years later, at Knock in Ireland, 15 people saw a vision standing on the village chapel roof of the Virgin accompanied by St Joseph, St John and a lamb. A shrine there now attracts more than a million pilgrims every year.

In 1917, the Blessed Virgin was said to have visited three children at Fátima in Portugal and entrusted them with three secrets. Now five million pilgrims a year visit their shrine. Believers claim that the Virgin told the children about forthcoming mass death in a second world war and an

Below Catholic pilgrims during the Holy Week praying at the first Station of the Cross on the Via Dolorosa in Jerusalem (Erich Matson, c.1900).

Above Pope John Paul II celebrated mass with a million believers in front of a statue of the Virgin in Fátima, Portugal, on 12 May 1991.

attempted assassination of a pope – both of which prophecies have come true.

ECHOES OF THE PAST

Modern pilgrims, in imitation of the difficult conditions of their medieval counterparts, and also to show penitence, may choose to walk the "pilgrim's way" to particular shrines.

A popular route is the trek to Santiego de Compostela on the Atlantic coast of Spain. During their journey, they may pass other

places of pilgrimage, such as the shrine to the Virgin Mary in Vézelay and at Conques, and can see the relics of the martyr, St Foy.

The main aim of the pilgrimage is to visit the tomb and relics of St James the Great at Santiago de Compostela. The Church gives a certificate to those pilgrims who have walked the last 100km/60 miles or cycled the last 200km/120 miles of the route. These awards echo the medieval habit of rewarding successful pilgrims with distinctive clothes and badges.

RECENT DEVELOPMENTS
Ever since 1717, the most devout have walked about 110km/70 miles from Warsaw to the Jasna Gora monastery in Poland to see the miraculous icon of Our Lady of Czestochowa, reputedly painted by St Luke. But since the ending of Communist rule in the late 20th century, many more throng the route. An estimated million pilgrims a year now go to the site.

The biggest crowds are found at Zihuatanejo in Guadalupe, Mexico, where St Juan Diego had a vision of the Virgin. Ten million pilgrims pay homage to Our Lady of Guadalupe at this shrine every year. And seven million people travel to the tomb of the humble stigmatic, St Padre Pio, at San Giovanni Rotondo in south Italy.

PERSONAL JOURNEYS
Other holy sites and shrines draw those seeking a significance particular to themselves. The pilgrim might be named after the saint, or be seeking one who is patron of a disease or other affliction.

Many visit Assisi, Italy, for St Francis, although an earthquake has left this site damaged. Pilgrims travel to the abbeys at Montserrat in France, or Trier in Germany, to seek intercession from the saints and wonder at the glorious holy

BEING A PILGRIM
Modern Roman Catholic and Orthodox pilgrims are serious in their intent when they undertake journeys to the places associated with the saints. This is often the site where their relics are enshrined. Pilgrims seek penance and offer prayers of gratitude, or request their intercession.

Walking the route to a shrine, the faithful will take time to pray or undergo some physical hardship in penance. They venerate those shrines they pass as they head toward their final destination. If that is Rome, they will climb, on hands and knees, the hard marble steps of the Holy Stairs of St Peter's Cathedral.

Popular pilgrimages are those to Assisi, the shrine of St Francis, or to places that honour St James the Great in South America, or visits to sacred sites of the Holy Land. But in the 21st century, the sites and festivals that attract most visitors are those associated with the Virgin Mary, the one figure from the company of saints who seems to have sustained an imaginative hold on believers – and non-believers.

Above Pilgrims kneel with crosses at the pass of Roncesvalles, Spain, on their way from south-west France to Santiago de Compostela.

buildings. Today, pilgrimages to the Holy Land have become almost as dangerous as they were during the Crusades.

Many aspects of modern pilgrimage resemble the medieval experience, as Chaucer described in his poetic work *The Canterbury Tales*. Hostelries proliferate along the routes, especially near the shrines, just as they did in the Middle Ages. Translators and guides find work, while merchants are busy selling souvenirs, often facsimiles of medieval relics.

Right Souvenir of the pilgrimage to Lourdes, made for the International Exhibition in Paris in 1867.

THE BLESSED

THE CHURCH DOES NOT GRANT SAINTHOOD LIGHTLY. HOLY SOULS MAY REMAIN FOR DECADES, EVEN CENTURIES, IN THE RANKS OF THE BLESSED OR THE VENERABLE, WHILE THE CLAIMS MADE ON THEIR BEHALF ARE CAREFULLY SCRUTINIZED BY THE VATICAN.

Above A photo of Blessed Father Joseph Damien de Veuster in 1873.

Mother Teresa of Calcutta lived a life that even the secular acknowledge was saintly. In the minds of many believers she is a saint. Yet she has not been canonized. Until a second miracle is officially attributed to her, she remains among the Blessed. Likewise, in the Rotunda of the Capitol Building in Washington, D.C., USA, stands a statue of the Blessed Father Joseph Damien de Veuster. This man was, and still is, deeply venerated by lepers and their families. For 16 years he nursed the lepers of Moloka'i in Hawaii. His gentle devotion and Christian faith were recognized as being worthy of a saint. He died in 1889 and was eventually beatified in 1995 by Pope John Paul II, but Catholics in Hawaii already regard Father Damien as a fully fledged saint.

UNKNOWN BUT HOLY

These are but two individuals who led lives of public service. Many others do not have national or global recognition. Cultuses have sometimes asked for obscure, private individuals to be named as saints. One such is Pierre Toussaint who was born a slave in Haiti in 1776 and taken by his master, John Berard, to live with him in New York. There Berard taught Pierre to read and write.

When Berard died, Pierre continued to care for the family of his late master by working as a barber. When Mrs Berard married again, Pierre set up his own home and with his wife cared for the homeless and destitute.

They purchased the freedom of many slaves, opened a school, and set up a religious order for black

Left The procession of the Beatified in The Last Judgement *(Giotto di Bondone, 1303).*

women. After his death in 1853, Toussaint became the only layman to be buried in the grand precincts of St Patrick's Cathedral in New York. He was recognized as Venerable by the Church in 1996, but in the local community people know him fondly as the "Barber Saint".

WILD MYSTIC

An Indian girl, Kateri Tekakwitha, endured a short wretched life, spent poor and lonely. Her father was a Mohawk chief and her parents died of smallpox. She survived but was scarred and left partially blind. Yet she claimed always to be filled with the joy of her faith.

Kateri, a mystic, revelled in the great prairie wilderness that was her home. She came to be known as the "Lily of the Mohawks", though some called her the "Mystic of the Wilds".

When she died in 1680, the local Jesuit missionaries were astounded to find her corpse transformed into the gracious form of a beautiful young woman. Their witness to her devotion and spiritual power formed the ground for her being granted beatification in 1980.

Right A statue of Blessed Kateri Tekakwitha, a Native American mystic who died in 1680.

Left A watercolour portrait of Pierre Toussaint, fondly known as the "Barber Saint" (c.1825).

PATRONS OF CAUSES

In some cases, the Blessed have been allowed to become patrons of causes. Maria Teresa Ledóchowska, who was born into a 19th-century noble Polish family, nevertheless devoted herself to mission work, especially to the abolition of slavery. The countess founded a community, first called the Sodality, now known as the Institute of St Peter Claver. Having taken vows as a nun, Maria worked tirelessly against slavery. She was beatified in 1976 by Pope Paul VI who declared her the patron of Polish missions.

Many saints are honoured for giving to the poor, but Blessed Bernardino of Feltre (d.1494) helped those too proud to accept welfare. He took over the Church's faltering little pawnshops, the *montes pietatis*, started in 1462 by Barnabas of Terni. Under Bernardino's care, the pawnshops were properly run and became very successful. They charged very low rates of interest and profits were used for charity. For centuries the shops could be found all over western Europe. His cultus was approved in 1728.

MOTHER TERESA OF CALCUTTA

Even as a small child in Skopje, Macedonia, Teresa showed a religious turn of mind and, at 17, announced she wanted to become a missionary. She was sent to India and took her vows as a nun in 1937.

Teresa worked as a teacher until 1946, when she claimed she heard the voice of Jesus calling for her help. Further voices told her to found the Missionaries of Charity. For the rest of her life she devoted her energies to the care of the ill and dying poor of Calcutta.

So inspirational was her example that her followers opened other centres of Missionaries of Charity, first in Venezuela and Tanzania, then in other countries. Women took vows as nuns, and laymen were encouraged to help. Later the Missionaries of Charity Brothers was founded for priests. Mother Teresa died in 1997 and her tomb in Calcutta is a site of pilgrimage. She was beatified in 2002.

Below Mother Teresa in Calcutta, India, in 1976.

PATRON SAINTS

EACH BELIEVER NURSES A PARTICULAR AFFECTION FOR ONE
OR MORE SAINTS, AND TURNS TO THESE HOLY SOULS FOR
HELP AND PROTECTION. EVERY ASPECT OF LIFE IS UNDER
SAINTLY GUARDIANSHIP, WHETHER IT IS BABYHOOD,
COURTSHIP, DOG BITES OR LOST POSSESSIONS.

Early Christians, believing the saints to be alive in heaven, found it logical to see them as patrons for mortals on earth.

Saints were thought to look after certain sectors of society, as well as support themes or activities with resonance in their personal story.

Above St Jerome Emiliani, the patron saint of lost children, with a young orphan boy (Giovanni Domenico Tiepolo, 1780).

Left Ferdinand III ruled as a king in Spain in the 13th century (illuminated manuscript, c.1250). He is the patron of prisoners and the poor.

Abandoned children – Ivo of Brittany, Jerome Emiliani
Asylums for the mentally ill – Dympna
Alpine travellers – Bernard of Montjoux
Babies – Holy Innocents, Maximus, Nicholas of Tolentino, Philip Zell
Beggars – Giles
Birds – Gall
Blind people – Thomas the Confessor, Cosmas and Damian, Archangel Raphael
Blood donors – Mary, the Blessed Virgin, Our Lady of the Thorns
Booksellers – John of God
Boys – Dominic Savio
Breastfeeding – Basilissa, Giles
Brides – Dorothy
Cemeteries – Michael, Anne
Childbirth – Margaret of Antioch, Raymund Nonnatus, Leonard of Noblac, Erasmus
Children, longing for – Rita of Cascia
Children, lost – Jerome Emiliani
Criminals – Dismas
Degree candidates – Joseph of Copertino
Dentists – Apollonia
Difficult situations – Eustace
Dog bites – Ubaldo

Doubters – Joseph (husband of Mary)

Drought – Genevieve

Emigrants – Frances Cabrini

Epilepsy – Dympna, Vitus

Falling – Venantius Fortunatus

Flying – Joseph of Copertino

Geese – Martin of Tours

Girls – Maria Goretti

Harvests – Antony of Padua

Heart patients – John of God

Hermits – Antony, Giles, Hilarion

Homeless – Benedict Joseph Labre

Horses – Eloi, Martin of Tours, Hippolytus

Hospitals – Camillus of Lellis, John of God

House hunting – Joseph (husband of Mary)

Housewives – Martha

Infertility – Rita of Cascia

Invalids – Roch

Journeys – Christopher, Nicholas of Bari, Archangel Raphael, Joseph (husband of Mary)

Kings – Edward the Confessor, Louis IX, Henry II

Knights – George, James the Greater

Learning – Catherine of Alexandria

Lost causes – Jude

Lost things – Antony of Padua

Lovers – Valentine

Married women – Monica

Marriage – John Francis Regis

Motherhood – Nicholas of Tolentino

Motorists – Christopher

Mountaineers – Bernard of Aosta

Music – Cecilia, Gregory the Great

Navigators – Brendan the Navigator, Erasmus, Nicholas of Myra

Old people – Teresa of Jesus Jornet y Ibars

Orphans – Ivo of Brittany, Jerome Emiliani

Paralysed – Osmund

Pets – Antony of Egypt

Pilgrims – Christopher, Nicholas of Myra

Poison sufferers – Benedict, John, Pirmin

Poor people – Antony of Padua, Ferdinand III

Pregnant women – Margaret of Antioch

Prisoners – Leonard of Noblac, Roch, Vincent de Paul, Ferdinand III of Castile

Rabies – Hubert, Ubaldo

Race relations – Martin de Porres, Peter Claver

Radio – Archangel Gabriel

Repentant prostitutes – Mary Magdalene, Mary of Egypt, Margaret of Cortona

Rheumatism sufferers – James the Great, Philip Neri

Restaurants – Martha

Retreats – Ignatius of Loyola

Shortsightedness – Clarus (abbot)

Shepherds – Cuthbert, Bernadette

Sleepwalkers – Dympna

Above St Giles, patron saint of beggars and cripples, was a hermit who probably lived in France in the 9th century (high altar of the Pacher School, c.1500).

Spas – John the Baptist

Stamp collectors – Archangel Gabriel

Television – Clare of Assisi

Teenage girls – Maria Goretti

Throat infections – Blaise

Toothache sufferers – Apollonia, Médard, Osmund, Cunibert of Cologne

Tourists – Francis Xavier

Unhappily married women – Wilgefortis, Rita of Cascia

Workers – Joseph (husband of Mary)

Youth – Aloysius Gonzaga

ALL SAINTS AND ALL SOULS

THE CHURCH CREATED TWO UNIVERSAL FEAST DAYS TO HONOUR
THOSE WHO HAVE LEFT THIS WORLD. CATHOLICS COMMEMORATE
ALL SAINTS ON 1 NOVEMBER, AND ALL THE DEVOUT SOULS WHO
HAVE NOT YET REACHED HEAVEN THE FOLLOWING DAY.

Precisely when the Roman
Catholic Church adopted the
practice of commemorating all
the saints is unknown. However,
it is known that the earliest
believers left inscriptions of general prayers for the dead in the
catacombs of Rome. Two later
saints, St Ephrem (d.AD 373) and
St John Chrysostom (d.AD 407),
describe in vague terms prayers
for "the martyrs of the whole
world". Yet, whether these prayers
referred only to officially sanctified individuals or more generally
to all devout souls who reside in
heaven is unclear.

A 7th-century AD manuscript
states that not only unknown
martyrs but unnamed saints, too,
were remembered in prayers
and rituals. Catholics believe, to
paraphrase St Paul's words, that
many of the faithful live not as
themselves but through Christ
who lives within them. These

*Above A man lights a candle at the
All Saints Memorial, to celebrate
fallen soldiers on Hungarian territory.*

*Below All Souls' Day in the
Churchyard at Glendalough
(Joseph Peacock, 19th century).*

souls, it is believed, reside in heaven but they are unknown. By the 9th century, the practice of praying to unknown saints had become widespread, and an official feast day was established on 1 November as All Saints, which is known also in England as All Hallows.

ALL SOULS' DAY

Believers pitied the faithful dead who might not be in heaven. Naturally, the living prayed for their dead relatives, priests and friends, in the belief that their prayers would help accelerate the passage of their beloved up to heaven. The faithful prayed for the purification of the souls of their beloved ones and their quick passage through purgatory. According to Roman Catholic belief, this is a transitionary abode where those souls who are not saints wait for redemption before passing to heaven. They depend for that redemption on the prayers of the living.

The origin of offering prayers for the unredeemed may date to before the 7th century. Certainly during the lifetime of Isidore of Seville (c.AD 560–636), prayers for this purpose were offered in churches. However, the Roman Church was reluctant to dedicate a liturgical place to those who hover on the edge of heaven.

It was not until the 10th century that the liturgy became fixed. According to tradition, a pilgrim returning from the Holy Land encountered a beggar who pointed to flames issuing from a fissure in the earth, believed to emanate from hell. Despairing moans of the dead were said to be audible. The pilgrim reported his terrible experience to St Odilo, abbot of Cluny, who immediately decreed that a day should be marked for "all the dead who have existed from the beginning of the world to the end of time". The feast day was set on 2 November to commemorate all dead souls.

CAKES FOR THE DEAD

Some have interpreted All Souls' Day in a more sinister light. They see the occasion as a time when the souls of the unredeemed return, briefly, to haunt the living. The angry dead, unsupported by prayers from their relatives and friends, turn into toads or witches to punish the living.

In parts of Catholic Italy, the dead are placated with alms in the form of food left on windowsills or the kitchen table, and bunches of flowers are heaped at gravesides in honour of the dead. In Poland, candles are lit on graves in the cemeteries and bread is left shaped in the figure of a body. In Ireland, the devout celebrate the eve of All Souls with a big feast, but the next day is spent fasting, with flowers laid on graves at cemeteries.

All Souls' Day has developed to become a time for feeding the poor and giving to charity. For centuries, believers in the Church of England used to offer alms to the poor on this day. Children would make lanterns from root vegetables, such as turnips, and go "souling" at the doors of friends and neighbours, asking for spiced buns known as soul-cakes.

The modern, secular world has added its own "spin" on these occasions. Halloween, a hybrid of All Saints and All Souls, has become a time for children to dress up in costumes and act as spooks, with rewards of sweets and money replacing traditional soul-cakes. These particular celebrations originated in the USA, but they have spread to areas where the Church is not as influential as it once was.

Above At a cemetery in La Digue, Seychelles, visitors bring gifts and flowers to dress the gravestones of their loved ones on All Souls' Day.

DIRECTORY OF SAINTS

The first Christian saints were recognized soon after Christ's death over two thousand years ago and new names have been added ever since. This Directory lists a selection of major saints chronologically in order of their deaths. A strong historical sense emerges from studying these biographies, while changing cultural systems form a background to their stories.

Many saints are surrounded by myths of super-human strength and startling powers of endurance. These legends can be viewed as entertaining tales, yet they linger in the mind because these impossible acts are underwritten by a sincere faith. But, generally, the lives show the humanity of the saints. Some were short-tempered, some had brilliant minds, while others were confused and bewildered. We see kings becoming humble, scullery maids honoured for their integrity, and pious illiterates making an impact on the world.

The difficulties and problems encountered in their lives mirror the political and social worlds they inhabited. The persecution of Christians during the Roman Empire is familiar to most readers, but perhaps less well known is the persecution of later times that proved equally horrific.

The company of saints is varied and complex, filled with eccentric personalities, but all are alike in their pious attachment to God.

Left St Francis Expels the Devils from Arezzo *(Giotto di Bondone, c. 1297–1299).*

Top *A bejewelled casket containing the relics of Thomas Becket (c. 1190).*

ARCHANGEL RAPHAEL

THIS ARCHANGEL IS THE HERO OF A LEGEND IN WHICH HE HELPS A POOR, BLIND MAN. HIS NAME MEANS "GOD HEALS", AND HE IS TRADITIONALLY SEEN AS BOTH A HEALER AND PROTECTOR.

KEY FACTS

Divine messenger of God
DATES: *Not human but a manifestation of God*
PATRON OF: *Travellers, young people leaving home, sad people, health inspectors, the sick, the blind and against eye disease*
FEAST DAY: *29 September*
EMBLEM: *Holding a bottle, carrying a fish or a staff, accompanied by a boy*

The Gospel of John tells us that in Jerusalem there was once a pool called Bethesda where, at a certain time every year, "an angel" stirred its waters. The first people to enter the pool after this visit would be cured of their illness or disability. By tradition, Raphael is credited as this very angel.

In the Apocryphal Book of Tobit, there are many stories about Raphael. Disguised as a man, he takes a journey with a boy, Tobias, and his dog. They travel to recover a debt owed to

Above Tobias and the Angel *(Andrea del Verrocchio, c. 1470–80).*

the boy's blind grandfather, and have many adventures. On their return home, Raphael restores the old man's sight by asking him to eat a particular fish. Most paintings of this archangel show him with a fish, the boy and the dog, and he is a patron of travellers.

ARCHANGEL MICHAEL

THE ARCHANGEL MICHAEL SAVED HEAVEN BY VANQUISHING THE DEVIL WHO WAS INTRUDING WHILE DISGUISED AS A DRAGON.

KEY FACTS

Divine messenger of God
DATES: *Not human but a manifestation of God*
PATRON OF: *Ambulance drivers, bakers, mariners, paramedics, soldiers and battles*
FEAST DAY: *29 September*
EMBLEM: *Frequently dressed in armour carrying a gatekeeper's staff, sword, scales, banner, dragon*

The Old Testament describes Michael as the protector of Israel, "always interceding for the human race". He was the angel who spoke to Moses on Mount Sinai. The New Testament says he "has authority over the people" and "gave them the law".

Archangel Michael fought the Devil when war broke out in heaven. Michael defeated the beast and the angels siding with it, so he was given the right to judge souls seeking entry into heaven.

Many medieval images show Michael weighing human souls

Above The Archangel Michael Defeating Satan *(Guido Reni, c. 1600–42).*

brought before him for judgement. He is very often pictured fighting the dragon. Michael is the patron of battles and soldiers, as well as those believed to be "possessed by the devil".

Archangel Michael appeared in visions at Monte Gargano in Apulia, Italy, in the 5th century AD. Many churches worldwide, especially those built on hilltops, are dedicated to him, such as Mont-St-Michel in France.

ARCHANGEL GABRIEL

THE ARCHANGEL GABRIEL DELIVERS SOME OF GOD'S MOST IMPORTANT MESSAGES TO MAN. HE INFORMED BOTH ELIZABETH AND MARY THAT THEY WOULD SOON GIVE BIRTH.

KEY FACTS

Divine messenger of God
DATES: *Not human but a manifestation of God*
PATRON OF: *Communications, postal workers, journalists, broadcasters*
FEAST DAY: *29 September*
EMBLEM: *Trumpet, often carries a lily, shield or spear*

In the Old Testament, Gabriel was present at the burial of Moses and at an Israelite victory over the Assyrians. He visited the prophet Daniel to warn him of the coming of the Messiah, saviour of the Israelites. He also helped Daniel interpret a dream that rescued the Israelites.

In the New Testament, the archangel Gabriel was charged with telling Zachary that his wife Elizabeth would bear a son who would play an important role in the Messiah's life. This son was John the Baptist.

THE ANNUNCIATION

The most important message Gabriel delivered was to the Virgin Mary. He appeared before her to announce she had been chosen, above all women, to give birth to Jesus, the Son of God. His greeting to Mary, reported in the Gospel of Luke, has become the start of the "Hail Mary".

The Annunciation, Gabriel's visitation to the Virgin Mary, has been the subject of hundreds of paintings. The archangel always has wings and often wears a courtier's clothes, or a white tunic covered by a cloak.

Some traditions hold that, accompanied by "a multitude of heavenly hosts", Gabriel appeared above the hills of Bethlehem where shepherds were tending their flock. He announced the birth of Jesus to them.

In an ancient chapel on the Appian Way in Rome there is an early image of Gabriel. Some medieval depictions show him carrying the staff of a doorkeeper to show that he is a guardian of the Church.

His feast day used to be 24 March, date of the Annunciation. In 1969, the pope decided he should share a feast day with archangels Michael and Raphael.

Below The archangel Gabriel appears before Mary for the Annunciation *(Sandro Botticelli, c.1489–90).*

"HAIL MARY, FULL OF GRACE.
THE LORD IS WITH THEE.
BLESSED ART THOU AMONGST WOMEN,
AND BLESSED IS THE FRUIT OF THY WOMB, JESUS.
HOLY MARY, MOTHER OF GOD,
PRAY FOR US SINNERS, NOW AND AT THE HOUR
OF OUR DEATH."

GABRIEL'S GREETING TO MARY MAKES UP THE FIRST TWO LINES OF THE "HAIL MARY" PRAYER

THE HOLY FAMILY

JOSEPH, MARY AND THE INFANT JESUS MAKE UP THE HOLY FAMILY. THE GOSPEL OF MATTHEW SAYS THAT THE MESSIAH WILL BE DESCENDED FROM THE HOUSE OF DAVID. THE SPIRITUAL RELATIVES OF THE HOLY FAMILY ARE THE HOLY TRINITY.

Joseph and Mary were humble and loving parents of the infant Jesus. They brought up their son in the Jewish faith and Jesus was taught to be a carpenter by his earthly father, Joseph.

OF ROYAL DESCENT?

In the first 16 verses of his gospel, Matthew demonstrates a direct line of descent from King David of the Israelites to Joseph and Jesus. Such an ancestry was essential if the Jewish prophecy that

the Messiah would come from the House of David was to be fulfilled. The same royal connections are ascribed to Mary, although nothing is known of her origins. Details of the lives of her mother, Anne, and of her father, Joachim, come only from apocryphal sources.

THE BIRTH OF JESUS

When the Roman authorities held a census of the population, Joseph was obliged to travel to

Above The Holy Family
(Luca Signorelli, 1486–90).
Christ is shown as a diligent child.

Below A fresco depicting The Flight into Egypt, *from the Lower Church at Assisi in Italy (Giotto di Bondone, 14th century).*

Bethlehem, the city of David, to record his name. The journey was slow because of his young wife's pregnancy. Mary was very close to giving birth, but as Joseph hurried round Bethlehem at nightfall all he heard was the cry, "No room at the inn". Many other people had crowded into the town to fulfil the Romans' demands.

At last, a kindly innkeeper led him to the stables and told the tired girl that she could rest there. It was here in the stable, alongside cows and donkeys, that Mary gave birth to Jesus and laid him in a manger for lack of a cradle.

Shepherds arrived because angels had told them to visit the new Messiah. A bright star hung over the stable and guided the shepherds who brought the baby the gift of a lamb. The Holy Family received more guests with the arrival some time later of the three Magi, or wise men. They had read signs and warnings that told them where to find the new "King of the Jews". They brought him costly gifts of gold, frankincense and myrrh.

Below Stained glass showing the holy family in the carpenter's shop, Steeple Aston, England (19th century).

Above A Nativity scene from the Bellieu Orthodox Church in Samokov, Bulgaria (16th century).

After Jesus was born, Joseph received a warning that Herod was planning to kill the baby, so the Holy Family fled to Egypt. Herod carried out his threat, killing all male infants in Bethlehem under two years, but the Holy Infant was not among them.

NO ORDINARY CHILD

Because the archangel Gabriel had appeared to both Mary, at the Annunciation, and to Joseph to explain the importance of their son, they knew that Jesus was a special child. In spite of this they were still horrified to find, a day

into their return journey from the annual trip to Jerusalem for Passover, that the 12-year-old Jesus could not be found among the family group.

Joseph and Mary returned immediately to the city and after searching for three days found him in the temple in the midst of doctors and rabbis, listening to the teachings and asking questions. Jesus calmly asked his mother why she had been so worried when she knew that he would be "about my Father's business".

THE CRUCIFIXION

We know from St John's Gospel that the Blessed Virgin was accompanied by her sister, Mary of Cleophas during her vigil at the foot of the cross. As Jesus hung from the cross, he asked the apostle John to care for his mother. This implies that she had no other sons or a husband to care for her after Jesus' death. By tradition Mary became surrogate mother to John, and travelled with him on missionary work abroad.

Below Twelve-year-old Jesus debating with the rabbis in the temple (Adolph Friedrich Erdmann von Menzel, 1851).

MARY, THE VIRGIN

MARY IS THE UNIVERSAL SYMBOL OF PURITY AND MOTHERHOOD. MANY CHRISTIANS BELIEVE SHE WAS FREE OF SIN FROM THE MOMENT SHE WAS CONCEIVED, A DOCTRINE KNOWN AS THE IMMACULATE CONCEPTION.

KEY FACTS
*Mother of the
Son of God*
DATES: *1st century BC*
BIRTH PLACE: *Unknown*
PATRON OF: *Motherhood,
virginity*
FEAST DAY: *15 August*
EMBLEM: *Blue robes, crown, lily*

The image of Mary, the Blessed Virgin, is instantly recognizable, whether as a mother with her child in her arms or with her dead son laid across her lap. A mother nurtures her child, and her suffering for the sake of that child is intense. Mary, in the role of the Holy Mother, represents feelings understood by everyone. No saint can match the mother of the Son of God.

EARLY LIFE

Little is known about Mary's early life. There are no dates for her birth or her death, and mention of her parents Anne and Joachim is only found in the apocryphal 2nd-century AD Gospel of James.

We do know, from the Bible, that the Blessed Virgin was a young Jewish girl, and that like her future husband Joseph, she was said to be descended from the family of the great Israelite king, David.

MOTHER OF CHRIST

It was the angel Gabriel who told Mary that she was to be the mother of Christ, an event known as the Annunciation. The angel said that the child would be

Left A sculpture of Mary cradling the body of her dead son (I. Günther, 18th century). Artistic images of this moment are known as "the Pietà".

Left Mary and the baby Jesus are depicted as playful and loving in this stained glass from Eaton Bishop, England (14th century).

the Son of God, not of a man. Mary accepted this extraordinary fate with great faith and courage.

The Roman population census obliged Mary and Joseph to travel to the home of their ancestor, David. Mary gave birth to Jesus in a stable in Bethlehem, surrounded by animals. Shepherds and later three wise men, the Magi, came to worship the young Messiah.

After the Nativity, Mary is mentioned only a few times in the gospels. Mary and Joseph took Jesus for his presentation at the Temple of Jerusalem, as was the custom. With Joseph and Jesus she fled to Egypt to save their child from slaughter by Herod's men. At the marriage feast at Canaan, Mary asked Jesus to intervene when the wine ran out. And when Jesus hung dying on the cross, Mary kept vigil close by.

The Blessed Virgin was also with the apostles at Pentecost, the time after Christ's Ascension when the Holy Spirit is believed to have descended upon them. There is no mention of Mary living with Jesus and his apostles or teaching during this time.

LEVELS OF VENERATION

Mary, the Mother of God, is universally admired by Catholic believers. The Catholic Church accords different levels of honour. The highest level is adoration, or latria, and is reserved for God and the Trinity (God the Father, God the Son and God the Holy Ghost). Veneration of the Blessed Virgin is granted the Church's second highest honour and is known as hyperdulia, as theorized by Thomas Aquinas. Veneration of the company of all other saints is known as dulia.

were generally richly decorated with gold. They were portrayed as formal, grand and majestic.

Images from the late medieval and early Renaissance periods show a tender young woman with a baby. She is often clothed in a heavenly blue gown and the child is naked. Images of the Virgin Mary in the developing world more recently often show her dressed in the most admired style of the local people.

In today's Catholic and Orthodox worlds, Mary is still remembered when many other saints are neglected. Holy icons and festivals held in Mary's honour continue to attract millions of believers across the globe.

Above A detail from Wedding at Canaan, *the occasion when Jesus performed his first miracle by turning water into wine at the request of Mary (Paolo Veronese, 1563).*

A MOTHER'S PLACE

Although nothing is known of Mary's death, members of the Roman Catholic and Eastern Orthodox Churches hold that she was lifted body and soul into heaven. This event is celebrated as the Assumption. Her role as the mother of Jesus placed her very close to God in heaven.

Many believers think that if a person asks Mary to intercede on their behalf, her great influence is bound to bring God's forgiveness and redemption of their sins.

MARY IN ART

In earlier times Mary's image could be seen widely throughout Christendom. During the early medieval era, depictions of the Virgin Mary and the infant Jesus

Right Mary with the twelve apostles and two archangels in a Russian icon showing The Ascension *(c. 1450).*

JOSEPH

THRUST INTO THE UNIQUE ROLE OF EARTHLY FATHER TO THE SON OF GOD, JOSEPH PROVED A KINDLY HUSBAND AND CARING PARENT. HE PROTECTED HIS YOUNG FAMILY BY FLEEING FROM KING HEROD.

Joseph, husband of the Virgin Mary, was a godly man. He is most often portrayed as both honourable and compassionate.

He makes few appearances in the New Testament. The Gospels of both Mark and Luke describe his royal descent from the House of David, although a carpenter by trade. According to the Jewish prophets, the Messiah would come from this House.

Joseph's age is unknown. As the betrothed of a young woman, it may be fair to assume he was also relatively young at the time of his engagement. An indication of his noble character is given by the nature of his reaction when he learned Mary was pregnant. Not wishing to shame her, he decided to end the betrothal quietly. His distress was dispelled when an angel appeared and explained the intervention of the Holy Spirit.

THE FLIGHT INTO EGYPT

After the Nativity and the visit of the Magi, an angel interpreted one of Joseph's dreams, warning

him of Herod's order to murder all the small boys in Bethlehem. This led Joseph to flee his home to save his wife and the baby Jesus. Numerous paintings depict Joseph as very protective of his family.

Later in Egypt, an angel let Joseph know when it was safe to return to Palestine, and he settled in Nazareth. He followed Jewish custom when he took his wife to the purification ceremony that all women underwent after giving birth. The scribes do not record Joseph's death but it is assumed he died sometime before the crucifixion of Jesus, as Joseph is not mentioned as present on this day.

OTHER INTERPRETATIONS

Joseph's actions show him worthy of his role as protector of the Son of God. Despite this, some apocryphal writings represent him as an old man and parent of other children. The travelling players of medieval theatre liked to present him as a clownish old fool.

Veneration for Joseph grew, however, and in 1870 he was declared patron of the Roman Catholic Church. A special day, 1 May, was dedicated to him as patron of manual workers.

Left A small angel reassures Joseph in The Doubt of St Joseph *(French School, c.1410–20).*

KEY FACTS
Husband of the Virgin Mary
DATES: *1st century BC*
BIRTH PLACE: *Palestine*
PATRON OF: *Canada, Peru and Mexico, families, fathers, manual workers (especially carpenters), the homeless, exiles, travellers*
FEAST DAY: *19 March and 1 May*
EMBLEM: *Bible, branch, carpenter's tools, ladder, lamb, lily*

ANNE

THE MOTHER OF THE BLESSED VIRGIN IS NOT MENTIONED IN THE CANONICAL GOSPELS, BUT APOCRYPHAL SOURCES PRAISE HER AND SHE HAS A LOYAL FOLLOWING NONETHELESS.

There is no firm evidence to determine the parentage or place of origin of the mother of the Virgin Mary. Yet believers longed to have information about the earthly grandmother of Jesus. There is an apocryphal text, the Gospel of James, that mentions her as a saint. Gregory of Nyssa, the brother of St Basil the Great and a saint in his own right, also refers to her with reverence.

In the Gospel of James, Anne is described as childless, and she "mourned in two mournings, and lamented in two lamentations". Her desperate prayers were answered when an angel visited her house to tell her she would bear a child.

Anne responded with the words, "As the Lord my God liveth, if I beget either male or female I will bring it as a gift to the Lord my God; and it shall minister to Him in holy things all the days of its life." So the Virgin Mary was consecrated to God even before her birth.

In the *Golden Legend*, stories of the saints from the 13th century, Anne's husband Joachim dies shortly after the birth of Mary. Anne remarries twice. She has a daughter by each of these new husbands, and both these girls are given the name of Mary. The girls grow up to produce many cousins for Jesus and two boy cousins become apostles. Despite the fictitious nature of both these sources, Anne became sufficiently important in the Church for her relics to appear at the church of Santa Maria Antiqua in Rome.

Above A young Mary is shown reading to her mother in this manuscript drawing (15th century).

Below The story of Mary's birth is here imagined within a contemporary Venetian domestic setting (Vittore Carpaccio, 1504–8).

KEY FACTS
Mother of the Virgin Mary
DATES: *1st century BC*
BIRTH PLACE: *Unknown*
PATRON OF: *Childless women, horsemen and miners*
FEAST DAY: *26 July (West)*
EMBLEM: *Basket, door*

LATER INFLUENCE

The figure of Anne remained in the public mind and artists favoured her as a subject. Paintings and stained glass illustrations show Anne as a tender mother to her little girl. Other images depict Anne teaching Mary how to weave and read.

An unexpected cultus grew in Constantinople (Istanbul) during the 6th century AD when Emperor Justinian I dedicated a shrine to St Anne. She was venerated in Europe from the 13th century. When England's King Richard II (1367–1400) married Anne of Bohemia in 1382, the English bishops petitioned the pope to grant a feast day for St Anne. Later, the official status of such an unsubstantiated figure aroused great anger in Martin Luther.

JOACHIM

JOACHIM IS HONOURED AS THE HUSBAND OF ANNE AND THE FATHER
OF MARY. HIS POPULARITY GREW IN THE WEST IN THE MIDDLE
AGES AS THE CULTUS OF THE BLESSED VIRGIN FLOURISHED.

KEY FACTS
Father of the Virgin Mary
DATES: *1st century BC*
BIRTH PLACE: *Unknown*
PATRON OF: *Fathers, grandfathers*
FEAST DAY: *26 July (West)*
EMBLEM: *Elderly man holding
doves, lamb*

This man became a saint by
virtue of being the husband
of St Anne and the father of the
Blessed Virgin. In Hebrew, his
name means "the Lord will
judge". The sources of information for him are entirely fictitious,
as they are for his wife.

In the *Golden Legend*, Joachim
is given a picturesque history. This
book tells how he was expelled
from the Jewish temple because,
after 20 years of marriage, he and
his wife remained childless.

Desolate and believing God
had cursed him, Joachim went to
seek refuge with a band of
shepherds. He decided to fast for
40 days. An angel visited and
comforted him with the news
that his wife would bear a child.
Excited, Joachim hurried home.

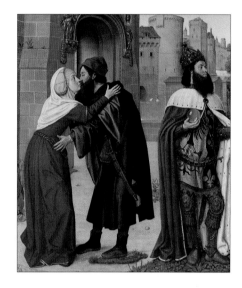

Above Charlemagne, and the
Meeting of Saints Joachim and
Anne at the Golden Gate
(the Master of Moulins, c.1500).

Below right Presentation of the
Virgin at the Temple *(Philippe de
Champaigne, 1639–40). Mary would
have been taken to a synagogue, but
this image depicts a Christian setting.*

But Anne, his worried wife,
was wandering through Jerusalem
looking for her husband. An angel
appeared and advised her to go to
the Golden Gate. There, Anne
found her husband. After this
happy reunion, she conceived the
child who would become the
Mother of God.

LATER RECOGNITION

The cultus of St Joachim began in
the East and was more popular
there than in the west. For several
centuries the Eastern Orthodox
Church has celebrated his feast day
on 9 September. The Roman
Catholic Church was less eager to
grant him sainthood, but the large
cultus could not be ignored. Pope
Gregory XV (1554–1623) allowed
him status as a saint, and Joachim
shares a feast day with his wife.

Below left A fresco scene showing
Joachim among the shepherds (Giotto
di Bondone, c.1303–10).

ELIZABETH

ELIZABETH WAS ELDERLY AND GENERALLY ASSUMED TO BE BARREN
WHEN SHE BECAME PREGNANT WITH THE BOY WHO WOULD BECOME
JOHN THE BAPTIST. THE ARCHANGEL GABRIEL DELIVERED THE NEWS.

It is assumed that Elizabeth was close to menopause when Gabriel announced that she was carrying a child. She was known to be childless, and the news must have brought her great joy.

Elizabeth, a descendant of the patriarch Aaron, is said to have been related to the Blessed Virgin. Their friendship was cemented by their fates as well as by blood.

KEY FACTS
Wife of Zachary,
mother of John the Baptist
DATES: *1st century* BC
BIRTH PLACE: *Probably Palestine*
PATRON OF: *Pregnancy*
FEAST DAY: *5 November*
EMBLEM: *Elderly woman*

Numerous paintings show these women together. Elizabeth was the first person to recognize Mary as the mother of the future Lord.

Left A detail of St Elizabeth from the church of Santa Maria di Porto Fuori, Italy (Ercole de' Roberti, c.1480–81).

ZACHARY

INITIALLY DOUBTFUL, ZACHARY
WAS JOYFUL AT THE PROMISE OF
A CHILD AND NAMED HIM JOHN.

The father of John the Baptist was a Jewish priest. He and his wife Elizabeth had long been married, but had no children.

Zachary was visited by the archangel Gabriel in the temple in Jerusalem, who announced that Elizabeth was to give birth to a child who would "make ready a people prepared for the Lord". Zachary doubted the words of the angel and was struck dumb.

At the baby's circumcision Elizabeth insisted that he was to be called John, going against the Jewish tradition that a child should be given a family name. Zachary supported her by writing on a tablet, "His name is John". Immediately, he regained his voice and began praising God. His words, known as the Benedictus, form part of the Church liturgy.

KEY FACTS
Father of John the Baptist
DATES: *1st century* BC
BIRTH PLACE: *Probably Palestine*
FEAST DAY: *5 November*

"AND THOU, O CHILD,
SHALL BE CALLED THE
PROPHET OF THE MOST
HIGH; FOR THOU
SHALT GO BEFORE THE
LORD TO PREPARE HIS
WAYS, TO GIVE HIS
PEOPLE KNOWLEDGE
OF SALVATION
THROUGH FORGIVENESS
OF THEIR SINS . . ."

THE BENEDICTUS
(CANTICLE OF ZACHARY)

Left In this Flemish early Renaissance painting, Zachary is displayed in the fine clothes of a medieval baron to indicate his high status as the father of John the Baptist (Jan Provost, 1510).

JOHN THE BAPTIST

JOHN THE BAPTIST DEVOTED HIS LIFE TO WARNING PEOPLE TO "REPENT, FOR THE KINGDOM OF GOD IS AT HAND". HE DECLARED THAT THE MESSIAH WOULD SOON APPEAR AMONG THEM.

KEY FACTS
Baptized Jesus
DATES: *d.c.AD 30*
BIRTH PLACE: *Nazareth*
PATRON OF: *Pilgrims to the Holy Land, Knights Hospitallers, hoteliers, birdwatchers*
FEAST DAY: *24 June, 29 August*
EMBLEM: *Lamb, cross, a scroll*

The writings of Sts Jerome and Augustine of Hippo suggested that John the Baptist was sanctified in the womb and never committed a sin. He certainly chose a "heroic" life of hardship and poverty, dressing only in animal skins and living on food he could scavenge.

John devoted his life to telling people to prepare for the coming of the Messiah and his Kingdom. He must have had a charismatic personality with great energy and determination, for he attracted a large following.

BY THE JORDAN

His youth was spent as a hermit, surviving on a diet of locusts and wild honey, a lifestyle that closely resembled that of some of the prophets of the Old Testament.

Crowds came to hear him preach, and John began to baptize them by dipping them in the River Jordan. When Jesus came through the crowd, a dove hovered over his head.

John took this bird to be a sign of the Holy Spirit, so he knew Jesus was the Messiah. He then baptized Jesus, saying he was "the Lamb of God who takest away the sins of the world". In paintings, John is often shown pointing at a lamb and holding a cross.

John the Baptist was later put in prison for denouncing an incestuous marriage between the governor of Galilee, Herod Antipas, and his niece, Herodias. His stepdaughter, Salome, pleased Herod so much with her dancing that he offered her anything she wanted. At her mother's prompting, the girl requested the head of John the Baptist. It was delivered to her on a platter.

TEACHINGS

The teachings of John the Baptist prepared the way for the work of Jesus. John preached about the presence of a "messianic kingdom" and the need for all to repent their sins. His lessons were

Left St John the Baptist in the Wilderness *(Hieronymus Bosch, c.1504–5). John the Baptist is shown in a landscape of strange plants with a lamb, one of his emblems.*

rooted in the Jewish belief that one day the Almighty would send a messiah to lead the people to righteousness. Many Jews who heard John speak were therefore sympathetic to the arrival of Jesus and accepted him as their long-awaited leader.

A large number of disciples followed John and imitated his severe ascetic mode of life. He taught them methods of prayer and meditation. Many ordinary, humble families were moved by his message, too.

Historians believe that John the Baptist's wanderings took him to the Dead Sea. Lessons similar to his message are recorded in the Dead Sea Scrolls – papyrus writings dating from the early Christian era. In Samaria, there is evidence of a community, the Mandaeans, or Sabaeans, who defined themselves as "Christians according to John". It seems these people preserved ideas and traditions that confused John the Baptist with Jesus.

Below Salome with the Head of Saint John the Baptist *(Bernardino Luini, c. 1525–30). Salome is shown as a young woman with a sly and cunning expression.*

Medieval Christians prayed to John the Baptist, believing that through him, Christ would enter their souls. He is reputedly buried in Sebaste, Samaria. Alone among the saints, his feast day is held on his birthday. However, the date of his death is also celebrated in the West on 29 August.

An important saint, some of his relics are claimed to be held in St Sylvester's Church in Rome, and in Amiens, France. Many churches in Britain and Europe have been dedicated to him.

Left Saint John the Baptist *(Titian, c. 1540). John may be dressed in skins and rags, but he is here presented as a powerful man and leader. The lamb lies at his feet.*

THE MEANING OF BAPTISM

Baptism is a religious purification ceremony in which a person is either immersed in water, or has water poured over their head. Baptism is part of the Christian tradition, but can be seen to have a precursor in the Jewish tradition of undergoing a *mikvah*, or cleansing ritual, for instance on conversion to Judaism.

Baptism has been subject to many interpretations by different Christian churches, and as a result has varied meanings. It can be seen as a path to salvation and a process by which a person is cleansed of their sins. In this way, baptism may help a convert to Christianity put their past behind them and start afresh.

Similarly, baptism may be seen as a symbolic death and rebirth, an interpretation put forward in the Bible by Paul who says that we share in the death, burial and rebirth of Jesus Christ through baptism. Baptism can also function as a symbol of conversion, through which a believer declares their faith and their membership of a particular church.

Right Mosaic in the dome of the Arian Baptistry in Ravenna, Italy (5th century AD). *The Holy Spirit, visible as a dove, hovers above the head of Christ during his baptism by John.*

DISMAS

JESUS COMFORTED DISMAS, THE "GOOD THIEF", AS TOGETHER THEY SUFFERED DEATH BY CRUCIFIXION. DISMAS FELT THAT UNLIKE JESUS HE DESERVED HIS PUNISHMENT AS HE HAD COMMITTED A CRIME.

KEY FACTS
Crucified next to Christ
DATES: *d.c.AD 30*
BIRTH PLACE: *Probably Galilee*
PATRON OF: *Thieves, condemned criminals, undertakers*
FEAST DAY: *25 March*
EMBLEM: *Tall cross, naked on cross*

Dismas, a common thief, was nailed to a cross next to Jesus on the day of the Crucifixion and spoke with him. The Eastern Orthodox Church has put in their litany the words that Dismas uttered to Jesus, "Lord," he said, "remember me when you come into your kingdom". Jesus gave the reassuring answer, "Today thou shalt be with me in Paradise".

Luke records the story in his gospel. Dismas reprimands the other thief, Gestas, who asks Jesus, as the Messiah, to prove it and save all three of them from death. According to a medieval story, some time previously, Dismas, in awe of the infant Jesus, had even ordered his fellow bandits to leave the Holy Family unmolested as they made their escape to Egypt.

In the Middle Ages, Dismas came to be seen as the patron saint of prisoners and thieves.

Right The Crucifixion
(Francesco Botticini, c.1471).

VERONICA

AN ORDINARY WOMAN WITH A KIND HEART TRIED TO SOOTHE CHRIST AS HE CARRIED HIS CROSS ON THE WAY TO HIS CRUCIFIXION AT CALVARY. THE VEIL SHE USED BECAME AN IMPORTANT RELIC.

KEY FACTS
Wiped the brow of Christ
DATES: *1st century AD*
BIRTH PLACE: *Probably Galilee*
FEAST DAY: *12 July*
EMBLEM: *Veil with Christ's image upon it*

There is a strong possibility that Veronica is a legendary figure. Even her name is likely to be a combination of *vera*, meaning "true" in Latin, and *icon*, meaning "image" in ancient Greek. However, she figures in the Stations of the Cross, the 14 events that mark the journey of Christ carrying his cross to the Hill of Calvary.

Veronica was a woman in the mob who followed Jesus on his last earthly trip. The crowds pushed and shoved to catch a glimpse of this man, the so-called "King of the Jews", and many yelled insults in bloodthirsty tones. But scattered among the crowds were frightened, anxious and distressed Christians. Veronica was one of these. Pitying Jesus as he sweated and struggled under his burden, she took off her veil and wiped his brow.

An imprint of his face was left on the veil and it was taken to St Peter's Basilica in Rome in the 8th century. The veil became a popular relic in the 14th and 15th centuries. Claims that Jesus had once cured Veronica of a blood illness remain unproven.

Left St Veronica's veil is clearly imprinted with the image of Jesus Christ (the Master of Saint Veronica, Germany, c.1420).

JOSEPH OF ARIMATHEA

A SECRET BUT WEALTHY CONVERT TO CHRISTIANITY RESCUED THE BODY OF CHRIST AFTER THE CRUCIFIXION. HE LAID IT TO REST IN THE TOMB HE HAD PREPARED FOR HIMSELF.

KEY FACTS

Cared for the dead body of Jesus

DATES: *1st century AD*

BIRTH PLACE: *Jerusalem*

PATRON OF: *Grave diggers, burial, cemetery keepers and caretakers*

FEAST DAY: *17 March*

Joseph was a wealthy Israelite who had secretly converted to Christianity. He did not take part in the Jewish condemnation of Jesus, nor did he speak against it.

Following the arrest of Jesus, the situation in Jerusalem was tense. Jewish leaders were calling for the punishment of this person who claimed to be the Messiah. But Pontius Pilate, the Roman governor, was reluctant to sentence Jesus to death.

To mark the Jewish festival of Passover, Pilate offered to pardon one prisoner, giving the Jews a

Below Joseph of Arimathea preaches to the inhabitants of Britain (William Blake, 18th century).

choice between Jesus and the common thief, Barabbas. Pilate was shocked by their choice and washed his hands to indicate his innocence. "Let his blood be upon us," the irate crowd replied. No doubt many Christians, like Joseph of Arimathea, did not dare face the mob.

THE TOMB OF CHRIST

Overwhelmed by shame at his cowardice after the Crucifixion, Joseph went to Pontius Pilate and asked for the body of Jesus. It was the custom to throw the bodies of criminals as carrion for animals to devour. But Joseph bought the mutilated body before this happened, and took it to a garden he

owned, close to Calvary where Jesus had died. Here, Joseph had carved out a rocky sepulchre intended as his own burial place. He wrapped the body in clean linen, pushing a huge rock against the opening to close the tomb.

LEGENDARY TRAVELS

It is said that the apostle Philip sent Joseph on a mission to England where he founded a church at Glastonbury and grew a tree that is said to flower on Christmas Day. Joseph is included in the Arthurian legends.

MARY MAGDALENE

LOVED FOR HER DEVOTION TO JESUS, MARY MAGDALENE IS THE GRAND EXAMPLE OF THE REFORMED SINNER. HER LIFE SHOWS THAT ANYONE MAY BE TRANSFORMED IF THEY TRULY REPENT.

KEY FACTS
First witness to the risen Christ
DATES: *1st century AD*
BIRTH PLACE: *Possibly Magdala, Palestine*
PATRON OF: *Repentant sinners, hairdressers, perfume-makers, contemplatives*
FEAST DAY: *22 July*
EMBLEM: *Jar of ointment, loosened hair*

Mary Magdalene was one of the many women who accompanied Jesus and the apostles on their travels, caring for them and supporting them. She was close to Jesus and played a major role in the events surrounding his death and resurrection.

CONTROVERSIAL FIGURE
Over the centuries Mary Magdalene has aroused much controversy among theologians.

In Western Christianity, she is often identified both as the sister of Martha of Bethany and as the sinner who dried Christ's feet with her hair. But in Eastern Christianity, Mary Magdalene, Martha of Bethany and the sinner are three different women.

Despite these problems, the existence of Mary Magdalene is not questioned. She is known for her sincere conversion, generous heart and contemplative mind.

Above Detail of Mary kissing Jesus' feet from Life of Saint Mary Magdalene *(attr. to Giotto di Bondone, Palmerino di Guido and others, 14th century).*

REPENTANT SINNER
The story of the sinner is perhaps the most significant of the earlier accounts thought to relate to Mary Magdalene.

While Jesus was dining at the home of a Pharisee called Simon, a woman crept in and knelt before him. Simon was angered by this interruption from a woman who was a known sinner.

The woman began to kiss Jesus' feet and weep, begging to be forgiven for her transgressions. She dried his feet with her long hair and rubbed them with

Left Mary Magdalene Reading *(attr. to Ambrosius Benson, 1540).*

Above Christ on the Cross with Saints (*Luca Signorelli and Pietro Perugino, 1482*).

expensive perfumed ointment. Jesus told the distraught woman that all her sins were forgiven.

MESSENGER OF CHRIST

To modern Christians, both Orthodox and Catholic, Mary Magdalene is important because she was a devoted and committed follower of Christ who witnessed some of the most significant moments of his life. She accom-

panied Jesus on his last journey to Jerusalem and was present at the Crucifixion, keeping vigil.

Three days after his death, Mary went to his burial cave, intending to anoint his body. When she arrived she found the rock that closed the cave opening had been rolled away and the body was gone. Mary ran to question a gardener nearby. But when he spoke she realized that he was the risen Christ. Jesus gave her the glory of telling the disciples that he had been resurrected.

PREACHER AND HERMIT

Eastern legend claims that, after the Resurrection, Mary Magdalene travelled to Ephesus with the Blessed Virgin and the apostle

> "Saint Mary Magdalene, teach us to forgive ourselves, and then to forgive others."
>
> PRAYER TO ST MARY MAGDALENE

Above Mary Magdalene carried by angels (Simon Vouet, 17th century).

John, where she later died and was buried. According to a Western legend, however, Mary, along with her sister Martha and brother Lazarus, travelled by boat to France. They landed in Provence and proceeded to Marseilles, where they preached the Gospel. Mary is said to have retired to a nearby cave to live as a hermit. When she died, angels carried her to the oratory of St Maximus near Aix-en-Provence.

MARTHA

Martha was either the sister of Mary of Bethany or, as in the Western Christian tradition, the sister of Mary Magdalene. Jesus was said to enjoy visiting Martha's house and loved her and her siblings. It was Martha's brother, Lazarus, whom Jesus raised from the dead.

A popular story reveals Martha's busy nature. On one of Jesus' visits to their home, she bustled about preparing food, while Mary sat in rapt attention at the feet of Christ. When Martha expressed irritation at her sister's idleness, Jesus rebuked her. He told her that Mary had made the better choice; the contemplative life is preferable to an active one that allows no time for thought or prayer.

Above The Raising of Lazarus (*the Coetivy Master, c.1460*). *Martha was chief among the mourners to witness the miracle.*

THE APOSTLES

THE 12 MEN CHOSEN BY JESUS TO AID HIM IN HIS WORK WENT OUT TO PREACH THE GOSPEL WITH AUTHORITY AFTER HIS DEATH. IT WAS EACH APOSTLE'S DUTY TO LIVE IN IMITATION OF CHRIST.

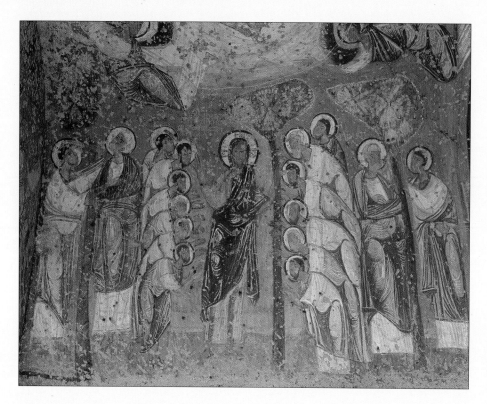

Above A very early fresco of Jesus Christ and his apostles, found in a church in Cappadocia, Turkey.

Jesus had at least 120, possibly thousands, of disciples. They were ordinary men and women who followed him wherever he went, learning from his teachings. He selected 12 special men to be his apostles (derived from the Greek word for "ambassador") from among these people. They became his closest companions and were witness to some of the most significant moments of Christ's life and resurrection.

FOLLOWERS OF JESUS

The earliest followers of Christ were two pairs of brothers – Peter and Andrew, and James and John – fishermen who worked along the coast of the Sea of Galilee. Tax collectors were generally despised at the time, and yet that was the profession of Matthew, the next apostle to be called.

It is thought that 11 of these 12 men were Galileans. Judas Iscariot, their treasurer and the man who betrayed Jesus, was the only non-Galilean. After the Crucifixion, Peter oversaw the replacement of Judas by Matthias.

FISHERS OF MEN

When Jesus called Peter and Andrew he said that if they followed him he would make them "fishers of men". Many Christians consider these words to be a metaphor for the apostles' role: to bring people to Jesus as a fisherman catches fish.

In the years of persecution, cautious Christians used the image of a fish, scratched on walls and rocks, as a secret sign. *Icthys*, the Greek word for "fish", is an acrostic, or word puzzle, consisting of the initial letters for five other words that described Christ to his believers: *Iesous Christos Theou Yios Soter* (Jesus Christ, Son of God, Saviour).

ROLE OF THE APOSTLES

Jesus defined the purpose of the work of his chosen few. They were to teach his message, to baptize, to rule by guiding the faithful, and to sanctify the grace of God through prayer. These roles were to be passed on to successors when an apostle died or became frail.

Roman Catholics believe that Jesus appointed these "men of the apostolate" to administer his Church. He put the organization into their hands with Peter, the first pope, as his chief. Peter was to rule the whole Church, make judgements and name his successor. This division of duties has remained the basis of the administrative structure of the Church ever since. All popes are believed to be Peter's successors.

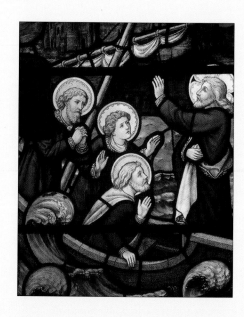

Above Christ calming a storm and saving fishermen in stained glass from Exeter Cathedral, England.

JUDAS ISCARIOT

This apostle is infamous for betraying Christ to the Jewish authorities. But it was his method of identifying his leader, Jesus, that is perceived as particularly repugnant. Judas knew that Jesus and the apostles had spent the night praying in the garden of Gethsemane. At dawn, he and the temple guards approached the group, and Judas told the guards, "The one I kiss is the man you want". For the sum of 30 pieces of silver, he kissed Jesus, who was then led to his death.

It was said that Judas, crazed with remorse, threw the "blood money" into the temple and then hanged himself. The kind of tree to which he tied his noose is still known as a Judas tree, and the field where Judas died is called "Áceldama" – the field of blood. His name is given to traitors, while any act of betrayal is often termed "the kiss of Judas".

Right The traitor's kiss is hewn from stone on this church wall in France.

Protestants were, and are, more ambivalent about the role of the individual apostles. Some credit them with divine authority. Other sects say they are simply the first evangelists or preachers. They are seen as early missionaries who were given significant qualities to fulfil their role as heralds of the gospel message.

SPREADING THE WORD

Soon after he had chosen the 12, Jesus gave his apostles the power to cast out evil spirits and cure disease. He sent them out in pairs to preach and use their gifts in the towns of Galilee, instructing them to "take nothing for their journey, except a mere staff".

After the Resurrection, the apostles dedicated themselves to spreading the teachings of Jesus around the known world. Peter was the first of them to perform a miracle and was also one of the first apostles to set out into the world as a missionary.

All the apostles undertook arduous journeys to fulfil their appointed roles. They set high standards of obedience, poverty and chastity, avoiding all worldly pleasures that might distract them from their mission.

DYING FOR THEIR FAITH

Such was the conviction of these men that they were prepared to die cruel deaths for their faith. A total of 11 apostles were martyred. The work of these brave men proved productive. After 300 years of continued apostleship the Emperor Constantine I made Christianity the religion of the Roman Empire, and from then on the "new" religion spread rapidly.

Below All the apostles were present with Jesus at the Last Supper (Justus van Gent, 1473–74).

59

JAMES THE GREAT

ABANDONING HIS FISHING NETS IN ORDER TO BECOME A "FISHER OF MEN", JAMES WAS ONE OF THE EARLIEST DISCIPLES TO FOLLOW JESUS, AND THE FIRST APOSTLE MARTYR.

KEY FACTS
Apostle
DATES: *d. AD 44*
BIRTH PLACE: *Galilee*
PATRON OF: *Spain, Guatemala, Nicaragua; and, with Philip, of Uruguay*
FEAST DAY: *25 July*
EMBLEM: *Shell, sword, pilgrim's staff, pilgrim's hat*

There were two apostles named James. One became known as James the Less and the other, James the Great – so-called because he was the elder of the two. James the Great was one of the leading apostles.

James and his brother John were fishermen who abandoned their nets to follow Jesus. Both brothers were known to be quick-tempered, hence their nickname "sons of thunder".

James also had qualities of reliability, leadership and loyalty. He witnessed the major events of Christ's life. He was one of those present at the Transfiguration, and was in the garden of Gethsemane to comfort his master during his most despairing moments.

The details of James' life after the Crucifixion are uncertain. He may have gone to Judea and Samaria to spread the Christian

Above The shell and pilgrim's staff identify St James the Great (Hans Klocker, c. 17th century).

Below Apostles Philip and James are often portrayed as men of learning (School of Fra Bartolommeo, c. 1400).

message. But it is known that he was beheaded by Herod Agrippa in Jerusalem.

His body, it is said, was carried to the shore where a boat suddenly materialized. His disciples placed the body in this miraculous vessel and it floated to the coast of Spain. There, Christians found the relics and buried them in a forest where the city of Santiago de Compostela now stands.

The shrine containing his relics in Compostela was of great importance during the Crusades, because soldiers believed St James could grant military prowess. Santiago de Compostela remains a major site of modern pilgrimage.

GROWTH OF HIS CULTUS

According to Spanish tradition James appeared to fight the Moors when they invaded Spain in AD 844. He rode through the sky on a white horse, holding a shield bearing a red cross and a sword. With his help, the Spanish vanquished their enemy.

In the 16th century, sailors allegedly saw St James resting on a cloud. It hovered protectively over the galleons carrying early Spanish explorers across the Atlantic to the Americas. He inspired them to convert the American people they encountered. The feast day of St James the Great is celebrated in major national festivals in South America to this day.

JAMES THE LESS

THIS APOSTLE IS IDENTIFIED AS "THE SON OF ALPHAEUS" BUT HE SLIPS QUIETLY, ALMOST ANONYMOUSLY, THROUGH THE CHRISTIAN STORY. SOME SOURCES IDENTIFY HIM AS CHRIST'S BROTHER.

KEY FACTS
Apostle
DATES: *d.AD 62*
BIRTH PLACE: *Galilee*
PATRON OF: *The dying*
FEAST DAY: *3 May*
EMBLEM: *Fuller's club*

There is little mention of James the Less during Jesus' ministry. But after the Crucifixion and Resurrection, this James communicated closely with Jesus before his Ascension into heaven.

James became an important figure in the new Christian community in Jerusalem where St Paul relied on his leadership. During the Council of Jerusalem (*c.*AD 50), James supported Paul in the call to accept Gentiles as Christians without demanding these converts be circumcized. This decision caused much controversy at the council. As men brought up in the Jewish tradition, the apostles tended to regard circumcision as an important symbol of faith.

James was stoned or possibly clubbed to death. Another version says James was thrown from a temple top, but as he lay dying, he forgave his tormentors. Even Jewish leaders of the time believed the city faced calamity after the death of this fine man. James is often linked with the apostle Philip, and many churches are dedicated to "Philip and James".

Right The Communion of the Apostle James the Less (*Niccolò Bambini, 1720*).

PHILIP

THIS PRACTICAL-MINDED APOSTLE HELPED IN THE FEEDING OF THE 5,000, AND THE SEARCHING QUESTIONS HE ASKED JESUS CLARIFIED IMPORTANT POINTS OF FAITH.

KEY FACTS
Apostle
DATES: *1st century AD*
BIRTH PLACE: *Bethsaida*
PATRON OF: *Uruguay*
FEAST DAY: *3 May (West)*
EMBLEM: *Loaf of bread, large cross, a dragon*

Philip heard John the Baptist preach and then sought out Jesus. Philip seems to have been an energetic and practical man. He arranged appointments, and introduced Nathanael, later St Bartholomew, to Christ.

When Jesus wanted to feed a crowd of 5,000 people who had gathered to hear his message, Philip commented, "Two hundred pennyworth of bread is not sufficient for them". But when a small boy offered five loaves and two fishes, Philip helped distribute the food, believing this would feed everyone as Jesus said.

Above The Apostle Philip (*Georges de La Tour, 1620*).

At the Last Supper, Philip asked, "Lord, show us the Father". The answer came from Jesus, "I am in the Father and the Father is in me."

Philip preached in Phrygia and is thought to have killed an evil dragon brought by the Scythians. He possibly died a martyr in Hierapolis (in Syria), but his relics are held in Rome. He is closely associated with James the Less. The two apostles share a feast day.

BARTHOLOMEW

BEST-KNOWN FOR THE CRUEL MANNER OF HIS DEATH FROM BEING FLAYED ALIVE, THIS SINCERE AND LOYAL APOSTLE IS THOUGHT TO HAVE PREACHED AS FAR AFIELD AS INDIA.

KEY FACTS
Apostle
DATES: *1st century AD*
BIRTH PLACE: *Probably Galilee*
PATRON OF: *Tanners*
FEAST DAY: *24 August*
EMBLEM: *Butcher's knife*

When Jesus first met Bartholomew, also known as Nathanael, he observed a man "in whom there is no guile". Bartholomew never doubted the truth of Jesus' teachings and was one of the early apostles. He was present at the Pentecost and then travelled to spread the message.

Bartholomew is said to have preached in Armenia and India, where he may have left behind a copy of the Gospel of St Matthew. Tradition says he defeated demons in India that encouraged idol worship. He converted the local king Polemius and his family. This action enraged the king's brother, Astrages, who captured him and ordered Bartholomew to be flayed alive and then beheaded.

Michelangelo shows Bartholomew holding his own flayed skin in *The Last Judgement* in the Sistine Chapel, Vatican City. His relics were enshrined on an island in the River Tiber in Rome.

Left A curved butcher's knife forms part of this statue of Bartholomew in San Gennaro in Italy, referring to his cruel death.

JUDE

TRADITIONALLY BELIEVED TO BE THE AUTHOR OF THE EPISTLE OF JUDE, THIS APOSTLE IS NOW BEST KNOWN AS THE PATRON SAINT OF LOST CAUSES. HE IS OFTEN TURNED TO BY THOSE IN DESPAIR.

KEY FACTS
Apostle
DATES: *1st century AD*
BIRTH PLACE: *Palestine*
PATRON OF: *Hopeless causes*
FEAST DAY: *28 October (West)*
EMBLEM: *Club, holding a boat*

The apostle Jude is not mentioned with any great frequency in the gospels, but he has a large modern cultus. For uncertain reasons, this apostle gained a reputation for offering sympathy and hope to those in despair. Worshippers turn to him when they are in dire trouble.

His name is often followed by the words "not Iscariot", so that he is not confused with Judas. He is also known as Thaddaeus.

It is claimed he wrote the *Epistle of Jude*. This tells of a mission to Persia with another apostle, Simon, who apparently was his cousin. Jude was martyred by being clubbed to death, although there is little evidence to verify how he died.

Sometimes Jude is pictured holding a ship while his cousin clutches a fish. These signs indicate that the men were both former fishermen.

Left A detail of The Apostle Thaddeus *from Siena Cathedral (Duccio di Buoninsegna, 1308).*

THOMAS

CHIEFLY REMEMBERED AS "DOUBTING THOMAS", THIS APOSTLE NEEDED PROOF BEFORE ACCEPTING ANY TRUTH. HE WAS THE FIRST TO ACKNOWLEDGE CHRIST'S DIVINITY AFTER THE RESURRECTION.

KEY FACTS

Apostle
DATES: *1st century AD*
BIRTH PLACE: *Probably Palestine*
PATRON OF: *Architects, carpenters, surveyors, builders, sculptors*
FEAST DAY: *3 July (West)*
EMBLEM: *Incredulity, holding T-square as a builder*

Thomas questioned things but, once he was given a satisfying answer, remained firm in his belief. He asked Jesus, "Where are you going? How can we know the way?" Jesus answered, "I am the way, the truth, and the life." Fiercely loyal, Thomas was ready to die with Jesus.

The apostle is most famously known as "Doubting Thomas" because he could not believe the Resurrection of Christ. When he met the Lord after his death, Thomas asked to touch the wounds left by a soldier's lance as he hung on the cross. Christ allowed him to do so and, now convinced of the reality, Thomas became ardent in his belief. Indeed, he was the first to publicly acknowledge the divinity of Christ by calling him "My Lord and my God".

A legend says that because Thomas did not witness the Blessed Virgin's Assumption to heaven, she appeared in person to reassure him. As a token of proof, she gave him her belt.

His life after the Pentecost is mysterious. There are claims that he travelled to India where he

Below A patient Christ offers proof of his resurrection in the painting Doubting Thomas *(Gian Francesco Barbieri, 1621).*

preached and built a cathedral for a prince. Such stories are perhaps confirmed by a community of Christians in Kerala, south India, who identify themselves as the "St Thomas Christians".

In 1522, Portuguese travellers claimed to have seen his grave in Mylapore near Madras. The *Acts of Thomas*, a document from the 3rd or 4th century, says he was killed by a lance. His relics ended up in Persia (Iran), but Ortona, in Italy, also laid claim to them.

PETER

CHRIST DESCRIBED PETER AS THE "ROCK OF THE CHURCH". AS THE LEADER OF THE APOSTLES, HE IS THE EARTHLY FATHER OF THE FAITH, AND IS SAID TO HOLD THE KEYS TO THE KINGDOM OF HEAVEN.

KEY FACTS
Leader of the apostles; called the rock of the Church by Jesus
DATES: *d.c.AD 64*
BIRTH PLACE: *Bethsaida, Sea of Galilee*
PATRON OF: *Fishermen, papacy*
FEAST DAY: *29 June*
EMBLEM: *Keys, ship, fish, cockerel*

Peter was warm and impetuous by nature, yet also rather cautious. He needed reassurance that Jesus was indeed the Messiah.

To his eternal shame, he was so overwhelmed by fear during the trial of Jesus that three times he denied his friendship with him. But Peter's passion and general boldness made him leader of the apostles. His name, Cephas in Aramaic, means "rock" and Jesus chose him as the "rock" upon which the Church was built.

Known as Simon Peter, he fished with his brother Andrew on the Sea of Galilee. Jesus came to them one day when they had failed to catch any fish. He told them to lower their nets and to their surprise they hauled up an enormous catch. "Come with

Below Peter enthroned and six scenes from the lives of Jesus and St Peter (the Master of St Peter, 1280).

Above A mural showing Peter's denial of Christ and the cock crowing (from the Church of the Holy Cross at Platanistasa, Cyprus, 15th century).

me," Jesus said, "and I will make you fishers of men." After this, Peter began his ministry with Jesus, and he is mentioned frequently throughout the gospels. He was very close to Christ and became the leader of the 12 apostles. He was with Jesus during the Agony in the Garden, the night Christ spent in tormented prayer before his arrest and death. And when the soldiers came that dawn to make the arrest, Peter was so enraged that he sliced off the ear of Judas Iscariot, the man who had betrayed Jesus to the authorities to his eternal shame.

Peter was one of three apostles to witness the Transfiguration when Jesus was surrounded by light with the prophets, Moses and Elijah, on either side. A voice said, "This is my beloved Son… Listen to Him." And after Pentecost, when the Holy Spirit gave the apostles the gift of tongues, Peter was the first to speak to the crowds.

FIRST CHURCH LEADER
Peter took administrative control of the apostles after Christ's death and chose Matthias to replace Judas Iscariot. He sent Paul and Barnabas to the Mediterranean as disciples and evangelists.

Peter cured a beggar who had suffered all his life from a lame leg, thus becoming the first apostle to perform a miracle. More significantly, he was ready to sit at a meal with a non-Jew, or Gentile. Peter converted a Roman centurion, Cornelius, who was the first Gentile to become a Christian believer.

The admittance of Gentiles caused controversy among the other apostles who had preached

only to other Jews. They regarded the diet of non-Jews as unclean. But Peter had the support of Paul, who, like him, was determined to spread Christianity to everyone. Peter's frequent public preaching led to his arrest by Herod, who imprisoned him under heavy guard. But the apostle escaped, helped – it was said – by an angel who broke his chains and opened the prison doors.

This convinced Peter that he had truly been chosen to lead. He wrote letters and preached unceasingly, while organizing from Jerusalem the appointment and missions of evangelists.

Some authorities credit Peter with introducing the concept of "episcopal succession". In finding a replacement for Judas Iscariot, he began a system of choosing leaders from men who were familiar with the first apostles. This gave rise to the tradition that bishops and priests had a special closeness to Christ, and ensured that the status of priests remained separate from their flock.

When Peter visited Rome, he was arrested for his Christian activities and tried by the

Below Peter is dressed in papal splendour as he observes the Crucifixion (Ottaviano di Martino Nelli, 1424).

CORNELIUS

Cornelius (not to be confused with the Gentile Roman centurion) was an heir to Peter who became "bishop" of Rome in 251. He followed Peter in teaching that the Church must be conciliatory in its embrace. He favoured a lenient approach towards Christians who had lapsed. Another priest, Novatian, thought those who committed adultery, murder or even made a second marriage, should be expelled from the Church. Cornelius asserted that the Church had the power to forgive and welcome the repentant back to the community. The inscription "Cornelius martyr" inscribed on his tomb can be seen in the crypt of Lucina, in Rome.

Right This reliquary of St Cornelius, dating from 1350–60, is made of gold and silver.

"YOU ARE PETER AND UPON THIS ROCK I WILL BUILD MY CHURCH."

JESUS SPEAKING TO PETER

Emperor Nero, who condemned him to death by crucifixion. Legend has it that Peter asked to be hung upside down on the cross because he was not worthy of dying in the same way as Christ.

Some claim that he died on the same day as Paul, and they share a feast day. For two centuries after Peter's death, letters which were supposedly written by him were distributed in order to revive his lessons and maintain his influence.

He was buried in a tomb beneath the Vatican. Believers consider him the keeper of the gates to heaven, the saint who can let them enter the kingdom, or deny them entry when they die. Peter's enduring popularity is shown by the dedication of 1,129 churches to him in England alone.

Below Peter was the first apostle to perform a miracle. In this painting St John and St Peter heal a lame man (Masolino da Panicale, 1425).

SIMON

SIMON LIVED TO A GREAT OLD AGE AFTER A SUCCESSFUL LIFE AS A WELL-TRAVELLED MISSIONARY.

Simon is featured in a number of legends and has long been venerated, especially in the East. He is also known as the Zealot or the Canaanite, possibly because he had belonged to a strict Jewish sect. He appears in the New Testament as one of the apostles, but is not much mentioned after the Pentecost, when the Holy Spirit granted Christ's followers the gift of tongues.

One story says he travelled with Jude and that they took their mission as far as Persia (Iran).

Above The Apostle Simon *in a chiaroscuro drawing (Mair von Landshut, 1496).*

KEY FACTS
Apostle
DATES: *1st century AD*
BIRTH PLACE: *Probably Galilee*
FEAST DAY: *28 October (West)*
EMBLEM: *Boat, sometimes the weapon of his murder, a falchion – a short sword bent like a sickle*

Here, pagan priests slaughtered both men. Some sources say Simon was sawn in two, others that he was stabbed to death.

A further interpretation has Simon dying in battle when he was bishop of Jerusalem, while others claim that the apostle trekked across North Africa until he reached the age of 120 years and was finally martyred.

BARNABAS

CHRIST DID NOT CHOOSE BARNABAS AS AN APOSTLE. HOWEVER, HIS MISSIONARY WORK OUTSIDE PALESTINE, FIRST WITH PAUL, THEN ALONE, BROUGHT HIM THE TITLE OF HONORARY APOSTLE.

KEY FACTS
Apostle
DATES: *1st century AD*
BIRTH PLACE: *Unknown*
FEAST DAY: *11 June*
EMBLEM: *Sometimes associated with a type of thistle that flowers on his feast day (in England)*

Barnabas was a Cypriot Jew who took the newly converted Paul to meet the other apostles in Jerusalem. Though not one of the 12 apostles, Barnabas was one of the earliest evangelists.

Peter described Barnabas as "a good man, full of the Holy Ghost and of faith", and sent him to Antioch. From there Barnabas sailed with Paul to Cyprus, where Barnabas showed the people what "wonders God had wrought".

He is believed to be the founder of the Church in Cyprus. He may have been martyred at Salamis in AD 61. *The Epistle of Barnabas* carries his name, but its authorship is uncertain.

Below Paul and Barnabas (attr. to Rombout van Troyen, 17th century).

ANDREW

PETER'S BROTHER ANDREW WAS THE FIRST OF THE DISCIPLES JESUS CALLED. THE CRUEL MANNER OF HIS REPUTED MARTYRDOM ON A SALTIRE CROSS IS COMMEMORATED ON THE SCOTTISH FLAG.

KEY FACTS

Apostle
DATES: *d.c.AD 60*
BIRTH PLACE: *Bethsaida, Galilee*
PATRON OF: *Scotland, Greece
and Russia, fishermen*
FEAST DAY: *30 November*
EMBLEM: *Small saltire cross*

Andrew heard John the Baptist preach and longed to meet Jesus. He and his brother Peter (then called Simon), worked as fishermen on the Sea of Galilee.

Initially, the brothers only joined Jesus at his preaching from time to time. But finally they abandoned their families and their work to follow him. The Greek Orthodox Church calls Andrew "Protoclete", meaning "first-called". They venerate him highly, as do the Roman Catholic and Russian Orthodox Churches.

Jesus granted the Miraculous Draught of Fishes to Andrew and Peter. This occurred when, after a day of poor fishing, the presence of Jesus produced a great haul for the two men. Andrew also played a part in the feeding of the 5,000 with loaves and fishes. Being an intense believer, he encouraged Gentiles to meet the Messiah, too.

MISSION AND DEATH

After the Crucifixion, it seems much of Andrew's mission work was in Greece, but he also went to Constantinople (Istanbul), a key place in the history of the early Church. Medieval worshippers claim he founded the Church there. Some believe he preached as far as Kiev in Ukraine before moving on to Scotland, but there is no evidence for this.

Legend gives Andrew a brave martyrdom at Patras. With dignity, he disrobed himself and knelt before the cross as his persecutors prepared him for crucifixion. He was bound to the wooden beams

Above Martyrdom of the Apostle Andreas *from Westphalia (artist unknown, c. 1500).*

of the saltire (X-shaped) cross. Even in his agony, Andrew is said to have carried on preaching. The crowd begged the consul to show mercy and take the dying man down. This he did after two days.

In 1204, Crusaders siezed Constantinople and took St Andrew's supposed relics to Amalfi, Italy. However, some say that St Regulus journeyed "to the ends of the earth" carrying his relics. Then an angel led him to Scotland, to the place now named after him, St Andrews.

Below St Andrew and St Peter Responding to the Call of Jesus, *Byzantine mosaic (6th century).*

PAUL

INITIALLY A PERSECUTOR OF CHRISTIANS, AFTER HIS DRAMATIC CONVERSION PAUL BECAME THE CHURCH'S FIRST MISSIONARY. HIS LETTERS DEVELOPED AND EXPOUNDED CHRISTIAN THEOLOGY.

On meeting Paul, a Roman centurion was struck by the apostle's air of nobility and courage. Others described him as having the spirit of a strong man who was generous and eager to create a cheerful atmosphere.

Paul was born in Tarsus to a strict Jewish family and was named Saul. His upbringing was steeped in strict Jewish Law. Although he applauded the killing of the Christian martyr, St Stephen, Saul was confused. How could this man find the strength to defy the Law, simply through the love of Jesus Christ? Even so, Saul decided that no one should break the laws that bind society.

CONVERSION
Saul tried to find Christians and deliver them to possible death. On one such errand Saul was travelling along the road to Damascus

Above This portrait of St Paul captures the expression of a noble man (Etienne Parrocel, c. 1740s).

Below Paul travelling on the road to Damascus with his troops in search of Christians to persecute in The Conversion of St Paul *(Pieter Bruegel the elder, 1567).*

KEY FACTS
Great missionary and theologian
DATES: *d. AD 64–65*
BIRTH PLACE: *Tarsus in Cilicia*
PATRON OF: *Malta, Greece, Catholic missions and lay teachers*
FEAST DAY: *29 June*
EMBLEM: *Sword and book; generally portrayed as elderly and balding with a long beard*

when suddenly he was blinded by a great light and overcome by the presence of Jesus. He understood from this vision that his mission was to spread the Christian faith to Gentile, non-Jewish people.

His sight was miraculously restored three days later, and shortly afterwards he was baptized. He then spent several years in Arabia living as a hermit.

He returned to Damascus and began to preach about Jesus, and took the name of Paul as a mark of his change. His preaching, however, aroused the fury of local Jews. Paul was forced to escape with the help of fellow disciples who lowered him in a basket over the city wall.

He travelled to Jerusalem to meet Peter who chose him and Barnabas as travelling evangelists.

APOSTLE TO THE GENTILES
Paul's first journey took him to Cyprus and Syria before he returned to take part in what came to be called the Council of Jerusalem in about AD 50. Here, he found Peter and others in dispute over the rules of conversion.

The apostles, all born as Jews, had tended to preach only to other Jews about Jesus the Messiah. Peter wanted Gentiles, or non-Jews, to be brought into the fold. Paul, who agreed Christ brought redemption to all of

humanity, managed to find a compromise. The Church, he argued, should be as catholic (universal) as the Roman Empire.

The disciples agreed that Gentiles must adopt certain Jewish rules, especially those regarding food. But they decided that the Gentiles must never be denied access to the Lord's message. Paul's diplomacy possibly saved Christianity from remaining a mere sect of Judaism, and opened the way for a whole new religious belief system.

Paul spent years travelling around the Middle East and the Mediterranean coast preaching the gospel. He was shipwrecked, mocked, arrested, but never deterred. While travelling, he wrote numerous letters which are included in the Epistles of the New Testament. These letters were read at gatherings so people might be inspired by his words to convert to the new faith.

His teaching was intimate and personal, related to his own experience of the vision of Jesus. His writings say that Jewish Talmudic Law teaches knowledge of sin, provoking people to dwell on evil thoughts. But the message

"FOR I AM PERSUADED THAT NEITHER DEATH, NOR LIFE NOR ANGELS, NOR PRINCIPALITIES, NOR POWERS, NOR THINGS PRESENT, NOR THINGS TO COME, NOR HEIGHT, NOR DEPTH, NOR ANY OTHER CREATURE, SHALL BE ABLE TO SEPARATE US FROM THE LOVE OF GOD, WHICH IS JESUS CHRIST OUR LORD."

ROMANS 8

Above St Paul's, Christopher Wren's magnificent cathedral in London, is dedicated to the man regarded as the greatest apostle of the Church.

of Jesus, said Paul, is one of love, "written on the heart". Jesus works inwards and outwards on people's thoughts, and Christians are "inspired to God-likeness".

ARREST AND DEATH

While visiting Jerusalem, Paul's preaching enraged the Jews who handed him over to the authorities. As a Roman citizen, he was able to claim trial in that city, though shipwrecked in Malta on the way. He was placed under house arrest and after some years, he was put on trial. Sources vary, and it was possibly on a later visit to Rome after further travels that he was found guilty of "anti-imperial activities" and beheaded.

It was claimed that his head bounced three times, and at each bounce a spring gushed from the earth. The place of his beheading is called Tre Fontane, in Rome. Tradition claims he died on 29 June in AD 64 or 65, the same

day as Peter's martyrdom (also in Rome), and thus they share their feast day.

Paul is the first great missionary and theologian of Christianity. He is regarded as second only to Jesus in inspiring Christian faith.

SAINT TITUS
St Paul's importance is confirmed by the enormous church dedicated to him in London. Yet little is heard of his close disciple, Titus, the Gentile who attended the decisive Council of Jerusalem where the apostles agreed that Gentiles should be accepted into the faith.

Titus travelled with Paul as secretary and companion on a mission and was entrusted with setting up a community in Crete. Paul warned him to be firm in converting the surly Cretans. Titus was to spend most of his life there, although he lived for a while in Dalmatia. He is recognized as the first bishop of Crete and was buried there in Gortyna. His head was taken as a relic to Venice in AD 823.

Above Titus helped Paul to escape the city walls of Damascus in a basket.

MATTHEW

THE PRESUMED AUTHOR OF THE FIRST GOSPEL WAS A FORMER TAX COLLECTOR.

There are few stories about Matthew, also known as Levi. Little is known too about his life as an evangelist. He is presumed to be the author of the first gospel, written in an easy style for public reading.

Matthew was a tax collector, one of the hated class of Jews who collected money on behalf of the Roman authorities. His fellow Jews not only regarded this close contact with Gentiles as unclean, but also distrusted tax-men and believed they were corrupt. When Jesus approached Matthew, and

Above Saint Matthew *from* The Book of Kells, *an illuminated manuscript,* c.AD 800.

was even prepared to eat with him, he immediately rose from his counting table and followed him.

KEY FACTS
Author of the first gospel
DATES: *1st century*
BIRTH PLACE: *Capernaum*
DEATH PLACE: *Possibly Ethiopia*
PATRON OF: *Bankers, accountants, tax collectors, bookkeepers*
FEAST DAY: *21 September*
EMBLEM: *Angel or man with wings, money bag, spear or sword*

After Christ's Ascension to heaven, Matthew became a missionary like the other apostles but his journeys are not recorded.

An apocryphal story says that Matthew was martyred in Ethiopia defending an abbess. His reputed relics were transported to Salerno in Italy via Brittany. Others say he died in Persia.

JOHN

THE DISCIPLE WHOM JESUS LOVED AND ENTRUSTED HIS MOTHER TO AFTER HIS DEATH IS THOUGHT TO BE THE AUTHOR OF THE FOURTH GOSPEL, THREE EPISTLES AND THE BOOK OF REVELATION.

John and James the Great were two fiery-tempered brothers, sons of Zebedee. Both were called from mending their fishing nets to follow Jesus.

John's ardour could turn him to brave and reckless endeavours. However, Jesus' faith in John was apparent at the Crucifixion. When he was facing death, Jesus put his mother, Mary, the Blessed Virgin, into John's care rather than choose anyone else.

The belief that he was a favourite disciple is confirmed by the facts of John's life. He was with Jesus at the Miracle of the Loaves and Fishes. With Peter and James, he witnessed the Transfiguration, and he was by the side of Jesus during the Agony in the Garden of Gethsemane.

John was placed at the right hand of Christ at the Last Supper, and he was the only disciple not to desert Jesus during the horrors

Left This woodcarving depicts John's anguish and horror during Christ's crucifixion at Calvary (Ferdinand Maximilian Brokof, 18th century).

KEY FACTS
Author of the Fourth Gospel and the Book of Revelation
DATES: *1st century AD*
BIRTH PLACE: *Galilee*
PATRON OF: *Booksellers, writers, artists, knights, theologians, typesetters*
FEAST DAY: *27 December (West)*
EMBLEM: *Eagle, chalice, sometimes a book*

of the Crucifixion. He kept vigil at the foot of the Cross, and then showed no hesitation in accepting Jesus had risen from the dead.

After the Ascension, John worked with St Peter organizing the early Christian Church. After some years, he was exiled to Patmos, a Greek island. One of the greatest Christian evangelists, it is thought he died at a great age in Ephesus, Turkey.

MARK

THE AUTHOR OF THE SECOND GOSPEL INTERPRETED AND RECORDED PETER'S TEACHING.

Mark was young when he first met Jesus. His mother's house was a favourite meeting place for the apostles and Jesus often visited.

Although Mark was not an apostle, he seems to have been charming and affectionate, though not brave or confident. It was rumoured that he ran away from the Roman soldiers who arrested Jesus. And he abandoned a difficult mission with St Peter to Cyprus. But when older, he gave St Paul much support during his arrest in Rome. St Peter even referred to him fondly as his son.

Mark travelled widely as an evangelist, visiting Jerusalem, Rome and Egypt. He may have travelled to Alexandria and become the first bishop of that city. Mark's gospel incorporates many of Peter's teachings and memoirs, so it is likely it was written in Rome where the two men spent long periods together.

Despite Mark's important role in the Christian story as the writer of the Second Gospel, his place and manner of death are uncertain. He is thought to have died sometime after Jerusalem was destroyed in AD 70. A legend claims he was tied round the neck and dragged through the streets of Alexandria. His bodily relics were carried by the Venetians to Venice where they were placed in the basilica named after him, St Mark's Basilica.

Right St Mark's famous emblem, the winged lion, sits at his feet (the Ulm Master, 1442).

The relics survived a fire in the church in AD 976, and were installed in the new building. A series of mosaics in the church tell the story of St Mark and the translation of his relics.

KEY FACTS
Writer of the Second Gospel
DATES: *d.c.AD 74*
BIRTH PLACE: *Jerusalem*
PATRON OF: *Notaries, translators, opticians, glass workers, Venice*
FEAST DAY: *25 April*
EMBLEM: *Winged lion*

Left A statue of St Mark by the early Renaissance sculptor Donatello (1411–15). St Mark's image appears widely in Italy.

His emblem is a winged lion. This refers to the inspiration Mark derived from John the Baptist, who lived in the wilderness with animals. Mark became the patron saint of Venice. His lion emblem can be found on the façades of many buildings across the Greek Ionian islands, where medieval Venice held dominion.

LUKE

THE PHYSICIAN AND WRITER OF THE THIRD GOSPEL WAS A MOST SYMPATHETIC MAN WHO, UNUSUALLY FOR THE TIME, INCLUDED IN HIS WORK THE WOMEN WHO WERE IMPORTANT IN THE LIFE OF JESUS.

St Luke was a Greek doctor. His writings contain observations of women and human suffering, and reveal him to be gentle and sensitive. St Paul probably converted Luke, a Gentile of Antioch, and persuaded him to travel with him on evangelical voyages around the Mediterranean.

More than any other New Testament writer, Luke shows us the women in Jesus' life. Thanks to him, we know more about Mary Magdalene and about the widow whose son Jesus restored to life.

Luke tells the story of Mary and the Annunciation, and also mentions Elizabeth, mother of John the Baptist. He is deeply respectful of the Virgin Mary and apparently knew her. The words

Above This enamel plaque showing St Luke was made in the workshop of the Kremlin (17th century).

Below St Luke Drawing the Virgin (Rogier van der Weyden, 15th century). Luke was a talented painter as well as writer.

KEY FACTS
Writer of the Third Gospel
DATES: *1st century AD*
BIRTH PLACE: *Antioch, Syria*
PATRON OF: *Surgeons, doctors, painters and glass artists*
FEAST DAY: *18 October*
EMBLEM: *Winged ox*

he puts into her mouth when he describes the Annunciation are known as "Mary's Prayer", and have become part of the liturgy.

A HUMANE APPROACH

Luke emphasizes gentle aspects of the faith. He repeats the most moving parables that Jesus told to show examples of goodness and kindness. However, his gospel does open with the story of the bull sacrificed by Zachary to celebrate the birth of his son, John the Baptist. This accounts for Luke's emblem, a winged ox.

He also wrote *The Acts of the Apostles*, a mixture of history and prophecy describing the spread of Christianity. He explains how the faith broke with Judaism, and extended beyond Jerusalem to Rome in the West.

Luke also has a reputation as a painter. There are many portraits of the Virgin attributed to St Luke in the Christian world, though unfortunately none are authenticated. The church of St Augustine in Rome has several such portraits. It is said Luke lived to a great age and never married.

"MY SOUL DOTH MAGNIFY THE LORD, AND MY SPIRIT HATH REJOICED IN GOD MY SAVIOUR"

LUKE 1:46

STEPHEN

THE FIRST CHRISTIAN MARTYR
WAS CRUELLY STONED TO DEATH
IN JERUSALEM FOR HIS BELIEFS.

The first ever Christian martyr was a learned Jew and one of the first deacons. After his conversion, Stephen took control of almsgiving to elderly widows in his community. When he began to preach he often criticized some aspects of Jewish Mosaic law.

After Stephen had made some particularly hostile allegations, his Jewish listeners became outraged. He accused them of resisting the true Spirit and being responsible for the death of Christ.

KEY FACTS
First martyr
DATES: *d.c.AD 35*
BIRTH PLACE: *Jerusalem*
PATRON OF: *Bricklayers, stonemasons, builders, deacons*
FEAST DAY: *26 December (West)*
EMBLEM: *Stones, the palm of martyrdom, a book*

The mob stoned him to death with the consent of a man called Saul, a Roman Jew. Saul later converted and became Paul, the great Christian leader.

Left The stoning of St Stephen as depicted in a stained glass window (St Edmundsbury Cathedral, Suffolk, England, 19th century).

EUSTACE

THE HERO OF THIS LEGEND CHASES A STAG THAT BEARS THE CROSS
OF CHRIST WITHIN ITS ANTLERS. THIS EXPERIENCE LEADS TO HIS
CONVERSION AND HIS UNTIMELY DEATH.

Fabulous stories surround the figure of St Eustace. Named Placidas at birth, he became a high-ranking Roman soldier and was a keen huntsman.

One day he stalked a stag deep in the forest. As he lifted his bow, the stag turned. A gleaming crucifix grew between its antlers. Then the stag said, "I am Jesus, whom you honour without knowing".

Placidas, his wife and children converted to Christianity and he was baptized as Eustace. They suffered many misfortunes and Eustace's faith was tested to the limits. His wife was seduced (or raped) and his children sold into slavery. Later, their luck changed for the better when Eustace was

KEY FACTS
Miracle appearance of the crucifix
DATES: *Unknown*
BIRTH PLACE: *Unknown*
PATRON OF: *Hunters and those in difficult situations*
FEAST DAY: *2 November (West; officially de-canonized)*
EMBLEM: *Stag bearing a crucifix*

reunited with his family in Rome. He was honoured for a military victory, but unfortunately this good luck did not last, and when he refused to make a pagan sacrifice, he and his family were thrown to the lions in the arena. The beasts refused to attack, so the entire family was burnt inside a brazen bull – a form of execution devised by the ancient Greeks, akin to being boiled alive.

Left The Vision of Saint Eustace (Albrecht Dürer, 16th century).

POLYCARP

A TRUE SHEPHERD TO HIS FLOCK, THE BISHOP OF SMYRNA WAS ONE OF THE APOSTOLIC FATHERS OF THE CHURCH. HE GUIDED IT THROUGH DANGERS OF HERESY AND INTERNAL DISPUTES IN ROME.

KEY FACTS
Apostolic Father of the Church
DATES: c.*AD 69–155*
BIRTH PLACE: *Possibly Syria*
FEAST DAY: *23 February*

Polycarp knew the apostles, particularly St John. He was the living link between those who had known Christ in the flesh and the next generation of believers. This made him an Apostolic Father, and with this authority he played a significant role in the early Church.

During a wave of paganism in Asia in the 2nd century AD, Polycarp kept an strong hold on the essentials of Christ's teaching. He fought heretical or radical interpretations and practices, and his firm stand strengthened the spread of the Church in the East.

A heretical sect leader who wished to have a debate with Polycarp was rebuffed with the phrase, "I recognize you as the first-born of Satan". In his own writing, Polycarp explained, "For every one who shall not confess that Jesus Christ has come in the flesh is the antichrist".

St Irenaeus of Lyons was a child when he first heard Polycarp preach and recount his memories of the apostles. Irenaeus has left letters mentioning Polycarp, who was the bishop of Smyrna for almost 50 years. These letters give

Left Saint Sebastian and Saint Polycarp Destroying the Idols *(Pedro Garcia de Benabarre, 15th century). Broken idols litter the floor.*

glimpses of his life and his high standing in the Church. Ignatius of Antioch, awaiting martyrdom in Rome, trusted Polycarp to receive and forward secret letters on his behalf.

In old age, Polycarp was called to Rome to discuss the timing of feast days, especially that of Easter. He met Anicetus, bishop of Rome. They agreed to disagree, and Polycarp returned to Smyrna, believing his community could now peacefully use the calendar that it preferred.

MARTYRDOM

He was over 80 when a mob bayed for his blood. Excited by pagan festivities that included lions attacking Christians, they shouted, "This is the father of the Christians". The Roman consul refused to throw Polycarp into the arena, but conceded to a death by burning. At the stake, Polycarp said, "May I be received among the martyrs in your presence today as a rich and pleasing sacrifice." A soldier stabbed him in order to spare him the pain of burning. Christians gathered relics from the ashes, and wrote an account of the trial and death of this martyr-saint, giving evidence of an early cultus.

Left St Polycarp spread the Christian faith in the sometimes rugged terrain of Palestine (left) and Syria.

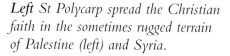

JUSTIN

THIS CHRISTIAN PHILOSOPHER EXPLAINED THE MESSAGE OF CHRIST IN HIS WRITINGS.

Justin was well educated and sought answers to life's problems through philosophy. But the teachings of Pythagorus, Plato and the Stoics brought him no closer to the Almighty.

CONVERSION

A chance encounter with a stranger directed him to look for meaning in the message of Christ. When Justin converted to the faith he was about 30 years old. The Christians he met were reluctant to discuss their rituals with an outsider. Justin said, "It is our duty to make known our doctrine, lest we incur the guilt and the punishment of those who have sinned through ignorance."

Justin wrote the *Apologies* and *Dialogues*, important fragments of which have survived. In these writings, he sets out the moral values of the faith and presents a philosophical proof of its truth.

He is recognized as the first Christian apologist. Dressed as a philosopher, he preached and taught throughout Palestine, Syria and other regions.

TRIAL AND DEATH

In Rome, he had a public debate with another philosopher, named Crescens. Justin presented the more convincing argument, and his adversary is believed to have later instigated his arrest. A record of his trial survives. The martyr confessed his faith unhesitatingly, and gave courage to six other Christians who were also on trial. Justin was decapitated, in accordance with Roman law.

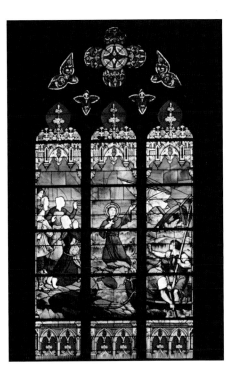

KEY FACTS

Apologist (vindicator) of the faith
DATES: c. *AD 100–65*
BIRTH PLACE: *Flavia Neapolis (now Nablus, Palestine)*
PATRON OF: *Philosophers*
FEAST DAY: *1 June*
EMBLEM: *Philosopher's clothes*

Left A stained-glass window depicting St Justin preaching to fishermen in stormy weather.

Below A Sailor Offering a Model Boat to St Justin *(Domenico Robusti Tintoretto, son of Jacopo, c. 17th century).*

IRENAEUS OF LYONS

THE BISHOP OF LYONS WAS AN INFLUENTIAL THEOLOGIAN WHO HELPED THE CHURCH TO CLARIFY THE ARTICLES OF CHRISTIAN FAITH, IN PARTICULAR THE UNITY OF THE FATHER AND THE SON.

KEY FACTS
Venerated as a martyr
DATES: *c.AD 130–200*
BIRTH PLACE: *Possibly Smyrna*
FEAST DAY: *28 June (West)*
EMBLEM: *Bishop's clothes*

As a theologian St Irenaeus was not only able to defend and explain Christianity theoretically, he could also preach it to laymen.

Irenaeus worked as a priest in Lyons. He was sent to Rome on a peacemaking mission by his bishop Pothinus in AD 177. He took a message to the pope to show leniency towards the North African Church whose practices differed from those of Rome. He also brokered a compromise between the East and Pope Victor III who wanted Rome to decree the dates for Easter.

On his return, Irenaeus became Bishop of Lyons as his predecessor had been killed. Under his care the faith spread through this rich merchant city. He was the first to make a systematic organization of Catholic beliefs. His writings distinguished faith from the then popular heresy, Gnosticism, and he enhanced the unity of the faithful.

He wrote the "rule of faith" that encompasses all "the riches of Christian truth", still delivered at baptisms. He died at Lyons, but unfortunately his shrine was destroyed in the Reformation.

Above St Irenaeus resurrects and baptizes a girl in this Belgian tapestry.

COSMAS AND DAMIAN

THE TWIN DOCTORS WHO NEVER CHARGED FOR THE MEDICAL CARE THEY GAVE HAVE LONG BEEN VENERATED FOR THEIR HEALING SKILLS AND THEIR KINDNESS. AS SUCH, THEY ARE PATRONS OF DOCTORS.

KEY FACTS
Doctors, miracle cures
DATES: *Unknown*
BIRTH PLACE: *Syria*
PATRON OF: *Doctors, dentists, barbers, chemists, hairdressers*
FEAST DAY: *26 September (West)*
EMBLEM: *Ampoules and medicine jars*

A widespread cultus followed Sts Cosmas and Damian in the 5th century AD. They practised as doctors in Cyrrhus, Syria, where a famous basilica was erected.

With wonderful powers of healing, aided by the Holy Spirit, they were known as the "holy moneyless ones" because their medical care was free. They also looked after sick animals.

Although Cosmas and Damian were persecuted by the Romans, it was said that rocks thrown at the twins simply flew backwards. Neither did the torture rack function. A further account says that after their eventual deaths by beheading, the twins returned to earth to save Justinianus, deacon of their church. He lost a leg and they replaced the pale limb with another one from a black-skinned Ethiopian man. Differing versions of this story have been depicted by artists over the years.

Sick believers took to sleeping in the twins' church, hoping this "incubation" would cure them – a practice known also to occur in other religions.

Right Healing of the Deacon Justinianus by the Saints Cosmas and Damian *(Fra Angelico, 1440). The new black leg is clearly visible.*

PERPETUA

A YOUNG MOTHER RECORDED HER EXPERIENCES AND VISIONS WHILE AWAITING MARTYRDOM.

KEY FACTS
Martyr
DATES: *d.AD 203*
BIRTH PLACE: *Carthage*
FEAST DAY: *7 March*

The daughter of a wealthy pagan in Carthage, Perpetua was arrested during a Roman persecution of newly converted Christians. Perpetua was first placed under house arrest, then imprisoned, even though she was the mother of a young baby.

She was 22 years old when she wrote about her extraordinary experiences. The work, finished anonymously, is an authentic record of Christian martyrdom.

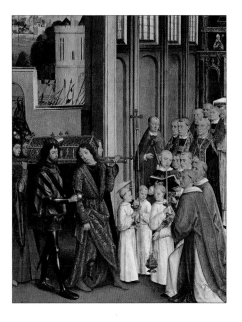

Above The shrine of St Perpetua is transferred to the Church of Bouvignes after the Siege of Dinant in 1466 (Flemish School, 15th century).

She mentions her worries about her father and baby and describes vivid dreams of ladders to heaven and her dead brother, but the most inspiring vision was one of herself, changed into a man, fighting the devil.

Perpetua was allowed to send her baby home before her death. Some say she entered the arena at Carthage singing joyfully. She was wounded by a mad heifer, then despatched by the sword.

FELICITAS

ST PERPETUA'S HANDMAIDEN RISKED HER OWN LIFE AND THAT OF HER UNBORN CHILD WHEN SHE ACCEPTED THE CHRISTIAN FAITH. SHE WAS MARTYRED AT THE SAME TIME AS HER MISTRESS.

KEY FACTS
Martyr
DATES: *d.AD 203*
BIRTH PLACE: *Carthage*
FEAST DAY: *7 March*

This young woman was a slave of St Perpetua in the Roman colony of Carthage. When her mistress was arrested, Felicitas (or Felicity) went with her to prison.

Felicitas was heavily pregnant at the time of their detention. Her husband, Revocatus, and two other slaves, Saturninus and Secundulus, were also caught up in the persecution. While under house arrest, they were all baptized before their transfer to prison.

Incarcerated in a filthy cell, Felicitas went into a difficult labour and brutal warders jeered at her pain. She knew her fate and that of her husband was death in the arena, so was grateful to give birth beforehand. A free Christian adopted the baby girl.

Above The ancient Punic city walls of Carthage in present-day Tunisia. For the saints' martyrdom in the city's arena, leopards and bears were prepared to attack the men, and a mad heifer directed toward the two women.

DENYS OF PARIS

CREDITED WITH THE FOUNDING OF THE CHRISTIAN CHURCH IN PARIS, THIS VIRTUOUS MAN WENT ON TO BECOME A BISHOP AND WAS LATER MARTYRED FOR HIS FAITH.

KEY FACTS
Early mission to France
DATES: *d.c.AD 250*
BIRTH PLACE: *Italy*
PATRON OF: *Paris and France, headaches*
FEAST DAY: *9 October*
EMBLEM: *Head held in his hands*

Said to be a fearless preacher, the Italian-born St Denys (or Dionysius) of Paris was sent on a dangerous mission to revive the persecuted Church of Gaul (France) in AD 250. Together with the deacon Eleutherius and the priest Rusticus, he established a Christian community on an island in the River Seine, close to Roman Paris.

St Denys' mission led to countless conversions, arousing the anger of the local pagan priests

Below The interior of the 12th-century monastery dedicated to St Denys, built on the site of his death in Paris. It is a fitting tribute to the patron saint of the city and France.

Above This baroque statue of St Denys is one in a group of the Fourteen Holy Helpers. Denys is shown carrying his severed head, still preaching, in accordance with the story.

who pushed for the missionaries to be stopped. The saint and his companions were eventually imprisoned and tortured before being beheaded on Montmartre (Martyrs' Hill) where the church of the Sacré Coeur now stands.

According to legend, a great miracle then occurred: St Denys picked up his head and walked two miles, preaching as he went. He eventually lay down and was buried with his fellow martyrs by a pious woman named Catulla.

Another version of events states that after they had been murdered the bodies of the martyrs were thrown into the Seine and retrieved and buried by converts. In both accounts, a shrine was built over the burial place, to be covered years later (c.AD 630) by a great abbey and church. This building, the Basilica of St-Denis later became the burial place of the kings of France.

A NATIONAL FIGURE
St Denys had become a figure of national devotion by the 9th century. This was partly due to a great medieval mix up. The Emperor Louis I of France had been given the writings of a certain Dionysius (or Pseudo Dionysius) in which the author claimed to know the apostles. To the people of the time this would have identified the author as Dionysius the Areopagite, who was converted to Christianity by St Paul.

When Louis commissioned Hilduin, Abbot of St-Denis, to write a biography of St Denys in 835, he asked the abbot to use the works of Pseudo Dionysius as his source. In Hilduin's book, Dionysius the Areopagite and St Denys became the same man. This fiction persisted for 700 years, until it was discovered that Pseudo Dionysius was in fact a 5th-century theologian and philosopher, and St Denys was a significant figure in his own right.

VALENTINE

TWO DIFFERENT VALENTINES WERE MARTYRS DURING THE ROMAN PERIOD, AND IT WAS ONLY DURING THE 14TH CENTURY THAT THE SAINT'S NAME BECAME ASSOCIATED WITH LOVERS.

KEY FACTS
Representative of hidden love and courtship
DATES: *3rd century AD*
BIRTH PLACE: *Unknown*
PATRON OF: *Lovers, betrothed couples, greetings*
FEAST DAY: *14 February*
EMBLEM: *Heart, birds, roses*

There seem to be two saints with this name. One was a 2nd-century bishop of Terni, Italy, the other a 3rd-century priest in Rome; both were martyred. Some hagiographers claim they were one and the same person.

The 3rd-century Valentinus was reportedly imprisoned for helping Christians, then tried to convert the Emperor Claudius II, cured his jailer's daughter of blindness, and was beheaded outside Rome's Flaminian Gate.

No one is sure why Valentine is associated with lovers. It may follow Lupercalia, an old pagan festival, celebrated in mid-February. On the eve of the Lupercalia, all the young women's names would be put into a container, and each young man would draw out a name. He would then be paired with the woman he had chosen for the remainder of the festival.

Another theory associates the courtship with a line by the English medieval poet Chaucer, who observed that birds choose their mates on 14 February.

Right St Valentine (painted glass, Hungarian School, 19th century).

VICTOR OF MARSEILLES

THIS CONVERT, A SOLDIER, WAS SEVERELY PUNISHED FOR HIS FAITH AND HAD A STRONG CULTUS IN THE MEDIEVAL ERA. HIS TOMB BECAME A POPULAR PILGRIM SHRINE.

KEY FACTS
Venerated as a martyr
DATES: *3rd century AD*
BIRTH PLACE: *Marseilles, France*
PATRON OF: *Millers, lightning, torture victims, cabinet-makers*
FEAST DAY: *21 July*
EMBLEM: *Windmill, millstone*

Archaeological evidence points to the burial of a total of three martyrs beneath the church of St Victor in Marseilles. Tunnels and caves show early habitation, probably of monks.

Victor may have been a Moor in the Roman army who was converted. His fellow soldiers, fearing for his life, begged him to return to traditional Roman beliefs, but he refused. Legend says he was betrayed by other militia.

He was thrown into prison but his profound faith converted the two military wardens charged with guarding him. These two

Below Victor of Marseilles is shown as a brave soldier of the faith destroying false idols (Hermen Rode, 1481).

men were executed, and legend describes the cruel treatment meted out to Victor. He was put on the rack, and burned. His foot was hacked off and then he was crushed and ground between two large millstones.

Many miracles were claimed in his name and he developed a wide cultus in the medieval era. His tomb became one of the most visited pilgrim centres in what was then Gaul, and St-Victor Church can still be visited today.

CECILIA

ANGELS AND HEAVENLY MUSIC HELPED CECILIA TO CONVERT HER HUSBAND AND OTHERS.

Above A terracotta statue of Cecilia in the cathedral in Le Mans, France (Charles Hoyay, 17th century).

When she was a young woman, Cecilia's family refused to accept that she had taken a vow of virginity and forced her to marry a pagan. During the wedding, Cecilia sang silently to the Lord, "My heart remain unsullied, so that I may not be confounded". The bride vowed that her marriage would never be consummated.

Cecilia kept strong in her faith and told her husband, Valerian, that an angel was guarding her. She said God would be angry if Valerian touched her, but if he desisted, God would love him. Furthermore, if her husband were baptized, he would see this angel.

Valerian converted and angels appeared and placed flowers on the heads of the young couple. Cecilia's brother Tiburtius chose to become a Christian after this incident. In fact, the two men became so ardent in their faith that the Romans beheaded them, as Christianity was proscribed. Cecilia buried the two martyrs at her home. She, too, attracted anger from the state, but officials sent to arrest her were so overwhelmed by her faith that they converted.

Cecilia converted 400 people who were later baptized by Pope Urban in her home, which was later dedicated as a church.

The authorities did not abandon their persecution of Cecilia. They tried locking her in her own bathroom and burning the furnaces high. She lived through this ordeal, and then survived for three days after a soldier hacked at her neck with a sword.

There is little firm evidence for Cecilia's story. Her patronage of music comes from the heavenly sound she heard in her head while the organs played at her wedding.

KEY FACTS
Virgin martyr
DATES: *3rd century AD*
BIRTH PLACE: *Rome*
PATRON OF: *Musicians, singers, composers*
FEAST DAY: *22 November*
EMBLEM: *Organ or lute*

ANASTASIA

Virgin martyrs such as Ursula and Cecilia have attracted legends of heroism and miracles. Other martyrs give their names to churches, or else linger in the religious folk memory.

One such figure is St Anastasia. Nothing is known about her. It is possible she was martyred at a place now known as Srem Mitrovica, Serbia. Her name is in the Roman Canon. A prayer is said to her at Mass, and a few antique Byzantine churches carry her name. She was a "matron", not a "maiden", so she is not counted as one of the virgin martyrs.

Below A stained-glass window depicting the martyrdom of St Anastasia (20th-century copy from a 13th-century original).

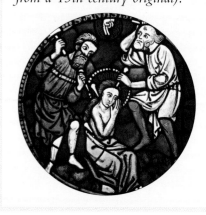

Left St Cecilia's tomb. Her body was found lying in this position in 1599, and the statue copies it exactly.

GEORGE

THE POTENCY OF HIS STORY ENSURES THAT ST GEORGE HOLDS A PLACE IN THE COMPANY OF SAINTS, BUT THE CHURCH SUSPECTS THAT THIS CHIVALROUS KNIGHT MAY BE MERELY A LEGEND.

In the 6th century, St George was described as good in so many ways that all his "deeds are known only to God". Sadly, most things about this saint remain known only by his maker, because evidence of his life is so sparse.

It seems certain, however, that George was a real martyr, a knight who came from Cappadocia in Turkey and died in Lydda (site of modern-day Lod) in Palestine.

GEORGE AND THE DRAGON
In what is undoubtedly his most famous legend, George was riding through Libya when he heard cries of mourning. Townspeople told him that they were being tyrannized by a dragon that they had to feed with two lambs a day. Now they had no lambs left and the dragon was demanding a human meal. They had drawn lots from the maidens and the king's daughter had been chosen. Dressed in a beautiful bridal gown, the princess had gone forth to meet her doom. St George dashed into action and crippled the monster by thrusting his lance into it. Tying her girdle round the dragon's neck, the princess led it limping to the town. The terrified citizens prepared to run, but George told them that if they would be baptized, the dragon would be slain. They all agreed. It was alleged that approximately 15,000 people were baptized. Four ox carts moved the beast's body to a distant meadow.

Right St George and the Dragon (Paolo Uccello, c.1439–40).

Above St George as depicted in a fresco in the Church of our Lady of the Pasture, Asinou, Cyprus (late 12th century).

CULTUSES AND CRUSADES
There are signs that St George's cultus was widespread early in Christian history. He was venerated across Europe and known in England before the Norman Conquest of AD 1066. His image can be found all over the Middle East, the Balkans and Greece.

During the Crusader battle of Antioch in AD 1098, Frankish (German) knights were blessed

KEY FACTS
Knight martyr
DATES: *d.c.AD 303*
BIRTH PLACE: *Cappadocia, Turkey*
PATRON OF: *England, Istanbul, boy scouts, soldiers, and many other groups*
FEAST DAY: *23 April*
EMBLEM: *Red cross on white background, dragon*

with a vision of George and another knight, St Demetrius. Possibly on his return from the Third Crusade a century later, Richard I promoted the veneration of St George in England.

PATRONAGE
St George is now the patron saint of England, as well as of boy scouts and soldiers, and many churches bear his name. In 1914, together with St John Chrysostom and St Roch, St George was declared a patron of Constantinople (Istanbul).

Because so little is actually known of St George, the Church downgraded him in 1960, and today his feast day is reduced to prayers during mass. But his name and his story of chivalry are loved across the world. His flag, a red cross on white background, was well known by the 14th century and is the national flag of England.

VITUS

A CHILD WHO DEFIED HIS PARENTS TO BECOME A CHRISTIAN, VITUS CURED SUFFERERS OF MENTAL ILLNESS AND EPILEPSY. FOLLOWERS DANCED ON HIS FEAST DAY TO ENSURE A YEAR OF GOOD HEALTH.

It is said that Vitus was a young boy when he elected to be baptized without his parents' knowledge. His angry parents beat him and threw him into a dungeon when he refused to give up his faith.

***Above** The façade of the neo-Gothic Cathedral of St Vitus in Prague.*

Angels, dancing in a dazzling light, came to comfort him. His furious father visited him and tried to persuade Vitus to abandon the faith. But the angry man was blinded by the light and flitting movements of the dancing angels. He restored his father's sight, but this did not bring Vitus any peace.

As various other miracles were attributed to him, he found that officials became suspicious of him. Fearing for his safety, he fled from his birthplace in Sicily. He landed with two companions at Lucania in Italy where they stayed a while, preaching to the people. Finally they reached Rome, where Vitus cured Emperor Diocletian's son by expelling evil spirits that possessed the child.

KEY FACTS
Miracle worker
DATES: *d.c.AD 303*
BIRTH PLACE: *Sicily*
PATRON OF: *St Vitus' dance, actors, comedians, against lightning and storms, against epilepsy, protection against dangerous animals, Sicily*
FEAST DAY: *15 June*
EMBLEM: *Dog or cockerel*

But after this healing, Vitus was expected to make a thanksgiving sacrifice to the Roman gods who, it was presumed, had given him the power. Vitus refused, and so was branded a dangerous sorcerer.

Vitus and his companions were subjected to various unsuccessful tortures and were reputedly lifted to safety by an angel during a great storm. The site of their death or martyrdom remains unclear. Both St-Denis in Paris and Corvey in Saxony claim to hold his relics.

DYMPNA

A PRINCESS WHO FLED FROM HER OBSESSED FATHER BECAME PATRONESS OF THE INSANE.

Legend explains that Dympna was a princess, the daughter of a Celtic or heathen king. She grew up to be beautiful, but she also bore an uncanny resemblance to her dead mother.

Her father developed a perverted passion for his daughter, and so she fled with her confessor or teacher, St Gerebernus. The two fugitives made their way to Gheel, near Antwerp, in Belgium. They lived as hermits but the king

***Above** This intricate decorated altar is found in the St Dympna Church in Gheel, Belgium (c.1490–1500). It is called the Passion Altar, and it depicts the last days of Christ on earth.*

KEY FACTS
Virgin, miracle worker
DATES: *c.7th century*
BIRTH PLACE: *Possibly Celtic Britain*
PATRON OF: *The mentally ill, against epilepsy and possession by the devil, sleepwalkers*
FEAST DAY: *30 May*

traced them and demanded her return. When the king's request was refused, he ordered his guards to murder Gerebernus and he beheaded his own daughter. Years later, the bones of the victims were discovered. After visiting these relics, numerous epileptics and lunatics claimed to be cured.

CHRISTOPHER

THE PATRON SAINT OF TRAVELLERS DERIVES HIS NAME FROM A GREEK WORD MEANING "ONE WHO CARRIES CHRIST". CHRISTOPHER IS LOVED FOR THIS HONOURABLE TASK.

KEY FACTS

Carried the child Jesus across a river
DATES: *Unknown*
BIRTH PLACE: *Unknown*
PATRON OF: *Wayfarers, travellers and motorists*
FEAST DAY: *25 July*
EMBLEM: *Pole to aid walking through the river, carrying a child on his shoulder*

One of the best-known saints, Christopher is now deemed legendary and no longer included in the Roman Calendar. However, this "de-canonization" has not stopped the popular veneration of St Christopher, whose image adorns cars and key rings. Travellers everywhere continue to pray for his intercession.

According to some stories, Christopher was a tall, muscular man. He is described in the *Golden Legend* as having a "fearful face and appearance".

Below This image from a German illuminated manuscript gives a realistic view of the agony St Christopher endured as he carried the small, but extraordinarily heavy infant Jesus across the river (15th century).

BECOMING A CHRISTIAN

Christopher found "a right great king" to serve, but soon observed he made the sign of the cross whenever hearing the word "devil". Christopher felt that needing such help was hardly fitting for a great monarch. So instead, he sought this powerful devil and worked for him.

With the devil leading him, Christopher travelled through the desert. The discovery that a cross, thrust into the sands, frightened the devil prompted Christopher to seek an explanation. A holy hermit told him about the power of this cross, and then converted him to Christianity.

Because of his size, Christopher dreaded fasting. Nor could he accept long hours of prayer and short periods of sleep. The hermit asked if Christopher could carry travellers across the river. In this way, the *Golden Legend* explains, he found a way to serve the Lord.

CARRYING CHRIST

A child once asked Christopher to carry him, so he hoisted the little boy on to his shoulders and stepped into the water. The child grew heavier, but Christopher persevered. On reaching the other bank, he felt "all the world upon me; I might bear no greater burden". The boy replied, "Thou hast not only borne all the world upon thee, but thou hast borne Him that made all the world, upon thy soldiers. I am Jesus Christ."

Christopher went to Lycia (southern Turkey) to preach but was arrested. He survived burning by iron rods, and when they shot him, the arrows stopped in mid-air. Finally they beheaded him.

The truth about Christopher is sparse. He was martyred in the Middle East, honoured in the 3rd century AD, and a church was dedicated to him in the 4th century AD. Early Christians prayed to his image to ensure safe travel, which has led to the practice today.

Below St Christopher is gaunt but noble in this sensitive wood carving (Gothic-style winged altar in the Kefermarkt, Austria, c. 1490).

CHILD SAINTS

THOUSANDS OF CHILDREN HAVE DIED ALONE OR WITH THEIR CHRISTIAN FAMILIES IN DEFENCE OF THEIR FAITH. YET FEW NAMES SURVIVE FROM THIS GROUP OF YOUNG MARTYR SAINTS.

Many children were named as saints not only for the purity and innocence of their youth, but for the horrible deaths they suffered as martyrs.

It is safe to assume that thousands of unnamed children, together with their families, were slaughtered by the Roman authorities. Some attracted a cultus and their names live on. These children mostly come from the early years of the faith when its members were subject to horrific, intermittent persecution.

EARLY MARTYRS
Legend describes St Foy (or Faith) as a defiant child who is said to have lived in Agen, Gaul (France) in the late 3rd century. Legend states that she was roasted alive and beheaded for her belief. Her bravery was venerated and thousands made the journey to visit her relics in Conques, France. Crusader soldiers, especially, pleaded for her protection.

The story of St Irene tells that this brave Macedonian girl was about 13 when she was arrested with her sisters

Above The Abbey church of St Foy in Conques, France, which holds her gorgeous relics.

in *c.*AD 303. While her sisters were killed, Irene was spared because she was so young. She was sent naked into the soldiers' brothel where no man dared approach her. She was eventually burnt alive in AD 304.

Although the 4th-century St Pelagia of Antioch is named in the church litany, all we know about her is that, when she was 15, soldiers invaded her home. To escape from them and avoid dishonour, the young virgin sacrificed her life by jumping off the roof of her house.

St Philomena's history is also obscure, but even now pilgrims visit her shrine in Naples. Her relics were unearthed in 1802 near an inscription bearing her

Left A sculpture of St Philomena made out of gilded wood (1890).

name in the Roman catacombs. Her relics were subsequently moved to Naples, and miracles began to occur.

Because of controversy surrounding the relics of St Philomena, in 1961 the Holy See removed her from the liturgical calendar of saints and wanted to dismantle her shrine; yet she continues to attract pilgrims.

Son of Coenwulf, King of Mercia (AD 796–821), Prince Kenelm was next in line for the throne. But according to legend his sister, Quendreda, was jealous of the seven-year-old Christian prince and ordered the boy's tutor to murder him so she would inherit the throne. It was said that a dove carried a document to Rome telling of his death, and his relics were translated to Winchcombe in Gloucestershire. His wicked sister's eyes fell out and she was blind for the rest of her life.

CHILD MARTYRS
Names with age at death; those in bold refer to martyrs described on these two pages:
Agape (Charity), 9
Agnes, 13
Christodoulos, 14
Dominic Savio, 15
Elpis (Hope), 10
Eulalia Mérida, 12
Foy (or **Faith**), unknown
Gabriel Gowdel, 7
Irene, 13
Justus of Beauvais, 9
Kenelm, 7
Kizito, 13
Maria Goretti, 12
Niño de Atocha, unknown
Pancras of Rome, 14
Paul Lang Fu, 9
Pelagia of Antioch, 15
Philomena, unknown
Pistis (Faith), 12
Rais, 12

19TH AND 20TH CENTURIES

There are only a few known child saints from the 19th and 20th centuries. They are symbols of the bravery of the thousands of unnamed children who suffered for their faith during this time.

One such child is Dominic Savio. He was only 12 when he entered a Turin monastery. A cheerful, peaceful child, he was famous for the hours he spent in prayer. Dominic suffered from tuberculosis and, during a fever, experienced a vision. Before his death in 1857 he cried out, "I am seeing the most wonderful things!" He was 15.

During the Boxer Rebellion in 1900, thousands of Christians were murdered for playing a part in the foreign domination of China. One of the youngest was Paul Lang Fu, just nine years old. He ran to his mother's side as soldiers tied her to a tree, but they hacked off his arm and burnt him to death.

Maria Goretti (1890–1902) was a martyr for chastity and the Christian life. She was only 12 years old when she was murdered by a man who tried to rape her. Before she died, she forgave him his sin. He was imprisoned and after eight years he became a Christian; he was present at her canonization in 1950.

AGNES

Agnes is probably the best-known child saint. Some stories claim she was 13 when she died in Rome around AD 305. She was buried on the Via Nomentana, and a church was built over her grave soon after her death.

This young Christian girl refused to marry the son of a Roman prefect because she had dedicated herself to Christ. When the son complained, the father tried to force the marriage. Agnes remained steadfast in her refusal. According to legend she was then dragged naked through the streets to a brothel, but her hair grew and hid her body. One man who tried to rape her was blinded, but Agnes prayed for him and his sight returned. The Romans finally put her to death by piercing her throat with a sword after flames would not burn her.

Agnes is often painted with a lamb to symbolize her purity and every year, on her feast day, two lambs are blessed inside her church in Rome. Their wool is woven by the nuns of St Agnes' convent into bands which the pope confers on bishops as a sign of authority. The superstitious believe virgins who go without supper on the eve of the feast of St Agnes will dream of the man who will become their true love.

Left St Agnes holding the palm of martyrdom (Lucas van Leyden, 1510).

EULALIA OF MÉRIDA

THIS YOUNG SPANISH GIRL DARED TO CONFRONT A ROMAN JUDGE, BOLDLY REPROVING HIM FOR HIS PERSECUTION OF CHRISTIANS. SHE WAS ACCOMPANIED AT HER DEATH BY A WHITE DOVE.

KEY FACTS
Virgin martyr
DATES: *d.c.AD 304*
BIRTH PLACE: *Mérida, Spain*
FEAST DAY: *10 December*
EMBLEM: *Oven*

Eulalia is widely venerated in Spain for being a courageous virgin, a martyr – and a child.

Early in the 4th century AD, under the Roman Emperor Maximian, the persecution of Christians was widely enforced. In Mérida, local believers were rounded up and arrested. The judge Dacian was presiding over their trials when a young girl confronted him. Her wealthy family were apparently austere and frugal, and it must be assumed they were among the persecuted. She was only 12 years old, but Eulalia was courageous and loyal to her faith and family. She informed the judge that he was wrong to condemn and oppress the Christians.

She said that his prisoners were following the way of the one true God, so the Romans should not

Above The interior of the Cathedral of Santa Eulalia, Barcelona (13th–15th century). The saint commemorated by this building may be merely legendary.

punish them. He tried to divert the child with bribes, but Eulalia became angry and stamped on the sacrificial pagan cake he offered her. Then she delivered a deadly insult. Eulalia spat at the judge.

Dacian gave orders that she be tortured by being torn with iron hooks. Finally, she was bound and burnt to death in an oven. Spectators said that, just as she was thrust into the flames, a white dove fluttered from her mouth and soared into the air. Then a short and unexpected snow fell,

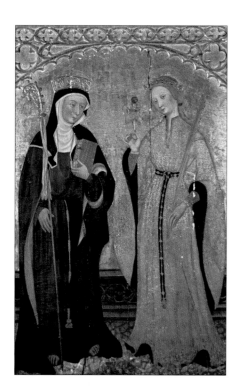

Left Sts Eulalia and Clare (Pedro Serra, 14th century).

soothing her burns and covering her body. Christians dug her body from the icy mound and buried her remains with the oven in which she had died. The burial site is in Mérida.

THE CULT OF EULALIA

Thousands of medieval pilgrims visited the young saint's shrine, and many sites claimed to house her relics during the 6th and 7th centuries. Numerous churches and monasteries were dedicated in her name.

Artists favoured her gruesome death as a subject. The cathedral of Palma and the Catalonian art gallery in Barcelona have paintings of Eulalia. The Venerable Bede refers to this child-martyr in one of his hymns, saying "scorched by fierce flames, Eulalia endures." The Spanish poet, Prudentius, describes the flight of the white dove from Eulalia's mouth.

FALSE CLAIMS

From time to time, it seems the longing to proclaim sainthood for a friend or relative overwhelms a community. There are examples of "duplicate saints" being given the name and even the legend of a known saint.

For instance, another girl named Eulalia, from Barcelona, has also been claimed as a saint. She has been accorded similar legends and status by false cultuses. Scholars have decided that the young girl from Mérida is the person who probably did exist, whereas the other girl never did.

JUSTUS OF BEAUVAIS

DURING ONE OF THE MOST SEVERE PERSECUTIONS OF THE CHURCH BY THE ROMAN AUTHORITIES, SOLDIERS CAME TO TAKE AWAY A CHRISTIAN FAMILY, BUT WERE GREETED BY A DEFIANT SMALL BOY.

KEY FACTS
Child martyr
DATES: *3rd or 4th century AD*
BIRTH PLACE: *Beauvais*
FEAST DAY: *18 October*

The persecution of Christians by edict of the Roman Emperor Diocletian in AD 303 was one of the worst in the history of the early Church.

It was possibly during this violent period that soldiers came to the family home of the young Justus demanding the arrest of his Christian father and brother. The boy, just nine years old, showed no fear, although he must have known that the soldiers were dangerous and brutal men. He refused to reveal where his family were hiding. Ignoring his youth and bravery, his persecutors lifted their swords and swiftly sliced off the boy's head.

According to legend, Justus' head continued to speak after his decapitation. The words remained defiant. Justus had a large cultus in France, Belgium and Switzerland.

Above The grave of a martyr from the 2nd or 3rd centuries AD; the fish was a secret symbol among Christians.

PANCRAS OF ROME

THIS SAINT'S HISTORY IS OBSCURE YET HIS NAME LIVES ON BOTH WITHIN THE CHURCH AND IN THE SECULAR WORLD, NOTABLY AS A PARISH AND RAILWAY TERMINUS IN LONDON, ENGLAND.

KEY FACTS
Child martyr
DATES: *Early 4th century AD*
BIRTH PLACE: *Phrygia*
FEAST DAY: *12 May*

There is no hard evidence about St Pancras. A martyr of that name was buried in the Aurelian Way in Rome. Legend has it that St Pancras was only 14 when he was killed.

In about AD 500, Pope St Symmachus built a church in Rome over the tomb of St Pancras. Miracles in his name were claimed at the site. The great St Augustine of Canterbury built a church in his honour in that city. This building, too, carried an atmosphere of great spirituality.

After their conquest of England in 1066, centuries later, the Normans dedicated a church in London to the boy saint. His name was given to a parish and a railway station in London. These facts make it easier to believe that the boy did exist, and that once upon a time his bravery and the circumstances of his death were well known.

Below An etching of St Pancras Church at Euston in London, designed by H.W. Inwood (Thomas Kearnan, 19th century)

DOROTHY

FEARLESS IN THE FACE OF TORTURE AND DEFIANT IN DEATH, DOROTHY RETURNED TO WORK A MIRACLE, DELIVERING A GIFT FROM PARADISE TO A MAN WHO HAD TAUNTED HER FOR HER FAITH.

KEY FACTS
Virgin martyr
DATES: *d.c.AD 304*
BIRTH PLACE: *Caesarea, Cappadocia*
PATRON OF: *Florists, gardeners, brewers and bridal couples*
FEAST DAY: *6 February*
EMBLEM: *Basket of flowers, especially roses, and of fruit*

Despite coming from a noble Roman family in Caesarea in Cappadocia, Turkey, Dorothy would not pay homage to her family's pagan gods. Punished for her Christian faith and refusal to marry, she experienced frightful torture. But the weapons used against her felt as mere feathers.

At the place of execution, Dorothy showed no fear and instead announced to the crowd around her that she was glad to leave this cold world for one that knew neither ice nor snow. A young man called Theophilus, taunted her for both her virginity and her faith. He then challenged her to send him roses and fruit when she reached her paradise.

In the winter after Dorothy's martyrdom, an angel delivered a basket filled with roses and fruit to Theophilus. He converted but the young man, too, was executed.

Left Theophilus taunts Dorothy in The Flower Miracle of Saint Dorothy *(Hans Baldung, 1516).*

VINCENT OF SARAGOSSA

SPAIN'S FIRST MARTYR SAINT WAS REVERED FOR HIS COURAGE AND STAMINA IN THE FACE OF REPEATED TORTURE. SYMBOLIC OF THIS RESISTANCE IS HIS SUPPOSED POWER AGAINST WINTER FROST.

KEY FACTS
Spain's first martyr
DATES: *d.AD 304*
BIRTH PLACE: *Saragossa, Spain*
PATRON OF: *Wine-growers, wine- and vinegar-makers, and of Portugal*
FEAST DAY: *22 January*
EMBLEM: *Dressed as a deacon holding a palm tree or on a gridiron*

There is little evidence about this early martyr saint, yet St Vincent of Saragossa was venerated across the Roman Empire. Every Christian community associated his name with Christ.

He is the protomartyr of Spain and his fate was horrible. Taken prisoner, Vincent was thrown into jail. He was kept on a starvation diet so that his body, and resolve, might weaken. Still he refused to recognize the pagan gods.

The authorities put him in the stocks, stretched him on the rack and roasted him on a gridiron. After that he was returned to his miserable prison and left to starve. Vincent endured all this brutal violence with defiance and took a long time dying.

Vincent is credited with the power to fight winter frost, hence his patronage of wine.

Left A depiction of the Martyrdom of St Vincent *(French manuscript illumination, 15th century).*

LUCY

YET ANOTHER VICTIM OF THE DIOCLETIAN PERSECUTION, LUCY WAS BELIEVED TO HAVE BEEN RESCUED BY THE HOLY SPIRIT. SHE IS REMEMBERED FOR THE MIRACULOUS RECOVERY OF HER EYES.

KEY FACTS
Virgin martyr
DATES: *d. AD 304*
BIRTH PLACE: *Syracuse, Sicily*
PATRON: *Against eye afflictions and throat infections*
FEAST DAY: *13 December*
EMBLEM: *Disembodied eyes, usually on a platter*

Lucy lost her father when she was a child but was, by all accounts, a resolute, devout young Sicilian. She had a loving mother, yet Lucy kept secret her Christian faith and her vow of virginity.

Her mother, Eutychia, was a wealthy noblewoman from Syracuse. She followed tradition by betrothing her adolescent daughter to a local youth. This expectation made Lucy confess her faith and she invited her mother to accompany her on a pilgrimage to the tomb of St Agatha. The two women prayed at this shrine and Eutychia was cured of haemorrhages from which she suffered. Grateful and convinced of Lucy's faith, she released the girl from the betrothal. But the young man was furious at the rejection of his marriage offer, and reported Lucy to the authorities who promptly arrested her.

MARTYRDOM

The persecution by the Emperor Diocletian was famous for its zeal in attacking Christianity, with many of its followers perishing.

The emperor sentenced Lucy to be taken to a brothel. However, it was said that the girl became immovable. Neither a gang of strong men nor a team of oxen could shift her. She had been filled by the Holy Spirit, making her miraculously heavy.

Her wardens could not lift her to take her to the stake for burning. So instead, it is claimed, they tore out her eyes and threw them on a platter. Lucy calmly

Above St Lucy displays her eyes on a platter (A. Colza, 1513).

took hold of them and put them back in their sockets. Her sight was magically restored. Frustrated by the failure of their cruel methods in persuading the saint to abandon her faith or her virginity, the soldiers beheaded the girl.

In many paintings, Lucy holds the platter bearing her eyes. Otherwise her eyes are dangling from a sprig of leaves or on her clothes. She has long been connected with light, partly because of the story of her eyes, and also because her name is linked to the Latin word for "light", *lux*.

Lucy is remembered in Sweden on the shortest day of the year with festivals at which young girls carry candles in her memory. She is likewise venerated in her birthplace, Sicily.

Below Detail of St Lucy resisting a team of oxen in front of the Judge Paschasius (Bartolo di Fredi, c. 1380).

PATRON SAINTS OF PROFESSIONS

IN THE WORLD OF WORK, SOME SAINTS ARE PATRONS BY CUSTOM, OTHERS BY PAPAL CONCESSION. SOME HELPED PARTICULAR PROFESSIONS; OTHERS ARE CHOSEN FOR THE LIVES THEY LED.

Accountants – Matthew

Actors – Genesius of Arles, Vitus

Actresses – Pelagia the Penitent

Advertisers – Bernardino of Siena

Air crew – Joseph of Copertino, Theresa of Lisieux

Anaesthetists – René Goupil

Apothecaries – Nicholas of Myra, Cosmas and Damian

Archaeologists – Jerome, Helen

Architects – Thomas, Barbara

Art dealers – John

Artists – Luke, Catherine de' Vigri of Bologna

Astronauts – Joseph of Copertino

Astronomers – Dominic

Athletes – Sebastian

Authors – John, Paul, Lucy, Francis of Sales

Bakers – Elizabeth of Hungary, Zita, Nicholas of Myra, Agatha

Bankers – Bernardino of Feltre, Matthew

Bar staff – Amand

Basket-makers – Antony of Egypt

Beekeepers – Ambrose, Bernard of Clairvaux, Valentine, Modomnoc

Bishops – Charles Borromeo

Blacksmiths – Dunstan, Eloi

Bookkeepers – Matthew

Brewers – Amand, Wenceslas, Augustine of Hippo, Boniface

Bricklayers – Stephen of Hungary

Broadcasters – Archangel Gabriel

Builders – Barbara, Blaise, Louis IX, Vincent Ferrer

Bus drivers – Christopher

Butchers – Adrian of Nicomedia, Luke

Cab drivers – Christopher, Eloi, Fiacre, Frances of Rome

Cabinet-makers – Anne, Joseph, Victor of Marseilles

Carpenters – Joseph, Thomas

Civil servants – Thomas More

Above St Bernardino of Siena *(Giovanni di Paolo, 1450). He is patron of advertisers.*

Clergy – Gabriel Possenti

Clowns – Genesius of Arles, Julian the Hospitaller

Cobblers – Crispin and Crispinian, Bartholomew

Cooks, chefs – Laurence, Macarius the Younger, Martha, Paschal Baylon

Craftsmen – Eloi, Catherine of Alexandria

Customs officers – Matthew

Dancers – Vitus, Genesius of Arles, Philemon

Dentists – Apollonia

Dietitians – Martha

Diplomats – Archangel Gabriel

Doctors – Blaise, Cosmas and Damian, Pantaleon

Domestic workers – Adelelmus, Martha, Zita

Ecologists – Francis of Assisi

Editors – John Bosco, Francis of Sales

Engineers – Ferdinand III

Farm-workers – Benedict, Isidore the Farmer, Eloi, Phocas of Sinope, George

Firefighters – Agatha, Laurence, Catherine of Siena

Fishermen – Andrew, Peter, Simon, Zeno, Magnus

Florists – Dorothy, Rose of Lima

Funeral directors – Joseph of Arimathea, Dismas, Sebastian

Above St Fiacre *(illumination, 15th century). Cab drivers in Paris plied their trade from the hotel St Fiacre and the saint has become their patron.*

Above St Ivo of Brittany is patron of judges because he mediated in church disputes (Gaudenzio Ferrari, 1520).

Goldsmiths – Dunstan, Eloi

Grocers – Archangel Michael, Leonard of Noblac

Gunners – Barbara

Hairdressers – Louis IX, Martin de Porres, Mary Magdalene

Hoteliers – Amand, Julian the Hospitaller, Martha

Housewives – Martha, Zita, Anne

Huntsmen – Eustace, Hubert

Jewellers – Eloi, Agatha, Dunstan

Journalists – Francis of Sales, Paul, Maximilian Kolbe

Judges – Ivo of Brittany

Labourers – Eloi, Isidore the Farmer, Guy of Anderlecht, Lucy

Lawyers – Ivo of Brittany, Thomas More, Robert Bellarmine

Leather-workers – Crispin and Crispinian, Bartholomew

Librarians – Jerome, Catherine of Alexandria, Laurence of Rome

Locksmiths – Dunstan, Eloi, Peter, Leonard of Noblac

Magistrates – Ferdinand III

Mechanics – Catherine of Alexandria

Merchants – Nicholas, Homobonus

Midwives – Dorothy of Myra,

Right Limestone statue of St Maurice, the patron of soldiers and armies (Magdeburg Cathedral, c.1240).

Brigid of Ireland, Peter of Verona, Raymund Nonnatus

Miners – Barbara

Musicians – Cecilia, Gregory the Great

Naval officers – Francis of Paola

Nurses – Agatha, Camillus of Lellis, John of God, Catherine of Siena

Obstetricians – Raymund Nonnatus

Painters – Catherine de'Vigri of Bologna, Benedict Biscop

Paramedics – Archangel Michael

Paratroopers – Archangel Michael

Pawnbrokers – Nicholas of Myra

Perfumers – Nicholas of Myra, Mary Magdalene

Philosophers – Albert the Great, Justin, Catherine of Alexandria, Thomas Aquinas

Photographers – Veronica

Poets – Columba of Iona, John of the Cross, Brigid of Ireland, Cecilia

Police officers – Archangel Michael, Sebastian

Politicians – Thomas More

Priests – Jean-Baptiste Vianney

Printers – Augustine of Hippo, John of God

Above St Vincent of Saragossa is surrounded by vines and grapes to indicate his patronage of wine-makers.

Publishers – John of God

Sailors – Nicholas of Myra, Francis of Paola, Phocas of Sinope

Scholars – Jerome, Brigid of Ireland, Catherine of Alexandria

Scientists – Albert the Great, Dominic

Secretaries – Genesius of Arles, Catherine of Alexandria

Silversmiths – Andronicus, Dunstan

Social workers – John Francis Regis, Louise de Marillac

Soldiers – Martin of Tours, George, Maurice, Fay, James the Great

Surgeons – Cosmas and Damian, Luke, Roch

Surveyors – Thomas

Tailors – Boniface, Homobonus

Tax collectors – Matthew

Teachers – John-Baptist de la Salle, Catherine of Alexandria, Francis of Sales, Gregory the Great, Ursula

Veterinarians – Eloi, Blaise, James the Great

Waiters – Martha, Notburga, Zita

Weavers – Maurice

Wine-makers – Amand, Vincent of Saragossa, Martin of Tours

PANTALEON

ONCE AMBITIOUS AND WORLDLY, PANTALEON ABANDONED A SUCCESSFUL CAREER IN MEDICINE TO LIVE "IN IMITATION OF CHRIST" AND WAS EVENTUALLY MARTYRED FOR HIS FAITH.

KEY FACTS
Martyr saint
DATES: *d.c.AD 305*
BIRTH PLACE: *Nicomedia
(now Izmit, Turkey)*
PATRON OF: *Doctors, midwives,
a Holy Helper*
FEAST DAY: *27 July*
EMBLEM: *Olive branch*

The Eastern Orthodox Church honours this saint as the "Great Martyr and Wonder Worker". (In the Greek language, Pantaleon means "all compassionate".) However, although his cult was well established in the East and West from an early date, there are no surviving authentic particulars of Pantaleon's life, which has become the subject of legends.

It is thought that he was the son of a pagan father, but was brought up as a Christian by his mother. He studied medicine and later practised as a doctor in Nicomedia (now Izmit) in Turkey, eventually gaining the important position of physician to the Emperor Galerius Maximianus.

However, being young and carefree, as well as ambitious and successful, Pantaleon abandoned his faith to enjoy the worldly pleasures of the royal palace. Fortunately, one of his friends from his former Christian life, Hermolaos, persistently reminded him of the truth of the Christian faith. When Emperor Diocletian came to power and started his fierce campaign of terror against Christians, Pantaleon realized where his feelings and loyalties lay. He distributed his wealth among the poor, treated the sick without receiving payment, and changed his life to one of discipline and austerity in imitation of Christ.

CAPTURE AND TORTURE

Other doctors, who had long envied Pantaleon for his success at court, took the opportunity to denounce him to the authorities.

***Above** The church of St Pantaleon (AD 966–80) in Köln, Germany.*

He was arrested with Hermolaos and two other friends. The other three men were all executed, but the emperor, reluctant to lose a good doctor, begged Pantaleon to deny his faith. He refused, and his statement of faith was reinforced when he miraculously cured a cripple during his trial.

According to the stories, six types of torture were devised for Pantaleon. He was thrown into deep water to drown, then burning lead was poured over him. They tried to burn him, and they set wild beasts upon him. Then they turned him on a wheel and thrust a sword through his throat. But no matter what mode of torture was employed, Pantaleon was miraculously protected from harm, suffering no wounds and feeling no pain. When at last his tormentors beheaded him, it is said that milk flowed from his veins and the olive tree to which he had been tied burst into fruit.

In Ravello, southern Italy, a reputed relic of St Pantaleon's blood allegedly liquefies every year on his feast day.

***Above** A fresco of St Pantaleon from Macedonia (12th century). Scarcely remembered now in the West, St Pantaleon is still venerated in the East, and many legends and miracles are associated with this martyr.*

LUCIAN OF ANTIOCH

THE MAN WHO ESTABLISHED THE IMPORTANT SCHOOL OF THEOLOGY IN ANTIOCH MADE AN AUTHORITATIVE TRANSLATION OF THE OLD TESTAMENT INTO GREEK BEFORE HIS MARTYRDOM.

KEY FACTS
Martyr saint
DATES: *d. AD 312*
BIRTH PLACE: *Samosata, Syria*
FEAST DAY: *7 January (West)*
EMBLEM: *Bishop's vestments, dolphins*

Orphaned at the age of 12, Lucian had Christian parents, who it is thought may have been martyred. He became the student of a famous teacher, Macarius of Edessa. After baptism, Lucian adopted a strictly ascetic life.

TEACHER AND SCHOLAR

His routine of disciplined habits allowed Lucian to write and study. He became a teacher, and is believed to be the man who established the school of theology in Antioch, which at that time was a significant Christian centre. One of his students was Arius, whose followers were sometimes known as Lucianists and who became the founder of Arianism.

Lucian is also known to have made an important translation of the Old Testament from Hebrew into Greek. His version, which corrected misleading translations in common use at the time, stressed the importance of maintaining the literal sense of the texts. His complete edition of the Bible, known as *Lucian Recension*, was used by St Jerome during his work on the *Vulgate*, and St John Chrysostom also regarded it as an authoritative text. Surviving manuscripts confirm this respect, and one such text, the Arundelian, is in the British Museum.

ORTHODOXY OR HERESY?

Lucian lived at a time of conflict within the Church in Antioch. Three successive bishops were hostile to his teachings, and for some years he was excluded from major meetings of Christian leaders. However, it seems that he otherwise enjoyed wide popular support. The people respected him for his great learning as well as admiring his noble character. He was later restored to office.

PRISON AND MARTYRDOM

During an outbreak of Christian persecution, Lucian was arrested and taken to Nicomedia, where he faced the Roman official Maximin Daza. He was thrown into prison, but, despite brutal treatment, his reputation for dignity and courage grew during the nine years he spent there. When dragged before the authorities for interrogation, he would always reply simply "I am a Christian".

At last, because he would not renounce his faith, his diet was reduced to sacrificial cake that had been dedicated to pagan idols. This he refused to eat. Some say he starved to death, but others relate that he was tortured and then beheaded. One legend even claimed he was flung into the sea and drowned, but that dolphins carried his body to shore where it was collected by his followers.

Lucian's relics were taken to Drepanum, where on the first anniversary of the saint's death, St John Chrysostom preached a tribute to this much-admired scholar and martyr.

Left The remains of the Roman Emperor Diocletian's palace at Nicomedia (now Izmit) in Turkey. Lucian suffered during Diocletian's persecution of Christians.

HELEN

THE MOTHER OF EMPEROR CONSTANTINE WAS AN ELDERLY WOMAN WHEN SHE CONVERTED. AN ANGEL IS SAID TO HAVE HELPED HER IDENTIFY THE TRUE CROSS WHILE SHE WAS VISITING THE HOLY LAND.

KEY FACTS
Mother of Constantine, finder of the True Cross
DATES: *c.AD 250–330*
BIRTH PLACE: *Drepanum (later Helenopolis, in modern-day north-west Turkey)*
PATRON OF: *Archaeologists*
FEAST DAY: *18 August (West)*
EMBLEM: *Crown, cross*

Helen came from humble origins, but she made a grand marriage and gave birth to a great son. According to tradition, she was born in Drepanum (later renamed Helenopolis after her, by her son Constantine) and her father was an innkeeper. Her husband, Constantius Chlorus, a Roman general, divorced her when he became Emperor of Rome in AD 292, but their son greatly honoured her.

FINDING THE TRUE CROSS

When in her sixties, Helen made a pilgrimage to Jerusalem. She had converted to Christianity by this time. Her son, who was by then emperor, had organized diggings to uncover the holy sites of Jesus and the apostles.

It is told that Helen was at the hill of Calvary, where foundations were being dug for the church of the Holy Sepulchre, when three

Left St Helen *(Altobello Meloni, 15th century).*

crosses were excavated. A woman with a terminal illness was touched by each of the crosses, and the True Cross cured her, thus revealing its sacred nature.

Relics of the Cross were taken to Rome, where they were housed in the Basilica of Santa Croce, built for the purpose. The Holy Stairs – allegedly the marble steps excavated from the hall of Pontius Pilate where Christ's trial was held – were also moved to Rome.

Helen was renowned for her generosity and work among prisoners and the poor, and she founded churches in both Palestine and Rome.

CONSTANTINE THE GREAT

Some biographies of Constantine claim his mother, Helen, was his father's paramour, not a wife. Though his father was emperor, Constantine still had to fight hard to win leadership of the Roman Empire. His cause was doubtless helped by his diplomatic skills.

Although he promoted Christianity after his conversion, he was reluctant to cause strife in a predominantly pagan Rome. As emperor, he founded Constantinople (now Istanbul) on the site of the old city of Byzantium, which in time became the centre of the Christian world.

Right Emperor Constantine and St Helen with the True Cross *(fresco, c.8th century).*

Above St Helena and the Miracle of the True Cross *(attr. to Simon Marmion, 15th century).*

PACHOMIUS

A COMPETENT ADMINISTRATOR, THIS FORMER ROMAN SOLDIER WAS HIGHLY INFLUENTIAL IN ESTABLISHING ORDERLY COMMUNAL LIFE FOR HERMITS IN THE REGION OF UPPER EGYPT.

KEY FACTS
Founder of the first monasteries
DATES: C.AD 290–346
BIRTH PLACE: *Esna,*
Upper Egypt
FEAST DAY: *9 May (West)*
EMBLEM: *Appearance of a hermit*

Life in the Roman army prepared Pachomius well for the path he chose to follow. Born to heathen parents in Egypt, he was conscripted into the Roman army, where he fought under Constantine the Great. He became a Christian after his return home, and immediately went to live in the wilderness, there putting himself under the guidance of an old hermit named Palemon.

Pachomius lived near the River Nile and became part of a small community of other ascetics committed to the austere life of a recluse. An angel is said to have visited Pachomius after a few years and told him to establish a monastery in the desert. It seems this Desert Father preferred the life of the community to that of the solitary. He was concerned, too, that some of his fellow hermits were extreme in their behaviour and that they were running the risk of madness from starvation and hardship.

Above This Byzantine mosaic includes Pachomius' name in Latin in the design (12th century).

The monks and nuns took vows of chastity, poverty and obedience, and regulations regarding diet and prayer were strict but humane. Fanaticism was outlawed and meditation and prayer were supervised. Members learnt by heart passages from the Psalms and other books of the Bible. Pachomius acted as an army general might do in running the monasteries. Monks were commanded to move from one house to another, superiors were put in charge of each house, and accounts were presented every year.

The order he founded was known as the Tabennisiots, after a place near his first monastery. Pachomius' manuscripts have not survived, but his Rule was translated into Latin by St Jerome, and this influenced Sts Basil the Great and Benedict, both of whom founded great monastic orders based on St Pachomius' methods.

St Athanasius the Aconite, patriarch of Alexandria, was a friend of Pachomius and visited the monk in his monastery at Dendera, near the Nile, where Pachomius lived out his life. The Eastern Orthodox Church holds this remarkable man in high veneration.

FOUNDING MONASTERIES

His life in the army had taught Pachomius about the organization of a dedicated community, and he also had a flair for administration. After his first monastery was founded in AD 320, he established nine others for men and two nunneries for women, and wrote rules for living in these communities.

Right St Pachomius (16th century). The saint, remembered for building the first monasteries, is shown in this fresco to be casting his saintly light on the construction of a grand tower.

RELIGIOUS ORDERS

MONASTERIES AND CONVENTS SUSTAIN COMMUNITIES DEVOTED TO A
STRICT RELIGIOUS LIFE. THESE RELIGIOUS ORDERS HAVE A ROLE IN
ROMAN CATHOLIC AND EASTERN ORTHODOX CHURCHES.

Although Christianity does not regard ownership of property or marriage as sinful, the Church recognizes that some people have a special calling to dedicate their lives to prayer and to God.

Those called to this religious life fall into two categories. The first are the eremites, who choose to pursue a life of solitary meditation, following the precepts formulated by St Antony of Egypt and other Desert Fathers. The second group, the coenobites, share a communal life of prayer that is influenced by the ideas of St Pachomius. Founders of the various orders laid down rules for monastic life, which continue to apply in Roman Catholic and Eastern Orthodox Churches.

The lives of all monks and nuns are guided by the primary disciplines of prayer, spiritual development, inner contemplation and physical labour.

EARLY MODELS
The earliest monasteries were self-supporting and independent of papal authority. Many monks were not even ordained as priests.

Some early founders, such as Martin of Tours and Cassian, maintained harsh regimes. But St Benedict, who established a monastery at Monte Cassino, Italy, rejected this military-like austerity. His rules were those of a well-ordered household with routine and sympathetic discipline. He encouraged labour to sustain the community and literacy to provide an understanding of the scriptures. By the 10th century, his rule was accepted throughout Western Christendom.

The Rule of St Augustine of Canterbury was also influential. He stipulated that monks should be ordained clerics, living within an order but going into the world to work as priests.

Above St Zeno (*Francesco Bonaza, 17th century*). *St Zeno founded the earliest nunneries and encouraged women to take vows.*

Above left St Hugo of Grenoble in the Refectory of the Carthusians (*Francisco Zurbarán, 1633*). *St Hugo helped establish their house in Grenoble, France.*

Over time, monastic orders lost their independent status and were required to obtain papal blessing and authorization.

LATE MEDIEVAL TIMES
During the Crusades, monastic rules of prayer and preaching were extended to include military and medical duties. The Knights Hospitaller of St John, which was founded in 1113, and the Knights Templar, established in 1119, both consisted of fighting men or soldier-nurses.

Above The monastery of Monte Cassino, originally established by St Benedict, had to be rebuilt after severe bombing by the Allies in WWII.

Other religious orders were established in the 13th century, which returned to the asceticism of the early Desert Fathers. They included the Franciscans, founded by St Francis of Assisi, the Dominicans of St Dominic, the Carmelites, and the Augustinian Hermits. These were all mendicant orders, relying on charity for survival. Although the monks were attached to a community, they functioned as individuals.

Nuns generally lived in their enclosed communities, isolated from the outside world. They followed the Rule of St Francis through St Clare, or that of the Dominicans or Benedictines.

COME THE REFORMATION

During and after the Reformation, orders developed to strengthen the faith. Priests concentrated on teaching, nursing, leading retreats or missions. Most famous were the Jesuits, a missionary order founded by Ignatius of Loyola in 1534.

The Reformation reinforced eremitical orders. The Capuchins evolved from the Franciscans in 1525, the Trappists from the Cistercians in 1664, and the Maurists from the Benedictines in 1621. The Discalced Carmelites developed from the rule of St Clare in 1593.

Below A 15th-century drawing of monks wearing the distinctive habits of their orders. The Carmelites wore white, the Franciscans brown or grey, the Benedictines black, and the Dominicans black and white.

KNIGHTS HOSPITALLER OF ST JOHN

For centuries, a nursing order ran a hospital in Jerusalem. Then, in the 1120s, Raymond du Puy turned the order into a military community known as the Knights Hospitaller of St John. Nursing was not abandoned, but during the Crusades, the monks became much-feared soldiers. Expelled from Jerusalem by the Turks in 1291, they went to Rhodes.

Later, in the 16th century, the order was forced to move to Malta, where it remained until 1798. In 1834, after demonstrating that they had left their military past behind them, the order was allowed to settle in Rome.

Above Order of St John of Jerusalem, a woodcut dating from the 14th century.

ANTONY OF EGYPT

THIS SAINT IS OFTEN REGARDED AS THE FATHER OF MONASTICISM, AND WAS KNOWN FOR HIS HEALINGS, BUT IT IS HIS LIFE OF SOLITUDE, PRAYER AND GENTLENESS THAT HAS HAD THE MOST LASTING IMPACT.

The popular view of saintliness is embodied by St Antony of Egypt. He was not tempted by worldly goods or comfort, he did no harm to others, he was not too proud to undertake humble work, and he spent his life in prayer.

SOLITUDE AND PRAYER

Born into a respectable Christian family in Coma in Upper Egypt, Antony was given a narrow education. When his parents died, he was 20 and heir to a considerable estate. But he recalled the words of Christ, "Go, sell what thou hast,

and give it to the poor, and thou shalt have treasure in Heaven." He gave away his land and wealth, keeping only enough for the care of his younger sister, and lived among local ascetics. Then for 20 years, from AD 286 to AD 306, he took to the desert, where he lived a life of complete solitude and extreme austerity, seeking the love of God in prayer and meditation.

When he was 54, Antony was asked to leave his hermitage and organize some nearby ascetics into a monastic order. Back on his mountain, the hermit cultivated a garden and wove baskets. A follower, Marcarius, guarded him from curious onlookers.

Toward the end of his life, Antony visited Alexandria to comfort persecuted Christians and refute Arianism. He was, by now, famous for his wisdom and miracles; crowds rushed to see him and many were converted.

Sufferers from ergotism (also known as "St Antony's Fire") visited his shrine at La Motte in France, where the Order of Hospitallers of Saint Antony was founded c.1100, to seek a cure.

KEY FACTS
Desert Father, ascetic
DATES: *AD 251–356*
BIRTH PLACE: *Coma, Egypt*
PATRON OF: *Skin diseases, domestic animals and pets, basket-makers*
FEAST DAY: *17 January*
EMBLEM: *Pig, bell*

Left St Antony in a stained glass from Suffolk, England (17th century). He was once a swineherd and St Antony's cross can be seen on his cloak.

Left The central panel of The Temptation of St Anthony *(Hieronymus Bosch, c.1505).*

BASIL THE GREAT

VENERATED FOR HIS ROBUST DEFENCE OF THE FAITH, THIS DOCTOR OF THE CHURCH WAS ALSO AN IMPORTANT FIGURE IN ESTABLISHING MONASTIC RULES DEDICATED TO CHARITABLE WORK AND POVERTY.

KEY FACTS

Doctor of the Eastern Church
DATES: *c.AD 330–79*
BIRTH PLACE: *Cappadocia, Turkey*
PATRON OF: *Russia, monks of the Eastern Churches*
FEAST DAY: *2 January (with St Gregory of Nazianzus)*
EMBLEM: *Bishop's vestments, often pictured with other early Doctors of the Church*

Basil's extensive writings reveal a humorous, tender person, yet he proved unyielding in his fight for orthodoxy.

He was born in Cappadocia, one of ten children in an extraordinary family: his grandmother, both parents, and three siblings were all destined for sainthood.

On returning from studies in Constantinople and Athens, where he had become good friends with Gregory of Nazianzus, he travelled widely, to Palestine, Egypt, Syria and Mesopotamia, studying the religious life, before taking up life as a hermit in Cappadocia. His brother joined him there in a life of contemplation and preaching.

Basil established the first monastery in Asia Minor, instigating a brotherhood of hard labour, charitable work and communal routine, a system that he believed better served God and his faithful than did solitary asceticism. His rule, unchanged, is followed by monks today in the Eastern Orthodox Church, and forms the basis of orders dedicated to him.

BATTLING ARIANISM

During Basil's lifetime, a schism threatened the Church, caused by the popular teachings of Arius, which denied the divinity of Jesus.

The harsh activities of the Arian Emperor Valens against traditionalism brought Basil back to Caesarea to protect his community from attack. Valens was too afraid of Basil's reputation to act against him, and withdrew from Caesarea, but he continued

Above *St Basil is the patron saint of Dubrovnik, and in this painting he cradles the city within the protective safety of his arms (18th century).*

to promote Arianism elsewhere. Basil preached daily to huge crowds and produced numerous texts on belief that remain in use in the Eastern Orthodox Church.

During a period of drought, he built hospitals and soup kitchens where his monks served the poor. But anxious that the faith might be waning in the east, he increased his preaching, emphasizing the Church's beliefs. His lessons were conveyed everywhere both by texts and through word of mouth.

In AD 378, Valens died and was succeeded by his nephew, Gratian, who discouraged Arianism. As Basil himself lay dying the follow-

ing year, he was confident that, with the emperor on his side, orthodoxy would prevail.

Christians, pagans and Jews all mourned the "father and protector" of Caesarea, while the Church honoured St Basil for keeping the faith alive. He is one of the great Doctors of the Church.

Below This reliquary (12th century) holds the skull of St Basil the Great and can be found in the cathedral dedicated to him in Dubrovnik.

BARBARA

THE LEGEND OF ST BARBARA IS A ROMANTIC ONE ABOUT A BRAVE AND BEAUTIFUL GIRL WHO REFUSES ALL SUITORS FOR CHRIST. HER CULTUS WAS POPULAR IN FRANCE DURING THE MIDDLE AGES.

KEY FACTS
Virgin martyr
DATES: *Unknown*
BIRTH PLACE: *Unknown*
PATRON OF: *Gunners, artillery, dying people, miners*
FEAST DAY: *Formerly 4 December, but removed from Roman calendar in 1969*
EMBLEM: *Tower*

It is highly unlikely that this saint ever existed: although she allegedly lived in the 3rd century, nothing was written about her until the 7th. She was officially de-canonized in 1969.

According to the *Golden Legend*, Barbara was the daughter of a pagan, who locked her in a tower so that no man could see her. But her beauty was so renowned that men still came to court her. When Barbara became a Christian, her father was so furious that he tried to kill her, but she miraculously escaped.

Above St Barbara (Flemish manuscript illumination, 1475).

Eventually she was handed over to a judge, who condemned her to death and ordered her father to carry out the deed. This he did, but he was immediately struck by lightning and died.

This is the reason that Barbara is regarded as a patron of those in danger of sudden death, originally from lightning, later from cannon-balls, gunfire or mines.

CYRIL OF JERUSALEM

THE LESSONS OF ST CYRIL FOR THOSE SEEKING BAPTISM ARE SO PROFOUND, AND HIS FIGHT FOR THE TRUE FAITH SO EARNEST, THAT HE IS HONOURED AS A DOCTOR OF THE CHURCH.

KEY FACTS
Doctor of the Church
DATES: c.*AD 315–86*
BIRTH PLACE: *Jerusalem*
FEAST DAY: *18 March*
EMBLEM: *Bishop's gown*

St Cyril was a clear thinker and an excellent teacher. But it was his misfortune to live during a time of schism among the Eastern Christian communities, when the ideas of the unorthodox Arians were gaining ground against the traditionalist concept of the Holy Trinity – the threefold godhead of Father, Son and Holy Spirit.

Cyril was born and educated in Jerusalem. After becoming a priest, his first assignment, from St Maximus, was to train converts preparing for baptism. His lessons of faith were – and indeed still are – much admired, and they brought him prestige and high office.

Left The Church of the Holy Sepulchre in Jerusalem where St Cyril was bishop during the 4th century AD. This scene has scarcely changed since.

When he first became Bishop of Jerusalem in AD 349, strange lights were said to fill the sky over the city. But during the 35 years Cyril served as a bishop, he spent much of his life in hot dispute with the dominant Arians. He was first exiled in AD 357, and although he was recalled two years later, he was banished twice more and spent a total of 16 years in exile.

However, in AD 381, Cyril took part in the First Council of Constantinople, which gave official endorsement to the concept of the Trinity. St Cyril was made a Doctor of the Church in 1882.

GREGORY OF NAZIANZUS

THE INSPIRED PREACHING AND WRITING OF ST GREGORY HELPED
TO UNIFY THE EASTERN ORTHODX CHURCHES IN TIMES OF STRIFE.
AS A RESULT HE WAS MADE A DOCTOR OF THE CHURCH.

KEY FACTS

*Doctor of the Eastern
Orthodox Church*
DATES: *AD 329–89*
BIRTH PLACE: *Arianzus, south-
west Cappadocia, Turkey*
FEAST DAY: *2 January*
EMBLEM: *Bishop's gown*

This shy, diffident poet-priest was the son of wealthy parents, Gregory, Bishop of Nazianzus and his wife Nonna, who were able to give him the best education. He attended the renowned theological school at Caesarea and continued his studies first at Alexandria and then at the University of Athens, where he rekindled his youthful friendship with St Basil the Great.

RELUCTANT PRIEST

Together, the two friends formed a common resolve to live a contemplative life, and when Basil set up a retreat in Pontus (now Turkey), Gregory joined him. Together they wrote the Monastic Rules.

After two years of the contemplative life, Gregory returned to Nazianzus. His father, now elderly, was not happy with his son's decision to live as a monk, and resolved to have him home. In AD 361, the bishop forced his son to be ordained as a priest.

Neither did his friend leave him in peace. Basil, who had by then become Archbishop of Caesarea, had Gregory consecrated as Bishop of Sasima, most probably to maintain his own influence in what was a disputed area. The place, however, was a hostile border settlement and Gregory spent little time there. The whole affair brought about a quarrel between the pair, from which their friendship never fully recovered.

After the death of his parents, Gregory, who had always desired the contemplative life, escaped briefly to a monastery in Seleucia.

Above These images depict the visions of the Old Testament prophet Ezekiel, and are part of The Homilies of St Gregory, *an illuminated manuscript held in Paris (9th century).*

AGAINST HERESY

Five years later, in 379, Gregory was recalled to serve the Christian community of Constantinople in their battle for orthodoxy. Church officials were determined to use Gregory's oratorial talents in their dispute with Arianism.

The heresy had been so successful in Constantinople that there was no longer an Orthodox Church active there, and Gregory was obliged to use his house to hold meetings. Here, he preached five discourses on the Holy Trinity. These teachings helped ensure that orthodoxy was confirmed at the First Council of Constantinople in AD 381. For a brief, unhappy period he was Bishop of Constantinople, but differences of opinion with the Eastern bishops led him to resign.

PEACE AT LAST

Gregory spent his last years in priestly duties in Nazianzus and in retreat. Many of his letters survive, as does an autobiography and some religious poetry.

After his death aged 60, St Gregory's relics were translated to Constantinople and later to Rome. He is one of the great Eastern Doctors of the Church alongside Sts John Chrysostom and Basil the Great.

Above St Gregory of Nazianzus, overseen by an angel while working at his desk, in a mosaic in the second dome of the Basilica San Marco, Venice (c. 1350).

AMBROSE

THIS POPULAR BISHOP OF MILAN BECAME A KEY COMBATANT IN THE STRUGGLE AGAINST THE ARIAN HERESY. HE ALSO WROTE IMPORTANT TEXTS ON CHRISTIAN ETHICS AND INTERPRETATION OF THE BIBLE.

KEY FACTS
One of the four great Latin Doctors of the Western Church
DATES: *AD 339–97*
BIRTH PLACE: *Trier, Germany*
PATRON OF: *Bees, beekeepers and those who work with wax*
FEAST DAY: *7 December (West)*
EMBLEM: *Whip, to symbolize his fight against heresy*

A vigorous intellect, energy and charm helped Ambrose in the murky political world he encountered as Bishop of Milan.

He was the son of a noble Roman family, and legend tells that, when he was child, a swarm of bees settled on him, which was deemed to symbolize his future eloquence (hence his patronage).

He studied law, Greek, rhetoric and poetry before becoming consular prefect of Liguria and Aemilia, with headquarters in Milan. He was a gifted administrator and diplomatic leader – and the citizens trusted him.

Left Enthroned Ambrose *(Alvise Vivarini, 1503).*

Then Ambrose took to studying Christianity. In AD 374, when the bishop of Milan died, he attended the council meeting to elect a successor. Ambrose was not a follower of Arianism, a sect that was strong in the Milan area, and gave a speech favouring orthodox beliefs. To his great surprise – he was not even baptized – he was elected bishop and was in office within a week.

TACKLING THE HERETICS

The new bishop took charge of a weak Church. The empire, too, was stricken by battles for supremacy between East and West.

The greatest demonstration of his moral strength was shown after the Massacre of Thessalonica in AD 390. The governor there had been assassinated and, in retribution, Theodosius, Emperor of the eastern Roman Empire, ordered thousands of citizens to be killed. Ambrose was horrified. He faced Theodosius and reminded him that God was more important than the state, and that even the emperor must submit to holy law. Contrite, Theodosius made a public penance for his savage act.

Left The Emperor Theodosius and Saint Ambrose *(Peter Paul Rubens, 17th century).*

AGATHA

ALTHOUGH LITTLE IS ACTUALLY KNOWN ABOUT THIS SAINT, HER ALLEGED BRAVERY IN THE FACE OF HORRIFIC TORTURE AND DEATH ENSURED HER A WIDESPREAD FOLLOWING IN MEDIEVAL TIMES.

KEY FACTS
Virgin martyr
DATES: *Unknown*
BIRTH PLACE: *Catania or Palermo in Sicily*
PATRON OF: *Protection from breast disease, volcanoes and fire; jewellers, nurses, bell founders, Catania*
FEAST DAY: *5 February*
EMBLEM: *Mutilated breasts, often carried on a dish*

Although there is some evidence that a virgin martyr named Agatha died in Catania in the first years of the 4th century, little is known about this saint. However, her memory persists and she is patron of Catania.

Her legend recounts that her parents were Christians from the nobility who openly refused to offer sacrifices to pagan gods. The local consul Quintinian, who tried unsuccessfully to seduce Agatha, raised a campaign against all Christians, and the young girl was arrested. As she approached the consul, she prayed, "Jesus Christ, Lord of all, Thou seest my heart… I am thy sheep: make me worthy to overcome the devil."

Her persecutors were aware that virginity was important to their Christian victims, so Agatha was sent to a brothel. It is said that her faith and piety shone from her, and no man dared approach her.

MUTILATION AND DEATH

Instead, she was taken away to be tortured. Agatha was not afraid of martyrdom because it meant she would soon join Christ. Quintinian devised a mutilation suited to horrify a beautiful young girl. His henchman pierced and severed Agatha's breasts.

St Peter is said to have visited Agatha and restored her breasts. However, she was then forced to walk across hot coals and shards of glass. But as she took her first step, Mount Etna erupted and an earthquake shook the earth. The watching crowd screamed for her release, convinced her God was

Above This marble altarpiece portrays the coronation of St Agatha in heaven (15th century).

punishing them all. Quintinian stopped the torture, but quietly starved her to death instead.

St Agatha is often the subject of paintings illustrating her mutilation. The resemblance in shape of bells to breasts is the reason for her patronage of bell founders.

Below Saint Agatha (Francesco Guarino, 17th century).

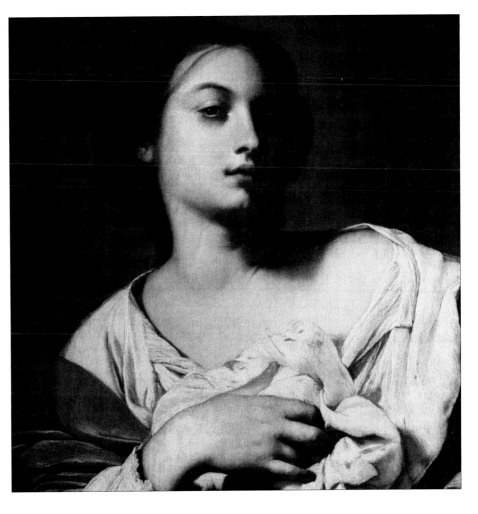

MARTIN OF TOURS

THE SON OF A MILITARY MAN, MARTIN JOINED THE ARMY BUT CHOSE INSTEAD TO BE A "SOLDIER OF CHRIST". HE FOLLOWED HIS FAITH WITH ENERGY AND CONVICTION.

KEY FACTS
Monk bishop
DATES: c.*AD 316–97*
BIRTH PLACE: *Pannonia (present-day western Hungary)*
PATRON OF: *Soldiers, infantry and cavalry, horses and their riders, geese, wine-makers*
FEAST DAY: *11 November (West)*
EMBLEM: *Armour, sword, cloak*

This saint is traditionally commemorated as having led a life of bravery as a "soldier of God". In fact, his first career was in the army – following his pagan father's footsteps – but he came to believe that war was incompatible with his commitment to Christ. When accused of cowardice, he offered to stand unarmed between the opposing sides, but was instead discharged from the army.

Martin became known for his charity as well as moral courage. One famous legend recounts that as a soldier riding to Amiens in bitterly cold weather, he saw a poor man dressed in rags. Filled with compassion for the man's plight, he cut his heavy army cloak in two and wrapped the man in one half. That night, as he slept, Jesus appeared to him wearing that half of the cloak.

Below Saint Martin Sharing His Cloak with a Poor Man *(Domenico Ghirlandaio and workshop, 15th century).*

Above The Mass of St Martin of Tours *(Eustache Le Sueur, 1654).*

MONK AND BISHOP

For ten years, Martin lived at Ligugé, a plot of land given to him by Hilary, the Bishop of Poitiers. Originally living a solitary life, Martin was soon joined by others, and founded a monastery there – the first one in Gaul. Then, in AD 372, at the acclamation of clergy and people, he was elected as Bishop of Tours.

After his ordination, he continued to live as a monk, moving to a solitary place, Marmoutier, where he later founded one of several other monasteries.

Martin travelled around his parish on foot and by donkey, preaching over a wide area with a desire to see the conversion of rural areas. He destroyed heathen temples and sacred trees and performed many miracles, notably healing lepers. It is said that he even raised a dead man to life.

He became involved in many doctrinal disputes. In AD 384, when some bishops appealed to the Roman authorities to execute local heretics, Martin begged (in vain) for their lives, claiming banishment was sufficient. Such a forgiving nature ensured his popularity into old age. A mausoleum marks his grave at Tours.

HILARY OF POITIERS

In AD 356, the Arian Roman Emperor Constantius II banished this bishop, whom he had branded a "mischief-maker". Throughout his life, Hilary was fierce in his fight against the Arian heresy.

Though born (c.AD 315) and brought up in a pagan family, Hilary converted to Christianity in AD 350, following a long process of study. He became a bishop around three years later, and went on to produce many influential writings, particularly discourses on the Holy Trinity. He was praised by Jerome and Augustine of Hippo, and was influential in the spiritual development of Martin of Tours.

PELAGIA THE PENITENT

THIS BEAUTIFUL AND TALENTED ACTRESS ABANDONED HER FORMER
LIFE AND WEALTH TO BECOME A CHRISTIAN. SHE LIVED THE REST OF
HER LIFE AS A RECLUSIVE HERMIT DISGUISED AS A MAN.

KEY FACTS

Penitent
DATES: *5th century*
BIRTH PLACE: *Antioch*
PATRON OF: *Actresses*
FEAST DAY: *8 October*
EMBLEM: *Hermit*

In the 5th century, St John Chrysostom wrote about a glamorous harlot of Antioch who repented and became a nun. The story of Pelagia the Penitent seems to follow this tale but it comes with embellishments.

Pelagia was a beautiful and immensely wealthy woman as well as an actress, which was considered a disgraceful profession.

She liked to sway through the promenades of Antioch, dressed in marvellous clothes to flaunt her attributes. A retinue of admirers followed in her wake. One day as she passed a solemn group of bishops attending a service given by bishop Nonnus of Edessa, a leading Christian, the men turned their backs on her. But Nonnus himself stopped preaching and admired the lovely woman. He was troubled that she was clearly so successful at her chosen yet despised profession, while he felt he had failed as bishop to his Christian flock.

PELAGIA'S CONVERSION
Nonnus prayed all through the night, then the next morning went to attend to his duties at the cathedral. Pelagia, who had heard his preaching, followed him and begged to be baptized. She was given instruction by a deaconess and accepted into the Christian community. After her baptism, she gave away all her possessions and disappeared from Antioch. She

crept off and, dressed as a man, she took up the life of a hermit on the Mount of Olives in Jerusalem.

Pelagia was forgotten by all her old companions although some Christians visited her. A deacon, known as James, was said to have sought an interview with the "beardless recluse", and afterwards wrote down her story. Only at her death did people realize that this hermit was not only a woman, but one with an infamous reputation in the city of Antioch.

The legend has been seen as a fine example of penitence. Others say it was written by a male hermit who longed for a female counterpart in his harsh life.

Pelagia's story has remained a popular one, and has been told in a number of versions over the centuries – from the fourth all the way to the thirteenth. Her name appears in many ports and villages around the Mediterranean Sea.

Right Sts Pelagia and Euphemia in a mosaic from San Apollinare Nuovo, Ravenna, Italy (AD 561).

NICHOLAS OF MYRA

LEGENDS ABOUT THE PATRON OF RUSSIA CREDIT ST NICHOLAS WITH BEING A MIRACLE WORKER BLESSED WITH THE VIRTUES OF KINDNESS AND GENEROSITY — ESPECIALLY TOWARD CHILDREN.

This saint is famous for his role as Father Christmas. The fact that he is patron of children may explain this status. Alternatively, the reason might lie in the legend that St Nicholas once found three dead children hidden in a brine tub and brought them miraculously back to life. There is also the story of his rescue of three young girls doomed to prostitution through poverty. As a gift, St Nicholas threw three bags of gold into their window, thus providing the girls with marriage dowries.

There is evidence that a bishop of Myra, named Nicholas, did live in the 4th century AD, but little else is known about him. Some claimed St Nicholas attended the Church's first General Council in

Above This fresco shows St Nicholas saving three condemned knights from death (Giotto School, c.1300–5).

Below Saint Nicholas Protecting the Sailors (Vitale da Bologna, 14th century). He is patron saint of sailors.

KEY FACTS
Identified with Santa Claus
DATES: *4th century AD*
BIRTH PLACE: *Possibly Patara, Lycia (modern-day Turkey)*
PATRON OF: *Children, brides, unmarried girls, Russia, travellers, sailors, maritime navigators*
FEAST DAY: *6 December*
EMBLEM: *Three balls or bags of gold, purse, anchor, ship*

Nicaea in AD 325. Or he may have been martyred before Constantine legalized Christianity in AD 313.

A PEOPLE'S SAINT

Despite his lost life story, St Nicholas has been, since early Christian history, a popular saint. His image can be found all over Russia and the Christian Middle East. Churches everywhere are dedicated in his name.

His many legends depict a strong, chivalrous man. He rescued three sailors from drowning, and saved three condemned men from execution. Sailors faced with a storm called upon his name, and it is said St Nicholas appeared at the shore and calmed the waves.

His physical strength was revealed as a newborn, when he sprang to his feet and stood firm. And as a small boy, he showed deep devotion, listening attentively to the sermons of the local bishop, his uncle.

Italians stole his relics in 1095 and gave them to the church in Bari, where they remain to this day. Europeans carried his name to the New World. Linguists have observed that Dutch settlers in the USA called him "Sinte Klaas". Following European tradition, they would have given presents on his feast day, thus starting the Santa Claus tradition.

BLAISE

KNOWN FOR HIS KINDNESS AND FOR HIS MEDICAL SKILLS, BLAISE WAS SOUGHT BY BELIEVERS TO INTERCEDE NOT ONLY FOR THEIR OWN HEALING BUT ALSO FOR THEIR PETS AND FARM ANIMALS.

KEY FACTS

Martyr saint
DATES: *4th century AD*
BIRTH PLACE: *Sebaste, Armenia*
PATRON OF: *Doctors, farmers, wool trade, laryngologists, builders, veterinarians, a Holy Helper*
FEAST DAY: *3 February*
EMBLEM: *Wool-comb, two crossed candles*

Although no historical details of his life exist, the stories of Blaise's healings have made him popular and his feast day is still celebrated in some churches.

It is said that Blaise was born into a wealthy, Christian home in the 4th century AD. Blaise became Bishop of Sebaste in Armenia while he was still young, but he lived during the reign of Emperor Licinius, a time of severe persecution of Christians.

Warned by his brethren that his life was in danger, Blaise fled to the hills, where he remained isolated from his community, and where, allegedly, wild animals would turn to Blaise when they were ill or hurt and he would heal them.

STORIES OF HEALINGS

Among many stories is one of a countrywoman who came to the saint's cave with her small son who was choking to death on a fishbone. Blaise touched the child's throat, the bone was dislodged, and the boy survived.

Eventually, Blaise was arrested. It is told that as he was marched off to jail, he passed a wolf loping off with a pig in its mouth, while nearby a poor woman wept at the loss of her animal. Blaise ordered the wolf to drop its prey and was instantly obeyed. The grateful woman later brought the prisoner food, and a candle to light his cell. Indeed, different traditions have varied tales of St Blaise, but all tell of farmers calling on him for help with their sickly animals. Water with the blessing of St Blaise is given to sick cattle.

PATRONAGE

The saint is also associated with mending sore throats, and some churches celebrate the Blessing of the Throat on his feast day. The priest ties ribbons to two candles, then touches the candle ends to the throat of the sufferer, saying, "May the Lord deliver you from the evil of the throat, and from all other evil."

Perhaps Blaise's torturers knew of his bond with animals because, before beheading him, along with numerous other tortures, they combed his flesh with an iron wool-comb. In time the wool comb came to be his emblem, and he became patron of the wool trade. For a long time, his feast day was celebrated with a procession in Bradford, once the centre of the English wool business.

St Blaise's cult is not known before the 8th century, but he became one of the most popular

Above Saint Blaise *(Giovanni Battista Tiepolo, 1740). His bishop's vestments give no hint of his hardships as a hermit.*

saints of the Middle Ages, most probably due to his association with miraculous cures. He was called upon to help diseased people and animals, and his name lives on in the village of St Blazey in Cornwall, England.

St Blaise also enjoys an international cultus. He is well known in Germany, for instance, and in Spain he is venerated under the name of San Blas; in Italy he is known as San Biagio. He is one of the Fourteen Holy Helpers.

Below A statue of St Blaise in Dubrovnik, Croatia (15th century).

JEROME

THE GREATEST BIBLICAL SCHOLAR OF HIS TIME WAS VENERATED FOR HIS AUTHORITATIVE TRANSLATION OF THE BIBLE FROM THE ORIGINAL HEBREW AND GREEK VERSIONS INTO LATIN.

KEY FACTS
One of the four great Latin Doctors of the Western Church
DATES: C.*AD 341–420*
BIRTH PLACE: *Strido, Dalmatia (Balkans)*
PATRON OF: *Scholars, students, archaeologists, librarians, translators*
FEAST DAY: *30 September*
EMBLEM: *Bishop's hat, book, stone and lion*

Numerous paintings of Jerome have created an abiding image of a lean old man, bent over his books in a remote cave. At his feet a large friendly lion keeps benevolent guard. But the reality was quite different.

Jerome seems to have been a man at war with himself. He longed to concentrate on his studies but also sought academic debate. A quick temper and impatient manner made this saint unpleasantly aggressive and

Left St Jerome *(Theodoricus of Prague, 14th century). Often his symbol in art is a book.*

intolerant of his colleagues' ideas. Critics bemoaned his lack of Christian meekness and surfeit of sarcasm and unkindness.

EARLY LIFE

Jerome received a classical education and went on to study further in Rome. During this time he nursed an ambition to experience the world and in order to fulfil this ambition, the young man travelled widely and actively sought out teachers and further intellectual stimulation.

At this early stage in his life Jerome was not devout, being too interested in the literature and philosophy of the Greeks. After a headstrong dispute in Rome with colleagues, he felt impelled to leave the city and travelled again, this time with two friends touring eastern Europe.

However, a chance occurrence changed his life. All three men fell dangerously ill with a severe fever. The subsequent death of both his companions had a profound impact on Jerome, who

Left Saint Jerome in a Landscape *(Giovanni Battista Cima da Conegliano, c.1500–1510).*

turned to the Christian faith. But his commitment to Christianity caused him great anguish.

He greatly enjoyed the company of women, and found too much pleasure in reading pagan Greek texts. Believing these joys would carry him away from God, he decided to abstain from them. To this end, Jerome went to live as a hermit in the desert where he could think and pray without distraction.

GREAT SCHOLAR

Somewhat against his will, he was ordained and sent back to Rome in AD 382. Pope Damasus I saw that this man would never do as a parish priest but believed his scholarship could serve well.

Jerome produced important texts about traditional dogma and monasticism, and expounded the virtue of celibacy. He wrote in praise of the Virgin Mary, asserting the view that she remained a virgin throughout her life.

Posterity honours him for translating the Bible from Greek and Hebrew into Latin. His version is known as the Vulgate or Authorized Bible. Jerome was the first scholar to make the distinction between the "true" texts and the dubious, or

"SHOW ME, O LORD, YOUR MERCY AND DELIGHT MY HEART WITH IT. LET ME FIND YOU FOR WHOM I SO LONGINGLY SEEK... I AM THE SHEEP WHO WANDERED INTO THE WILDERNESS – SEEK AFTER ME AND BRING ME HOME TO YOUR FOLD. AMEN"

PRAYER OF ST JEROME

Above Annunciation to Mary with the Saints Jerome and John the Baptist *(Francesco Raibolini, c.1448–1517).*

"apocryphal", texts. His work has proved invaluable to theologians ever since.

As was his wont, however, Jerome became embroiled in theological dispute, this time with the heretical Arians, about whom he wrote a scathing attack. And in the process it is possible he made one too many enemies.

SCANDAL AND FLIGHT

Jerome's promotion of a study group for girls and widows in Rome proved to be too risky. Soon rumour was rife that Jerome shared more than his religious teachings with the ladies. Despite protests of his innocence, he did not have the support of friends and was forced to flee.

Jerome travelled to Cyprus and Antioch where two Roman women, the widow Paula and her daughter, joined him. Together they went to Egypt, then returned to Bethlehem in the Holy Land.

Paula established three nunneries in Bethlehem, and she built a monastery for men which Jerome headed. Living in a cave nearby, he

continued to analyse scripture. Even from this remote spot, his sharp tongue aroused fury among fellow theologians. He went into hiding again, before returning to Bethlehem in AD 418.

By then Jerome was old and sickly. It is said he died with his head resting on the manger where baby Jesus was born. Jerome was buried under the Church of the Nativity in Bethlehem.

JEROME AND THE LION

A lion had crept into the monastery in Bethlehem and its presence was frightening the monks. But the animal was limping, and Jerome, realizing its distress, and impatient no doubt with the squeals of his colleagues, strode over and removed a thorn from the lion's paw. For the rest of his days, the lion padded along next to him. Perhaps a dumb beast suited the saint's social temperament better than could a human. After Jerome's death, the lion protected the monastery's domestic animals.

Above Saint Jerome Reading *(Rembrandt Harmensz van Rijn, 1634).*

JOHN CHRYSOSTOM

BOTH LOVED AND HATED FOR UPHOLDING CHRISTIAN PRINCIPLES, ST JOHN CHRYSOSTOM WAS A GREAT PREACHER, WHO ALSO PRODUCED PROFOUND INSIGHTS INTO SCRIPTURE.

A man of high intellect, John Chrysostom knew how to touch the hearts of his listeners. A committed ascetic, he aroused fury among those churchmen who preferred ease and luxury to the simplicity of a devout life.

John grew up in the major Christian centre of Antioch (in Syria). After his father died, his mother brought him up as a Christian. He studied law, but opted instead for a religious life. After his baptism, *c.*AD 370, he retired to the desert.

For health reasons, he returned to Antioch where he was ordained a priest in AD 386. His eloquent preaching won him many followers in the city.

REFORM AND OPPOSITION
In AD 398, he was appointed Archbishop of Constantinople, and began to instigate moral reform. He dedicated church money to hospitals, forbade the clergy from keeping servants, and put idle monks to work.

It was not long before he faced opposition. Empress Eudoxia took his attacks on the morals at court as a personal affront, and Theophilus, Bishop of Alexandria, demanded that John be exiled from Constantinople.

He was briefly recalled, but then banished again a year later, and eventually died of exhaustion after he was forced to travel long distances on foot in bad weather.

Left Detail of St John Chrysostom *from the Apse Mosaic, San Paolo fuori le Mura, Rome (Edward Burne-Jones, 19th century).*

A RENOWNED TEACHER
St John Chrysostom is remembered for his preaching – his name means "golden mouth" in Greek. He emphasized literal interpretation and practical application of scripture and wrote treatises on the Psalms, St Matthew's Gospel and St Paul's Epistles. He is admired in the West, where he is one of the four Great Doctors of the Eastern Orthodox Church.

Right St John Chrysostom exiled by the Empress Eudoxia *(Benjamin Constant, 19th century).*

AUGUSTINE OF HIPPO

THIS INFLUENTIAL THINKER FROM NORTH AFRICA WAS THE ARCHITECT OF EARLY CHURCH DOCTRINE. HIS WRITINGS, *CITY OF GOD* AND *CONFESSIONS*, BECAME FAMOUS CHRISTIAN TEXTS.

As a young man of Roman Carthage, Augustine had considerable intellect and charm. His vivacity brought him, by the age of 20, a concubine and small son, Adeodatus. But he matured into a disciplined theologian and bishop, kindly towards his flock.

His pagan father ensured Augustine was well educated. His mother, St Monica, was a Christian but her son rejected her beliefs. Driven by ambition, he moved with his family from North Africa to Rome, and then to Milan. He was a restless man, searching for a vocation. His widowed mother insisted he send the

Below St Augustine *(the Master of Grossgmain, c.1498).*

"O GOD OUR FATHER, WHO DOST EXHORT US TO PRAY, AND WHO DOES GRANT WHAT WE ASK, HEAR ME, WHO AM TREMBLING IN THE DARKNESS, AND STRETCH FORTH THY HAND TO ME, HOLD FORTH THY LIGHT BEFORE ME, RECALL ME FROM MY WANDERINGS, AND MAY I BE RESTORED TO MYSELF AND TO THEE. AMEN."

PRAYER OF ST AUGUSTINE

Above A view of St Augustine's Cathedral at Hippo Regius, a Roman town in Algeria.

concubine, his companion of 15 years, back to Africa. Shortly after this separation, Augustine claimed to hear a heavenly child's voice bearing a divine message.

CONVERSION

His subsequent conversion to Christianity, however, was marred by the emotional conflict between, on the one hand, his love of comfort and women, and on the other, the austerity demanded by his faith. These feelings are recorded in his autobiography, *Confessions*.

He and his son were baptized in AD 387 and, with a group of friends, retired to his estates in Africa. The group took vows of chastity, poverty and obedience, and undertook charitable work in the community. The rules that Augustine made for monastic life formed the basis of future orders.

In AD 396, Augustine became Bishop of Hippo and never left North Africa again. From this corner of the empire, he set down his beliefs about spiritual redemption, which had a lasting impact on Church teachings.

Augustine lived in a period when the Roman Empire was crumbling under the burden of invading barbarians. Civic order was breaking down. However, Christianity was spreading, albeit haphazardly, across Europe.

Augustine believed the Church to be superior to the state, because its secular duties were based on spiritual qualities. He introduced the doctrine of man's salvation through the grace of God, and his ideas laid the foundations of a Christian political culture.

KEY FACTS
One of the four great Latin Doctors of the Western Church, Bishop of Hippo
DATES: *AD 354–430*
BIRTH PLACE: *Tagaste (now in Algeria)*
PATRON OF: *Printers and theologians, brewers, against eye diseases*
FEAST DAY: *28 August*
EMBLEM: *Bishop's staff and mitre, dove, pen, shell, child*

CATHERINE OF ALEXANDRIA

THIS COURAGEOUS AND INTELLIGENT WOMAN OUT-ARGUED LEARNED PHILOSOPHERS IN DEFENCE OF CHRISTIANITY. SHE WAS TORTURED ON TWO SPIKED WHEELS AND THEN BEHEADED.

KEY FACTS
Virgin martyr
DATES: *4th century AD*
BIRTH PLACE: *Unknown*
PATRON OF: *Philosophers, young female students, librarians, nannies and wheelwrights*
FEAST DAY: *25 November*
EMBLEM: *Jagged wheel and the sword that beheaded her*

The legend of St Catherine of Alexandria is a gorgeous and romantic tale of heroism and faith.

Catherine was the beautiful young daughter of King Costus of Cyprus. She was also clever and courageous. A Christian, she confronted Emperor Maxentius about his persecution of her community.

He was amused and intrigued, and challenged her to a debate with 50 philosophers. On learning that her arguments had converted these learned men, he ordered all 50 to be burnt on a pyre, and had Catherine beaten. Unfortunately for the emperor's wife, she and 200 soldiers were converted too, and also executed.

Isolated in prison, Catherine had doves come to feed her. Then she was "despoiled naked and beaten with scorpions". But no punishments affected her body or her convictions. Maxentius then tried to tempt her with wealth and status, and asked the beautiful Christian to become his wife.

CATHERINE'S DEATH

When Catherine refused he devised a cruel death. She was to be turned between two wheels spiked with blades. But the blades broke and the splinters killed and injured the onlookers. An angel rescued Catherine. No torture could make the girl forsake her faith or her virginity. Even her beheading confounded the emperor. Instead of blood, milk flowed from her virginal veins.

Angels, or perhaps monks, are said to have lifted her body and carried it to Mount Sinai. There it remains, in a monastery built in AD 527 by Emperor Justinian.

Left St Catherine poses, calm and fearless, against her torture wheel (detail from a painting by the studio of Lucas Cranach, 1510).

Catherine had an early cultus in the East, possibly originating near Mount Sinai, and it seems the Crusaders brought her story to the West. Her story is featured in the *Golden Legend*.

Catherine was removed from the Church's Calendar of Saints in 1969, but people continued to venerate her as the bride of Christ (for refusing to marry) and patron of advocates and the dying. A limited recognition of her cultus and sainthood was allowed in 2001.

Above A medieval woman depicted as St Catherine (Dante Gabriel Rossetti, 1857).

URSULA

THIS BEAUTIFUL DAUGHTER OF A CHRISTIAN KING OF ENGLAND IS SAID TO HAVE TURNED DOWN AN OFFER OF MARRIAGE FROM ATTILA THE HUN ON ACCOUNT OF HER FAITHFUL VOW OF VIRGINITY.

KEY FACTS
Virgin martyr
DATES: *4th or 5th century AD*
BIRTH PLACE: *Unknown*
PATRON OF: *Girls, students, the Ursuline Order*
FEAST DAY: *21 October*
EMBLEM: *Crown and huddle of women under her opened cloak*

It is uncertain in which century St Ursula lived, or even that she lived at all. A mound of bones in a burial ground was uncovered in Germany in the 8th century, and in the 10th century an inscription bearing the name Ursula, a 12-year-old girl, was found at the same site. From this "evidence", a medieval legend grew.

Ursula was a British princess during the 4th or 5th century. As a dedicated follower of Christ, she vowed to remain a virgin. She is said to have refused a marriage arranged by the court. In other versions she was betrothed to a pagan and did not refuse him but, instead, set out to convert him.

PILGRIMAGE TO ROME
She requested that, before the wedding, she make a pilgrimage. Either she ran away, or was allowed to board a ship with 11,000 young women, also avowed to Christ and virginity.

This crowd reached Rome where they venerated the saints and their relics. Ursula apparently had a meeting with the pope, one Cyriacus (unknown in papal records). Ursula and her hand-maidens then turned back and sailed the Rhine to Germany.

They stopped in Cologne but invading Huns had taken the city. These barbarians slaughtered the 11,000 Christian women, but not Ursula. The princess was spared because her beauty had been noticed by Attila, warrior leader of the Huns. He desired her, even offering marriage. But her refusal, on account of her vows angered

Above St Ursula Bidding Farewell to her Parents *(the Master of the Legend of St Ursula, before 1482).*

Below St Ursula and her companions are martyred *(16th century).*

the Hun, whereupon he ordered his archers to shoot her through with arrows.

In Cologne, the romance of Ursula and her maidens was supported by old rumours of an early martyrdom of many young women in the city. The city's basilica was rebuilt to honour them. The story led to a brisk circulation of relics and forged inscriptions. Then, in the 11th century, Elizabeth of Schönau claimed visions of Ursula, and made revelations in her name.

The Roman Catholic Church removed Ursula and her Companions from the Calendar of Saints in 1969.

LEO THE GREAT

KNOWN TO HAVE BEEN AN ASTUTE DIPLOMAT, LEO I IS VENERATED PARTICULARLY FOR STRENGTHENING THE ROLE OF THE POPE, AND FOR HIS ARTICULATE WRITINGS ON THE INCARNATION OF JESUS.

KEY FACTS
Doctor of the Church
DATES: *d.AD 461*
BIRTH PLACE: *Rome*
FEAST DAY: *10 November (West)*
EMBLEM: *Papal clothing*

This pope embodied the belief that the Church brings a beneficial authority to affairs of state. He was diplomatic and his decisions were supported by a strong faith and conviction in the spiritual discipline of the Church.

Born in Rome, Leo took office as pope in AD 440 when the Church was in upheaval. Not helped by the destruction of the Roman Empire, he soon went to parley with Attila, leader of the invading Huns, who had reached the River Mincio, close to Rome.

Leo persuaded Attila to withdraw beyond the Danube. When the Vandals invaded Rome in AD 455, Leo's diplomacy once again prevailed, preventing widespread massacre of the city's citizens. Leo's strong leadership was important in Church affairs. The faith's foothold in Europe was shaky, and heresies were rife, especially Monophysitism (a sect declaring "one nature" of Christ).

This doctrine held that Jesus was completely absorbed by his divinity, thus had no humanity. In contrast, Leo maintained that God had made his Son a man in order to preach the truth and to suffer in a sacrificial offering to redeem the sins of mankind.

CHAMPION OF RIGHT

Leo wrote his tome to rebut the Monophysites and presented it at the Council of Chalcedon in AD 451. His views were upheld, confirming the orthodox belief that Jesus is both man and God. Also at the Council, the balance of power in the Eastern Church was maintained because Leo refused to grant Constantinople primacy over Antioch and Alexandria.

His energy and mission work ensured the growth of the faith in Spain, France and North Africa. Leo implemented papal authority in these countries as well as in Italy. He was convinced that for the Church to survive, believers needed to respect the spiritual guidance embodied in the papacy.

To support his conviction, Leo spoke of St Peter's role as leader. He reminded his followers that this succession had been passed in an unbroken line to every pope since St Peter. Leo's teachings, particularly those expressed in a sermon one Christmas, brought many Christians a deeper understanding of the Incarnation of the Word.

Of Leo's numerous and articulate writings, 96 sermons and 143 letters survive. It was the long-lasting influence of these texts on the Christian Church that inspired Pope Benedict XIV to pronounce St Leo as a Doctor of the Church in 1754.

Left St Peter and St Paul can be seen floating above the scene here in The Meeting of Attila the Hun and Pope Leo I *(Raphael, 1509–11).*

SIMEON STYLITES

FOR 37 YEARS ST SIMEON LIVED ON TOP OF A PILLAR, FROM WHERE HE PREACHED SERMONS THAT DREW CROWDS FROM FAR AND WIDE.

KEY FACTS

Stylite (pillar hermit)
DATES: *AD 390–459*
BIRTH PLACE: *Cilicia*
FEAST DAY: *5 January (West)*
EMBLEM: *Saint on pillar*

This saint's story is as fantastic as any legend. Simeon was a shepherd's son who hated comfort and longed for solitude. His self-mortifications included tying plaited palm leaves round his body, causing a flesh infection that nearly killed him. He chained himself to a rock on a mountain, and spent the 40 days of Lent with neither food nor water. Priests usually had to rescue him.

His fame spread when he built a pillar, 3m/9ft high, and lived on it for four years. But feeling this altitude did not give him enough solitude, he moved to ever higher pillars until eventually he climbed atop a pillar 20m/60ft

Right A Byzantine mosaic of St Simeon Stylites living on top of his pillar in the Basilica San Marco, Venice.

high and 2m/6ft wide. There he stayed for 20 years until his death. Food and water were hauled up by rope. But still he had no solitude. Throngs of spectators came to gawp and ask questions. Unfazed, Simeon gave informal sermons about kindness, fairness, and not cheating on God.

Above A monument in a sanctuary to Simeon Stylites, on the site in Syria where he lived as a pillar hermit.

GENEVIEVE

BARBARIAN INVASIONS OF HER HOMELAND INSPIRED GENEVIEVE TO PERFORM HEROIC ACTS OF DEFENCE IN ORDER TO PROTECT THE CITIZENS OF PARIS. IN TIME, THEY ADOPTED HER AS THEIR PATRON.

KEY FACTS

Heroic virgin
DATES: *c.AD 420–500*
BIRTH PLACE: *Nanterre*
PATRON OF: *Paris, against fever and plague*
FEAST DAY: *3 January*
EMBLEM: *Carries a candle, the devil at her side, shepherd's crook, bread*

As a child, Genevieve confided to Bishop Germanus that she lived only for God. In Paris, her young life was spent in prayer and caring for the poor.

When the city was threatened by a Hun invasion, Genevieve begged the frightened citizens not to flee but to pray. To everyone's relief, the Huns turned away at Orléans and Paris was saved.

Later, Genevieve ran sorties up the River Seine to fetch food for Parisians when under siege by the Franks. She also persuaded

Above St Genevieve praying to save Paris (French School, 17th century).

barbarian kings to show leniency to French prisoners-of-war. In 1129, her relics were paraded through Paris during a plague of the deadly disease, ergotism. The sick were said to be miraculously cured. The event is commemorated annually in Paris, but without her relics, which were burnt in the French Revolution.

CELTIC SAINTS

THE CELTIC CHURCH WAS THE PRODUCT OF UNCONVENTIONAL IRISH MONKS WHO, INDEPENDENTLY OF THE ROMAN CHURCH, CREATED A GOLDEN AGE OF SPIRITUALITY, ART AND LEARNING.

Christianity arrived as early as the 2nd century AD in Wales, England and Ireland, which became the Celtic branch of the Church, albeit in scattered communities. Then in the 5th century AD, the Irish missions of two saints, Patrick and Brendan the Navigator, took the faith across the North Sea to Scotland.

These Irishmen are also thought to have introduced the austere monasticism of the Desert Fathers to the British mainland. Ascetic ideals, conceived in Egypt and Syria, might have made their way to Ireland via the distribution of religious texts, or through trade and pilgrimage in Europe.

Two other saints, Finnian of Clonard (d.AD 549) and Columba of Iona (d.AD 597), played key roles in establishing monastic life in Ireland and on the British mainland respectively. By the middle of the 6th century there were

"WHAT WRETCHES WE ARE, GIVEN UP TO SLEEP AND SLOTH SO THAT WE NEVER SEE THE GLORY OF THOSE WHO WATCH WITH CHRIST UNCEASINGLY! AFTER SO SHORT A VIGIL WHAT MARVELS I HAVE SEEN. THE GATE OF HEAVEN OPENED AND A BAND OF ANGELS LET IN..."

FROM BEDE'S
LIFE OF ST CUTHBERT

Above St Cuthbert turns water into wine, from Bede's Life of St Cuthbert *(English School, 12th century).*

Below A Celtic cross outside the Iona Monastery, Scotland.

monasteries at Glastonbury and Tintagel in Cornwall. St Columba founded a community at Iona, Scotland, in AD 565. And St Aidan established the abbey of Lindisfarne, on the coast of Northumbria, in the 7th century.

BEACONS IN THE DARK

These times were the Dark Ages. The old Roman Empire was in disarray. Rome herself was under constant attack from the Huns, and she neglected the distant Celtic churches.

The British Isles were wild, backward and uncivilized, except in the monasteries, where Latin and learning were kept alive. Irish monks were to become famous for the quality of their scholarship and all Celtic monasteries became beacons of study and literature.

When St Augustine of Canterbury's mission arrived in AD 597, the Celtic Church, though not heretical, was regarded with some suspicion. It had a peculiar administrative structure, with no dioceses, and bishops performing mainly ritual duties. Monasteries were built on land owned by the abbot, not the

monks were not bound by rules of a founder. They lived together in monasteries, which allowed, within the usual vows of austerity and obedience, independence and individual expression.

Perhaps this freedom from a more rigorous communal routine accounts for the extraordinary flowering of art and craft among the Celtic monks. Beautiful ornamental ironwork and stone work developed to a high degree of sophistication.

Some monks wrote poetry and biographies of religious figures. Others transcribed scriptural texts into lovingly made manuscripts, adorned with intricate decoration and illustration. The writing of history and biography formed an important part of the monks' literary output. The best-known examples of this genre come from a writer who was the epitome of a Celtic monk, the Venerable Bede. Bede died in AD 735 and spent his entire life within cloisters, devoting himself to scholarship and prayer. Bede is most famous for his

Above The Venerable Bede, St Wilfrid and St Cuthbert in St Augustine's Chapel, Ramsgate, England.

Ecclesiastical History of the English People. Examples of biography include Bede's *Life of Cuthbert* and Eddius Stephanus' *Life of Wilfrid.*

Christianity gradually came to replace the old pagan practices. Saxon kings of the 7th and 8th centuries AD led mass conversions, strengthening the Church in England, especially Northumbria in the north-east.

PRESSURE FROM ROME

As the mission of St Augustine gained ground, the Celtic Church came under pressure to conform to Roman authority. The Irish tradition, with its archaic rituals and odd calculations of the Church calendar, particularly Easter, was finally rejected at the Synod of Whitby in AD 664.

The influential monk St Wilfrid (c.AD 633–709) approved this turn toward Rome. And by early in the 8th century, even Iona and Lindisfarne, centres of Celtic culture in the north, had rejected the old Irish practices.

From the 9th to 11th centuries, invading Vikings destroyed many monasteries, dispersing the monks. Thus the "Golden Age" of the Celtic church was ended, and little of its identity remained.

Left Illumination depicting three monks sitting at desks, diligently copying manuscripts (13th century).

CELTIC ARTISTRY

The monks of Northumbria and Ireland produced illuminated manuscripts, the quality of which has rarely been surpassed. Until the 14th century, the material used for manuscripts in Europe and the Celtic fringe was vellum or parchment. Some of the finest early medieval artwork is found in these books. Celtic monks exhibited extraordinary skill in the art of interlacing patterns of animal and geometric designs. The text, written in a script known as *literae saxonicae*, consisted of letters inked in decorative shape and subtle hue. Little illustrations appear in the margins around the text, providing a detailed record of contemporary rural and courtly life. The finest examples are the Lindisfarne Gospels, produced in honour of St Cuthbert, and the Irish *Book of Kells.*

Right Ornamental page from The Book of Kells *(8th century).*

PATRICK

THE FEAST DAY OF ST PATRICK IS CELEBRATED WITH MUCH FANFARE, NOT ONLY IN HIS NATIVE IRELAND, BUT ALSO IN THE USA AND AUSTRALIA WHERE COLONISTS AND SETTLERS SPREAD HIS CULT.

It is said that St Patrick alone converted Ireland, and banished all snakes from the island. His own life story is also extraordinary.

Patrick grew up somewhere between the Rivers Clyde and Severn. Irish pirates kidnapped and enslaved him. He escaped after six years of servitude.

After a long period of aimless wandering he found his way home. Patrick studied the Latin Bible in preparation for joining the priesthood, but was criticized for his lack of scholarly education. He was ordained and, inspired by a dream, returned to Ireland as a missionary. He was appointed Bishop of Ireland in about AD 435.

Patrick divided the country into dioceses, and encouraged the setting up of monastic orders. He devoted himself to the delicate task of spreading the Christian faith across a land in which sun worship prevailed at the time. Every year the pilgrims of Croagh Patrick commemorate his retreat for 40 days on Cruachan Aigli.

Right St Patrick and a king (vellum, Irish School, 13th century).

BRIGID OF IRELAND

LONG VENERATED IN IRELAND, ST BRIGID WAS SO LOVED BY THE NUNS AT HER MONASTERY THAT THEY KEPT A FIRE BURNING AT HER SHRINE IN KILDARE FOR CENTURIES AFTER HER DEATH.

Irish Catholics have a special affection for Brigid, placing her second only to St Patrick. Although the Church has de-canonized her, Brigid's cultus continues. Her legends reflect a generous, kindly personality, but historical facts are hard to find.

She was born, it is believed, near Kildare, and St Patrick baptized her. A very young Brigid took vows as a nun. In the convent she was a milkmaid, hence the legends of Brigid giving butter to the poor, or of cows giving her milk three times a day to cope with the thirst of visiting bishops. Brigid founded the monastery of Kildare and helped spread Christianity through Ireland and beyond her shores. Churches dedicated in her name span Europe, showing her wide veneration. A brass reliquary of her shoe, set with jewels, is kept at a museum in Dublin.

Left Stained-glass windows depicting St Patrick and St Brigid (Paul Vincent Woodroffe, 1919).

BRENDAN THE NAVIGATOR

A LEGEND CLAIMS THAT ST BRENDAN CROSSED THE ATLANTIC OCEAN IN A CORACLE. CERTAINLY, HE WAS VENERATED BY CELTIC PEOPLES FOR HIS MISSIONARY OUTREACH TO UNKNOWN LANDS.

KEY FACTS
Founder
DATES: c.*AD 486–575*
BIRTH PLACE: *Possibly Tralee,
Ireland*
FEAST DAY: *16 May*
EMBLEM: *Sitting in a small boat*

Best known as the hero of an adventure legend of the 10th century, St Brendan became widely known as "the Navigator". Translated from the Anglo-Norman into several European languages, the story of his life was one of the first books to be published after Caxton's invention of the printing press in 1476.

EARLY LIFE

Brendan was fostered by Ita, a much-loved Irish nun and saint who founded a small convent where she lived in solitude. Her nuns were encouraged to care for the sick and Ita herself educated needy boys, instilling into them her own faith.

As a youth, Brendan studied with St Erc, the bishop of Kerry. Brendan became a monk and later was appointed as abbot of Clonfert monastery. Some reports also claim he became abbot of Llancarvan in Wales.

He founded four monasteries in Ireland, one in Scotland, and evangelized in Wales and Brittany. In imitation of the apostles, Brendan was an indefatigable missionary. His life of extensive travel, criss-crossing the Irish Sea and the English Channel to France, became the source of legends about St Brendan.

TO PARADISE

In the legend of St Brendan, he and his band of monks take to the sea in search of the Island of Promise. They sail in a traditional vessel, a coracle, made of leather stretched over a wicker frame. During the journey, unwittingly, they make camp on the back of a whale and light a fire there.

One Christmas Eve, they come upon Judas Iscariot. Every year on this night, Christ's betrayer is allowed to sit on a rock in the middle of the ocean to cool off before returning to fiery hell.

Within these stories of adventure there are hints that Brendan reached the shores of distant America. Researchers say that a close study of the text allows for an interpretation that confirms that he conducted an expedition across the Atlantic Ocean. Brendan's popularity is shown by the survival of 116 Medieval Latin manuscripts of his story.

Below Painting on vellum depicting St Brendan and his companions meeting a siren on their travels from the Navigatio Sancti Brendani Abbatis *(German School, c.1476).*

BENEDICT

ST BENEDICT CREATED A MONASTIC LIFE OF SIMPLICITY, WORK AND PRAYER FOR THE RELIGIOUS. HIS RULES REJECTED THE GRIM HARDSHIP IMPOSED BY FOUNDERS OF MORE AUSTERE ORDERS.

The best way to appreciate the character of St Benedict is by studying his Rule. These guides to daily living reveal a man who understood the perils of power. He knew that extreme forms of discipline were unkind and could even drive men and women mad.

The system Benedict set up was inspired by his own experiences as a young man. Born into a good family in Umbria in the 5th century AD, he was sent as a student to Rome. However, he disliked the riotous living of the city and wandered off through the

Left Saint Benedict with His Monks at the Refectory (*Il Sodoma, c.1505*).

forested valley between Lazio and Abruzzo. Finding the ruins of Nero's palace beside a lake at Subiaco, he settled in a cave there and spent most of his time in prayer and meditation.

Only one person knew of his whereabouts, a monk named Romanus, who secretly delivered him food. Gradually, knowledge of the hermit became common and his fame spread.

MONASTIC BEGINNINGS

Benedict was persuaded to join a nearby monastery, where he was disturbed by the lax, even dissolute, ways of the monks, and set about reforming them. The monks enjoyed their easy life, and determined to poison the abbot.

Legend tells that when the deadly draught was served to Benedict he made the sign of the cross over the cup. It immediately shattered, and a raven carried the shards away.

He returned to the life of a hermit, but he was not left alone, and soon disciples gathered about him. Benedict founded 12 small monasteries, in each placing

Left St Benedict, *shown wearing the black garb of his monastic order (Pietro Perugino, c.1495–98).*

12 monks, over whom he served as abbot. The houses all gained a reputation for orderly, learned living, without austerity.

RULE OF THE ORDER

Benedict perceived that prayer, routine and purposeful activity were the paths to serenity and to God. Authority was to be controlled. If a monk were to commit a major transgression, the abbot must, before fixing on a punishment, seek the advice of everyone in the monastery, even the youngest.

Though the abbot's decision was final, he must be minded that his decisions would be judged by God. Benedict recommended a simple but ample diet, though no flesh should be served, and the first meal should be around noon.

Benedict allowed for sensible hours of sleep. Property was communal, and the monks had to work, either producing food, maintaining the monastery, or spending time reading and writing the scriptures. But more important than any other duty was regular communal prayer. This he called "divine work".

MONTE CASSINO

Soon Benedict's order became established and noble families sent their sons to his monasteries. These boys were destined to be monks and their training began

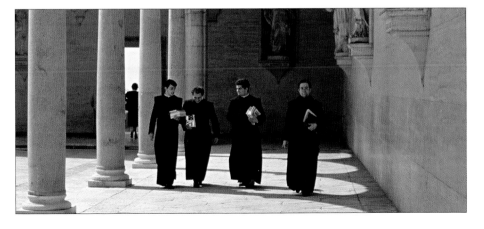

SCHOLASTICA

Scholastica, the sister of St Benedict, followed her brother to Monte Cassino. She founded a nunnery about five miles from her brother's monastery. They met once a year, and on one visit Scholastica begged him to stay, for she longed to converse with him. But he refused, so she prayed for rain. It is said that a thunderstorm started and so he stayed the night. Alas, she died three days later, and Benedict then wrote about his conversation with Scholastica during which they discussed their faith.

Above John the Evangelist, Scholastica and Benedict *(the Master of Liesborn, c. 1470-80).*

early. It is said that Benedict saved two of these youths from drowning by walking across water to rescue them.

They became his favourite disciples, Maurus and Placid, and were also venerated as saints. When a powerful, jealous priest complained about the abbot, Benedict left Subiaco, taking with him a few disciples, including Maurus and Placid. He climbed a mountain above the village of Cassino. On a plateau he built Monte Cassino, the monastery that would become the centre of religious life in western Europe and which still operates today.

It was the kindly, humane interpretation of the monastic life that made Benedict so popular. He found a way of allowing the religious to live with an austerity suited to their calling, without risking their health or wellbeing.

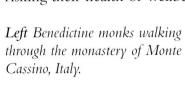

Left Benedictine monks walking through the monastery of Monte Cassino, Italy.

DAVID OF WALES

AN AUSTERE PRIEST RENOWNED FOR THE HARSHNESS OF THE MONASTIC REGIME HE ESTABLISHED IN WALES, HE NEVERTHELESS BECAME ONE OF THE BEST-LOVED SAINTS IN HIS COUNTRY.

KEY FACTS
Founder
DATES: *c.AD* 540–601
BIRTH PLACE: *Possibly Ceredigion, Wales*
PATRON OF: *Wales, poets*
FEAST DAY: *1 March*
EMBLEM: *Dove, later associated with a leek or daffodil*

St David is known as Dewi Sant in Wales, and his name is also sometimes translated as Dafydd. He is also given the title Dewi Dyfyrwr, or David Aquaticus, meaning "David, the Water Drinker". This is attributed to the teetotal regime of his monks who drank neither wine nor beer.

Tradition says David had a grand lineage. His father was thought to be of a princely family named Sant, and his mother, St Non, was also well connected. Possibly born in AD 540, David chose the life of a religious and went to study under the Welsh St Paulinus on a remote, unidentified island. He is said to have found the old hermit blind from weeping for the sins of the world, and restored his sight.

There is another report that David made a pilgrimage to the Holy Land where he was consecrated as an archbishop by the patriarch of Jerusalem.

AUSTERE ORDERS

When David attended the Synod of Victory at Caerleon he was uncompromsing in his stand against the Pelagian movement. This heresy claimed it was possible to find salvation without the help of divine grace. A decisive victory for the established Church outlawed the British movement. David then focused on founding monastic orders.

He settled with his disciples in Mynyw, a remote corner of Wales, and set up the first of many monasteries. David's rule was renowned for its severity. His monks had to live by hard labour and were not even allowed oxen to help them plough the fields.

Their diet was bread, salt and vegetables, and only water could be drunk. Speech was permitted only when absolutely necessary. The monks prayed without break from Friday evening till dawn on Sundays. The monks were described as "more abstemious than Christian".

David was also a powerful preacher. Once, as he was denouncing Pelagianism to a crowd, the earth swelled into a small hill so that more people could see him. He was made head of the Church in Wales by popular acclaim, and died at Mynyw. Leeks and daffodils are worn to mark his feast day.

There are more than 50 place names and dedications to David in South Wales, with further dedications in Devon, Cornwall and Brittany. David's cult was approved by Callistus in 1120, and two pilgrimages to St David's (Mynyw) in Pembrokeshire were said to equal one pilgrimage to Rome, while three were said to equal a pilgrimage to Jerusalem.

Left Detail from a manuscript depicting St David (15th century).

Right Detail from a manuscript depicting St David playing the harp (French School, 11th century).

LEANDER

IN HIS CAPACITY AS BISHOP OF SEVILLE, THE SON OF THE DUKE OF CARTHAGENA BECAME A PROMINENT DEFENDER OF ORTHODOXY IN THE ARIAN DEBATE, AND DREW UP A RULE FOR SPANISH NUNS.

As a member of the Spanish aristocracy, Leander was well disposed to influence those around him. He was a man who carefully selected projects, then applied his energy to completing them successfully.

In about AD 584, he became Bishop of Seville and turned his attention to the unwelcome dominance of the unorthodox Arians in Spain. He used his position to ensure that, at the Council of Toledo, the orthodox concept of the Holy Trinity was officially confirmed. He then concentrated on converting the Arian Visigoths, a strong presence in the Seville region. Patiently, he set about convincing these people of the truth of the Church.

His third concern was for the lives of nuns, for whom he drew up a Rule that proved highly influential. Leander introduced the practice of singing the Nicene Creed at Mass. His younger brother was St Isidore of Seville.

KEY FACTS

Bishop
DATES: *c.AD 550–600*
BIRTH PLACE: *Carthagena*
FEAST DAY: *27 February*
EMBLEM: *Bishop's vestments*

Below The region around Seville today, where Leander was a bishop in the 6th century AD.

JOHN THE ALMSGIVER

WHEN ST JOHN BECAME PATRIARCH OF ALEXANDRIA, HE APPLIED IDEALS OF CHARITY AND JUSTICE TO THE ADMINISTRATION OF THE CITY EARNING HIM THE EPITHET OF ALMSGIVER.

Though it is known John was born in Cyprus, it is uncertain where he lived as an adult with his wife and children. At some point he moved to Egypt where, in about AD 610, he became the Bishop and Patriarch of the archdiocese of Alexandria.

John observed that the heretical Monophysites had been busy in the city. They were persuading Christians to accept their view that Jesus had no humanity and was wholly divine.

Instead of confronting the sect, John thought to weaken them through his own example of humble but generous Christian living. His work included establishing a system of welfare reform, and the

Above Detail from a manuscript depicting St John the Almsgiver (French School, c.550–616).

KEY FACTS

Bishop, Patriarch of Alexandria
DATES: *c.AD 560–620*
BIRTH PLACE: *Amathus, Cyprus*
PATRON OF: *Formerly patron of the Knights of Malta but replaced by John the Baptist*
FEAST DAY: *23 January*
EMBLEM: *Bishop's vestments*

building of maternity hospitals and homes for the aged and frail. Citizens with legal or financial problems were invited to seek John's advice at twice-weekly meetings. And he organized relief for refugees after the Persians sacked Jerusalem in AD 614.

These efforts at ameliorating hardships and difficulties much endeared him to the people of Alexandria. Many were persuaded to follow his orthodox beliefs. John died soon after retiring to Cyprus in AD 619.

GREGORY THE GREAT

FACED WITH MILITARY THREATS FROM GERMANIC TRIBES AND UNEASY RELATIONS WITH CONSTANTINOPLE, ST GREGORY DID MUCH TO STRENGTHEN CHRISTENDOM AT A DIFFICULT TIME.

KEY FACTS
One of the four great Latin Doctors of the Church
DATES: *c.AD 540–604*
BIRTH PLACE: *Rome*
PATRON OF: *Music, protection against plague*
FEAST DAY: *3 September*
EMBLEM: *Three-tiered papal crown, dove of the Holy Spirit*

Although Pope Gregory I dreamed of a life of solitude and prayer, he was the obedient son of a wealthy family and so took up a worldly career. Self-assured and clever, he studied law and then, just 30 years of age, was appointed governor of Rome.

A year later, his father died and Gregory found himself one of the richest men in Rome. At last he revealed his true longings by giving up his position and all his wealth. His house became a monastery and he a simple monk.

The Church was reluctant to miss out on such talented leadership. First it made Gregory deacon of Rome, then an ambassador to the Byzantine court in Constantinople. He spoke no Greek and seemed to use this deficiency as a reason for living a monastic life among the monks of the city.

After a few years, in AD 586, he was recalled to Rome. Although he returned as deacon of the city, again he sought the monastic life. But when Pope Pelagius II died four years later, the people of Rome elected Gregory to succeed him. Rome was in a terrible condition when Gregory became pope. Over the previous century, the state had been conquered, sacked and pillaged many times. The city was dilapidated, without leadership or administration.

AS POPE
When Gregory took office, a plague was raging through the city. One of his first duties was to seek penitence from the citizens in order to end the disease. And so he led a great processional litany through the ruined streets.

Soon after taking office, he wrote to all his clerics, reminding them to treat their flocks with compassion and generosity. He recommended that church money be given to those in dire straits. The granaries of Rome were filled to feed the needy in times of

Right *An altarpiece depicting Gregory the Great (Pedro Torres, 16th–17th century).*

Below *Canterbury Cathedral where Gregory based his English mission (Wenzel Hollar, c.1650).*

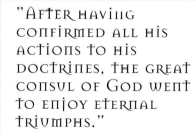

"AFTER HAVING CONFIRMED ALL HIS ACTIONS TO HIS DOCTRINES, THE GREAT CONSUL OF GOD WENT TO ENJOY ETERNAL TRIUMPHS."

EPITAPH ON ST GREGORY'S TOMB

Right A detail of Saints Augustine and Gregory in The Fathers of the Church *(Michael Pacher, 1480).*

food shortage. Jews were allowed to practise their faith and keep their property without fear of being persecuted.

AFFAIRS OF STATE

A greater worry to Gregory was the barbarian foe. From the very outset of his papacy, Gregory had to find energy to deal with the Lombards, a well-organized Germanic group intent on settling in the Roman Empire.

Their presence threatened Christianity. Gregory induced them to remain beyond the border, and arranged an uneasy truce between their leaders and the Byzantine emperor in Constantinople. However, his relationship with the Byzantines was also tense. He resented the grand titles of office assumed by

the Patriarch of Constantinople, who he feared wanted to wrest power from the West. Gregory insisted Rome was the centre of the Church and was successful in strengthening papal authority.

MISSION TO ENGLAND

Denied a life of solitude, Gregory found other ways to serve God directly. After once saving some English boys from slavery, Gregory set his mind on converting England. To this end, he dispatched St Augustine and 40 missionaries to Canterbury. Their success among the Anglo-Saxons gave Gregory deep satisfaction.

His writings about the liturgy were of special value, and his text is still used in the Roman Missal. Gregory died in Rome and was buried in St Peter's Cathedral.

ANGELS IN SLAVERY

When wandering the streets of Rome one day, Gregory noticed three boys with golden hair and fair skin. They were Anglo-Saxons to be sold in the slave market. On inquiry, he was informed that the youths were "Angels".

Gregory observed, "They are well named, for they have angelic faces and it becomes such to be companions with the angels in heaven. And who is the king of their province?"

"Aella," came the reply.

"Then," announced Pope Gregory, "Alleluia must be sung in Aella's land."

He felt such pity for these little golden creatures that he determined to spread the gospel to their country.

Below Saint Gregory the Great is visited by a dove representing the Holy Spirit as he sits writing letters (Carlo Saraceni, c.1620). The dove of the Holy Spirit is one of his emblems.

ISIDORE OF SEVILLE

KNOWN AS THE "SCHOOLMASTER OF THE MIDDLE AGES", ISIDORE OF SEVILLE WAS FAMOUS FOR WRITING A HUGE ENCYCLOPEDIA, WHICH BECAME A STANDARD REFERENCE WORK FOR CENTURIES.

KEY FACTS
Bishop, historian
DATES: c.*AD 560–636*
BIRTH PLACE: *Carthagena*
FEAST DAY: *4 April*
EMBLEM: *Bishop's vestments, books*

The veneration of St Isidore of Seville rests on his scientific and historical research. For the intellectual discipline involved in academic work, he had to thank his brother Leander, who educated him.

Although not a monk, Isidore learnt the monastic habits of deep thinking and discipline of work. When he succeeded his brother as Bishop of Seville in about AD 600, he continued Leander's mission to lead the Visigoths away from the unorthodox views of Arianism. He made the Church run more efficiently and emphasized duty of service and charity. Above all, believing in the importance of education, Isidore recommended that every diocese should have a Church school.

EDUCATIONIST

His writings were to become major texts in the education of generations of theologians, students and researchers. Isidore wrote 86 biographies of biblical figures, and a handbook on morals and theology. He also produced various liturgical analyses.

But his most important work was a massive encyclopedia, called the *Etymologies* (or *Origines*). This opus covered the arts, medicine, law, theology, history, zoology, anthropology, cosmology, agriculture, science and other subjects. Almost 1,000 medieval manucrips

Above Isidore of Seville gives a book to his sister in this Latin manuscript.

of the *Etymologies* are still in existence. Isidore intentionally did not apply any original thinking when he compiled this text. He wished to present all the knowledge then available to the European world and drew on numerous sources.

His other important writings include *On the Wonders of Nature* and *Chronica Majora,* a history from creation to AD 610, though with emphasis on Spanish history. His scholarship was admired across Christendom and medieval intellectuals thought him equal to St Gregory the Great.

Right Scenes from the Life of St Isidore, *from* Le Miroir Historial *by Vincent de Beauvais (French School, 15th century).*

CUTHBERT

Λ PURPORTED PROPHET AND HEALER, THE POPULAR ANGLO-SAXON
ST CUTHBERT PERSUADED HIS CELTIC FLOCK OF THE
CORRECTNESS OF FOLLOWING ROMAN CHURCH CUSTOMS.

After becoming a monk in Melrose in AD 651, Cuthbert spent ten years striving to be a model ascetic. He followed the practice of the time of standing for hours waist-deep in freezing sea water, and walked miles to visit the sick, whom he was said to heal miraculously.

His appointment as abbot put him in a position of influence. His winning manner and frequent local missions laid the groundwork for replacing the ideas of the Celtic Church with those of the Roman Church. The Synod of Whitby endorsed his view.

KEY FACTS
Bishop, missionary
DATES: *c.AD 634–87*
BIRTH PLACE: *Possibly Jarrow*
PATRON OF: *Formerly of Lindisfarne*
FEAST DAY: *20 March*

After a spell at Lindisfarne Abbey, he retired to Inner Farne as a hermit, only to be recalled to become Bishop of Lindisfarne. The gentle monk had a special affinity with the birdlife of the Farne Islands. After he died, his body reputedly stayed incorrupt.

Left King Siegfried visits St Cuthbert and asks him to accept the bishopric of Lindisfarne, from the Latin manuscript of Life and Miracles of St Cuthbert *by the Venerable Bede (English School, 12th century).*

THE VENERABLE BEDE

NO HARDY MISSIONARY OR INSPIRED LEADER, THIS HOMELY MONK
SPENT HIS ENTIRE LIFE IN CLOISTERS. YET HE BECAME THE MOST
RESPECTED HISTORIAN IN MEDIEVAL WESTERN CHRISTENDOM.

At the age of seven, Bede was given to a monastery in Jarrow, Northumbria, and stayed there for the rest of his life. From an early age, he loved singing, studying, reading and writing.

He produced numerous texts on many different subjects and the fame of his learning spread far beyond his native county. The best known of his works, *Ecclesiastical History of the English People*, was written in AD 731, and is still in print.

The book was compiled at a time when Christianity was still relatively new to the Anglo-Saxons

Above Bede is shown here dictating a translation of St John's Gospel into Anglo-Saxon (James Doyle Penrose, 1906).

KEY FACTS
Writer, historian
DATES: *AD 673–735*
BIRTH PLACE: *Sunderland, England*
FEAST DAY: *25 May*
EMBLEM: *Monk with pen at a manuscript*

of Britain, and the faith is presented as a unifying force for the nation. Unusually for his time, Bede took the trouble to differentiate between fact and hearsay in writing history.

An important biography was his *Life and Miracles of St Cuthbert*. His last work was a translation into Old English of the *Gospel of St John*. It is said he dictated the closing sentences of this work from his deathbed.

RUPERT

KNOWN AS THE "APOSTLE OF THE BAVARIANS", ST RUPERT IS CREDITED WITH ESTABLISHING CHRISTIANITY IN LANDS BORDERING THE RIVER DANUBE AND WITH FOUNDING SALZBURG.

KEY FACTS
Missionary, bishop
DATES: *d.c.AD 710*
BIRTH PLACE: *Unknown*
PATRON OF: *Bavaria, Austria, Salzburg*
FEAST DAY: *27 March*
EMBLEM: *Barrel of salt*

Little is known about Rupert's early life, including his birthplace. He may have been a Frank or an Irishman. However, having committed himself to becoming a missionary, Rupert attained high office in the Church, being elected Bishop of Worms in southern Germany.

At the invitation of the Duke of Bavaria, Theodo II, the saint went to Regensburg in Bavaria. There he founded a church near the Wallersee and dedicated it to St Peter. Rupert moved on to Salzburg and gathered disciples around him. For these followers, he founded a monastery at a site

Left St Rupert in a detail from the Altar of St Hildegard of Bingen, Chapel of St Roch (1896).

now known as the Mönchberg, and a convent, the Nonnberg. His sister, Ermentrude, was appointed as abbess to the nuns. He built a house to accommodate clerks and dedicated another church to St Peter. It is possible that Rupert wished to emulate the great apostle in his life of fearless travel, spreading the faith.

MISSION TO THE DANUBE

Having been appointed Bishop of Salzburg, Rupert made that city his headquarters while he travelled extensively through the lands along the River Danube. This region was still a wild part of Europe. The Frankish empire had not yet extended this far east, so Rupert was blazing a trail into hostile barbarian territory.

He must have been a charismatic preacher, for his success as a missionary was immense. He is credited, too, with opening the salt-mining industry at a place which, before his efforts, held only the crumbling ruins of an old Roman town, Juvavum. He renamed the place Salzburg. Because of this activity, paintings often depict St Rupert with a barrel of salt beside him.

Left A statue of St Rupert located outside the Ruprechtskirche, the oldest church in Vienna.

BONIFACE

ONE OF THE GREAT MISSIONARY SAINTS, ST BONIFACE PLAYED A MAJOR ROLE IN ESTABLISHING CHRISTIANITY IN GERMANY WHERE HE IS SAID TO HAVE CONVERTED FOLLOWERS OF NORSE GODS.

KEY FACTS

Missionary martyr, archbishop
DATES: *c.AD 680–754*
BIRTH PLACE: *Possibly Crediton, Devon, England*
PATRON OF: *Germany, brewers, tailors*
FEAST DAY: *5 June*
EMBLEM: *Axe*

Boniface was born in England but he spent many years in Europe where he became known as the "Apostle to the Germans". For the first 40 years of his life he was a monk, mainly at Nursling, near Southampton. Learned and devoted to biblical studies, Boniface was nevertheless no timid scholar.

The Church recognized his qualities of boldness and effective preaching, and sent him on a hazardous mission to lands still in heathen hands. It is said that in AD 718, armed with an axe, Boniface marched into a shrine dedicated to Thor, the Norse god of thunder.

With one mighty swing of the axe, Boniface is said to have felled the oak that was a key cultic object. The amazed onlookers were so impressed with the power of this man's God that tradition says the Germanic tribes converted to his faith en masse.

TIRELESS MISSIONARY

It is much more likely that these conversions happened over a period of time. But Boniface quickly established a reputation among the people of Bavaria, Württemberg, Westphalia and Hesse as "a man who moved with power", in the words of contemporary reports. Pope Gregory II was equally impressed and gave him the bishopric of Mainz.

Right Detail from a manuscript showing Germans being baptized and the martyrdom of St Boniface at Dokkum (AD 975).

Above St Boniface is here shown in proselytizing mode with his axe (Alfred Rethel, 1832).

Boniface summoned more male and female missionaries from his native country.

In about AD 732, the pope made him archbishop. Boniface increasingly handed over the outward missionary work to his English evangelists, while he concentrated on organizing the new Church in West Germany.

Once satisfied that Christianity had taken firm root in Germany, Boniface turned to France. Many sees were vacant or poorly managed. With the help of the Frankish King Pepin, Boniface reformed those dioceses.

He then turned northwards to Frisia, where pagan communities still existed. He was over 70 when he undertook this mission. Travelling with a small band of disciples, he stopped at a place called Dokkum. Here, Boniface and his fellow missionaries were slaughtered by the very people he had hoped to convert.

St Boniface's surviving Latin correspondence reveals a man of courage and determination, who deserves as high a profile in his native England as he enjoys in Germany. The faithful continue to make pilgrimages to his shrine at Fulda, where his remains lie.

CYRIL AND METHODIUS

THESE BROTHERS ARE VENERATED AS APOSTLES OF THE SOUTHERN SLAVS AND FATHERS OF SLAVIC LITERATURE. ST CYRIL GAVE HIS NAME TO THE MODERN SCRIPT CYRILLIC, DEVISED FROM HIS WORK.

KEY FACTS
Translators of Christian texts and apostles to the Slavs
DATES: *Cyril AD 826–69, Methodius c.AD 815–85*
BIRTH PLACE: *Thessalonica, Macedonia*
PATRON OF: *Europe*
FEAST DAY: *14 February (West)*
EMBLEM: *Books, Cyrillic script*

In 1980, Pope John Paul II decided the brothers, Cyril and Methodius, should share the patronage of Europe with St Benedict. Together, these three saints symbolize the religious and political unity of Eastern and Western Europe.

Cyril and Methodius were scholarly men from Thessalonika, Macedonia. Cyril studied in Constantinople where he earned the nickname, "the philosopher".

MISSION TO MORAVIA

His older brother, Methodius, went on a mission to the Khazars of Russia. He then returned to Greece as abbot of a monastery.

At the request of Prince Rostislav of Moravia, both men were sent on a mission to the Slavic province of Moravia (now part of the Czech Republic). The two missionaries were unique in being Greek monks sent off with

Above This icon from Bulgaria shows Sts Cyril and Methodius in their role as the inventors of the Cyrillic alphabet.

Below A fresco depicting Cyril and Methodius meeting Pope Adrian II (Lionello de Nobili, 1886).

the blessing of the pope in Rome. Until 1054, the Eastern and Western Churches remained in communion with each other.

The brothers not only preached in Slavonic but began translating the Bible and liturgy into the vernacular. Using Greek letters as a model, they invented an alphabet for Slavonic, later named Cyrillic, after Cyril, the younger brother.

But their mission, while finding converts, aroused much political and theological opposition. Their early supporters, Rostislav and Pope Adrian II, had died, and their replacements condemned the use of Slavonic, asserting that no vernacular language was suitable for use in the Church.

METHODIUS ALONE

After Cyril died in Rome in AD 869, Methodius continued the mission alone. But he was persecuted by Bavarian princes and forces within the Church, and imprisoned by German bishops.

After he had spent two years in a damp cell, Pope John VIII had him released and he continued his work in Moravia. He endeavoured to finish translating the Bible into Slavonic but opposition went on, and he died of exhaustion. Cyril and Methodius are admired for their ecumenism – the desire to unite worshippers, East and West.

WENCESLAS

VENERATION OF ST WENCESLAS FOLLOWED HIS RULE AS A GOOD CHRISTIAN DUKE OF BOHEMIA. HE WAS CRUELLY MURDERED FOR HIS FAITH.

Left St Wenceslas is depicted here in armour, bearing a banner of an eagle, oil on panel (Czech School, 16th century).

Despite the conversion of much of Bohemia (now part of the Czech Republic), pagan culture persisted and often took a political hue. When Wenceslas' father, the Duke of Bohemia, died, opposition factions mobilized. His grandmother, St Ludmilla, who had educated the boy as a Christian, was murdered and his mother was banished.

However, the people of Bohemia defeated these factions and chose Wenceslas to be their leader. He allied himself with the Christian Henry I (known as Henry the Fowler) of the Holy Roman Empire. Some nobles, including his pagan brother Boleslav, resented the power the clergy of the new court now had.

Boleslav feared his brother's marriage would produce an heir, further strengthening Christian rule and jeopardizing his own chances of power. Following celebrations at the Feast of Sts Cosmas and Damian, Wenceslas died. Boleslav was implicated in the murder but he later repented and had his brother's relics translated to St Vitus's Church, Prague.

The popular hymn "Good King Wenceslas" reflects his reputation for strength and generosity.

KEY FACTS
Ruler of Bohemia
DATES: *AD 907–35*
BIRTH PLACE: *Prague*
PATRON OF: *Brewers, Czech Republic*
FEAST DAY: *28 September*
EMBLEM: *Crown, dagger*

ODO OF CLUNY

SO ADMIRED WAS ST ODO FOR HIS LEADERSHIP THAT EVEN THE SECULAR AUTHORITIES TURNED TO HIM FOR GUIDANCE.

Above A view of the 12th-century Benedictine monastery at Cluny in Burgundy, France.

Reports say Odo had a good sense of fun and was a sympathetic person. Yet he was also a leader who instilled strict monastic observances across France and Italy.

Brought up by the Duke of Aquitaine, he founded the monastery of Cluny. When Odo was made abbot, he introduced the Rule of St Benedict, with its emphasis on vows of chastity, communal poverty and long periods of silent meditation. Cluny rose to become the most important monastery in Europe and Odo was instrumental in it.

He attained papal protection from secular interference for this monastery and others in Western Europe. By the time he retired from the world, Odo's stature was such that Italian politicians often referred to him for help as an impartial mediator in disputes.

KEY FACTS
Abbot of the Benedictine Monastery of Cluny
DATES: *AD 879–942*
BIRTH PLACE: *Tours, France*
PATRON OF: *Rain*
FEAST DAY: *18 November*

ULRIC

BELOVED FOR HIS GENEROSITY AND CARE OF THE POOR, ST ULRIC SERVED AS BISHOP TO THE DIOCESE OF AUGSBURG, BAVARIA, FOR 50 YEARS BEFORE DYING ON A CROSS OF ASHES.

KEY FACTS
Bishop
DATES: c.*AD 890–973*
BIRTH PLACE: *Near Zurich, Switzerland*
FEAST DAY: *4 July*
EMBLEM: *Bishop's vestments*

His father placed Ulric in the care of his uncle, Bishop of Augsburg, as a child, and Ulric lived at the monastery of St Gall. He never forgot the care shown to him there.

Ulric developed a deep piety and strong sense of duty toward the poor and afflicted in the community. But his office as Bishop of Augsburg was beset with strife from constant Magyar raids on Bavaria. Ulric devoted himself to easing the hardships suffered.

He founded a number of religious houses, and built a small church where he hoped to live as a monk. However, the trappings of high office kept him from fulfilling this wish. He once caused consternation by trying to hand his bishopric to a nephew, thus infringing canonical law. As a symbol of Christian sacrificial love, Ulric died on a cross of ashes marked out on the floor. His canonization is the first known case of a pope becoming a saint.

EDWARD THE MARTYR

COMING TO THE THRONE AT A YOUNG AGE, EDWARD WAS THRUST INTO A POLITICAL HORNET'S NEST IN ENGLAND. HIS MARTYRDOM A FEW YEARS LATER WAS RECEIVED WITH HORROR BY THE NATION.

KEY FACTS
Martyr
DATES: c.*AD 962–79*
BIRTH PLACE: *Possibly Corfe Castle, Dorset, England*
FEAST DAY: *18 March*
EMBLEM: *Dagger*

Aged just 13, Edward became king of England. At such a tender age he inherited a country troubled by disputes within the Church and faced a rival claim to the throne from his stepbrother Ethelred. His bid for the throne was supported by a rebellious party led by his stepmother, Aelfthryth. Together they plotted to overthrow the young king.

Riding home one day after hunting, Edward was greeted by Aelfthryth, who offered him a chalice of wine. As he leant to take the drink, a courtier stabbed him with a dagger. Edward slumped from his horse, but a foot caught in the stirrup and he was dragged over the ground, leaving behind a trail of blood.

Though this was not technically a martyr's death, kings were regarded as representatives of God. His murder was described as "the worst deed in English history". A pillar of light was said to hover over his abandoned body, and folk claimed their ailments were cured when they visited his grave. By common consent he was deemed a martyr, while his stepmother retired to a convent.

Left Edward the Martyr shown about to be murdered at Corfe Castle.

WOLFGANG OF REGENSBURG

DURING HIS LIFETIME, THE HOLY ROMAN EMPIRE EVOLVED AS A CONFEDERATION OF DUCHIES IN GERMANY. ST WOLFGANG WAS ENTRUSTED WITH EDUCATING ITS FUTURE EMPEROR HENRY II.

KEY FACTS
Bishop
DATES: c.AD *924–94*
BIRTH PLACE: *Duchy of Swabia, Germany*
FEAST DAY: *31 October*
EMBLEM: *Bishop's vestments*

Though content to lead a life as an abstemious monk devoted to prayer, Wolfgang was recognized for his wisdom and qualities as a teacher. He was handed the responsibility of educating the young prince and future emperor Henry II.

Wolfgang was put in charge of the Benedictine monastery school at Einsiedeln in Switzerland before progressing to become bishop of Regensburg in AD 972. He set about reforming the lax ways of the monks and nuns in his diocese. This meant reinforcing the vows of poverty and prayer, for which Wolgang set an admirable example.

Despite Wolfgang's talents as an evangelist, his mission into Hungary was largely unsuccessful. Wolfgang's cult remains strong and his relics at Regensburg continue to attract pilgrims.

Left A woodcut depicting St Wolfgang (P.M. Vogel, 1860).

OLAF

A SOLDIER KING WHO ROVED AS A PIRATE BEFORE COMMITTING TO THE FAITH, ST OLAF OF NORWAY IS CREDITED WITH INTRODUCING CHRISTIANITY TO HIS COUNTRY AT A TIME OF POLITICAL TURMOIL.

KEY FACTS
King
DATES: *AD 995–1030*
BIRTH PLACE: *Norway*
PATRON OF: *Norway*
FEAST DAY: *29 July*
EMBLEM: *Battle-axe, loaves of bread*

The son of a Norwegian lord, Olaf began his adult life as a Viking pirate raiding the shores of the Baltic and France. But one trip to Normandy ended with Olaf's conversion to Christianity.

His new faith inspired him to fight for the English who were suffering invasions from the Danes. On returning to Norway, he seized power and determined to make his country Christian.

Just though his rule was, its severity spawned dissent. Olaf's erstwhile enemy, King Cnut of Denmark and England, took advantage of the situation and sponsored a rebellion in Norway.

Their combined forces succeeded in exiling Olaf in 1029. On trying the following year to regain his throne with the aid of Swedish allies, Olaf was killed in battle. After his death, Norwegians longed for his Christian rule and claimed many miracle cures from a spring issuing at his grave.

Left The church of St Olaf in Wasdale in Cumbria is one of the smallest churches in England. Its beams are said to have come from a Viking longship.

STEPHEN OF HUNGARY

ALSO KNOWN AS STEPHEN THE GREAT, THIS NATIONAL HERO IS CONSIDERED THE ARCHITECT OF AN INDEPENDENT CHRISTIAN HUNGARY AND FOUNDER OF A CHURCH WELFARE SYSTEM.

KEY FACTS
King
DATES: c.*AD 975–1038*
BIRTH PLACE: *Esztergom, Hungary*
PATRON OF: *Hungary*
FEAST DAY: *16 August*
EMBLEM: *Crown*

Filled with reforming zeal, King Stephen was inspired by his faith and sympathy for the oppressed. As king, he reduced the power of the nobles and established a semi-feudal, but secure, social system.

If the hallmark of his rule was charity, it was also fundamentalist. Adultery and blasphemy were crimes not to be tolerated, and marriage between Christians and pagans was forbidden. On the other hand, he helped the poor through his church-building programme. By ensuring there was a church in virtually every diocese, tithes demanded from landlords could feed and clothe the underprivileged.

Stephen encouraged missions and finished building the great monastery of St Martin, begun by his father. His last years were spent in dispute over his successor, because his only son had died.

Right The crown of St Stephen, now held at the Magyar Nemzeti Galeria in Budapest (11th century).

EDWARD THE CONFESSOR

ADMIRED FOR HIS DEVOTION TO GOD AND CARE FOR HIS POORER SUBJECTS, EDWARD WAS THE LAST NATIVE KING TO RULE ENGLAND BEFORE THE NORMAN CONQUEST.

KEY FACTS
King
DATES: *1003–66*
BIRTH PLACE: *Islip, England*
PATRON OF: *Once of England*
FEAST DAY: *13 October*
EMBLEM: *Ring*

The term "Confessor" refers to the fact that Edward lived his life as a devout follower of Christ. It was said that the king and his wife, Edith, were so holy that they did not consummate their marriage.

Edward became King of England in 1042 during a time of great political turbulence. His father-in-law, Earl Godwine, plotted against him while the Danish king threatened to invade England. Edward was generous to the poor. His subjects believed he could "touch for the king's evil", meaning that simply through touch, the king was able to cure scrofula, a kind of tuberculosis.

Another story surrounded a ring which the king supposedly gave to a beggar. Years later, English pilgrims in the Holy Land met an old man who claimed to be John the Apostle and he gave the travellers the king's ring.

Edward started building Westminster Abbey, however he died before it was consecrated. He was canonized in 1161, and since then many sick people have visited his shrine in Westminster Abbey to pray for a cure. The worn steps to the shrine are evidence to the number of pilgrims. The shrine was dismantled during the Reformation that began under Henry VIII and Edward's body was removed. His relics lie behind the high altar in to this day.

Left A sculpture of Edward the Confessor in the church of San Marco, Florence (Pietro Francavilla, 1589).

STANISLAUS OF CRACOW

THE PATRON OF POLAND WAS A BRAVE REFORMER WHO WOULD NOT ALLOW SPECIAL DISPENSATION TO AN UNREPENTANT KING. ST STANISLAUS WAS MARTYRED FOR HIS UNCOMPROMISING STAND.

KEY FACTS
Martyr saint, bishop
DATES: *1010–79*
BIRTH PLACE: *Szczepanow, Poland*
PATRON OF: *Poland, soldiers in battle*
FEAST DAY: *11 April*
EMBLEM: *Bishop's vestments, sword*

Born into a noble Polish family, Stanislaus was well educated, possibly studying in Paris. He was consecrated a bishop in 1072, having made a reputation as a stern reformer of lapses in Christian behaviour.

In the 11th century, Boleslav II was King of Poland and said to be violent and headstrong. Once he abducted a nobleman's wife and imprisoned her in his palace.

Refusing to repent of this demeaning act, the king incurred the wrath of Stanislaus who publicly excommunicated him from the Church. King Boleslav II chased his bishop from the church at Cracow and cornered him in the chapel of St Michael.

The knights who hunted down Stanislaus refused to raise their swords against him, so Boleslav committed the murder himself. The king was later deposed and Stanislaus was acknowleged as a martyr saint.

Below The Death of St Stanislaus *(Hungarian, 15th century).*

CANUTE

KING CANUTE OF DENMARK WAS DETERMINED TO TURN HIS NATION TO CHRISTIANITY, BUT HE PAID WITH HIS LIFE FOR IMPOSING RELIGIOUS LAWS AND TAXES THAT RILED THE NOBLES.

KEY FACTS
Martyr king
DATES: *d. 1086*
BIRTH PLACE: *Denmark*
PATRON OF: *Denmark*
FEAST DAY: *10 July*
EMBLEM: *Crown, dagger, lance, barefoot king with hair in a fillet*

Two passions drove this King of Denmark. He wished to impose the Christian faith on his subjects and he was determined to gain the English throne.

Twice he tried to invade England. Its countrymen, who resented the rule of French invaders brought by William the Conqueror in 1066, sided with the Danish pretender. His first attack on England was a minor raid on York, but for his second campaign, in 1085, he prepared huge numbers of men.

Not all his subjects supported the invasion. Much had been spent on church buildings, and new laws empowered priests at the expense of secular nobles. Annoyed by high taxes and heavy-handed religious laws, they sided with Canute's rebellious brother, Olaf. Under siege in the church of St Alban at Odensee, Canute took the sacrament. As he knelt before the altar, he and 18 followers were stabbed to death.

Left Stained glass depicting King Canute from the west window of Canterbury Cathedral.

PATRON SAINTS OF NATIONS

NATIONS EVERYWHERE HAVE CHOSEN PATRON SAINTS AS SPECIAL
GUARDIANS OVER THEIR COUNTRY. IN TIMES OF NATIONAL PERIL,
COUNTRYMEN ASK THEIR SAINT TO PRAY TO GOD FOR THEM.

Albania – Mary
Algeria – Cyprian
Andorra – Our Lady of Meritxell
Argentina – Francis Solano
Armenia – Bartholomew
Australia – Francis Xavier
Austria – Leopold III, Rupert
Belgium – Joseph
Bolivia – Francis Solano
Borneo – Francis Xavier
Bosnia – James the Great
Brazil – Peter of Alcantara,
Antony of Padua
Bulgaria – Cyril and Methodius
Canada – Anne, George, Joseph
Chile – Francis Solano
China – Francis Xavier
Colombia – Luis Bertran,
Peter Claver
Corsica – Devota
Costa Rica – Mary
Crete – Titus
Croatia – Joseph
Cuba – Mary

*Below Detail from a 13th-century
mosaic showing scenes from the life
of St Mark.*

Cyprus – Barnabas
Czech Republic – Wenceslas
Denmark – Anskar, Canute
Dominican Republic – Dominic
Ecuador – Mary
Egypt – Mark
El Salvador – Mary
England – George
Ethiopia – Frumentius
Finland – Henry of Finland
France – Denys of Paris, Joan of
Arc, Theresa of Lisieux
Georgia – George
Germany – Boniface
Gibraltar – Bernard of Clairvaux
Gozo – George
Greece – Nicholas of Myra, Paul
Guatemala – James the Great
Haiti – Mary
Honduras – Mary
Hungary – Stephen of Hungary
Iceland – Thorlac of Skalholt
India – Rose of Lima, Thomas
Indonesia – Mary
Iran – Maruthas
Ireland – Brigid, Patrick
Italy – Catherine of Siena, Francis
of Assisi

*Above Saint Rose of Lima (Carlo
Dolci, 17th century).*

Jamaica – Mary
Japan – Francis Xavier, Peter
Jordan – John the Baptist
Korea – Joseph
Kosovo – Methodius
Lithuania – Casimir of Poland
Luxembourg – Willibrord
Macedonia – Clement of Okhrida
Madagascar – Vincent de Paul
Malta – George, Paul
Mexico – Our Lady of Guadalupe,
Joseph
Monaco – Devota
Montenegro – George
Moravia – Wenceslas
Netherlands – Willibrord
New Zealand – Francis Xavier
Nicaragua – James the Great
Nigeria – Patrick
Norway – Olaf, Magnus
Oceania – Peter Chanel
Pakistan – Francis Xavier, Thomas
Palestine – George
Panama – Mary
Papua New Guinea – Archangel
Michael
Paraguay – Francis Solano
Peru – Francis Solano, Rose of Lima

Far Left St Francis Xavier Blessing the Sick *(Rubens, 17th century).*

Left Nicetas *(Giovanni Antonio Guardi, 18th century).*

Philippines – Rose of Lima
Poland – Stanislaus of Cracow,
  Casimir of Poland
Portugal – Antony of Padua,
  Francis Borgia
Puerto Rico – Mary
Romania – Cyril and Methodius,
  Nicetas
Russia – Nicholas of Myra, Andrew,
  Vladimir
Sardinia – Maurice
Scotland – Andrew, Margaret
  of Scotland
Serbia – Sava of Serbia
Sicily – Andrew Avellino
Slovakia – John of Nepomuk
Slovenia – Virgilius
South Africa – Mary
Spain – James the Great
Sri Lanka – Thomas
Sudan – Josephine Bakhita
Sweden – Bridget of Sweden,
  Eric of Sweden
Switzerland – Gall, Nicholas
  of Flue
Syria – Barbara
Tanzania – Mary
Tunisia – Mary
Turkey – John the Evangelist, John
  Chrysostom
Uganda – Mary
Ukraine – Josaphat
USA – Mary

Below Stained-glass window depicting St Andrew from the church of St Neot in Cornwall (16th century).

Uruguay – James the Less
Venezuela – Mary
Vietnam – Joseph
Wales – David
West Indies – Rose of Lima
Zaire – Mary

MARY, THE BLESSED VIRGIN

Many nations around the world have adopted Mary, mother of Jesus, as their patron, often in addition to other saints. In this feature she is listed only beside those states where she is sole patron.

Mary, the Blessed Virgin, is believed to appear in symbolic and visionary form at times of national crisis. The Philippine navy, for example, was convinced Mary hovered over their ships and helped them to repulse the enemy.

Another example comes from Albania. Catholics believe a canvas painting of the Virgin, lodged on a cliff, prevented bombs in World War II falling on their land.

Above Enthroned Madonna with Child, Angels and Saints *(Lorenzetti, c. 1340).*

MARGARET OF SCOTLAND

AN ANGLO-SAXON ROYAL WHO MARRIED A SCOTTISH KING DID MUCH TO REVIVE THE FLAGGING CHURCH IN HIS COUNTRY.

KEY FACTS
Queen
DATES: *1046–93*
BIRTH PLACE: *Hungary*
PATRON OF: *Scotland*
FEAST DAY: *16 November*
EMBLEM: *Crown*

Left A portrait of Margaret published in the Memoirs of the Court of Queen Elizabeth *(c.1825).*

This cultivated granddaughter of the English king Edmund Ironside was one of the last members of Anglo-Saxon royalty before the Norman Conquest. Indeed, at the invasion she fled northwards and took refuge at the court of Malcolm III of Scotland.

The king was beguiled by her charm and intelligence, and they married in 1069. Her Christian devotion inspired her to revive the Church in Scotland, which had declined since the Celtic heyday of St Columba of Iona and St Aidan. She reformed the abbey at Iona and encouraged pilgrimages and the building of monasteries.

Margaret built Dunfermline church to be a burial place for the Scottish royal family. Her adoring husband, who was at first rough and illiterate, grew to be proud of her generosity toward his subjects, and became as devout a Christian as she was.

Two of her sons became kings of Scotland. She died shortly after hearing of the death of her husband and son in battle.

BENNO OF MUNICH

TORN BETWEEN LOYALTIES, ST BENNO HAD TO SEARCH HIS CONSCIENCE TO MAKE THE RIGHT DECISIONS. HE WAS IMPRISONED AND CASTIGATED, BUT IN ALL HE STROVE ONLY TO SERVE HIS FLOCK.

KEY FACTS
Bishop
DATES: *d.1107*
BIRTH PLACE: *Saxony*
PATRON OF: *Munich*
FEAST DAY: *16 June*
EMBLEM: *Fish and key*

Born to a noble Saxon family at a time of political strife, Benno was frequently caught up in the agitation. Having been appointed Bishop of Meissen by the German Emperor Henry IV, Benno found himself torn between allegiances. He opted to support his fellow Saxons in their uprising against the emperor.

Henry IV promptly had Benno imprisoned, but then released him on oath of fidelity. However, he reneged on this promise, siding again with the emperor's enemies.

When, as a punishment, his bishopric was removed, Benno vowed allegiance to the anti-pope Guibert in the hope that he might

recover his position as bishop and return to his flock. When this move failed, Benno revived his loyalty to Pope Urban II.

A legend says that when the emperor was excommunicated, Benno decided the best way to stop him entering his cathedral was to throw the key into the river. Benno later found his key miraculously stored inside a fish. The saint's relics were later moved to Munich for safekeeping.

Left The Martyrdom of St Benno (Carlo Saraceni, 1618). Benno was venerated throughout Saxony.

ANSELM

DESPITE FALLING OUT WITH TWO KINGS OF ENGLAND, THE ITALIAN
MONK WHO BECAME ARCHBISHOP OF CANTERBURY WAS WIDELY
ADMIRED FOR HIS LEARNING AND "PROOF" OF GOD'S EXISTENCE.

KEY FACTS

Doctor of the Church
DATES: *1033–1109*
BIRTH PLACE: *Aosta, Italy*
FEAST DAY: *21 April*
EMBLEM: *A ship, symbolizing
spiritual independence*

As a boy, Anselm longed to be a monk. After his mother died when he was 20, Anselm left home to wander as a lone ascetic. He passed through Burgundy and found himself in Normandy, where he was inspired by the teaching of the abbot Lanfranc.

He stayed at Lanfranc's monastery of Bec and in time became its abbot. It was a wealthy establishment. Once Anselm was obliged to visit England to oversee property owned by Bec, and it was on this trip that the Italian monk first met the king.

IN AND OUT OF FAVOUR

He so impressed King William II (Rufus) that, in 1093, he made Anselm archbishop of Canterbury. Though preferring to stay in Bec, Anselm nevertheless accepted the office.

The Italian's reluctance was soon justified when William declared his hand and demanded that he, the king, should appoint all English bishops and abbots henceforth. Anselm claimed that such power resides solely within the Church, and went to Rome to discuss the problem.

In his absence, the king took his opportunity and seized the church revenues. Anselm condemned the action as theft and abandoned Canterbury to live as an exile in Europe.

In 1100, the new English king, Henry I, summoned Anselm back. Again monk and monarch disagreed over appointments, and again Anselm went into exile. By 1107, they finally reached a

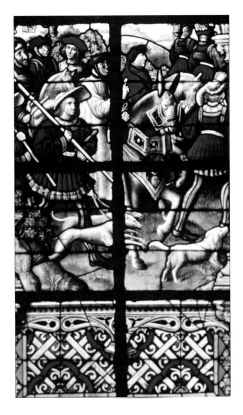

Above A 15th-century window in Tournai Cathedral, Belgium, shows Anselm travelling to consult the pope.

compromise and Anselm returned to office to live out his last years in relative peace.

Exile had provided him with a chance to put down his ideas in writing. Unlike his predecessors, Anselm defended his faith by reason, rather than using scripture as his authority.

Anselm is famous for his "ontological argument" for the existence of God, in which he asserts that the mere idea that there is a God necessarily proves his existence.

Anselm's cult grew slowly, but was helped by a well-written and sympathetic biography of his life

written by his friend and disciple, Eadmer of Canterbury. In 1734, in recognition of his position as the most influential Christian writer in the period between Augustine of Hippo and Thomas Aquinas, Anselm was named a Doctor of the Church. He is admired to this day for his steadfastness and piety, and is remembered as an intellectual and philosophical man.

Below Scenes from the Life of St Anselm of Canterbury, *from Le Miroir Historial by Vincent de Beauvais (French School, 15th century).*

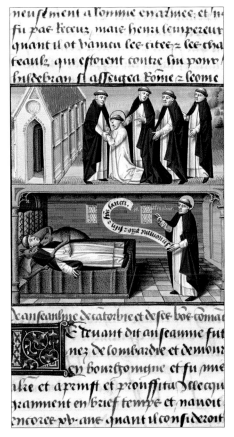

STEPHEN HARDING

ESTABLISHING THE MONASTIC SYSTEM OF THE CISTERCIANS WAS ST HARDING'S GREAT ACHIEVEMENT. HIS IDEAS SPREAD ACROSS WESTERN EUROPE AND REFORMED NEARLY 700 MONASTERIES.

KEY FACTS
*Founder of Cistercian
monastic order*
DATES: *d.1134*
BIRTH PLACE: *England*
FEAST DAY: *28 March*
EMBLEM: *Cistercian habit*

Having settled in France, Stephen Harding, who was English by birth, made a huge impact on the religious history of Europe by helping to found the great monastery of Citeaux. Under his 25-year leadership, this first of the Cistercian monasteries became a model for the austere religious life.

In a bid to return to a strict observance of the Benedictine Rule, Stephen demanded wholesale changes to the dissolute lifestyle of contemporary monks. Luxuries were banned. The monks could no longer enjoy the monastic income derived from their mills, serfs and tithes. They now had to farm the fields themselves and live on their produce alone. Many new monasteries were built in remote places to avoid contact with town folk.

Stephen expected each abbot to visit the monasteries under his care and report to Citeaux. Thus he maintained his high standards.

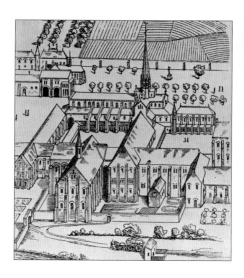

Right A woodcut of the Cistercian monastery at Citeaux, France, founded in 1098.

NORBERT

NORBERT GAVE UP A WEALTHY LIFE TO BECOME A MONASTIC REFORMER. HE SET UP THE SO-CALLED "WHITE CANONS", WHICH SPREAD QUICKLY OVER WESTERN EUROPE, ESPECIALLY HUNGARY.

KEY FACTS
Founder of order, archbishop
DATES: *c.1080–1134*
BIRTH PLACE: *Xanten, Prussia*
FEAST DAY: *6 June*
EMBLEM: *Bishop's vestments*

Like St Francis of Assisi, Norbert was born into a wealthy family and then abandoned his worldly privileges. Norbert almost died in a thunderstorm in 1115. This experience inspired him to give away his possessions and beg the pope for forgiveness for his past life. To atone for his sins, he became a wandering preacher in northern France and the Low Countries.

Norbert's sternness of faith and eschewing of worldly things did not endear him to all the clergy. To put his beliefs into practice, he founded a community in Prémontré in the Rhineland,

where he instituted an austere regime following the rules of St Augustine of Hippo. Norbert was a friend of St Bernard of Clairvaux and shared his reforming zeal.

Although there were clergy who resented his ideas, Norbert was generally popular. In 1126, he was appointed Archbishop of Magdeburg. His monastic order, known as the Premonstratensians, or "White Canons", after their vestments, gained ground quickly.

Left A portrait of St Norbert from an illuminated manuscript (11th–12th century).

BERNARD OF CLAIRVAUX

UNDER THE LEADERSHIP OF ST BERNARD, THE CISTERCIAN ORDER GREATLY INFLUENCED THE SPIRITUAL DIRECTION CHRISTIANITY WOULD TAKE DURING MEDIEVAL TIMES.

KEY FACTS

Doctor of the Church
DATES: *c. 1090–1153*
BIRTH PLACE: *Fontaines, near Dijon, France*
PATRON OF: *Gibraltar*
FEAST DAY: *20 August*
EMBLEM: *Beehive, beekeepers, candle-makers, Eucharistic host*

St Bernard was one of the most charismatic figures of the medieval Church. His powerful preaching, energy and dedication to leading a model Christian life made him an influential force in the Church, though not one that always met with approval.

Fervent in his commitment to reforming monastic life, Bernard followed the example set by Stephen Harding, and joined his monastery at Citeaux. His clarity of vision for the developing Cistercian Order naturally led to Bernard's appointment in 1115 as abbot of the poverty-stricken Clairvaux, the third Cistercian monastery.

Critical of the gentler, parallel order at Cluny, known as the "Black Benedictines", Bernard was determined to establish an austere discipline without compromise, surviving on minimal rations and hard labour.

Starting with just 30 fellow devotees, his way blossomed despite its rigours. It is said that his charm and facility to heal the sick attracted thousands of pilgrims. By his death, the number of monks at Clairvaux alone had risen to 700, while some 400 Cistercian monasteries were established across Europe.

POLITICS AND CRUSADE

Bernard's enthusiasm, coupled with his eloquence, inevitably drew him into church politics. At this time, the authority of the Roman Church was jeopardized by disputes over who should be pope. The princes of Europe tended to back one candidate or another. Bernard's successful promotion of Eugenius III to the papacy in 1145 did much to raise his public profile. Soon he was being asked to combat the rising Albigensian heresy in southern France, which he condemned with characteristic fervour.

Perhaps Bernard's greatest challenge was promoting the Second Crusade (1145–49) to recover the Holy Land from Muslim control. His stirring speeches inspired thousands of the good, the bad, even criminals, to "take the Cross". To protect Christians travelling to Palestine, Bernard took control of the Cistercian Order of Knights Templar and devised a chivalric code of conduct. Following the failure of the crusade, Bernard's esteem suffered a great deal, allowing his enemies to make capital out of the disaster.

Bernard's eloquent articulation of his faith is nowhere more evident than in his surviving letters and sermons, and in his treatise on the Love of God.

Below St Bernard of Clairvaux *(Ferrer Bassa, 14th century).*

HENRY OF FINLAND

AN ENGLISH BISHOP OF UPPSALA, SWEDEN, HENRY JOINED A CRUSADE TO FINLAND IN ORDER TO CONVERT ITS WAR-LIKE PEOPLE, AND REMAINED THERE AS A MISSIONARY.

KEY FACTS
Martyr bishop
DATES: *d.1156*
BIRTH PLACE: *England*
PATRON OF: *Finland,
sea fishermen*
FEAST DAY: *20 January*
EMBLEM: *Bishop's vestments*

Henry was a soldier for Christ. In 1154, he joined King Eric IX of Sweden's war against the Finns. The king saw his military expedition as a crusade and offered the Finns peace if they became Christian. They refused and were defeated in battle.

Henry stayed in Finland and he baptized many of the people. He built a church at Nousis, which became the centre of his missionary work. Eventually, he was killed

by a Finnish convert when he refused to grant him forgiveness for killing a Swedish soldier. His cultus spread and he became Finland's patron saint.

Left St Henry of Finland from the Sforza Hours, *one of the most beautiful Renaissance manuscripts extant (Giampietrino Birago, c.1490).*

ERIC OF SWEDEN

ERIC HOPED TO INTRODUCE CHRISTIAN RULE TO HIS COUNTRYMEN BUT WAS MURDERED IN DENMARK WHEN HE TRIED TO USE HIS MILITARY MIGHT TO SPREAD HIS CHRISTIAN MESSAGE.

KEY FACTS
Martyr king
DATES: *d.1160*
BIRTH PLACE: *Sweden*
PATRON OF: *Sweden*
FEAST DAY: *18 May*
EMBLEM: *Crown*

Through his marriage to Christine, of the Swedish royal family, Eric was able to claim the throne in 1156. Committed to his faith, he instituted a Christian legal system and channelled funds into the Church.

However, disgruntled Swedes opposed to his reforms sought allies abroad to back a rebellion. In 1154, one such ally arose in Denmark. Determined to spread Christianity across Scandinavia, Eric waged war against any neighbouring peoples who would not accept Christianity as their faith. He began by invading Finland. When he continued into Denmark, he was outnumbered by a united force of Danes and rebel Swedes. As Eric left Mass on Ascension Day, he was cut down by Danish soldiers. Lying humiliated at their feet, he was subjected to terrible torture and beheaded.

A cultus quickly developed around Eric. Ironically, Nordic mythology possibly played its part in raising his profile to that of national hero, residing in the heavenly abode of Valhalla.

Eric's body and kingly regalia were laid in a new cathedral built in Uppsala, and he was adopted as patron of Sweden. Until the Reformation, farmers would hold annual processions begging Eric's intercession for good harvests.

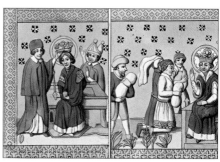

Left The coronation of Eric of Sweden (Italian School, 19th century).

THOMAS BECKET

THE TRAGIC MURDER IN CANTERBURY CATHEDRAL OF THIS DEVOUT PRIEST CREATED SUCH A SENSATION THAT PILGRIMS CAME FROM ALL OVER MEDIEVAL CHRISTENDOM TO VISIT HIS SHRINE.

KEY FACTS
Martyr, archbishop
DATES: *1118–70*
BIRTH PLACE: *London*
PATRON OF: *Clergy*
FEAST DAY: *29 December*
EMBLEM: *Tonsured (crown of head shaved), holding archbishop's cross, mitre*

The clever son of a wealthy family, Thomas was a man of the world in his early career as archdeacon of Canterbury. He was just the sort of pleasure-loving priest that appealed to the young King of England, Henry II.

The king soon appointed him Chancellor of England. In this capacity, Thomas entertained lavishly and travelled abroad on diplomatic missions on behalf of his friend, the king.

ARCHBISHOP

Henry ensured Thomas was made Archbishop of Canterbury in 1162 but, to his intense annoyance, Thomas repented of his former ways. Instead, he became a dutiful, austere religious, wearing a hairshirt and holding long prayer vigils.

No longer the carefree friend, Thomas began to upbraid the king on matters of taxation, reminding him of the Church's rights and privileges. Henry was further enraged when Thomas insisted God and Rome were the supreme authorities, not the King of England. Henry wished to try the clergy in the courts of England, but Thomas claimed this was unacceptable, that they had the right to appeal to Rome.

EXILE AND MURDER

The differences between the two men descended into bitter squabbles, including disputes over money. Thomas went into exile, seeking refuge in a Cistercian monastery in France. After six

Above Detail from a medieval manuscript showing the murder of Thomas Becket (English School).

years, he believed reconciliation had been reached, and returned to Canterbury in hope.

To his great dismay, he discovered his land had been appropriated and his followers alienated. But Thomas continued to assert his allegiance to God over the state. Henry, demanding and quick-tempered, was exasperated. In an outburst, his uttered wish to be rid of "this turbulent priest" was taken at face value by four nearby barons.

His henchmen sped off to the cathedral in Canterbury and, after a brief altercation with Thomas, set upon him with their swords. The king did public penance for this savage murder, but the veneration of Thomas as a martyr spread fast. Hundreds of miracles were claimed in his name and his shrine became one of the most popular in all Christendom.

Below Henry II of England arguing with Thomas Becket (English School, 14th century).

HILDEGARD OF BINGEN

A MEDIEVAL RENAISSANCE WOMAN, HILDEGARD WAS A VISIONARY NUN, POET, PAINTER, MUSICIAN AND WRITER OF BOOKS NOT ONLY ON MYSTICAL THEOLOGY BUT ALSO ON BOTANY AND NATURAL CURES.

KEY FACTS
Abbess, theologian
DATES: *1098–1179*
BIRTH PLACE: *Bokelheim, Germany*
FEAST DAY: *17 September*
EMBLEM: *Books*

Born the tenth child of a noble German family, the "Sibyl of the Rhineland", as she was dubbed, became aware of receiving visions as early as three years of age. At eight, she was entrusted to the care of a reclusive nun, Juetta, who lived beside a Benedictine abbey at Diessenberg in Germany.

Hildegard took vows at the age of 15, and entered a small convent established by Juetta. Under her guidance, the young nun grew in stature to eventually succeed Juetta as abbess at the age of 38.

MYSTICAL VISIONS

The depth and quality of Hildegard's mystical experiences prompted her contemporary, St Bernard of Clairvaux, to urge her to record them on paper. This she did in abundance.

The best known of her mystical works is *Scivias* (short for *Sciens vias Domini*, "Know the ways of the Lord"). In the book

HILDEGARDIS a Virgin Prophetess, Abbess of St Ruperts Nunnerye. She died at Bingen A° Do. 1180. Aged 82 yeares. W. Marshall sculpsit.

Above An engraving of Hildegard (William Marshall, 1648).

she describes visions as coming to her through "the eyes of her soul". Fully awake, she saw luminous images of figures and scripture bathed in divine light.

This light, she wrote, ignited a flame in her chest, "not like a burning, but like a warming flame, as the sun warms everything its rays touch." The experiences deepened her understanding of scripture, and she felt impelled to write widely on whatever inspired her.

Morality plays, hymns and prayers flowed from her pen. Her illustrations to *Scivias* have been likened to those of the English visionary William Blake.

DIVERSE INTERESTS

Besides religious subjects, Hildegard compiled a survey of natural history, and a medical handbook of ailments and their treatment by natural remedy. Her breadth of knowledge prompted her to correspond with the theologian, Guibert of Gembloux, who sought her views on dogma. She gave written advice to King Henry II of England, the German Emperor Frederick Barbarossa, and even the pope himself.

Despite all this creative output, Hildegard did not neglect her duties. When it became necessary, she moved her convent to a larger building near Bingen. She founded a new house at Eibingen, and made reforms elsewhere.

Keen to pass on her spiritual insights, she preached in Germany and beyond, before dying of old age. In the modern feminist movement, she is lauded for her independence and creative energy.

Left The Vision of St Hildegard (attributed to Battista Dossi, c.1474–1548).

LAURENCE O'TOOLE

THE INVASION OF IRELAND BY ENGLISH ADVENTURERS IN 1170 TURNED LAURENCE'S DUTIES FROM TENDING TO HIS FAMINE-STRICKEN FLOCK TO PROTECTOR OF THE IRISH CHURCH.

KEY FACTS
Archbishop
DATES: *1128–80*
BIRTH PLACE: *Co. Kildare, Ireland*
FEAST DAY: *14 November*
EMBLEM: *Bishop's vestments*

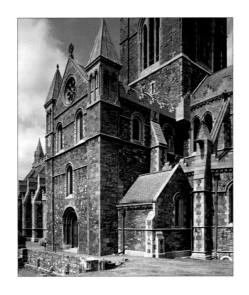

As abbot of Glendalough monastery, one of the five suffragan dioceses to Dublin, O'Toole was mainly involved in preventing his rural congregations from starving. But eight years after his election in 1162 as Archbishop of Dublin, O'Toole had to contend with invading Anglo-Normans led by Strongbow, Earl of Pembroke.

Two years later, the archbishop went to Rome where he was made papal legate. He also secured the pope's protection of all Church property in Ireland. This upset the English king who had told the Irish archbishop to remind the pope that he, Henry II of the Angevin Empire, now controlled Ireland. In a tricky meeting with the king, it is a measure of O'Toole's talents that he won the king's agreement not to threaten Irish Church property.

Left Christ Church Cathedral, Dublin (built 1172–1240).

DOMINIC

THE FOUNDER OF THE "BLACK FRIARS" ORDER UNDERSTOOD THAT LEADING AN EXEMPLARY LIFE OF VIRTUE WAS THE BEST WAY TO BRING CONVERTS TO THE FAITH.

KEY FACTS
Founder of an order
DATES: c. *1170 1221*
BIRTH PLACE: *Caleruega, Spain*
FEAST DAY: *8 August*
EMBLEM: *Lily, black-and-white dog*

Of noble birth in Castile, Dominic de Guzmán led an uneventful life until he joined his bishop on a mission to the heretical Cathars of southern France. The movement was growing into a menacing force.

Though avowedly Christian, the Cathars did not regard Jesus as Saviour, but merely a teacher. Other groups joined the effort but failed. A warrior knight, Simon de Montfort, mounted a crusade against them in 1208, and caused much grief and bitterness.

But Dominic took no part in such confrontation. His bishop having left him to his own devices, Dominic discovered his gift for preaching. Direct and personal, his style appealed to the listener's heart, rather than the contemporary Franciscan friars' emphasis on creation's beauty.

Basing himself in Toulouse, Dominic founded an order in which he trained priests as itinerant preachers. His eagerness to guard the teachings of Christ meant his priests were nicknamed *domini canes*, "dogs of God".

His order multiplied rapidly. Even now, Dominican men and women play an important role in teaching and preaching the faith.

Above St Dominic (Cosmé Tura, c.1430-95).

HOLY BEASTS

CHRISTIANITY HONOURS ANIMALS AS PART OF GOD'S CREATION. THE SAINTS TURNED TO THEM FOR HELP AND COMPANIONSHIP, AND STORIES TELL OF SAINTS PERFORMING MIRACLE CURES ON ANIMALS.

From the very beginning of the Christian story, beasts have played their role. Mary, the Blessed Virgin was said to have given birth in a stable, witnessed by cows and donkeys. She was visited by shepherds who brought a lamb as a gift for the infant Jesus.

Legend states that Christ trusted animals. He even used one to deliver his message. When St Eustace went hunting, his prey, a stag, turned to display a crucifix between his horns, thus converting the hunter to Christianity. The cross marking the back of the donkey is also seen as Christ's legacy to this humble beast who bore him on his final entry into Jerusalem.

Above St Bernard dogs were used by members of the St Bernard fathers to rescue Alpine travellers from the snow.

Above A wooden carving showing St Roch with an angel and a dog (Antwerp School, early 16th century).

As with Christ, so the saints' lives are linked to animals. Some saints had them as companions, others were reputed to have performed miracle cures on the sick and maimed. In turn, stories tell of animals rescuing saints from hardship and mortal danger.

DIVINE SYMBOLS

Certain creatures came to symbolize human qualities. Dogs stood for loyalty and can be spotted in numerous paintings of saints. A lion represents courage and a dove symbolizes the Holy Spirit of peace.

St Bernard of Clairvaux is shown with a little dog at his feet. His mother, pregnant with her son, dreamt of a dog, which is regarded as the guardian of God's house, and security against evil. But the highest status in the Christian world is held by the lamb. The holiest of saints have a lamb as their attribute in emulation of Christ's figuration as

Left Detail from Annunciation to the Shepherds *(attributed to Simone Martini and others, 14th century).*

> "PRAISE BE TO THEE, MY LORD, WITH ALL THY CREATURES."
>
> ST FRANCIS OF ASSISI

the Lamb of God. This symbolism is based on the Paschal Lamb, sacrificed at the Jewish Passover. John the Baptist and St Agnes are both depicted with the creature.

RESCUE AND CARE

A wolf is said to have looked after St Antony of Egypt when he lost his way in the wilderness. And St Roch was indebted to a dog. As the saint lay in a forest, dying of the plague, a little dog appeared carrying bread in his mouth and saved St Roch from starvation.

St Bernard mountain dogs, employed to track people lost in the Swiss Alps, were named after St Bernard of Aosta. In the 11th century, this saint founded a monastery in the Alps to provide shelter for crusaders trekking to the Holy Land.

As well as coming to their rescue, animals have worked closely with saints. St Antony was once a

Below The stag appears in The Vision of Saint Eustace *(Antonio Pisano Pisanello, 15th century).*

swineherd and St Brigid a dairymaid. The Welsh St Beuno worked with, and cared for, his cattle and sheep. At his death, these animals were taken to visit his tomb, and thereafter were said to produce strong offspring.

TENDING TO ANIMALS

St Francis of Assisi is famous for his empathy with wild creatures. His sermon to the birds and taming of the wolf of Gubbio illustrate the saint's appreciation of creatures, which he sees as objects of God's love. St Cuthbert also had a special affinity with birds, particularly eider ducks on the Farne Islands of northern England. It was said that birds inhabiting these barren rock stacks fell under the protection of the saint who was a sort of prototype conservationist.

Famously, St Jerome drew a thorn from the paw of a lion who became his life companion. St Blaise was said to have the power to heal animals. Farmers brought him their ailing cattle, and beasts

came of their own accord. St Antony of Padua, often aloof with people, had sympathy with the animal world. He preached to fishes who were said to swarm toward him to hear his wisdom. It is said that a badly treated mule once refused its owner's fodder in indignation, but knelt at the eucharist St Antony offered it.

Below St Francis of Assisi Preaching to the Birds *(Giotto di Bondone, c.1295–1300).*

PATRON SAINTS OF ANIMALS

Animals – Francis of Assisi, Antony of Padua
Bees – Ambrose, Bernard of Clairvaux
Birds – Francis of Assisi
Cats – Gertrude of Nivelles
Deer – Francis of Assisi
Domestic animals – Antony of Egypt
Diseased animals – Blaise
Dogs – Hubert
Dogs, mad – Sithney
Fish – Francis of Assisi
Horned animals – Cornelius
Horses – Martin of Tours, Giles, Hippolytus
Rams – Giles
Wolves – Francis of Assisi

FRANCIS OF ASSISI

THROUGHOUT THE WORLD TODAY, FRANCISCAN MONKS AND NUNS
CONTINUE THE CHARITY WORK BEGUN BY THEIR FOUNDER, WHOSE
PURE LOVE OF CREATION INSPIRED A NEW ATTITUDE TO THE WORLD.

KEY FACTS
*First saint to receive the
stigmata, in 1224*
DATES: *1181–1226*
BIRTH PLACE: *Assisi, Italy*
PATRON OF: *Animals and birds,
ecologists, merchants*
FEAST DAY: *4 October*

Few saints are held in such high esteem for their spirit of devotion as is St Francis. The humble friar wished for nothing other than to imitate Christ. For him the world was an expression of God, and this conviction gave him a special affinity with nature.

REJECTING WEALTH

Francis was born into a rich Italian family and as a youth enjoyed his privileged status. But in the course of a war between Assisi and Perugia, he was imprisoned and began to question his spiritual life. After the war he

Left Scenes from the life of St Francis of Assisi *(Bonaventura Berlinghieri, 1235). This panel is the earliest known depiction of this saint.*

started to give away money to the poor and once, so overcome with compassion, he kissed the diseased hand of a leper.

His father was so angry at this bizarre behaviour that he demanded his son renounce his inheritance. In fact, Francis was glad to do so, for he had heard a voice telling him to live without property, and to preach the word of God. Francis left his family to take up a life of poverty.

NEW ORDER

Francis lived near the ruined chapel of St Mary of the Angels, known as the Portiuncula, near Assisi. He took shelter in a bare hut, and cared for the local lepers.

His preaching and devotion attracted followers, impressed by the simplicity and humility of Francis's faith. In 1210, Pope Innocent III authorized Francis and 11 companions to be "roving preachers of God".

Franciscans travelled in pairs preaching his philosophy of poverty and living by begging. The order soon spread across Europe as far as England.

Left The Lower Church of San Francesco in Assisi, Italy, built in the 13th century.

Mountains where he fasted for 40 days with his followers. While there he had a vision of an angel who enveloped him with light.

Francis then famously received the stigmata. His hands, feet and side are said to have manifested the same wounds that Christ received at the Crucifixion. The marks stayed with him for the rest of his life. In 1226, blind yet filled with joyous faith, Francis died at Portiuncula.

Despite poor health, Francis made several journeys to convert Muslims living around the Mediterranean Sea. Once, when he was taken prisoner during a battle in Egypt between Crusaders and Muslims, the local sultan was so touched by his

Above St Francis Prays to the Birds*, fresco from the church of San Francesco in Assisi (c.1260).*

devotion and disdain of wealth that he was released. In 1219, he reached the Holy Land, but the following year the Franciscans recalled him to Europe.

SPIRITUAL RETREAT
The order had grown hugely in his absence and Francis handed control to the able administrator, Elias of Cortona. It was he who now maintained the Franciscan Rule, which insisted on possessing no money or property, teaching the word of Christ, and caring for the sick and needy. In 1224, Francis retreated to the Apennine

> "LORD GRANT ME THE SERENITY TO ACCEPT THE THINGS I CANNOT CHANGE, THE COURAGE TO CHANGE THE THINGS I CAN, AND THE WISDOM TO KNOW THE DIFFERENCE."
>
> ST FRANCIS OF ASSISI

> "MOST HIGH, ALL-POWERFUL, ALL GOOD, LORD!
> ALL PRAISE IS YOURS, ALL GLORY, ALL HONOUR
> AND ALL BLESSING.
>
> TO YOU ALONE, MOST HIGH, DO THEY BELONG.
> NO MORTAL LIPS ARE WORTHY
> TO PRONOUNCE YOUR NAME.
>
> ALL PRAISE BE YOURS, MY LORD, THROUGH ALL THAT YOU HAVE MADE,
> AND FIRST MY LORD BROTHER SUN,
> WHO BRINGS THE DAY; AND LIGHT YOU GIVE TO US THROUGH HIM.
>
> HOW BEAUTIFUL IS HE, HOW RADIANT IN ALL HIS SPLENDOUR!
> OF YOU, MOST HIGH, HE BEARS THE LIKENESS."
>
> THE FIRST FOUR VERSES OF THE CANTICLE OF BROTHER SUN

ANTONY OF PADUA

THIS CHARISMATIC SAINT FROM LISBON, BELIEVED TO BE A GREAT MIRACLE WORKER, WAS MOSTLY REVERED FOR HIS PREACHING TO THE UNCONVERTED, TO HERETICS, AND TO THE MOORS OF AFRICA.

KEY FACTS
Doctor of the Church
DATES: c.*1193–1231*
BIRTH PLACE: *Lisbon, Portugal*
PATRON OF: *Portugal, lost articles, the poor, and animals*
FEAST DAY: *13 June*
EMBLEM: *Loaves of bread*

Stout and overweight, St Antony looked an unlikely person to radiate holiness. Yet it was said that when people heard his eloquent words, they were filled with the wonder of his faith.

Having joined an Augustinian monastery at the age of 15, Antony was impressed more by some visiting Franciscan friars. The simple modesty of the way taught by his contemporary St Francis of Assisi persuaded him to join their order in 1221. On a dangerous mission to Muslims in North Africa, he was lucky to suffer only fever, not martyrdom.

On returning to Italy, Antony made his way to Assisi. While staying at a nearby hermitage, he attended an ordination of Franciscan monks. Speakers who were expected to give addresses failed to appear, and Antony was prompted to step up in their place. His speech was so impressive that he was asked to become a wandering preacher.

His renown as such spread beyond his province of Romagna. Soon he was preaching against the Cathars in France, and was known as the "hammer of the heretics."

MIRACLE WORKER

Many miracles were attributed to this popular figure. The most famous example causes the faithful to ask for his intercession now to find things lost or stolen.

Tradition says that a novice at his monastery stole Antony's psalter. When the saint prayed for its return, the thief was duly moved to do so, and rejoined the order, too. At Rimini, a mule was said to have refused its diet of oats for three days, then accepted the eucharist when Antony offered it.

It was also claimed that fish once swarmed a river to hear him preach; a tale symbolic of his powers as a preacher.

Left The Vision of St Anthony of Padua (*Giovanni Battista Pittoni, 18th century*).

Right St Antony is shown here holding the infant Christ (c.*16th century*).

ELIZABETH OF HUNGARY

THE NOBLE WIFE OF A GERMAN PRINCE WAS HAPPILY MARRIED BEFORE HIS TRAGIC DEATH PROPELLED HER INTO A LIFE OF SUCH SELFLESS CHARITY AND MORTIFICATION THAT SHE DIED YOUNG.

KEY FACTS

Princess

DATES: *1207–31*

BIRTH PLACE: *Pressburg, Hungary*

PATRON OF: *Catholic charities, bakers*

FEAST DAY: *17 November*

EMBLEM: *Alms of a pitcher, a basket of bread, fruit, and fish, an apron of flowers*

The tragic story of Elizabeth is set in the royal society of medieval central Europe. At the birth of Elizabeth, a wandering poet-musician predicted she would marry the German prince Louis of Thuringia. Aged four, she was duly betrothed to Louis, and her father, Andrew II of Hungary, sent her to live with his family.

Expectations were fulfilled when the couple married when she was 14 and he 21 years old. Furthermore, the marriage was a happy one, with each partner allowing the other to be free to do as he or she wished.

Elizabeth was committed to helping the poor in her adoptive province. The couple's castle home was sited at the top of a cliff. Elizabeth built a hospital at the foot of this rock, and daily took down food and clothing.

She worked tirelessly as a nurse there, tending the sick and orphaned children, as well as the poor of the diocese. At her own expense, it is said, she fed over 900 people a day.

CHANGING FORTUNES

When she was pregnant with their third child, her husband joined the Sixth Crusade (1228–29). They parted, vowing they would never marry anyone else, should anything happen to either of them. Within months of departing, Louis died of the plague. His death proved to be a turning point in

her life. His brother-in-law Henry, for some unknown reason, expelled Elizabeth and her children from the castle. The family was forced into a life of hardship, without home or protection.

At last, elderly relatives came to their rescue. An uncle, the Bishop of Bamberg, let her live in his castle and provision was made for the children.

In a state of continuing grief, she assumed the life of a Franciscan tertiary (lay member). In time the urge to return to her former place of work prompted a move back to Marburg where she lived in a small hut attached to the hospital she had built. Here she resumed nursing.

Although Master Conrad of Marburg offered her protection, he was alarmed by the harsh regime Elizabeth imposed upon herself. Extreme acts of self-mortification and utter devotion to others took a toll on her health. The restrictions Conrad placed on her, and the beatings given if she disobeyed, only served to strengthen and harden Elizabeth's will.

Despite an offer of sanctuary from a Magyar noble, she could not bear to leave the place she believed the poor needed her. She died weak from lack of nutrition and austerity, aged just 23. In 1235, she was declared a saint.

Right St Elizabeth of Hungary *holding a basket of flowers (Ambrogio Lorenzetti, 14th century).*

CLARE OF ASSISI

LIKE HER NEIGHBOUR, ST FRANCIS, ST CLARE ABANDONED A LIFE OF INHERITED EASE TO SERVE GOD. FOLLOWING THE FRANCISCAN WAY, SHE FOUNDED THE ORDER NOW KNOWN AS THE POOR CLARES.

KEY FACTS
Founder of Poor Clares
DATES: *1194–1253*
BIRTH PLACE: *Assisi*
PATRON OF: *Embroiderers, television*
FEAST DAY: *11 August*
EMBLEM: *Lilies for purity, holding a monstrance, and scimitar for triumph over Saracens*

Having declined two offers of marriage, Clare decided that her greatest desire in life was not to be found in the aristocratic world into which she was born, but in devotion to God. She knew that Francis in the same village of Assisi had made the same decision a few years earlier, and now she determined to emulate him.

Clare was 18 when she made her way to the chapel of the Portiuncula, where Francis based himself, two miles from Assisi. As a test of her commitment, he told Clare to don sackcloth and go and beg in the streets of her home town. Francis then asked her to dress as a bride, and in his chapel he solemnly shaved her head and received her vows.

POOR CLARE

Francis set up a house for her nearby at San Damiano. He drew up a Rule following the example he had set himself, of poverty, chastity and obedience, and in 1216 she was made abbess.

Clare added another rule, forbidding ownership of any property, personal or communal. The order, which her widowed mother and sister also joined, was known as the Second Order of St Francis, and later the Poor Clares.

The nuns survived by begging, but the Church disapproved of this undignified public display. At the time, nuns lived in enclosed communities,

Right The Miracles of St Clare of Assisi, *fresco (Lorenzo Lotto, 1523–24).*

Above St Clare (attributed to Simone Martini and others, 14th century).

financed by church rents. She also struggled to have her rules of austerity approved, but eventually won her way in 1253.

However, these measures of self-denial seriously affected her health. During bouts of illness, she would lie in bed embroidering religious vestments. It was said that once, when too ill to attend Christmas Mass, Clare saw the Nativity crib projected on her cell wall and heard singing as if she were in church. As a result, she has become the patron of television.

She never wavered in her belief in God's protection. When the Saracens attacked Assisi, she was said to have held up a monstrance (vessel for the Eucharist) on the city walls in defiance, and the infidel army withdrew.

For 40 years, Clare lived with poverty and prayer, guiding her nuns, who later adopted an even harsher regime than her own. The order spread through Europe, but the English convents did not survive the Reformation.

HYACINTH OF CRACOW

THE EXPANSION OF THE DOMINICAN ORDER OF FRIARS ACROSS NORTHERN AND EASTERN EUROPE WAS SPEARHEADED BY ST HYACINTH. HE ALSO FOUNDED THE CHURCH IN POLAND.

KEY FACTS
Evangelist
DATES: *1185–1257*
BIRTH PLACE: *Kammien (Grosstein), Poland*
FEAST DAY: *15 August*
EMBLEM: *Dominican friar's habit*

A determined missionary, he was one of the key first-generation evangelizers of the Dominican Order. He helped to establish Christianity in his native Poland, and some claim he also took the faith to Russia, Lithuania and Sweden, though the historical accuracy of this is uncertain.

Legends abound of him working miracles and travelling great distances to spread the gospel. The crucial moment in his life came during a visit to Rome accompanied by his uncle, the Bishop of Cracow. Hyacinth was already a priest, but on meeting St Dominic, he was overwhelmed

by the founder's strength of faith and compassion. Thus inspired, the young priest felt a profound conversion and was received into the order of preachers.

In 1221, he went to Cracow, where he set up five Dominican monasteries as centres of learning. However, his missions to the East were severley hampered by invasions from Tartar hordes that began in 1238.

Left Vision of St Hyacinth *(Domenikos Theotocopoulos, El Greco, late 16th or early 17th century).*

ALBERT THE GREAT

THIS GERMAN DOMINICAN HELPED LAY THE FOUNDATIONS OF MODERN SCIENCE.

KEY FACTS
Doctor of the Church
DATES: *1200–80*
BIRTH PLACE: *Swabia*
PATRON OF: *Students of the natural sciences*
FEAST DAY: *15 November*
EMBLEM: *Dominican friar, scientific instruments*

An inspiring teacher, Albert was the only scholar of his time to be called "Great". After joining the Dominicans in Padua, he taught in Germany, where Thomas Aquinas was his student.

After spells in Paris and Cologne, Albert was made Bishop of Ratisbon in 1260. But Albert longed to pursue his writings on geology, astronomy, chemistry, and geography, so asked to be released from office after just two years. His scientific observations

filled 38 volumes. His theological texts also contain insight. Like Aquinas later, Albert asserted there was no conflict between faith and reason. The two are joined in harmony, he said, but some truth can only be grasped through faith. Albert was made a Doctor of the Church in 1931.

Left Portrait of St Albertus Magnus *(Joos van Gent, c.1475).*

FOURTEEN HOLY HELPERS

IN THE 14TH CENTURY, THE BLACK DEATH STRUCK TERROR IN THE POPULATIONS OF EUROPE. AS A SOURCE OF RELIEF TO ROMAN CATHOLIC VICTIMS, THE POPE SET UP A SPECIAL GROUP OF SAINTS.

A magnificent chapel was built in the 18th century to house the statues of the Fourteen Holy Helpers. Within its Baroque interior, massed in a circle around the altar, stand 14 figures, each representing a saint. The Vierzehnheiligen Sanctuary was built in Germany in veneration of these saints, who were first grouped together during the Black Death of the 14th century.

IMMORTAL PERIL
This disease was terrifying in its symptoms and caused rapid death. People were dying before they received the last rites.

"REMEMBER THE DANGERS THAT SURROUND US IN THIS VALE OF TEARS, AND INTERCEDE FOR US IN ALL OUR NEEDS AND ADVERSITIES. AMEN"

A PRAYER OF INVOCATION TO THE FOURTEEN HOLY HELPERS

This both saddened and frightened the faithful, who believed that without receiving this sacrament, they would forego the essential final step on the journey to heaven. To compensate in some measure for the lack of a priest available to serve the last rites, sufferers could call upon any one of these specified saints to intercede on their behalf for the absolution of their sins.

Some of the Helpers are martyrs, others are associated with certain diseases. Some, such as St Christopher, are even legendary. A collective feast day was assigned for all Holy Helpers on 8 August.

MEANING THROUGH ART
As well as the statues in the sanctuary in Germany, there are many other representations of the Fourteen Holy Helpers, particularly from the 14th and 15th centuries.

Images of the figures were usually placed near church altars, often with Mary, the Blessed Virgin, cradling the Baby Jesus, or with St Christopher carrying the Christ Child on his shoulders.

Left St Roch Praying to the Virgin for an End to the Plague *(Jacques-Louis David, 1780).*

Above View of the Town Hall of Marseilles During the Plague of 1720 *(Michel Serre, 18th century).*

Paintings and sculptures often represent these saints as distorted, or holding awkward positions to indicate the symptoms they are believed to cure. Clothes or an animal companion might give a symbolic meaning or denote their traditional significance.

Indeed, some paintings are so grotesque in their depictions of diseases and suffering that the artists seem intent on bringing home the full horror of the Black Death to the viewer.

CULTUS IN EUROPE

For centuries, these images attracted large crowds. The cultus was strong in Germany, Hungary and Scandinavia. But it never commanded much of a following in Italy, France or England.

The numbers of pilgrims decreased after the Reformation. Now this group of saints is relatively obscure to most Roman Catholic worshippers.

THE PROTECTORS

- **Acacius** and **Denys of Paris** are called upon for headaches.
- **Barbara** intercedes for fevers and sudden death.
- **George** and **Pantaleon** protect domestic animals.
- **Blaise** guards against sore throats.
- **Catherine of Alexandria** and **Christopher** are patrons of sudden death.
- **Cyricus** helps to ward off temptation.
- **Margaret of Antioch** aids women in childbirth.
- **Vitus** prevents epilepsy.
- **Erasmus** is associated with intestinal troubles.
- **Eustace** helps out in difficult situations.
- **Giles** is invoked by lepers, the physically handicapped, and nursing mothers.

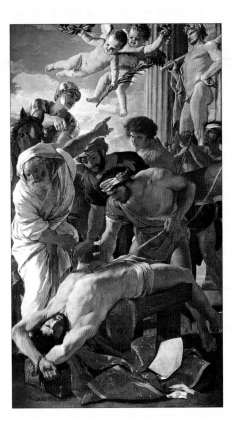

Above Martyrdom of St Erasmus *(Nicolas Poussin, 1629).*

The list of saints is generally stable, but substitutions were made in some regions or cities where the veneration of particular saints was strong. The Holy Helpers were invoked to guard against specific illnesses – and these included diseases suffered by animals as well as humans.

THE BLACK DEATH

The origin of this plague remains a mystery. It was a virulent epidemic that swept across Europe in 1348. It caused rapid putrefaction of the sufferer's body, which turned black before death occurred. In Europe, 25 million died, including one-third of the English population. The numbers of victims in Asia and North Africa are unknown.

There were other outbreaks of plague in Europe but none so devastating as the Black Death. Its cause has been attributed variously to unknown substances, germs introduced by sailors, or a predominance of rats. The lack of hygiene found in medieval cities was a major factor.

Above Black Death at Tournai *(Gilles Le Muisit, 1349).*

ALEXANDER NEVSKI

A WARRIOR COUNT WAS CANONIZED BY THE EASTERN ORTHODOX CHURCH FOR HIS VALIANT DEFENCE OF RUSSIA, AND FOR ASSURING PEACE FOR HIS COMPATRIOTS DURING THE MONGOL OCCUPATION.

KEY FACTS
National hero of Russia
DATES: *1220–63*
BIRTH PLACE: *Novgorod, Russia*
PATRON OF: *Russia*
FEAST DAY: *23 November*
EMBLEM: *Knight's armour*

As the Grand Duke of Vladimir, Alexander Nevski spent much of his early life in wars against neighbouring nations of Europe. His title "Nevski" was earned by his decisive victory over the Swedes at the River Neva in 1240.

Born a prince and patriot of Russia, military pride rode next to devotion to God. Integrity of faith was an essential component of all Nevski's military expeditions. The belief that God was not on the side of force but on the side of truth and justice was one of the guiding maxims of his faith.

Major campaigns included repelling the Swedes from Novgorod and Pskov. Lithuanians were other foes, as were the Knights of the Teutonic Order, a

Left Alexander Nevski *(Afanasiy Yefremovich Kulikov), 20th century.*

noble Germanic troop formed during the Crusader wars. In a triumphant battle on the banks of the frozen Lake Peipous in 1242, Nevski repelled the enemy. In so doing he put an end to all future claims of conquest by the Knights.

TARTAR OVERLORDS

Perhaps equally as important for Russia as these military conquests was the time Nevski had to spend placating the occupying Tartars. Between 1237 and 1240, these fearsome successors of Genghis Khan invaded the principalities of eastern and central Russia.

The control these menacing hordes exerted over his country posed quite a different problem, requiring careful handling. From 1240, Russia was held in servitude, paying high tribute and penalties.

Through clever diplomacy, Alexander Nevski achieved some key concessions, which boosted national morale. He persuaded the Mongols to drop compulsory military service, and negotiated reductions in the tribute demanded by these overlords.

His reputation as a national hero has grown since his death. In recognition of his national status, the Russian Orthodox Church raised a division during World War II named after this patriotic saint. Many street names in Russia are also named in his honour.

Below The silver gilt tomb of Alexander Nevski, held in The State Hermitage Museum, St Petersburg (1747–52).

BONAVENTURE

RECOGNIZED AS THE "SECOND FOUNDER" OF THE FRANCISCANS, ST BONAVENTURE INTRODUCED REFORMS THAT EDUCATED THE FRIARS AND MODERATED AUSTERE TENDENCIES WITHIN THE ORDER.

KEY FACTS

General of the Franciscan Friars, known as the Seraphic Doctor
DATES: *c.1218–74*
BIRTH PLACE: *Bagnoreggio, Italy*
PATRON OF: *Theologians, farmers, porters, weavers*
FEAST DAY: *15 July*
EMBLEM: *Franciscan gown, bishop's mitre. His cloak is bordered with images of seraphim, the highest order of angels*

The "Seraphic Doctor", as Bonaventure was known for his intellectual and mystical qualities, established a high reputation in the Church for his reforming theology. Choosing not to follow in his father's footsteps as a medical doctor, Bonaventure opted instead to become a Franciscan in 1243. It was an interesting choice for a clever man, since the Franciscan order discouraged intellectual pursuits. But he was happy to lead a life of frugal simplicity.

REFORMS

In 1257, Bonaventure became general of the Franciscan Order in Paris, where he had studied. Because the founder, St Francis of Assisi, was detached from formal learning, there were no books to be found in the monasteries.

Yet Bonaventure could see that if the friars were to be effective as teachers they needed to be educated. They would need books and libraries to house them.

Another problem was that St Francis' Rules forbade the ownership of property. So Bonaventure had to persuade his followers to accept a different model. Being a patient man with moderate views, he was prepared to travel to the many Franciscan monasteries and Poor Clare convents to convince the religious that these changes made sense.

For the reforms he thus achieved, as well as the curbs he placed on the more austere practices of some members, he is regarded as the "second founder" of the Franciscans. Disliking high office, he once refused to become Archbishop of York, but later was compelled to be cardinal-bishop of Albano. In this role, he brokered a reconciliation with the Greek church at Constantinople.

The peace turned out to be a temporary one, though Bonaventure never knew this, since he died shortly afterwards.

Below Saint Bonaventure Taking the Franciscan Habit *(Francisco Herrera the Elder, 17th century).*

THOMAS AQUINAS

THE "ANGELIC DOCTOR" WAS AN INTELLECTUAL GIANT OF THE MEDIEVAL CHURCH WHO EXPANDED CHRISTIAN THINKING TO ESTABLISH A COMPREHENSIVE DOCTRINE OF THE CATHOLIC FAITH.

This well-built man was dubbed the "dumb ox" for his gentle courtesy and because he was thought to be a little slow of mind. But as his energy and output was to demonstrate, Thomas Aquinas outstripped all his contemporaries in intellectual capacity.

One writer said that the amount of study required to produce all Aquinas' books would take several normal lifetimes. However, his aristocratic family did not share the young man's enthusiasm to join the Dominicans, a mendicant order that lived by begging.

HOUSE ARREST

His family, who regarded the mendicants' activities as shameful, had educated Thomas at the reputable Benedictine monastery at Monte Cassino, whose abbot was related to the Aquino family. When the determined prodigy nevertheless joined the Black

KEY FACTS
Theologian and writer
DATES: *c.1225–74*
BIRTH PLACE: *Rocca Secca, near Aquino, Italy*
PATRON OF: *Academics, universities, schools, students, theologians, pencil-makers*
FEAST DAY: *28 January*
EMBLEM: *Star shedding light, ox, books, lily*

Friars at the age of 21, his brothers kidnapped him and imprisoned him at the family home.

But Thomas would not relent. His family even sent a beautiful girl to tempt him from his chosen path. Paintings depict him brandishing a burning stick to ward away the temptress.

FAITH AND REASON

Eventually released, Thomas went to Cologne, Germany, to study under St Albert the Great. This teacher provided the groundwork for much of Aquinas' theology. Thenceforth, he was to spend his

Left Temptation of St Thomas Aquinas *(Diego Rodríguez de Silva y Velásquez, 17th century).*

> "WE SHOULD SHOW HONOUR TO THE SAINTS OF GOD, AS BEING MEMBERS OF CHRIST, THE CHILDREN AND FRIENDS OF GOD, AND OUR INTERCESSORS. THEREFORE, IN MEMORY OF THEM WE OUGHT TO HONOUR ANY RELICS OF THEIRS IN A FITTING MANNER."
>
> ST THOMAS AQUINAS

life moving back and forth between France and Italy as a teacher and academic.

In tandem with St Albert the Great, Thomas Aquinas believed in the harmony of faith and reason. Hitherto, theological points of debate had taken the Bible as their authority. Now Aquinas was asserting that reasoned argument was authority in itself because God gave mankind the power of reason.

ARISTOTLE AND ISLAM

Aquinas held that everything comes from God. He said that at the end of their lives humans return to God as to their home.

A perfect life was one that combined contemplation with action, since it is only through prayer that we can know the will of God. At the time that Aquinas

Below St Thomas Aquinas *(Abraham Jansz Diepenbeeck, c.1640–50).*

lived, Islamic scholars were bringing ideas of the ancient Greek philosophers, such as Aristotle, back to Europe. In debate with Muslims, Aquinas produced an entire book responding to their writings.

His intellect aimed not only at the higher reaches of the Church. Some of the most beautiful hymns written for Mass have been ascribed to him and he produced prayers and expositions of the Creed for the ordinary believer. He was also a preacher, giving sermons on the Ten Commandments and key tenets of the Christian faith.

SPIRITUAL END

In about 1266, Aquinas began his *Summa Theologica*, a study of all the Christian mysteries, which ran to five volumes. He never finished the work because in 1272 he had a profound mystical experience while attending Mass.

The effect of receiving a vision of God, as he reported, was so overwhelming that he felt his intellect no longer adequate. Indeed, he is famously reputed to have said that all he had written to date was "like straw" compared to this spiritual experience.

Not long after this event, he prepared to attend the Council at Lyons but was taken ill on the journey. He died at the abbey of Fossanuova aged 43.

Left St Thomas Aquinas wearing Dominican garb and praying at the altar, from Libro de Horas de Alfonso el Magnifico, *the vellum prayer book of Alfonso V of Aragon (Spanish School, c.1442).*

SUMMA THEOLOGICA

Having produced a text, *Summa contra Gentes*, that presented the faith to non-believers, Thomas Aquinas set about writing his *magnum opus* to instruct beginners in Roman Catholic theology. Running to five volumes, *Summa Theologica* covers a great variety of subjects.

The first volume explains all that emanates from God. The second volume explains the psychology of human activity and its organization. The third asserts that humans return to God as to their natural home. The fourth volume discusses the Holy Spirit, and a life of meditation and action. And the fifth, unfinished, summarizes faith.

Above Title page from Summa Theologica *on vellum (French School, 14th century).*

AGNES OF BOHEMIA

PRINCESS AGNES USED HER WEALTH TO FINANCE HER LIFE AS A HUMBLE NUN WORKING WITH LEPERS. SHE WAS CANONIZED BY POPE JOHN PAUL II IN 1989.

KEY FACTS
Princess, abbess
DATES: *d.1282*
BIRTH PLACE: *Bohemia*
FEAST DAY: *6 March*
EMBLEM: *Poor Clare habit*

The daughter of the King of Bohemia (now part of the Czech Republic) was once betrothed to Emperor Frederick II of the Holy Roman Empire. However, this marriage was not one she wished to fulfil, so she wrote to the pope asking to be released from the engagement.

Frederick retreated with grace, and accepted that his fiancée preferred to "wed the king of heaven". Agnes' family were also supportive. On becoming king, her brother funded various projects of hers, including new monasteries, a hospital and the first Poor Clare convent north of the Alps, located in Prague.

Agnes became its abbess, having taken her vows in 1236. St Clare herself sent five nuns to help establish the convent. The severe rules of poverty demanded by the order were faithfully followed by Agnes for 40 years until her death.

Left St Agnes in Prison *(José de Ribera, 1641).*

NICHOLAS OF TOLENTINO

THIS AUGUSTINIAN FRIAR SPENT MANY YEARS AS AN ITINERANT PREACHER AND GAINED A REPUTATION AS A MIRACLE HEALER. AT TOLENTINO HE BROUGHT HARMONY TO A TOWN TORN BY STRIFE.

KEY FACTS
Augustinian friar, miracle worker
DATES: *1245–1305*
BIRTH PLACE: *Sant'Angelo, Italy*
PATRON OF: *The dying and souls in purgatory, babies and mothers, fires, sick animals*
FEAST DAY: *6 March*
EMBLEM: *Augustinian habit, basket of bread rolls, star on his chest*

On hearing an Augustinian friar preaching that the best form of love comes from beyond the world, Nicholas became so inspired that he decided to join the order.

For some years, he lived successfully as a wandering preacher in the Italian district of Ancona, on the Adriatic coast. He gradually aquired a reputation for healing people, including, in about 1270, restoring the sight to a blind woman in Cingoli.

Shortly afterwards, he heard heavenly voices calling him to Tolentino, a town devastated by family feuds and religious schism. For the rest of his life, Nicholas devoted his energies to mending broken relations in the little town.

He fostered harmony at domestic level, caring for children and the dying and criminals. Not surprisingly, Nicholas became much loved for his kindness and sincerity of faith – it is said the entire city turned up to listen to his preaching. After a long illness, he died and was deeply mourned.

Above Nicholas at the Battle of San Romano *(Paolo Uccello, c.1450–60).*

ELIZABETH OF PORTUGAL

A SPANISH PRINCESS, MARRIED TO A PORTUGUESE KING, BECAME A SYMBOL OF RECONCILIATION BOTH AT THE DOMESTIC LEVEL AND AT THE HIGHEST LEVEL OF INTERNATIONAL DIPLOMACY.

KEY FACTS
Queen of Portugal
DATES: *1271–1336*
BIRTH PLACE: *Aragon, Spain*
PATRON OF: *Difficult marriages*
FEAST DAY: *4 July*
EMBLEM: *Crown*

The daughter of Peter III of Aragon was married at the age of 12 to King Denis of Portugal. Though her husband became cruel and abusive to Elizabeth, she followed the Christian teaching of turning the other cheek. In time, her husband converted to the faith.

Elizabeth founded hospitals and orphanages, and cared for abused prostitutes. After the death of her husband, she made a pilgrimage to

St James the Great's shrine at Compostela and became a Franciscan tertiary (lay member).

Although Elizabeth wished to live in modest obscurity, she was called upon to soothe the poor relations between Portugal and Castile. She died at Estremoz but was buried in the Poor Clares convent at Coimbra.

Left St Elizabeth of Portugal
(Francisco Zurbarán, 1640).

ROCH

THIS MYSTERIOUS SAINT, WHO WORKED HEROICALLY DURING A PLAGUE IN ITALY, WAS SAID TO HAVE MIRACULOUSLY SURVIVED THE DISEASE HIMSELF, BUT THEN PERISHED IN PRISON FALSELY ACCUSED.

KEY FACTS
One of the Fourteen Holy Helpers
DATES: c. *1350 80*
BIRTH PLACE: *Montpelier, France*
PATRON OF: *Istanbul, contagious diseases, physicians, surgeons, prisoners, cattle*
FEAST DAY: *17 August*
EMBLEM: *Plague sore on his thigh, dog at his feet, angel, bread*

Also known as Rocco or Roc, Roch is remembered chiefly for nursing plague victims in medieval Italy. It was in a time of great desperation that this young man came to do good public service. Born to a wealthy merchant family in Montpelier, France, Roch chose early in life to be a hermit and pilgrim.

It is believed he lived in Rome but was staying in Piacenza when a plague broke out. By all accounts, he exhausted himself nursing humans, and even animals, before falling victim to the disease himself. Not wishing to become a focus of concern, Roch crawled to a wood to face

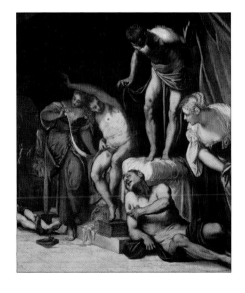

Above St Roch is shown healing *victims of the plague (Jacopo Robusti Tintoretto, 1549).*

death. But legend has it that a dog brought him bread to eat and an angel cured him of the disease.

On recovering, he returned home whereupon his uncle did not recognize him, or refused to do so. Roch was then imprisoned, accused of being a fraud or spy.

He died behind bars in Lombardy. Miracle cures were later claimed at his grave, and believers started calling upon him for help at times of epidemic.

CATHERINE OF SIENA

CATHERINE'S AGGRESSIVE SPIRITUAL BELIEFS DIVIDED PUBLIC OPINION ABOUT HER TRUE UNDERSTANDING OF THE FAITH. SOME THOUGHT HER HYSTERICAL, OTHERS AN EXEMPLARY VISIONARY.

KEY FACTS
Dominican tertiary
DATES: *1347–80*
BIRTH PLACE: *Siena*
PATRON OF: *Italy, Italian nurses*
FEAST DAY: *29 April*
EMBLEM: *Dominican tertiary habit, stigmata, holding a cross, crown of thorns, lily*

Like Hildegard of Bingen, this remarkable woman was a mystic who experienced visions and wrote meaningful religious texts. Both also became involved in worldly affairs.

Catherine was the youngest in a family of 25 children. Her twin sister died at birth. And aged six, she is said to have had her first vision of Jesus.

She used to say a Hail Mary on each step of the staircase while ascending or descending. Frightened and angered by her behaviour, her family insisted on her working incessantly, never allowing her to be alone. However, her patience

Left Saint Catherine of Siena *(Giovanni Battista Tiepolo, 1746).*

style. Some thought her hysterical. But she won respect from the pope after admonishing people to go on a crusade to the Holy Land. In 1375, while visiting Pisa, Catherine suffered pangs of pain, and claimed she was marked by the stigmata (wounds identified with those of the Crucifixion). Again, none could see the scars, but on her death they became clearly visible.

THE AVIGNON POPES

In all her contact with the public, Catherine had developed a talent for mediation, which brought her into Church politics. For some 75 years, the popes had lived in exile at Avignon. Now Catherine became involved in persuading Pope Gregory XI to return to the papal seat in Rome. Gregory responded to her quasi-mystical call and sailed for the city in 1376.

After Gregory's death, French factions in Avignon selected a rival pope in opposition to his successor, Urban VI. Catherine tried to settle the dispute but aroused such anger in her opponents they threatened her life. In 1380, she dreamt she was being crushed by a ship that symbolized the Church. Shortly afterwards, she was paralysed for days by a stroke before she died.

Below Saint Catherine of Siena Exchanging Her Heart with Christ *(Giovanni di Paolo, 15th century). Her heart is held in her fist.*

and obedience convinced her father of her holiness and he permitted her to become a Dominican tertiary.

ZEAL AND STIGMATA

She lived a solitary life of prayer until 1366, when she was said to have received a vision of Mary, the Blessed Virgin, who led her to Christ. Catherine was convinced she had received a wedding ring given by Christ, though no one else could see the jewellery.

After this experience, Catherine went out into the world and began to preach. A band of followers gathered round her, referring to her as "mama".

She was energetic as a preacher and not all the citizens of her hometown, Siena, admired her

BRIDGET OF SWEDEN

ROYAL ADVISOR, NURSE OF THE BLACK DEATH, AND MORAL CRUSADER, BRIDGET STOPPED AT NOTHING IN PURSUIT OF RIGHT. SHE PROPHESIED DAMNATION, AND EVEN CRITICIZED THE POPE.

KEY FACTS
Founder of Order
DATES: *1303–73*
BIRTH PLACE: *Uppland*
PATRON OF: *Sweden, pilgrims*
FEAST DAY: *23 July*
EMBLEM: *Monogram of Christ (HIS), candle, book, pen, dressed as a widow or pilgrim*

The daughter of the governor of Uppland served in the Swedish court as lady-in-waiting, moral adviser to the feckless royal family. In 1344, Bridget (or Birgitta) went with her nobleman husband on the long pilgrimage to Compostela in Spain, but he died on their return journey.

Now widowed, though with eight children from her marriage, Bridget for a time directed her energy into founding a monastic order, called the Most Holy Saviour, or Bridgettines.

Despite the Black Death then sweeping across Europe, Bridget travelled to Rome and nursed the

PEREGRINACION.

sick there. After reputedly receiving a vision of St Francis, she went on to Assisi and spent two years visiting Italian shrines.

It was said Bridget had the power of prophecy about political events. She is believed to have used this facility to condemn to damnation weak or corrupt heads of state. The fearless nun even dared once to criticize the pope.

Left St Bridget in a Portuguese vellum from the 17th century.

JOHN OF NEPOMUK

A DEVOUT ADVISER TO THE ARCHBISHOP OF PRAGUE UPHELD HIS CLERICAL DUTIES TO THE POINT OF MARTYRDOM RATHER THAN COMPROMISE THE CHURCH IN THE FACE OF A POWERFUL TYRANT.

KEY FACTS
Martyr
DATES: *c. 1345–93*
BIRTH PLACE: *Nepomuk, Bohemia*
PATRON OF: *Slovakia, of confessors, bridges and protection against slander*
FEAST DAY: *5 January*
EMBLEM: *Seven stars*

As vicar general, John of Nepomuk (or Nepomucen) became the close aide of the Archbishop of Prague on matters of church-state relations. When, in 1378, Wenceslaus IV became King of Bohemia, these relations took a turn for the worse.

A legend says that being a man given to violent rages, Wenceslaus became insanely jealous of his wife and harassed John to reveal her confessional secrets. The king so mistrusted priests that he planned to set up a monastery manned by his own priests. To this end, when

the abbot of the rich Benedictine monastery at Kladruby died, Wenceslaus wanted to appoint his successor in order to gain control of the revenues from the land.

However, in anticipation, the priests appointed a new abbot the moment the old incumbent died. Learning this, Wenceslaus believed John to be the instigator.

He first beat the priests, then tied John up, his ankles bound to his head, and hurled him into the River Moldau at Prague. Seven stars were said to glow over the site of his drowning. John was

greatly mourned when his body was found the next day.

Right A statue of St John of Nepomuk with a halo of stars, on the Charles Bridge in Prague.

WARRIOR SAINTS

WHETHER SOLDIERS OF WAR OR FOR PEACE, MANY MEN AND WOMEN SINCE THE BIRTH OF CHRISTIANITY HAVE BEEN CANONIZED FOR DEFENDING THEIR FAITH AND GOING INTO BATTLE.

Throughout history, soldiers have often claimed that the saints have aided and protected them in battle. Many warriors have converted to Christianity and died for their faith, or fought bloody wars to protect their right to worship their God. There are others whose inspiration came from Christ himself and who took to the path of peace.

HEAVENLY INSPIRATION

The archangel Michael, "captain of the heavenly host" and protector of Christian soldiers, has often appeared above battlefields or kept company with troops in combat. Joan of Arc identified him as helping spur her into battle.

In their long battle against Moorish invasion, the Spanish frequently called upon the apostle St James the Great, patron saint of Spain. After the miraculous victory at the Battle of Clavijo (AD 844), the soldiers claimed that James had appeared in their midst in full armour, sword in one hand and banner in the other, riding a white charger.

SOLDIER SAINTS

Since the days of the Roman Empire, there have been military men who have rejected their earthly masters and pledged to serve only Christ.

Known in the Eastern Orthodox Church as the "Great Martyr", St Demetrius was much admired as a warrior saint. He was a soldier in the Roman army in the early 4th century, who converted to Christianity and was subsequently put to death.

Above St Maurice, fresco detail (artist unknown, 15th century).

A great soldier saint and inspiration to warriors and crusaders, St George is always depicted as a knight in armour. Although most of what we know is legendary, he is venerated throughout the Christian world. St George is thought to have been martyred at Lydda in Palestine around AD 303.

St Theodore, known as "the recruit", was a young Roman soldier. After his conversion to Christianity he refused to join his comrades in the worship of pagan gods. Tradition says that he also set fire to a pagan temple. He was martyred in the 4th century at Pontus (part of modern Turkey).

During birthday celebrations for the Roman emperors Diocletian and Maximian, a centurion named Marcellus threw off his soldier's belt crying, "I am a soldier of Christ, the eternal king, and from now I cease to serve you." Other Roman soldiers who

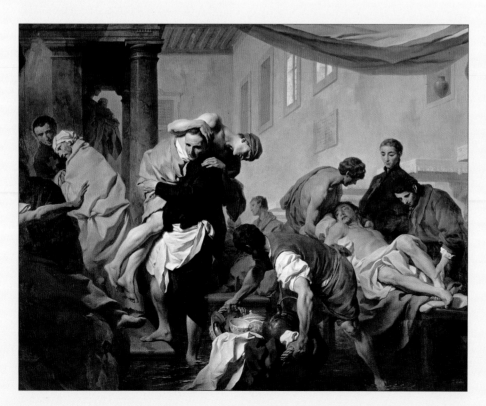

Left Camillus of Lellis rescues hospital patients during the flooding of the Tiber in 1598 (Pierre Subleyras, 1745).

converted expressed the same anti-military sentiments, such as St Julius who chose to die by the sword rather than serve a master on earth.

There are also great leaders who are much venerated because they were soldiers in service of Christ. St Stephen of Hungary, a skilled military strategist, set out to conquer the pagans in his country and force them to convert to the Christian faith. St Vladimir of Kiev is revered throughout Orthodox Russia as the man who brought Christianity to his country, although initially he used the army to impose the new faith.

PEACEFUL PATH
Some soldier converts came to realize that the Christian life was not compatible with violence.

Martin of Tours, a young officer in the Roman army, asked for a discharge after his conversion. He announced, "I am Christ's soldier; I am not allowed to fight."

Left Alexander Nevski (artist unknown, 1855).

Much later, in the 16th century, St Camillus of Lellis was a mercenary or "soldier of fortune" who began nursing the sick and injured after his conversion. He is credited with organizing the first field ambulance unit, going into the battlefield to care for the wounded. St John of God was another mercenary whose conversion made him seek peace. He also turned to nursing and founded the Brothers Hospitallers.

During the Spanish Civil War of 1936–39, thousands of Christians fought for a country that was guided by the faith against their fellow citizens who wanted a secular regime. Hundreds of the Catholics who died were beatified by Pope John Paul II and are known as the Martyrs of the Spanish Civil War.

Below St Demetrius (Serbian icon, 18th century).

THE CRUSADES
In the Middle Ages, European Christian countries mounted military campaigns to oust the Muslims from Jerusalem and give support to Christians isolated in the East.

There were eight Crusades in all, lasting from 1095 to 1272 and ending with the Muslims still in control. Vast sums of money and huge numbers of men were involved. The journey to the Holy Land involved travelling great distances and was often disrupted by battles on land and sea. The Crusaders often fought while weak with hunger and ravaged by disease.

The Crusaders believed they had God on their side and often experienced heavenly visions. They adopted St George and St Demetrius as patron saints after they appeared above the demoralized soldiers and led them to victory against the Saracens at the Siege of Antioch (1097–98).

King Louis IX of France led two disastrous crusades in 1248 and 1270. Although he was not victorious, he was venerated for his zeal in fighting for the Holy Land.

Left The archangel Michael (Greek, c.14th century).

***Above** Manuscript illumination showing soldiers departing for the Crusades (c.1240–84).*

JOAN OF ARC

AS THE GIRL WARRIOR, JOAN OF ARC, PERISHED IN THE FIRE PREPARED BY ENGLISHMEN, ONE SOLDIER WAS HEARD TO CRY OUT, "WE ARE LOST. WE HAVE BURNED A SAINT."

Joan of Arc is one of the most remarkable women in history. Her life has inspired books, films, poems and paintings, yet she remains mysterious. She was courageous and indifferent to pain, a good horsewoman and deft with her sword. Yet she began as a simple illiterate peasant, at home with domestic work.

How did she convince a royal court that she could be a military leader? Where did she learn to lead an army on horseback and wield a weapon? Brought up in the Champagne area of France during the Hundred Years War between England and France, Joan was used to living in a war-torn environment.

Her village was sympathetic to the royal house of Orléans. But across the river to the south, the peasants sided with the dukes of

Below Joan of Arc Kissing the Sword of Deliverance *(Dante Gabriel Rossetti, 1863).*

KEY FACTS
Visionary, military leader
DATES: c.*1412–31*
BIRTH PLACE: *Domrémy, France*
PATRON OF: *France, French soldiers*
FEAST DAY: *30 May*
EMBLEM: *Armour, battle banner*

Burgundy and the English. When she was 13, Joan said she heard God speak to her. As a result, she vowed to remain a virgin, devoted to the will of Christ.

DIVINE VOICES
At 16, Joan claimed frequent visits by the archangel Michael and two saints, Catherine of Alexandria and Margaret of Antioch. She said the saints were dressed as queens and they instructed her to save France and crown the dauphin, Charles, as King of France.

Ignoring pleas from her father to remain, Joan prepared to travel to the court of Charles. To help her cause, she dressed as a man.

Entering the royal quarters, Joan unerringly approached the dauphin. He was a frivolous youth who hid among his courtiers to trick the girl. But she was said to have had a divine recognition of

"IT IS BETTER TO BE ALONE WITH GOD: HIS FRIENDSHIP WILL NOT FAIL ME, NOR HIS COUNSEL, NOR HIS LOVE. IN HIS STRENGTH I WILL DARE, AND DARE, AND DARE, UNTIL I DIE."

WORDS GIVEN TO JOAN IN *ST JOAN* BY G.B. SHAW

him. Confounded, the young royal listened to her announcement that God had sent her to help him and his kingdom. After close questioning from religious and military leaders, Joan won permission to raise arms.

INTO BATTLE

Stealing a sword from behind a church altar, Joan prepared for battle bearing a banner painted with the words "Jesus Maria". The people of nearby Vaucouleurs gave her a horse and a man's suit of white armour.

On 7 May 1429, Joan led her soldiers into war and banished the English from Orléans. She went on to win victories in Patay and Tours as well. But her greatest moment of triumph came when she stood beside the dauphin as he was crowned King Charles VII of France, at Rheims in July of that year. However, the indolent Charles neglected Joan, who took

Below The Burning of Joan of Arc on 30 May 1431 *(lithograph of the French School, 19th century).*

Above The Entrance of Joan of Arc into Orléans on 8 May 1429 *(Jean-Jacques Scherrer, 1887).*

it upon herself to continue the fight. But in Compiègne she was captured by the Burgundians who then sold her to the English.

WITCHCRAFT

Joan suffered nine months of brutal confinement charged with witchcraft and heresy. Her decision to dress as a man was deemed to be proof of her heresy. Barely 19 years old, the transcript of her trial in Rouen, then in English hands, makes sad reading. The court found her guilty of heresy.

As she approached the scene of her dreadful punishment in Rouen's market square, she asked for a crucifix. This she kissed and was heard to cry "Jesus" as the flames licked round her. Before her body was consumed, her corpse was displayed naked to the crowd to prove she was indeed a woman who had "wickedly" paraded as a man.

To prevent any veneration of the relics, her ashes were thrown into the River Seine. Her family petitioned to clear her name. In 1456, the pope overturned the

guilty verdict. For centuries she was popularly held to be a saint but the Church waited until 1920 before granting canonization.

Joan was not a martyr, but a virgin who lived her faith. She is the first Christian patriot, her love of country entwined with her religion. Even the English went so far as to erect a statue of St Joan in Winchester Cathedral.

VOICE OF A LEGEND

There is a tradition that Margaret of Antioch, who may never even have existed, spoke to Joan. Legend claims Margaret was a Christian exiled from home by a pagan father. She lived as a poor shepherdess until the governor of Antioch tried to seduce her. When she refused him, he tortured her. A dragon is said to have swallowed her, but she burst from it and survived. She promised divine protection, safeguards against devils, and fertility to the childless.

Above St Margaret *(Raffaello Sanzio Raphael, 16th century).*

RITA OF CASCIA

AFTER CARING FOR HER WAYWARD FAMILY, ST RITA BECAME A NUN AND SUFFERED THE PAINS OF MORTIFICATION. HER RENOWN AS A HEALER MADE HER ONE OF THE FOURTEEN HOLY HELPERS.

KEY FACTS
Widow, mystic
DATES: *1377–1447*
BIRTH PLACE: *Roccaporena, Italy*
PATRON OF: *Those in desperate situations, parenthood, help for the infertile*
FEAST DAY: *22 May*
EMBLEM: *Crown of thorns, stigmata on forehead*

Born in a village in Umbria, Rita was brought up a pious girl. Indeed, she longed to devote herself to God. But she owed greater allegiance to her parents' wishes than to her own and so she submitted to a marriage that they arranged.

Unhappily, Rita found herself bound to a violent, unfaithful husband. Furthermore, their sons followed his example. Despite the difficulties she had to endure, she patiently cared for her family.

Rita prayed unceasingly that Jesus might be revealed to them. And in time the husband seemed to repent and convert to the faith, only to come home one day mortally wounded in a vendetta.

Her sons swore vengeance for his death, so Rita prayed for their death before they committed any dreadful deeds. They then fell ill. Inspired by their mother's gentle nursing, the two sons repented of their evil ways and were forgiven before they too died.

THORN OF GOD

Now widowed, Rita applied to join an Augustinian convent in Cascia. She was refused on the ground of not being a virgin. But persistent entreaties on her part eventually succeeded and, at the age of 52, Rita was admitted to the convent.

She proved a devout sister who never flinched from the austere rules. Rita made it her special duty to nurse the sick and counsel sinners outside the nunnery. Her kindliness was said to inspire many converts.

At the age of 60, Rita attended a sermon centred on the crown of thorns. As she listened to the words describing Jesus as "king of the Jews", being forced to wear a mock crown, Rita suffered a dreadful stab of pain. She later found a wound, such as that which a thorn might cause, on the middle of her forehead.

The wound did not disappear but suppurated. It became so offensive that, for the last 16 years of her life, Rita lived largely as a recluse. On a pilgrimage to Rome in 1450, her wound disappeared, only to return when she was back

Below Detail from Three Depictions of St Rita of Cascia *(colour lithograph of the French School, 20th century).*

Above Detail from Three Depictions of St Rita of Cascia *(colour lithograph of the French School, 20th century).*

in her convent. Rita contracted tuberculosis, and thus a life of devotion, prayer and obedience was ended in 1447.

Miracles were attributed to Rita after her death. Her body, housed in a grand tomb, has remained incorrupt to the present day. A school, a hospital and an orphanage have been built around the tomb, which forms part of the Cascia convent buildings.

FRA ANGELICO

THE PRIOR AT A MONASTERY IN TUSCANY BECAME KNOWN AS THE "ANGELIC BROTHER" FOR HIS BEAUTIFUL SPIRITUAL PAINTINGS. FRA ANGELICO REGARDED HIS ARTISTIC WORK AS ACTS OF PRAYER.

KEY FACTS
Artist monk
DATES: *1387–1455*
BIRTH PLACE: *Vicchio, Italy*
PATRON OF: *Artists*
FEAST DAY: *18 February*
EMBLEM: *Paintbrush*

Guido di Pietro, as he was christened, was born in the mountains beyond Florence, Italy. He joined the Dominican Order in Fiesole as a young man and soon became known as Fra Angelico, or "angelic brother".

An artist who thought of painting as an act of prayer, Fra Angelico produced works entirely religious in subject. Indeed, the spirituality of his work prompted the Victorian art critic, John Ruskin, to declare that the talented monk was an inspired saint rather than an artist.

MEDICI PATRONS

Initially, the monastery trained Fra Angelico in manuscript painting under guidance from an older monk, Lorenzo Monaco. When the monks were moved to San Marco convent in Florence, the powerful and wealthy Medici family paid for enlargements of the building.

With his teacher, Fra Angelico painted the new walls with a series of murals depicting sacred scenes. He coupled the elements of medieval work with the new scientific knowledge of his own Renaissance era.

Thus his style appealed to the contemporary tastes but did not alienate traditional viewers. It is the beauty of his work, with its mystical quality, that still inspires.

In 1445, he was called to Rome to produce wall paintings at the Vatican, in St Peter's

Right The Annunciation *(Fra Angelico, c.1440–45).*

Above Fresco detail from The Deeds of the Antichrist *(Luca Signorelli, c.1499–1502). In the foreground, Fra Angelico (right) is depicted standing next to Signorelli (left).*

Cathedral and the pope's private rooms. And four years later he went to Orvieto in Spain to decorate the vault of the chapel, though he was called to monastic office before finishing the work.

PRIOR AT FIESOLE

From 1449 to 1452, he was prior of the monastery at Fiesole. He then returned to Rome, where he died after three years.

His works, which serve a contemplative purpose, are regarded as "visual prayers". They brought him recognition from a public who would gaze at them in admiration. Many are preserved in religious buildings. Almost 600 years later, at the beatification of Fra Angelico, Pope John Paul II exclaimed, "Why do we need miracles? These are his miracles."

CASIMIR OF POLAND

ST CASIMIR IS CLAIMED AS PATRON BY POLAND, RUSSIA AND LITHUANIA, REFLECTING THE COMPLICATED GEO-POLITICS OF MEDIEVAL EASTERN EUROPE.

KEY FACTS
Prince of Poland
DATES: *1458–84*
BIRTH PLACE: *Cracow, Poland*
PATRON OF: *Poland, Russia, Lithuania, the youth of Lithuania*
FEAST DAY: *4 March*
EMBLEM: *Crown*

Numerous reports from the medieval period describe well-born children possessed of a deep spirituality. But Casimir is an extraordinary example. From infancy, it was said, he had a natural tendency to be ascetic.

His father was King Casimir IV of Poland, yet his small son would admit no luxury, choosing to sleep on a bare floor and spend hours at prayer. He frequently recited a long Latin hymn in praise of Mary, the Blessed Virgin. Under plain clothes, he wore a hair-shirt to mortify the flesh. He visited the poor regularly, using his royal position to gain concessions on their behalf.

When Casimir was 15, the king appointed this unworldly

son to lead the Polish army in a bid to take the throne of Hungary. As both the boy's officers and the pope were opposed to this war, Casimir decided to turn back home during the campaign. His angry father imprisoned him in Dobzki Castle for months.

Yet nothing would induce Casimir to take up arms, nor would he abandon his vow of celibacy. He continued to follow his stern, simple ways, ultimately to his death. He died in what is now Lithuania, aged 26.

Left St Casimir of Poland (Carlo Dolci, 17th century).

NICHOLAS OF FLUE

POPE PIUS XII DECLARED ST NICHOLAS OF FLUE TO BE THE FATHER OF SWITZERLAND, A TRIBUTE TO HIS ROLE IN UNITING THE VARIOUS FACTIONS THAT HAD PLUNGED THE REGION INTO CIVIL WAR.

KEY FACTS
Hermit
DATES: *1417–87*
BIRTH PLACE: *Sachseln, Switzerland*
PATRON OF: *Switzerland*
FEAST DAY: *21 March (25 September in Switzerland)*
EMBLEM: *Hut, hermit's clothes*

The life of St Nicholas falls into two halves. At first, he lived as a soldier, magistrate and judge in Switzerland. His family belonged to the Friends of God, a Christian brotherhood that stressed the personal union of their souls with God.

On turning 50, the second part of his life began. Nicholas decided to become a hermit. With his wife's blessing, he set off for France, but on the way observed what he described as a fiery sign calling him back to Switzerland. So he settled on a high pasture, living under the shelter of a tree.

The faithful sought him out, and built him a hut and a chapel. At this time, Switzerland was in the grip of civil war, and delegates from both sides visited Nicholas. His words are said to have resolved the political differences and a national unity was achieved by the Edict of Stans (1481).

Left Nicholas of Flue praying in the wilderness, with a skull by his side as a memento mori (woodcut, artist unknown, 1860).

THOMAS MORE

AT HIS EXECUTION, THE LORD CHANCELLOR THOMAS MORE TOLD THE CROWD THAT HE WAS "THE KING'S GOOD SERVANT – BUT GOD'S FIRST". TO THE END, MORE WOULD NOT COMPROMISE HIS FAITH.

KEY FACTS
Martyr saint
DATES: *1478–1535*
BIRTH PLACE: *London, England*
PATRON OF: *Politicians*
FEAST DAY: *22 June*
EMBLEM: *Lawyer's hat*

A scholar of great integrity, Thomas More was granted high office by his friend, King Henry VIII of England. He read law at Oxford University and, at the age of 23, became a Member of Parliament.

Thomas had a witty, light-hearted personality, and the king delighted in his company. When appointed Lord Chancellor, he wrote his most famous work, *Utopia*, a fantasy about an ideal community living in harmony, with equality of opportunity.

His first wife, by whom he had four children, died young but he made a happy second marriage. His family was a source of love and comfort, and Thomas drew great strength from his faith.

Much of his work was written in support of the Catholic Church and against Martin Luther's ideas of reformation. He corresponded with theologians across Europe, including Erasmus

RUPTURE WITH THE KING

Thomas was deeply distressed by Henry VIII's decision to break with Rome and set himself up as supreme head of the Church in England. The king's reasons were not theological.

He simply wished Rome to nullify his marriage to Catherine of Aragon, but the pope refused. Henry followed fashionable ideas of reformation and revolt against Rome, and declared religious independence.

But Thomas More was a pious man and could not support his wayward king. He resigned as

Above An engraving of Thomas More after a painting by Holbein (Francesco Bartolozzi, 1792).

Lord Chancellor in 1532. Two years later, More was called to take an oath denying papal authority over English Christians. He refused and was dispatched to the Tower of London. His lands were confiscated and his family forced into poverty.

During his imprisonment there, he wrote often to his beloved daughter, Margaret Roper. He also produced his *Dialogue of Comfort*, a moving text on the meaning of faith.

The following year he was taken to Westminster Hall where he faced charges of treason because he refused to accept the king's authority over the pope's. Thomas More was sentenced to death and was beheaded in public on Tower Hill, London.

JOHN FISHER

A distinguished scholar-priest, John Fisher was Chancellor of Cambridge University and Bishop of Rochester. He was involved in reforming the Church, but preferred dialogue to confrontation as a means of bringing change.

Fisher was a good friend of Thomas More and, like him, was asked to accept the Act of Succession, which gave Henry VIII authority over English Catholics. John refused and was taken to the Tower. While there, the pope made him a cardinal. The infuriated king condemned John to death.

The saint was so ill, he had to be carried to the executioner's block. He died in 1535, a month before Thomas More.

Above Portrait of Martyr and Prelate John Fisher (artist and date unknown).

THE SAINTS IN ART

PAINTINGS OF THE SAINTS INSPIRED BELIEVERS TO FEEL THAT, IN CONTEMPLATING HOLY IMAGES, THEY WOULD DRAW CLOSER TO GOD. PERSONAL ATTRIBUTES WERE ADDED TO IDENTIFY THE SAINTS.

Gregory the Great observed that paintings do for the illiterate what texts do for readers. There can be little doubt that the medieval faithful, most of whom could not read, were uplifted by illustrations of the saints' lives.

Despite the passing of centuries, believers who gazed upon these images were not dismayed by various artistic developments. Changes to the style of clothing worn by the saints or altered settings tended to cause no discomfort among the faithful. Neither did the portrayal of particular saints with different faces in successive paintings.

Above The Martyrdom of St Catherine of Alexandria *(Lucas Cranach the Elder, 1506).*

SYMBOLS OF IDENTITY

From early in the history of Christian art, a convention arose to identify saints through symbols. These emblems served to clarify the narrative being told, and to identify the characters.

Mary, the Blessed Virgin, and infant Jesus are instantly recognizable. Likewise, Mary holding her dead son, a scene known as the Pietà, is universally understood, as is the image of the crucifix, representing the crucified Christ.

But other characters needed their individual code of identity in order to be recognized, since no one knew what the saints looked like. To modern eyes, medieval and Renaissance Christian paintings can look quaint, even bizarre.

Doves emanate rays of light, lions lie meekly on cathedral floors, and a stag might display a crucifix within its antlers. Angels have blue duck-feathered wings, and men stand, pierced by arrows or even holding their own heads. For some 1,700 years, these unlikely elements possessed a beautiful logic, easily understood by all Christians, from the bogs of Ireland to the deserts of Syria.

Above St Lucy with her eyes on a plate (Umbrian School, c.1550).

LIONS TO ALABASTER

The medieval faithful knew the scholarly man with the lion was St Jerome. Likewise, the man with an arrow was Sebastian, who by tradition was shot in this manner.

The shepherdess, St Margaret of Antioch, carried a staff and was shown with a dragon because she escaped from such a beast. St James the Great had a seashell and pilgrim's staff near him. The shell

Below St Jerome in the Desert (Pietro Perugino, c.1499–1502).

> "THE WORK SHINES NOBLY,
> BUT THE WORK WHICH SHINES NOBLY SHOULD CLEAR MINDS,
> SO THAT THEY MAY TRAVEL THROUGH THE TRUE LIGHTS TO THE TRUE LIGHT
> WHERE CHRIST IS THE TRUE DOOR."
>
> ABBOT SUGER (C.1081–1151)

indicated his body was found in a drifting boat, the staff that he was a journeying evangelist.

All Christendom recognized Mary Magdalene because a jar of ointment and loosened hair marked her apart. With oil of alabaster she anointed Christ's feet before drying them with her hair.

ART AS IDOLATRY

The Church regarded artistic representations as an expression of the holiness of the saints. In the

Below A fresco showing the popular subject of St Luke painting the Madonna (Andrea Delitio, 1477).

Orthodox Church, they were used to concentrate the mind during meditation. But these artistic works aroused anxiety during the Reformation.

Protestant leaders forbade the erection of any kind of image in religious buildings. Images were regarded as idolatrous on the ground that the Old Testament forbids worship before idols.

Paintings, shrines and statues of saints were cleared away and frescoes were concealed behind a covering of wall paint. These zealous reformers even showed hostility toward music. The Roman Catholic Church uses

music for worship. The Eastern Orthodox Church retains a sung liturgy so revered it has remained unaltered to this day.

The reformer John Calvin declared that music had no place in a church. The less stern Martin Luther, on the other hand, composed his own church hymns.

SAINTLY ARTISTS

There are saints who were artists, the first being the Apostle Luke, reported to have made studies of Mary, the Blessed Virgin. Perhaps the greatest painter is Fra Angelico whose spiritual paintings are famous, but the drawings and music of Hildegard of Bingen also carry a mystical quality.

Musicians and poets can be found in the company of saints. It is assumed Gregory the Great was a musician – one reason for this assumption is that the Gregorian Chants bear his name.

There are contemporary reports that describe Nicetas of Remesiana as a poet and composer who wrote the beautiful Latin hymn, *Te Deum*. He used music as a form of preaching.

Above Manuscript illumination from Cantigas de Santa Maria (Alphonse Le Sage, 13th century).

ANGELA MERICI

THE ITALIAN FOUNDER OF THE FIRST ORDER OF WOMEN DEVOTED SPECIALLY TO EDUCATING CHILDREN HAS BECOME A PATRON OF MANY CAUSES RELATED TO THE UNDERPRIVILEGED IN SOCIETY.

As an orphan from an early age, Angela Merici suffered great deprivation and neglect. Vulnerable, malnourished and unloved, orphaned children were a pitiable class in Italian society at this time.

Forced to be independent as a child, Angela developed a special sympathy for the plight of orphans. While she could not help their loss of parentage, she could work to improve their lot.

To this end, she first joined the Franciscan tertiaries and then founded a special Christian community. Its members were women who were not cloistered but free to move among those who most needed education – children. The sisters, who went wherever it was convenient to deliver lessons, taught local children in the villages. Aged 42, Angela went to educate the children at Brescia.

The lay nun made pilgrimages to Rome and the Holy Land, where she was strangely struck blind. She recovered her sight on returning home.

Once again, Angela gathered a group of women in Brescia who dedicated their lives to educating children. The women made no vows of chastity or obedience, and shared no communal life. But from this nucleus grew the Company of St Ursula (known as the Ursuline nuns), named after the legendary virgin martyr.

Right St Angela Merici
(Moretto da Brescia, date unknown).

KEY FACTS
Founder of Ursuline nuns
DATES: *1474–1540*
BIRTH PLACE: *Lake Garda, Italy*
PATRON OF: *Disabled people*
FEAST DAY: *27 January*
EMBLEM: *Book*

CAJETAN

DEVOTING MOST OF HIS LIFE TO WORKING AMONG THE POOR IN THE SLUMS OF NAPLES OPENED ST CAJETAN'S EYES TO THE REALITY OF RENAISSANCE SQUALOR FOR LARGE SECTIONS OF THE COMMUNITY.

Though not ordained until he was 36, Cajetan had seen enough in his working life to realize that the Church was in dire need of reform. Being an active charity worker made him acutely aware of the suffering and loss of faith in the community.

In partnership with Pietro Caraffa, a mistrusted fanatic who in fact became Pope Paul IV, Cajetan founded the Theatines (named after the diocese of Theate). This fundamentalist group of priests were trained to follow the first teachings of Christ, avoiding all sophisticated theology.

Their purpose was to preach the basics of the Christian faith in the hope of bringing back the disaffected into the Church. Cajetan also devised a system of alleviating poverty. He set up pawnshops owned by the Church to allow the poor access to loans. These non-profit organizations operated for centuries. He lived briefly in Rome but left during an invasion by troops of the Holy Roman Emperor.

Cajetan spent most of his life in Naples, then a corrupt diocese. He died there, having tried to improve its moral culture.

KEY FACTS
Founder of the Theatines
DATES: *1480–1547*
BIRTH PLACE: *Vicenza, Italy*
PATRON OF: *Job seekers*
FEAST DAY: *7 August*
EMBLEM: *Theatine habit*

JOHN OF GOD

A PORTUGUESE MADMAN RESCUED FROM AN ASYLUM TURNED ROUND HIS LIFE BY DEDICATING IT TO THE RELIEF OF SOCIETY'S OUTCASTS. A HOSPITAL SERVICE WAS FOUNDED IN HIS NAME.

KEY FACTS
*Founder of the Brothers of
St John of God*
DATES: *1495–1550*
BIRTH PLACE: *Monte Mor il
Nuovo, Portugal*
PATRON OF: *Nurses and nursing
associations, bookbinders*
FEAST DAY: *8 March*
EMBLEM: *Poor clothing, cross*

John of God, a Portuguese, spent his youth as a soldier for Spain, roaming the battlefields of Europe, before working first as a shepherd in Andalusia, and later as a merchant, peddling religious images and pamphlets in Granada.

Attending a sermon given by John of Avila, the merchant went mad with remorse for his sins. He began to scream and tear at his hair. He was confined to a lunatic asylum until John of Avila visited him, asking him to serve God. John of God began to sell wood, feeding the poor with his profits.

He built a house where he sheltered vagabonds, prostitutes, and nursed the ill.

He never founded an order, but his hospital service became the Order of the Brothers of St John of God. He tried to hide his ill health but when a noblewoman insisted on nursing him, he wept, believing he was unworthy of comfort while others suffered. When John died, all Granada followed his funeral procession.

Right St John of God *(the School of Pedro Nolasco y Lara, 18th century).*

THOMAS OF VILLANOVA

FROM SIMPLE FRIAR TO ARCHBISHOP OF VALENCIA, ST THOMAS ENDEAVOURED TO MEET THE NEEDS OF ALL WHO CAME HIS WAY, REGARDLESS OF THEIR WEALTH OR STATUS IN SOCIETY.

KEY FACTS
Archbishop
DATES: *1488–1555*
BIRTH PLACE: *Near Villanova,
Castile*
FEAST DAY: *22 September*
EMBLEM: *Franciscan habit,
archbishop's crook*

A dreamy man by nature, fond of meditation, Thomas of Villanova was destined to join a religious order. When admitted to the Spanish Franciscan friary at Salamanca, he developed a deep faith and became a significant preacher for 25 years.

Somewhat against his will, Thomas was then appointed Archbishop of Valencia. What he found, on taking office, was a Church in need of inspiration.

A lazy, dissolute clergy required discipline, but Thomas knew that high-handed methods achieved nothing. Instead, he adopted patience and diplomacy. His gen-

Above The Charity of Saint Thomas of Villanova *(Bartolomé Murillo, c. 1670).*

tle faith served many quarters of the community. Among his congregation were disturbed *Moriscos*, Moors who had been forcibly converted to Christianity. His spirituality and reputed gift for healing brought much solace to these people.

Preferring the solitary life, Thomas asked to be allowed to step down as archbishop. But his leadership was so vital the Church ignored his requests. Worn out by duties, Thomas died in Valencia and was canonized in 1658.

IGNATIUS OF LOYOLA

AS FOUNDER OF THE POWERFUL MISSIONARY ORDER, THE
SOCIETY OF JESUS (ALSO KNOWN AS THE JESUITS), ST IGNATIUS
SPEARHEADED THE COUNTER-REFORMATION IN EUROPE.

KEY FACTS
*Founder of the Society of Jesus,
or "Jesuits"*
DATES: *c.1491–1556*
BIRTH PLACE: *Azpeitia, Spain*
PATRON OF: *Spiritual exercise
and retreats*
FEAST DAY: *31 July*
EMBLEM: *Black cassock, heart
pierced by thorns, the monogram
of Christ (HIS), and a crown
of glory*

The youngest of 11 children of a noble Basque family, Ignatius was born in the Castle of Loyola at Azpeitia. He followed the course taken by many young men of the period and trained as a soldier in the Spanish army.

But for a severe wound to his leg while fighting the French at Pamplona, Ignatius would probably have joined the ranks of the conquistadors on their expeditions to the Americas.

Instead, he was forced to take a long convalescence, during which he is said to have had a conversion

Left *Colour engraving of Ignatius of Loyola (c.1500).*

experience. Having no strong convictions of faith up to then, he reported suddenly having a vision of Mary, the Blessed Virgin, with Jesus beside her.

The experience inspired Ignatius to go to the Benedictine abbey at Montserrat. There he duly laid his sword and dagger upon the altar, and sought a cave nearby to take up life as a hermit.

TRAINING THE SPIRIT

Ignatius imposed a harsh lifestyle on himself, going without food for long periods, scourging his body daily, and immersing himself in prayer.

As word spread, people started visiting him to seek his advice and join him in prayer. But his life of deprivation took its toll and his health suffered. He came to realize that he should not shut himself away from people, but serve them in their spiritual needs.

At the age of 32, Ignatius walked to Jerusalem, despite a permanent limp caused by his war injury. He hoped to convert Muslims but the Franciscan

Left *Detail of Heaven and angels from* The Glorification of Saint Ignatius *(Andrea Pozzo, c.1691–94).*

brothers discouraged him and, fearing for his safety, sent him home. Back in Barcelona, he took up studying and began to preach and to help the needy. However, since he was no priest, this did not endear him to the Church.

SOLDIERS OF CHRIST

In Paris to do further studies, the ambitious young man formed a brotherhood with six friends. Among them was St Francis Xavier who would become the great missionary to the East.

Having now been ordained, Ignatius instructed the group using his own spiritual manual, *Spiritual Exercises.* This work consisted of a four-week course designed to induct new "soldiers of Christ", as Ignatius refered to the members of his brotherhood. They gave themselves to chastity and poverty, and determined to teach those without education.

Calling themselves the Society of Jesus, they also pledged to conduct missions in Europe to reclaim souls lost to the Protestant reformers. The pope gave the society his blessing in 1540, and Ignatius was chosen as its general.

RETRIEVING CATHOLICS

Ignatius spent the rest of his life in Rome. He founded a house for converted Jews and hostels for prostitutes. But it was his work in organizing foreign missions that

earned his reputation. His writing and teaching played a pivotal role in drawing believers back to the Roman Catholic Church after the Reformation.

His conviction in the power of prayer and sympathy towards those struggling with Christian principles endeared him to believers. His influence over Church doctrine and teaching has been immense.

Yet Ignatius was criticized in some quarters for being too militaristic and authoritarian. Likewise, the Jesuits, as they were popularly known, have been attacked for their power and political meddling.

Under Ignatius' leadership, the society grew rapidly. By his death, after 16 years of development, the number of Jesuits had increased to more than 1,000 members.

Right Detail of The Vision of St Ignatius of Loyola *(Peter Paul Rubens, 17th century).*

Left St Francis Borgia Helping a Dying Impenitent *(Francisco José de Goya y Lucientes, 1795).*

THE SOCIETY OF JESUS

This order made the usual commitments to chastity, poverty and obedience, but added a fourth vow: absolute loyalty to papal authority. It proved an effective mission in post-Reformation Europe.

Chief among their European missions was that led by St Francis Borgia (1510–72), described as the order's "second founder". St Aloysius Gonzago (1568–91) nursed plague victims and wrote important texts. And St Stanislaus Kostka (1550–68) gained fame as a Jesuit mystic.

In the 16th century, missions were set up in Brazil, China, India, Japan and Malaysia. Two martyrs, St Francis Xavier (1506–51) and St Modeste Andlauer (1847–1900), served these missions. The society has since spread worldwide.

"DEAREST JESUS, TEACH US TO BE GENEROUS;
TO SERVE THEE AS THOU DESERVEST;
TO GIVE, AND NOT TO COUNT THE COST;
TO FIGHT, AND NOT TO HEED THE WOUNDS;
TO TOIL, AND NOT TO SEEK FOR REST;
TO LABOUR, AND TO SEEK FOR NO REWARD,
SAVE THAT OF KNOWING THAT WE DO THY
   HOLY WILL."

PRAYER OF ST IGNATIUS OF LOYOLA

FRANCIS XAVIER

THE JESUIT WHO DEVOTED HIS LIFE TO SPREADING THE GOSPEL TO DISTANT LANDS PLANTED THE FAITH AS FAR EAST AS JAPAN. HE EXTENDED THE CHURCH FURTHER THAN ANY OTHER MISSIONARY.

KEY FACTS

Missionary to the East
DATES: *1506–51*
BIRTH PLACE: *Xavier Castle, Navarre*
PATRON OF: *India, Pakistan, Outer Mongolia, missions, Spanish tourism, and the pelota players of Argentina*
FEAST DAY: *3 December*
EMBLEM: *Jesuit cassock, holding a crucifix, baptism bowl, heart and pilgrim's hat*

A poor linguist and sufferer from seasickness, St Francis Xavier was nevertheless eager to carry the message of Christ to far-off lands. He was born in the Basque region and studied in Paris, where he met Ignatius of Loyola. With him and five others, they formed the Society of Jesus, popularly known as the Jesuits.

After the men were ordained as priests in 1534, Ignatius sent Francis to join Father Simon Rodriguez in Lisbon. Seven years later the young missionary set sail for Goa, western India.

After a journey lasting over a year, he landed to find a decadent Portuguese community of clerks and merchants who had abandoned their Christian ideals and virtues. Francis lived simply among the people and hoped to encourage them as converts by setting lessons to their music.

Through his example as a Christian, he tried to counteract the greed of the cruel colonists.

For seven years he travelled through southern India, Ceylon (now Sri Lanka) and Malaysia, sleeping on the floor and living off rice and water.

Always having a bowl to hold water for baptism, Francis converted many, especially among the Parava tribe, who still follow the faith to this day.

TO THE FAR EAST

In 1549, Francis ventured to Japan where he translated the key tenets of Christianity. By currying the favour of the ruling Mikado, he was given the use of an empty

Left St Francis Xavier (artist unknown c.1545).

Buddhist temple to practise his faith. He established a Christian community, but it was subject to persecution in future years.

In 1552, Francis briefly returned to Goa but felt compelled to reach out to new horizons. The conviction that the unbaptized were condemned to an eternity in hell drove Francis to preach in China, then a country closed to all foreigners.

Horribly seasick during the journey, he asked to be left on a small island, Chang-Chuen-Shan, near Hong Kong. Unable to make the crossing to the mainland, he took a gamble and went with a Chinese man who promised to sneak him into China.

Alas, he was abandoned. Being exposed to bad weather and weak from malnutrition, Francis died before arriving. His coffin was packed with lime, to preserve the corpse, and taken to Goa. His body proved incorruptible and is enshrined in a church there.

Left St Francis Xavier and his entourage in a detail from a folding screen (Japanese School, 16th century).

PIUS V

A STERN REFORMER WHO TOLERATED NO LAXITY AMONG HIS OWN KIND WAS JUST AS RUTHLESS IN STAMPING OUT THE MUSLIM PRESENCE IN EASTERN EUROPE.

KEY FACTS
Pope
DATES: *1504–72*
BIRTH PLACE: *Bosco, Italy*
FEAST DAY: *30 April*
EMBLEM: *Papal vestments*

St Pius V entered the Church when he was a youth of 15, and became a diligent priest. He held office as bishop, cardinal and inquisitor-general before being appointed pope in 1566.

At this time the Church was in a fragile state. Congregations had turned to the new churches of the Reformation. Morale was low among the clergy. The previous pope was infamous for his nepotism. The pope before him was the unpopular Paul IV, the fanatical priest Caraffa, who suppressed Protestantism by violent means.

PAPAL POLICY

Pius V started his reign as he meant to continue it. The Church was to be an example of discipline, modest living and charity. The usual lavish party to celebrate papal ordination was cancelled. Instead, the money went to fund hospitals and the poor.

He insisted bishops live in their own diocese, not luxuriate in Rome. Priests were commanded to teach the faith to the young within their parishes. The Roman Catechism, the statement of belief, was completed after years of preparation, and translated into different languages. The Missal was reformed as well.

Although Pius's methods were stern, congregations approved of his reforms. During his papacy, he led the Inquisition, determined to stamp out Islam inside Europe. At a political level, he allowed papal ships to join those of Spain and Venice in an alliance that defeated the Turks at the Battle of Lepanto in 1571. This victory proved decisive in breaking Muslim power in the eastern Mediterranean region.

In England, however, Pius V disappointed Catholics by not insisting they fall under the authority of the Roman Church. Indeed, his excommunication of Queen Elizabeth I only led to further persecutions of Catholics in that country, including the destruction of their legal rights.

But in Europe, many Catholics admired his leadership. They saw him as a hero against the Turks and Protestantism, and as a pope who strengthened the Roman Catholic Church and encouraged his flock.

Right Pope Pius V *(Scipione Pulzone, 1570).*

THERESA OF ÁVILA

THIS DEVOUT NUN COURTED CONTROVERSY DURING HER LIFETIME BY CHALLENGING THE ESTABLISHED CARMELITE ORDER AND BY CLAIMING NUMEROUS VISIONS AND COMMUNICATIONS WITH CHRIST.

KEY FACTS

Mystic, virgin
DATES: *1515–82*
BIRTH PLACE: *Avila, Spain*
PATRON OF: *Spain, Spanish Catholic writers, Carmelites*
FEAST DAY: *15 October*
EMBLEM: *Pen and book, an angel, burning lance or arrow*

Theresa de Capeda y Ahumada was born at Ávila to a wealthy Castilian family. She was a bright, independent girl whose piety was evident from an early age. After her mother's death, her father sent her to an Augustinian convent, where she discovered her calling to the Church. Aged 20, and against her father's wishes, she entered a Carmelite convent. Within a short time, however, Theresa was taken gravely ill and left the convent to be cared for by her family. Although she never regained full health, she returned to the Carmelites where she enjoyed the sociable, relaxed environment of the Order.

Following the death of her father in 1543, Theresa became committed to a more private,

Above Detail of the Ecstasy of Saint Theresa, *held in the Church of Santa Maria della Vittoria in Rome (Gianlorenzo Bernini, c.1645–52).*

contemplative life. One particular incident changed her life: she collapsed in front of an image of Christ, later waking and realizing she must renounce all worldly emotion and live only for Him.

VISIONARY

From the moment of her conversion, Theresa had visions and went into deep spiritual trances when she prayed. She felt misunderstood by her fellow nuns who were dismissive of her mystic experiences. For the rest of her life she continued to have rapturous visions. In particular, she suffered a pain in her side, inflicted, she claimed, by an angel who thrust a burning lance into her heart. Her powers of contemplation developed into a deep devotion and she referred to herself as "Theresa of Jesus".

REFORMER

After meeting Peter of Alcantara, Theresa was moved to follow his example of strict penance and mental prayer. She requested permission from the pope to open a small house. The order would be named St Joseph after her patron saint. When the secret plans were revealed, the Carmelite nuns and influential people of Ávila asked the pope to stop them. Theresa appealed to Spain's King Philip II, who resented Rome's authority. This caused angry confrontation between Church and state and Theresa was imprisoned for two

Below Theresa of Ávila's Vision of a Dove (Peter Paul Rubens, c.1614).

"ST THERESA, GRANT THAT MY EVERY THOUGHT, DESIRE AND AFFECTION MAY BE CONTINUALLY DIRECTED TO DOING THE WILL OF GOD, WHETHER I AM IN JOY OR IN PAIN, FOR HE IS WORTHY TO BE LOVED AND OBEYED FOREVER. OBTAIN FOR ME THIS GRACE, THOU WHO ART SO POWERFUL WITH GOD; MAY I BE ALL ON FIRE, LIKE THEE, WITH THE HOLY LOVE OF GOD."

PRAYER OF INTERCESSION TO ST THERESA OF ÁVILA

years before she was permitted to open a Carmelite sub-group. Her nuns, known as Discalced, or Barefoots, wore coarse brown habits and rope sandals to show their lives of poverty.

During the next few years, Theresa travelled across Spain establishing convents. Her nuns were separated from the world, lived on alms, were forbidden to eat meat, and were instructed by Theresa in meditation.

She founded 16 convents and 14 monasteries, because men, too, wanted to take the vows of the Discalced. These male orders were organized with the help of another mystic, John of the Cross.

Below The Communion of St Theresa of Ávila *(Claudio Coello, 17th century).*

Left Saint Theresa of Ávila *(Gregorio Fernandez, 1625).*

Theresa's writings are testament to her great personal devotion and her thoughts on a life of prayer and contemplation. Chief among her works are *The Interior Castle* and *The Way of Perfection*. The books, which describe the journey of the "soul toward a perfect unity with God", continue to be published in numerous languages.

Theresa of Ávila died at the convent of Alba de Tormes. The odour of violets and sweet oil emanated from her tomb. It was opened and a hand was cut off illicitly, and this was found to work miracles. Her remains were reburied in 1585 in a tomb built by the Duke of Alba. Theresa was canonized by Pope Gregory XV in 1622, and declared a Doctor of the Church in 1970, the first woman to win this recognition. Her order continues to prove the need for retreat and prayer in the modern world.

ST PETER OF ALCANTARA

St Theresa of Ávila was inspired by the life and teachings of another great mystic, Peter of Alcantara. Born Peter Garavito, he was ordained a Franciscan, but longed for a more rigorous discipline. In 1538, he became head of the strict order in Estremadura, Spain, but met with opposition when he tried to reform them further. He went on to found a small, reformed Alcantrine Franciscan order at a friary in Pedrosa. Peter encouraged Theresa to follow his rules of avoiding meat and wine, and walking barefoot. His treatise on prayer and meditation has been translated into many languages. He was canonized in 1669.

Above St Peter of Alcantara *visited by a dove (engraving by A. Masson after a painting by Francisco de Zurbarán, c.1560).*

LUIS BERTRAN

LUIS BERTRAN WAS A GIFTED PREACHER WHO CONVERTED THOUSANDS OF SOUTH AMERICAN INDIANS AND CARIBBEAN ISLANDERS TO CHRISTIANITY.

KEY FACTS
Missionary in the New World
DATES: *1526–81*
BIRTH PLACE: *Valencia, Spain*
PATRON OF: *Colombia*
FEAST DAY: *9 October*
EMBLEM: *Dominican habit*

A Dominican priest with a serious nature, Luis Bertran was a great preacher and apostle, known for his austerity. For many years, he trained Dominican novices and was admired for his teaching, profound wisdom and counselling skills. Theresa of Ávila is said to have turned to him for advice when she was reforming the Carmelite Order.

Athough he spent most of his life in his native Valencia, Luis' most significant work was carried out during his six years as a missionary to Latin America. In 1562, he was sent to a Dominican priory in Cartagena, Colombia, where he began to preach through an interpreter.

There are stories that his mission was successful because he inspired his listeners through an exhilarating combination of prophecy, miracles and talking in tongues. Certainly, his conversion rate was high – he baptized thousands of people during his travels around South America and the Caribbean Islands.

Recalled to Valencia in 1568, Louis began to train preachers for the missions. He emphasized the importance of prayer, simple Christian living and the need to reinforce words with actions.

Luis Bertran was one of the very first missionaries to speak out against the greed, cruelty and violence of many of the Spanish conquistadors. He was taken ill in Valencia Cathedral and died 18 months later.

JOHN OF THE CROSS

JOHN OF THE CROSS IS ONE OF SPAIN'S GREATEST MYSTICAL THEOLOGIANS, LOVED FOR THE BEAUTY OF HIS POETRY AND PITIED FOR THE SUFFERING THAT HE WAS MADE TO ENDURE.

KEY FACTS
Poet and mystic
DATES: *1542–91*
BIRTH PLACE: *Near Avila, Spain*
PATRON OF: *Mystics, poets*
FEAST DAY: *14 December*
EMBLEM: *Carmelite habit, book*

B orn to a poor but noble Spanish family, John of the Cross attended a Jesuit college and became a Carmelite friar in 1563.

Theresa of Ávila inspired John with her reform of the Carmelite Order, the Decalced (Barefoot) Carmelites. With Theresa's help, he set up a Decalced Carmelite friary in a hovel in Duruelo.

The Carmelite Order rejected their reforms, and in 1575 John of the Cross was imprisoned. Subjected to extremely harsh treatment, John found expression for his suffering in poetry dedicated to his search for, and love of, God. After nine months he escaped and continued his spiritual work,

founding a college at Baeza and working at monasteries in Granada and Segovia.

At the end of his life, John was once again harshly treated, this time by the Decalced Carmelites who now found his views too moderate. He died in 1591 after having written some of the most moving poetry in Christian literature, such as *The Dark Night of the Soul*, *The Spiritual Canticle* and *The Living Flame of Love*.

Left St John of the Cross *(Joaquín Vaquero Turcios, 20th century).*

PETER CANISIUS

CATHOLICS AND PROTESTANTS ALIKE ADMIRED ST PETER CANISIUS FOR HIS MODERATION DURING A PERIOD OF STRIFE AMONG CHRISTIANS IN THE 16TH CENTURY.

Peter Canisius rejected a legal career and marriage in Holland to join the Society of Jesus, or Jesuits. In 1552, he was sent to revive the Roman Catholic Church in Vienna, where he found deserted monasteries and many lapsed believers.

He applied all his energy to teaching the faith and strengthening the Catholic Church. He skilfully avoided confrontation with the Protestants by emphasizing a common belief in Christ's teachings. He also won the respect of the Viennese by nursing the sick during the plague.

KEY FACTS
Jesuit Doctor of the Church
DATES: *1521–97*
BIRTH PLACE: *Nijmegen, Holland*
PATRON OF: *Germany, Catholic press, catechism writers*
FEAST DAY: *21 December*
EMBLEM: *Jesuit habit*

Canisius quickly recognized the importance of the printing presses flourishing at this time. His numerous writings persuaded thousands to return to the Church, and his Catechism (1555), was translated into 15 languages. He helped found the University of Fribourg in Switzerland, where he died in 1597.

Left Peter Canisius the Preacher *(attr. to Pierre Wuilleret, c.1635).*

PHILIP NERI

PHILIP NERI, THE APOSTLE OF ROME, WAS A MAN OF GREAT INTUITION AND HUMOUR WHOSE PATIENCE AND GOOD ADVICE WON HIM MANY SUPPORTERS AMONG THE PEOPLE OF ROME.

Kindly and charismatic, Philip Neri founded a brotherhood devoted to welfare. In 1533, he abandoned business to live in poverty in Rome. His charisma drew loyal followers to him. In 1548, he set up a fraternity to care for the sick and the many pilgrims to the city.

After he was ordained in 1551, he formed the Congregation of the Oratory in San Girolamo. His followers took no vows and did not abandon their property or dedicate their lives to a monastic community. Pope Gregory XIII approved the order in 1575.

KEY FACTS
Founder of the Congregation of the Oratory in Rome
DATES: *1515–95*
BIRTH PLACE: *Florence, Italy*
FEAST DAY: *26 May*
EMBLEM: *Bell, book*

The Holy See called for Philip's advice in 1593 when it was reluctant to recognize Henry IV of France, a former Protestant. Philip told them to forgive the king for his lapse.

Philip died in 1595 and was so well loved that he was instantly recognized as a saint. The Oratory Order is found all over the Catholic world.

Left The interior of the 19th-century Brompton Oratory in London, dedicated to Philip Neri.

ROYAL SAINTS

MANY MONARCHS ARE VENERATED FOR THEIR BRAVE DEFENCE OF CHRISTIANITY. SOME GAVE THEIR LIVES FOR THAT CAUSE; OTHERS RULED WITH ESPECIAL WISDOM AND BENEVOLENCE.

It may be difficult to reconcile the virtuous qualities of sainthood with the characteristics of the rich and mighty, but many saints were, in fact, also powerful monarchs. In their privileged positions, these holy men and women ruled with great fortitude, promoting Christianity through example and sacrifice.

Left St Cunegund, empress and wife of Henry II, holding the model of a church (the Master of Messkirch, c.1530–38).

Right Edward the Confessor in stained glass from Canterbury, England (15th century).

WARRIOR SAINTS
Many kings have been involved in warfare, protecting their borders and Christianity on behalf of their countrymen. Some, including Vladimir and Alexander Nevski, were soldiers. These early rulers of Russia used arms to quell invaders but proved righteous monarchs.

Henry II, another militant man, went to war to establish the borders of Germany and became emperor in 1014. After this, he turned to his religion and prayer, built monasteries, and promoted welfare for the poor. He was said to be so pious that his marriage was never consummated. Henry II was canonized in 1146, while his wife Cunegund was canonized in 1200.

Other saintly warrior kings include Stephen of Hungary, who limited the power of the nobles, reduced tribal tensions and installed a judicial system. Stephen made Hungary a Christian country, and was a heroic leader.

SPREADING THE FAITH
As Christianity began to take root in Europe, monarchs played a vital role in imparting the faith to their subjects. English kings, such as Ethelbert of Kent and Oswald, were pioneers of the faith and venerated for encouraging the

first Christian missions. Edward the Confessor was known for his visions and miraculous cures of the ill. He devoted much of his time to the establishment of the Church and the monasteries in England and was loved for his kind and fair rule.

Norway's patron saint, King Olaf, established the Christian faith among his people and, after

"DEAR SON, IF YOU COME TO REIGN, DO THAT WHICH BEFITS A KING, THAT IS, BE SO JUST AS TO DEVIATE IN NOTHING FROM JUSTICE, WHATEVER MAY BEFALL YOU."

ST LOUIS, KING OF FRANCE

Above A statue of Stephen of Hungary near the Freedom Bridge in Budapest, Hungary.

his death in battle, was credited with miracles and a healing spring that began to flow from his grave.

MARTYRED MONARCHS

Several Christian monarchs have been martyred for their faith. One was the English boy king, Edward the Martyr, who was killed in AD 979 in a power struggle for the throne. Another, Edmund of Abingdon, was cruelly murdered by Viking invaders when he refused to deny his faith.

Two Scandinavian kings, Canute of Denmark and Eric of Sweden, also gave their lives for their Christian beliefs. Canute's murder at an altar was followed by many miracles and wonders. Sweden became a Christian country under Eric, but he was tortured and beheaded by attacking soldiers. These Scandinavian kings had large cultuses until the Reformation, when the Protestant movement began to overwhelm the Roman Catholic Church in northern Europe.

QUEENLY SAINTS

By the 11th century, the Scots had a pious queen. Margaret of Scotland was recognized for both her devotion to her family and her deep faith, as witnessed by her charitable work for the poor and for prisoners.

Elizabeth of Portugal was married to King Denis of Portugal. He was a violent man, but she converted him to the faith. She brought comfort and aid to orphans and "fallen women", and founded hospitals. Pilgrims and the very poor turned to her for hospitality and care.

Her distant relative, after whom she was named, Elizabeth of Hungary, likewise established hospitals, as well as founding the first orphanage in central Europe. The final part of her life was austere, poverty-stricken and devoted to prayer and charity. Her relics at the church of St Elizabeth at Marburg drew hordes of pilgrims until, in 1539, the Lutheran Philip of Hesse removed them and hid them in an unknown site.

Right A portrait of St Vladimir (anonymous Russian artist, 1905).

Although many later monarchs continued to support the Catholic Church and to exercise their rule with Christian values, few European kings or queens were canonized after the Reformation.

KING LOUIS IX OF FRANCE

Louis IX took up arms for his faith, but he dedicated much of his life to spiritual causes. His subjects knew him as a man who was severe in his habits, devoting long hours to prayer. He built monasteries and a hospital for the poor. He was also admired for his efforts to show justice, even though his courtiers sometimes thwarted his good intentions. His courage in fighting for Christendom aroused great respect and he led two crusades, meeting his death at Tunis in 1270. During this last expedition, Louis tried to reconcile the Greeks to the Church of Rome.

Above King Louis IX of France (St Louis) embarking on his first Crusade in 1248 (manuscript illumination, c.1325).

185

TURIBIUS OF LIMA

TURIBIUS WAS A TIRELESS APOSTLE, BLESSED WITH INTELLIGENCE AND A STRONG MORAL SENSE. HE SPOKE NUMEROUS LOCAL DIALECTS, WHICH ENDEARED HIM TO THE PEOPLE OF PERU.

KEY FACTS
Archbishop and missionary
DATES: *1538–1606*
BIRTH PLACE: *Mayorga, Spain*
PATRON OF: *Bishops of Latin America*
FEAST DAY: *23 March*
EMBLEM: *Archbishop's vestments*

Turibius Alfonso de Mogrobejo was born in Spain and studied law at the University of Salamanca. His reputation as a scholar and professor led to his appointment as chief judge of the Inquisition Court, and to his becoming Archbishop of Lima. He protested his inadequacy for the latter post – an unusual appointment as he was a layman – but took orders and was made archbishop before travelling to Peru in 1581.

As he visited the members of his vast new diocese, he found immorality and tyranny to be rife amongst the Spanish colonists. He saw that their Peruvian converts were not given the benefit of good Christian teaching and set about reforming the communities by building churches and hospitals. In 1591, he established the first seminary in the Americas.

Turibius was sensitive and considerate to his congregation, and his kindness encouraged trust. His implacable stand against tyranny was so effective that many converted to the faith. He died in Santa, Peru, having achieved considerable success in his mission.

Above The monastery of St Turibius of Lima in Potes, Spain.

FRANCIS SOLANO

THIS DEDICATED MISSIONARY SHOWED PROFOUND COMPASSION FOR HUMAN SUFFERING AND BECAME KNOWN AS "THE APOSTLE OF AMERICA", WINNING NUMEROUS CONVERTS TO CHRISTIANITY.

KEY FACTS
Missionary
DATES: *1549–1610*
BIRTH PLACE: *Montilla, near Córdoba, Spain*
PATRON OF: *Peru, Bolivia, Paraguay, Uruguay, Chile and Argentina*
FEAST DAY: *14 July*
EMBLEM: *Franciscan habit*

Local legend has it that Francis Solano addressed his congregation in one language but was understood by everyone, irrespective of their tongue. In fact, the Franciscan priest was a gifted linguist and this talent helped him make many converts.

Ordained as a priest in Seville in 1576, Francis spent several years in the Franciscan convent before travelling to the Americas in 1589. His ship was destined for Peru but was wrecked on the way and abandoned by the Spanish crew. Francis rescued 80 African slaves, who were on board, encouraging them to cling to a section of the ship. Inspired by his prayers, they landed in Lima after two months at sea.

Left Seville Cathedral, Spain, where Francis Solano was ordained in 1576. It is the largest Roman Catholic cathedral in the world.

Francis spent the next 20 years evangelizing in Argentina, Chile, Colombia and Peru. He charmed his congregation by playing his lute in veneration of Mary, the Blessed Virgin, and they often joined him in song. Later, as Guardian of Lima, Francis aroused anger because of his attacks on corrupt colonists. Nevertheless, his death was the cause of widespread grief. His relics are kept in Buenos Aires and Rome.

ROSE OF LIMA

IN 1671, ROSE OF LIMA WAS CANONIZED BY POPE CLEMENT X, THUS BECOMING THE FIRST OFFICIALLY RECOGNIZED SAINT OF THE NEW WORLD. SHE IS THE PATRON OF SOUTH AMERICA.

KEY FACTS

First saint of the New World
DATE: *1586–1617*
BIRTH PLACE: *Lima, Peru*
PATRON OF: *Peru, Bolivia, Central and South America, the Philippines*
FEAST DAY: *23 August*
EMBLEM: *Crown of roses*

As a young woman, Rose was so mortified by her own beauty that she rubbed her face and hands with pepper and lye to ruin her complexion. This pious child was born to modest parents and christened Isabel, though she was always known as Rose. She chose to model herself on St Catherine of Siena by living a life of purity and self-denial. Though her parents were anxious for her to marry, Rose vowed to remain a virgin and became a tertiary of the Dominican Order. However, she remained a conscientious daughter, working to help her parents by growing flowers and making exquisite lace to sell at the local market.

EXTREME PENANCE

To bring herself closer to God, Rose built a hut in her parents' garden and lived there in virtual seclusion. In imitation of Christ, who was forced to wear a crown of thorns, she wore on her head a circlet of silver studded inside with small spikes. She prayed for long hours, often in spiritual despair because she felt she was not worthy of God's love.

Throughout this time, she faced constant ridicule from her community and fierce opposition from her parents. Her self-inflicted penances were so extreme that she attracted the attention of the Church, which held an inquiry into her behaviour. Her friend, the

Below A ceiling painting in Rome showing Mary crowning St Rose of Lima (Lazzaro Baldi, 17th century).

archbishop St Turibius of Lima, defended her, and the Church eventually conceded that her visions and mystic exaltations were holy and true.

CARE FOR THE SICK

In spite of her own suffering, Rose spent much time among the sick and needy of Lima. However, after many years of physical deprivation, her health

Left A statue of Rose of Lima outside the Mission San Francisco de Asís, California (20th century).

declined and she was taken to live with the government official Don Gonzales de Massa and his wife, who nursed her through a long and painful illness. They later testified as to the words she used in prayer, "Lord, increase my sufferings, and with them increase thy love in my heart".

By the time Rose died in 1617 – still only a young woman at the age of 31 – her holiness was widely recognized. The people of Lima went into mourning. Dominicans, city dignitaries and officials took it in turn to carry her coffin to the grave. Her example still holds much power.

ROBERT BELLARMINE

AMONG HIS MANY ACHIEVEMENTS, THE BRILLIANT THEOLOGIAN ROBERT BELLARMINE WAS RESPONSIBLE FOR CORRECTING THE VULGATE BIBLE AND WRITING A CATECHISM, BOTH IN USE TODAY.

KEY FACTS
Archbishop and theologian
DATES: *1542–1621*
BIRTH PLACE: *Montepulciano, Tuscany, Italy*
PATRON OF: *Catechists and catechumens*
FEAST DAY: *17 September*
EMBLEM: *Archbishop's vestments*

This great Italian archbishop chose a life of service to God over a secular career. Despite his father's wishes that he become a politician, Robert Bellarmine entered a novitiate in Rome and went on to teach in Jesuit colleges in Rome and Florence.

GIFTED THEOLOGIAN

After his ordination in 1570, Robert became the first Jesuit professor of the University of Louvain. It was here that his writings and lectures began to stir strong feelings and debate. The Church brought him to Milan as professor of controversial theology at the Roman College. The lectures he gave there formed the basis of one of his greatest works, *Disputations on the Controversies of the Christian Faith*, which is described as "the most complete defence of Catholic teaching yet published". It was read eagerly by all Christians, although his enemies

Above St Robert Bellarmine, in a painting from the church of Sant-Ignazio in Rome.

Below The trial of Galileo by Pope Urban VIII during the Inquisition in 1633 (Italian School, 17th century).

denounced it as being so clever it must have been the joint effort of several Jesuit scholars. The work was banned in England.

CONTROVERSY

Robert continued to attract controversy when his stand on the power of the Church was opposed by the French and by James I of England because he insisted the pope had complete authority above that of any monarch. His *De potestate papae* on this subject was burnt by the Paris parlement. Then, contrary to other Church leaders at the time, Robert was gentle with Galileo, asking him only to produce better evidence about the sun's movements.

Appointed Archbishop of Capua in 1602, Robert dedicated his time to preaching and to attending to his parish. His last appointment, in 1605, was as Prefect of the Vatican Library.

SIMPLE LIFE, NOBLE DEATH

All his life, Robert Bellarmine lived on the bread and garlic diet of a peasant, denied himself fires in winter and gave his possessions to the poor. In old age, he continued to write, and his *Art of Dying* was translated into many languages. He died in Rome, but he had asked beforehand that the day of his death be marked each anniversary as a time to honour the Stigmata of St Francis of Assisi. The Church granted this request.

FRANCIS OF SALES

THE FIRST SOLEMN BEATIFICATION TO TAKE PLACE IN ST PETER'S IN ROME WAS THAT OF ST FRANCIS OF SALES, A SAINT WHO WAS ADORED FOR HIS GENTLE LEADERSHIP.

KEY FACTS
Founder, Doctor of the Church
DATES: *1567–1622*
BIRTH PLACE: *Château de Sales, Savoy, France*
PATRON OF: *Journalists, editors and writers*
FEAST DAY: *24 January*
EMBLEM: *Archbishop's vestments*

Francis of Sales was physically frail from birth, but had a determined spirit and an unwavering faith. From an early age, he longed to join the Church. But his father refused his permission, instead sending Francis to study at the University of Paris. He later became a Doctor of Law at Padua in Italy. When a relative found Francis a position as provost to the Jesuit chapter in Geneva, his father finally relented and Francis was ordained.

MISSIONARY PRIEST

Francis volunteered as a missionary to Chablais, where he distributed notices explaining his work and Christ's message to attract his reluctant congregation. Trekking through isolated hamlets, he met many dangers, including an attack by a wolf and another by an angry mob. Yet, slowly, lapsed Catholics began to seek his guidance.

His success was acknowledged, and in 1602, the Church appointed him Bishop of Geneva. Francis lived in Annecy, where he was a popular preacher and began to compile his handwritten texts into books. His most famous work is the *Introduction to the Devout Life*. In addition to his writing, Francis was instrumental in the founding of the Order of the Visitation with his friend, St Jane Frances de Chantal in 1610.

In 1622, Francis accepted an invitation to join the Duke of Savoy at Avignon, hoping to gain

Left St Francis de Sales in the Desert *(Marco Antonio Franceschini, c.1700–10).*

privileges for his community. In every village he passed, people wanted him to stop and minister to them. It was bitterly cold, but Francis continued to preach throughout Advent and Christmas, before becoming ill and dying at a Visitandine convent in Lyons.

Right St Francis of Sales *(Noel Halle, 18th century).*

ROQUE GONZALEZ

ALTHOUGH ROQUE GONZALEZ SPENT TWO DECADES PROTECTING THE FREEDOM OF INDIGENOUS PEOPLE IN SOUTH AMERICA, HE WAS MARTYRED FOR HIS FAITH, ALONG WITH TWO FELLOW MISSIONARIES.

KEY FACTS
Martyr of Paraguay
DATES: *1576–1628*
BIRTH PLACE: *Asunción,
Paraguay*
PATRON OF: *Posadas, Argentina,
and Encarnación, Paraguay*
FEAST DAY: *17 November*

Roque Gonzalez was born into a noble Spanish family in Asunción, Paraguay, and raised a strict Catholic. He was ordained in 1599 and ten years later joined the Jesuits to pursue his dream of becoming a missionary.

THE REDUCTIONS

Gonzalez was instrumental in founding the Reductions, an organization that created settlements for local tribes in which they could learn about Christianity. The Jesuits were passionately opposed to slavery and sought to teach, nurse and bring solace to the converts.

Without complaint, Roque endured bad weather, insects, illness and hunger, but his biggest problems came from the European "guardians". The Spanish authorities demanded that these officials be present on every mission, but they were disdainful, even brutal,

Left A statue standing in the ruins of a Jesuit mission near Encarnación in Paraguay.

toward the indigenous people. This did not reflect on Roque, whose courtesy and simplicity won the admiration of numerous converts. He taught them valuable skills such as building and farming, and established churches and schools. After three years in the

Reduction of St Ignatius of Loyola, Roque travelled east of the Parana and Uruguay Rivers, establishing six more communities.

In 1628, he was joined by Alonso Rodriguez and Juan de Castillo, also brothers of the Jesuit Reductions. They opened another Reduction near the Ijuhi River. Juan de Castillo was selected to stay there, while Roque and Alonso trekked to an even wilder area – Caaró, now part of southern Brazil.

OPPOSITION AND MURDER

Now, however, the missionaries met with hostility from the local medicine man, who incited some local tribesmen to attack the priest. Giving him no opportunity to defend himself, they brutally murdered him with their tomahawks. They killed Alonso, too, then dragged their bodies into the church the men had built and set it alight. A few days later, Juan de Castillo was beaten and murdered at the Ijuhi River mission.

Although these sad events were reported, the records were lost until the 19th century, when they were discovered in archives kept in Argentina. All three men were canonized as the Martyrs of Paraguay in 1988.

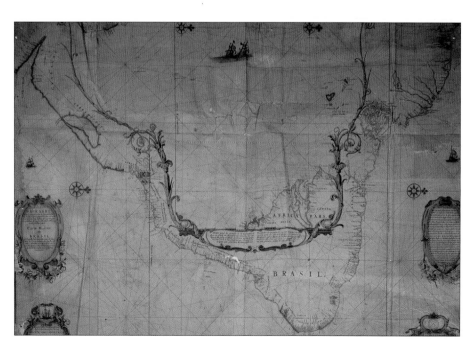

Left A map of Brazil by a Dutch cartographer in the early 17th century.

LORENZO RUIZ

THE FIRST FILIPINO SAINT WAS AFRAID OF MARTYRDOM, BUT HIS FAITH SUSTAINED HIM SO THAT, FACING DEATH, HE PROCLAIMED, "I AM A CATHOLIC AND HAPPY TO DIE FOR GOD".

KEY FACTS
Martyr of Japan
DATES: *1600–37*
BIRTH PLACE: *Binondo, Manila, Philippines*
PATRON OF: *Filipino youth*
FEAST DAY: *28 September*

Married with three children, Lorenzo was a member of the lay brotherhood, the Holy Rosary. In 1636 he was falsely accused of murder and, fearing an unfair trial and imprisonment, he sought refuge with the Dominicans. He sailed to Japan with Father Antonio Gonzalez and others.

On their arrival in Okinawa, the Emperor Tokugawa Yemitsu ordered the ship's Christians to be arrested. Faced by a tribunal in Nagasaki, a frightened Lorenzo asked if a denunciation of Christianity would bring release.

His translator consulted the judges, but Lorenzo found his courage and cried out, "I am a Christian." His brave confession brought terrible retribution. He was burnt, hung upside down and beheaded, and his body was thrown into the sea. Lorenzo was one of 17 people martyred by the Emperor. They were canonized as Martyrs of Japan in 1987.

Left The Franciscan Martyrs in Japan *(Don Juan Carreño de Miranda, 17th century).*

MARTIN DE PORRES

THE LIFE OF MARTIN DE PORRES WAS ONE OF HUMBLE DEVOTION. HE IS VENERATED FOR HIS CONSTANT, UNASSUMING SERVICE TO THE POOR AND HIS MIRACULOUS CURES OF THE SICK.

KEY FACTS
Charity worker
DATES: *1579–1639*
BIRTH PLACE: *Lima, Peru*
PATRON OF: *Social justice, public education, public health service, people of mixed race, Italian barbers and hairdressers*
FEAST DAY: *3 November*

Martin de Porres was one of two illegitimate children born to a Spanish knight and a freed black woman. His mother apprenticed the 12-year-old Martin to a barber-surgeon, from whom he learned to care for the sick. Three years later, he was admitted to the Dominican Convent of the Holy Rosary, first as a lay brother and later as a coadjutor brother.

Here, Martin helped to establish a hospital and an orphanage. He also welcomed African slaves, who were comforted on their arrival in Lima. Animals loved

Above St Martin de Porres *(artist and date unknown).*

him, and it was said he could feed a dog, cat and mouse from the same bowl. One of his many duties at the convent was to handle the alms for the poor, and his careful budgeting allowed him to feed and clothe hundreds of needy people in the city.

Martin was acquainted with St Rose of Lima, and when he died, as at her funeral, noblemen and Church officials were honoured to carry his coffin to its grave.

PETER CLAVER

THIS SPANISH MISSIONARY WAS BLESSED "BY GOD WITH THOSE GIFTS THAT PARTICULARLY PERTAIN TO APOSTLES, OF MIRACLES, OF PROPHECY AND OF READING HEARTS".

KEY FACTS
Missionary
DATES: *1580–1654*
BIRTH PLACE: *Verdu, Catalonia, Spain*
PATRON OF: *Colombia; missions to slaves and African Americans*
FEAST DAY: *9 September*

In the late 16th century, the port of Cartagena in Colombia was the centre of a thriving slave trade. Thousands of captive Africans arrived at the port every month. Here, Peter Claver baptized about 300,000 enslaved people and ministered also to traders, sailors, prisoners and others in need.

Born in Catalonia in Spain and educated at the University of Barcelona, Peter Claver's spiritual journey began at the Jesuit college in Majorca. Here, he met Alphonsus Rodriguez, who foretold that they both had a future in South America.

Peter left for Cartagena in 1610, and was ordained there by the Jesuits five years later. Inspired by working alongside Father Alfonso de Sandoval, who had been ministering to the slaves for 40 years, Claver declared himself "the slave of Negroes forever".

Below Sts Peter Claver and Aloysius Gonzaga (St Xavier Church, Amsterdam, Holland).

SAINT PIERRE CLAVER

Left A stained glass showing St Peter Claver (La Chapelle de La Colombière, Chalon sur Saône, France, 1930).

MISSIONARY TO THE SLAVES

Peter would meet the slave ships as they came into the harbour. Conscious of the need for immediate emotional and physical care, he comforted the slaves with his gentle manner and gave them gifts of medicines, food, brandy and lemons. He carried pictures to convey Christ's life and his promise of redemption explaining to his helpers, "we must speak to them with our hands before we try to speak to them with our lips". He later visited the plantations and mines where these slaves were put to work. Refusing the hospitality of the owners, who were not all happy to see him, he stayed in the slaves' quarters.

In 1650, Peter succumbed to a plague, which left him weak and incapacitated. He was confined to his cell. He was neglected by everyone until Dona Isabel de Urbina, who had funded his charities, came to his rescue, and with her sister nursed him. Four years later, Peter took mass before falling into a coma. The people of Cartagena, realizing they were losing an extraordinary priest, were anxious to kiss his hands. Even plantation owners sensed his greatness, and after his death his cell was stripped of relics. He was canonized, along with his friend Alphonsus Rodriguez, in 1888.

JOSEPH OF COPERTINO

CREDITED WITH POWERS OF LEVITATION, AS WELL AS WITH MANY
OTHER MIRACLES, THIS SIMPLE, THOUGH MISUNDERSTOOD, PRIEST
GAINED THE NICKNAME "THE FLYING FRIAR".

KEY FACTS
Mystic, miracle worker
DATES: *1603–63*
BIRTH PLACE: *Copertino, near
Brindisi, Italy*
PATRON OF: *Aviation,
astronauts, students and students'
examinations*
FEAST DAY: *18 September*
EMBLEM: *Flying in Franciscan habit*

The story of Joseph of Copertino is a sad one. His father's death left his mother penniless and she considered the slow-witted Joseph a tiresome burden. He was widely ridiculed and known for his violent temper. He seemed incapable of learning a trade and was rejected by local monasteries until Franciscans at Grottella accepted him as a servant The young boy became serious in his devotions and performed menial tasks without complaint.

Despite his academic struggles, Joseph was ordained in 1628 and legends began to surround him. The mere sight of religious imagery or the mention of holy names sent Joseph into a state of ecstasy during which his body would rise in the air.

INQUISITION AND EXILE

In Joseph's 17 years at Grottella, witnesses recorded 70 incidents of levitation. One extraordinary occurrence reportedly took place during the construction of a cross of Calvary. The centre strut was 11m/36ft high and very heavy. Ten men couldn't lift it, but during the night, Joseph flew through the air, raised the strut and fixed it to the earth.

This behaviour so worried his superiors that he was prohibited from celebrating mass, eating with his brethren or attending processions. As his trances continued, and the public interest in him increased, Joseph was taken for questioning by the Inquisitors in Naples. Finding no fault with him, they sent him to Rome,

Above Pope Urban VIII *(Gianlorenzo Bernini, c. 1625–30), before whom Joseph experienced a religious ecstasy.*

Below St Joseph of Copertino levitates *in front of an image of the Virgin. The saint was known for such ecstasies.*

where, at an audience with Pope Urban VIII, Joseph fell into an ecstasy and the pope decided to send him to Assisi.

With crowds of people seeking out the "Flying Friar", Joseph was exiled to a monastery at Pietrarossa, and was forbidden to speak or write to anyone. When pilgrims continued to clamour for a glimpse of his miracles, he was sent to an even more remote monastery at Fossombrone, and then to Assisi, where he was kept in strict isolation. Although consoled by his visions, Joseph died in solitude. In 1767, he was canonized for his humility and patience.

VINCENT DE PAUL

A CLEVER AND DIPLOMATIC FRENCH PRIEST, ADEPT AT PERSUADING THE WEALTHY TO BE GENEROUS TO THE POOR. TODAY, HIS SOCIETIES CONTINUE HIS TRADITION OF CHARITY AND SOCIAL WELFARE.

KEY FACTS
Founder of charitable orders, hospitals and orphanages
DATES: *1581–1660*
BIRTH PLACE: *Landes, France*
PATRON OF: *Charity workers, hospitals, prisoners, Madagascar*
FEAST DAY: *27 September*
EMBLEM: *White cloak, begging bowl*

Vincent de Paul was born in Gascony to a peasant family, but he escaped the harsh life of a farmer by studying under the Franciscans at Dax and later attending Toulouse University. He was ordained at 19 and undertook a journey to Rome, at which point he seemed to vanish for two years. Historians suspect that he obscured, or even invented, the truth about this time.

In fact, Vincent himself perpetuated the most famous account of these two years through letters he wrote to his patron, a Gascon judge called Monsieur de Comet. He claimed that, on his way from

Above St Vincent de Paul *(attributed to Daniel Dumonstier, 17th century).*

Below St Vincent de Paul and the Sisters of Charity *(Jean Andre, c.1729).*

Toulouse to Narbonne, his ship was overwhelmed by Barbary pirates. He was sold into slavery at Tunis and endured two years there before, appealing to the Christian faith of one of his captors, he managed to escape to Marseilles.

Following this uncertain period, Vincent appeared in Rome, where he was given instructions by Pope Paul V to travel to the French court of Henry IV. Vincent remained in Paris as chaplain to the queen, which gave him access to the rich and powerful members of court. He was charming and kind and able to persuade many wealthy patrons to devote funds to his worthy causes.

CHARITY WORKER

Vincent's sensitivies to the suffering of others came to dominate his thinking. He met, and was profoundly influenced by, Francis of Sales, and expanded his work to found hospitals and orphanages. He also worked to improve the lives of galley slaves and gave missions to prisoners in Bordeaux.

Then, in 1625, he founded an order of priests to preach in remote villages, where they cared for convicts and the poor. From 1633, the men lived in small communal groups and became known as the Vincentians, or Lazarists. The order was so successful in its mission that the Archbishop of Paris

Above An old people's home run by the Sisters of Charity at St Vincent de Paul's hospital in Peking (1900).

asked Vincent to train priests for parish work. For 27 years, Vincent gave weekly conferences, and his priests taught at seminaries around France. They also travelled as missionaries to Madagascar, Poland, Ireland, Scotland and countries in Africa.

Also in 1633, Vincent asked his friend, Louise de Marillac, to help him form an order of women to nurse the sick. At this time, nuns lived in enclosed houses, cut off from public lives. This new order, the Sisters of Charity, took a vow of obedience for one year only,

Above The Church of St Vincent de Paul in Paris (Rouargue Frères, 19th century).

> "IT IS OUR DUTY TO PREFER THE SERVICE OF THE POOR TO EVERY-THING ELSE, AND TO OFFER SUCH SERVICE AS QUICKLY AS POSSIBLE... OFFER THE DEED TO GOD AS YOUR PRAYER."
>
> ST VINCENT DE PAUL

this being the time the Church allowed noviciates to enjoy social contact. They renewed their vows yearly, but Vincent's rule allowed them to take their good works into the wider world.

INFLUENCE
Vincent de Paul had a profound effect on Church reform and was extremely popular and influential in his lifetime. He inspired count-less men and women to care for the dispossessed, and the rich to fund the work. His Sisters of Charity and Vincentians continue to work all around the world, helping the homeless, the debt-ridden, orphans and prisoners. In 1833, Frederick Ozanam, a Frenchman, instituted a lay broth-erhood in the name of Saint Vincent de Paul. The modern worldwide membership of SVP, as this charity is called, includes men and women, Catholics and

LOUISE DE MARILLAC
When Louise de Marillac was widowed in 1625, she devoted herself to the charity work of Vincent de Paul. He depended on her good sense, and she helped found the Sisters of Charity, "whose convent is the sickroom; their chapel their parish church; their cloister, the city streets". She was an inspiring teacher and, under her guidance, women were committed to 40 houses of the Charity, working with the sick and giving shelter to distressed women. She was canonized in 1934. Her feast day is 15 March.

Above Louise de Marillac distributing alms to the poor (Diogène Maillart, 1920).

Protestants. Vincent always insisted that Protestants be treated with courtesy and understanding.

Vincent's teaching of care and service, his gentle faith, and res-olute belief in the sustaining love of God brought him many friends and admirers. He died peacefully and was buried at the church of Saint-Lazare. He was beatified in 1729 and Pope Clement XII canonized him in 1737.

SAINTLY POPES

THE FIRST POPES ARE VENERATED AS MARTYRS OF THE FAITH, BUT MANY OTHERS ARE REVERED FOR THE WISDOM, STRENGTH AND SPIRITUAL LEADERSHIP THEY DEMONSTRATED IN OFFICE.

The role of the papacy has often been fraught with spiritual and political strife. When Christianity was just beginning to be established, during persecution by the Roman Empire, a number of early popes were martyred for their faith. Later, popes struggled to unite the Church, which was being damaged by warring factions and corruption. Many of these holy men have been canonized in recognition of their faithfulness and spiritual leadership.

THE MARTYRS
One of the first popes, Clement I, who died around AD 100, was a contemporary of Sts Peter and Paul. He was credited with miraculous powers, and some of his writings are extant, revealing him as a thoughtful theologian. His Epistle to the Corinthians is significant because it marks the first

> "WHEN THE WORK OF GOD IS FINISHED, LET ALL GO OUT WITH THE DEEPEST SILENCE, AND LET REVERENCE BE SHOWN TO GOD."
>
> FROM THE RULE OF ST BENEDICT

time a bishop of Rome intervened in the business of another Church. Clement I was martyred by having an anchor tied to his neck and being pushed into the sea. Allegedly, angels built him a tomb on the seabed, and this could be seen when the sea was at low tide.

Pope Callistus was born a slave and rebelled against Roman law by promoting marriage between freeborn Christians and slaves. Kind and forgiving, he was thrown

Above A fresco of Leo the Great (Italian School, 8th century AD).

down a well and drowned in AD 222. Pope Cornelius was likewise resented for his policy of forgiveness to those who truly repented their sins. His attitude caused a split among churchmen, and the Romans beheaded him.

Sixtus II, who became pope in AD 257, was killed by the sword one year after he took office.

LEADERS OF THE FAITH
One of the most influential early popes was Leo the Great. During his reign, he freed Rome from the barbarians and healed a Church fractured by war and the spread of pagan beliefs. Both the people and the clergy needed clarification on Christian dogma. In a letter to the Council of Chalcedon, Leo explained that Jesus Christ is one person, in whom the divine and the human are united, but not mixed. This became a fundamental teaching of the Church.

Left Coronation of Pope Celestine V in August 1294 (French School, 16th century).

The Church continued to strengthen under the rule of Pope Gregory the Great, an austere, devout man, who succeeded in establishing the primacy of Rome against claims from the Eastern Orthodox Church. He developed the Church liturgy and mounted a successful mission to England.

Gregory II, too, was an energetic apostle. He instigated reforms in the clergy, built churches and sustained the Church's authority against secular power. The monastery at Monte Cassino was revived under his care, and he built another in Rome, St Paul's-outside-the-Walls.

DIVISION AND REFORM

The problems between the Eastern and Western branches of the Church became urgent during the office of Pope Leo IX (1002–54). Under his rule, the Church increased its independence from secular authority, and he sent legates to confer with Michael Cerularius, Patriarch of Constantinople. Leo died before the schism between the East and West had widened into total separation. Leo was a holy man, and many miracles were attributed to him after his death.

Pope Gregory VII continued his predecessors' reformation of the Church and alienated many powerful people in the process. He was determined to stop the practice of laymen appointing officers of the Church, because these laymen were often the rich

and powerful, who used the clergy to extend their secular ambitions. The German Emperor Henry IV was infuriated by this reform and tried to depose Gregory, though he later famously repented by standing at the palace gates for three days in the snow.

Peter Celestine (or Celestine V) founded the Celestine Order, but was an unwilling and unworldly pope. He abdicated his office but was still canonized for his devout nature in 1313.

In the 16th century, while the Church was still reeling from the Reformation, Pope Pius V provided vigorous leadership. A key figure in the Counter-Reformation, he helped rid the Church of heresy and corruption, controlled excessive spending by the bishops, and reformed the liturgy, making the words and rituals accessible to ordinary worshippers.

Indeed, throughout the centuries, the popes who have attained sainthood are often men who have brought remarkable devotion and wise leadership to the papal office.

Left St Peter's Basilica and Square, Rome, as depicted in the 18th century.

Left Gregory the Great dictating a manuscript (illuminated manuscript, 9th century).

POPE PIUS X

Pope Pius X wanted "to renew all things in Christ". He opened the Church and her liturgy to ordinary people, encouraged daily attendance at Mass and welcomed children to partake of the Holy Eucharist. Church music was modernized, and on Sundays, Pius X would deliver a short sermon in a Vatican courtyard, which anyone was welcome to attend. He faced problems with the French state, and was forced to sacrifice Church property in exchange for freedom from secular control. He also restated the Christian doctrine against what he saw as heretical interpretations, in what he termed the "Modernist" crisis. After his death in 1914, a cultus came quickly into being.

Above Pope Pius X (c. 1905).

MARGUERITE BOURGEOYS

THIS PIONEERING EDUCATOR, WHO ESTABLISHED THE FIRST RELIGIOUS ORDER IN CANADA AND THE FIRST SCHOOL IN MONTREAL, BECAME KNOWN AS THE "MOTHER OF THE COLONY".

KEY FACTS
Educator, founder of a religious order
DATES: *1620–1700*
BIRTH PLACE: *Troyes, France*
PATRON OF: *Poverty*
FEAST DAY: *12 January*

Born into the large family of a rich merchant, Marguerite Bourgeoys enjoyed a privileged upbringing. After her mother's death in 1639, she cared for her younger siblings but soon felt the calling of a religious vocation.

She joined a lay order of women called the Congregation of Troyes, an organization devoted to teaching the poor children of the area.

CALLED TO CANADA

In 1652, Marguerite's future took a dramatic turn when she met Monsieur de Maisonneuve, a governor in New France (now Canada). He was recruiting teachers for an outpost called Ville-Marie, and because she was not a cloistered nun, Marguerite was able to accept the challenge.

She arrived at the fort in 1653, finding herself both teacher and nurse for the tiny community. As there was no permanent place of

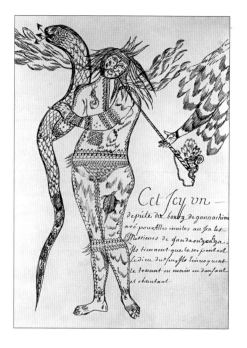

Above *An engraving of a tattooed Iroquois Indian holding a snake and smoking a peace pipe (c.1701).*

Below *Marguerite Bourgeoys with Canadian Indian converts (artist and date unknown).*

worship, she organized the building of the stone chapel of Notre-Dame-de-Bon-Secour in 1655. A year later, seeing an urgent need for education in this new land, she established the first Montreal school, teaching domestic, spiritual and academic subjects. The school thrived and she travelled back to France three times in the following years to enlist teachers.

FOUNDING EDUCATOR

Marguerite and her fellow teachers were very courageous women, spreading their schools across the wilderness of Quebec. They were resolved to educate the children of the Iroquois tribes as well as those of the French colonists, but they faced hardships of illness, hunger, fires, and violent attacks from the very people they hoped to help. In 1676, determined to persevere with her cause, Marguerite founded the Sisters of Notre Dame.

Sadly, by 1698, she had become exhausted by hardship, and chose to resign as the superior. In keeping with the selflessness of her life, she nursed a young nun who was dying. She prayed, "God, why do you not take me instead, I who am useless and good for nought!" The young nun lived and, a few days later, Marguerite died. Thousands mourned the loss of her wise, steady guidance.

Today, giving testimony to her faith and ambition, there are 200 convents and missions around the world following Marguerite's ideals of Christian education.

LOUIS GRIGNION DE MONTFORT

THIS UNCONVENTIONAL PRIEST ENRAGED CHURCH AUTHORITIES BUT HIS MISSIONS TO THE POOR AND INSPIRATIONAL SERMONS ENSURED HIM RECOGNITION AS A FAITHFUL APOSTLE.

KEY FACTS

Missionary apostolic and founder

DATES: *1673–1716*

BIRTH PLACE: *Montfort, Brittany*

FEAST DAY: *28 April*

As a student in Paris, Louis de Montfort experienced such squalid poverty that his future course as a missionary to the poor was decided. After his ordination in Paris in 1700, he was sent to work in Poitiers. There he founded the Daughters of Wisdom, an order of nuns that nursed in hospitals, and took his own mission to the poorest quarters.

EVANGELIST TO THE POOR

He was very popular with the public, but his flamboyant speeches caused concern among his superiors. To enhance his lessons, Louis would make an effigy of the devil dressed as a rich woman, then burn irreligious books before it. Or he would act out the role of a dying sinner caught between the angels and the devil. His writing, too, was dramatic. The *True Devotion to the Blessed Virgin* gained a wide readership, except among theologians.

Banned from Poitiers for his evangelistic style, Louis was given the office of "missionary apostolic" by the pope. This allowed him to roam Brittany and Poitiers, which well suited his personality. The singing of the hymns that he wrote reinforced his intense and emotional preaching, and he encouraged the use of the rosary in prayer.

Right Pope Pius XII canonized Louis Grignion de Montfort in 1947.

Above Louis Grignion de Montfort in a church dedicated to him in Saint-Laurent-sur-Sèvres.

Wherever he went, churches were restored and charity to the poor was revived. Lapsed believers returned to faith after attending his sermons, while in La Rochelle, a number of Calvinists returned to the Roman Catholic Church.

In 1712, Louis founded an association of missionary priests called the Company of Mary. These men, and the women of his Daughters of Wisdom, were trained to follow his emotional approach to faith. The orders have since become highly successful international apostolic and educational missions.

Louis Grignion de Montfort died in Saint-Laurent-sur-Sèvres and was canonized in 1947.

JOHN-BAPTIST DE LA SALLE

THIS SAINT MADE A PROFOUND DIFFERENCE TO THE EDUCATIONAL SYSTEM IN 17TH-CENTURY FRANCE, AND HIS INFLUENCE IS EVIDENT TODAY IN THE CONTINUING SUCCESS OF HIS SCHOOLS.

KEY FACTS
Educator, founder of the Brothers of the Christian Schools
DATES: *1651–1719*
BIRTH PLACE: *Rheims, France*
PATRON OF: *Schoolteachers*
FEAST DAY: *7 April*

John-Baptist de La Salle, a French nobleman, became one of the most distinguished educators in Europe. He studied in Rheims and at Saint-Sulpice, in Paris, where he was ordained in 1678.

In 1679, he met Adrian Nyel, a layman hoping to start a school for poor boys. While he encouraged him, John-Baptist did not foresee the great role he himself would play in this endeavour. He later wrote, "God, who guides all things with wisdom and serenity …willed to commit me entirely to the development of the schools."

CHRISTIAN SCHOOLS

John-Baptist used his family home to house the schoolmasters. Patient and confident in his methods, he slowly gathered men dedicated to the profession. He sold his home, resigned as canon of Rheims, and with his 12 followers, drew up a Rule.

Teachers were to make a vow of obedience, renewable ever year, and they agreed on a name – the Brothers of the Christian Schools. Rural congregations appealed to him to train youths who would then teach in the villages, so John-Baptist opened the first training school for teachers in Rheims in 1686, followed by others in Paris and Saint-Denis. He also opened free schools for poor boys in Paris.

He drew up statutes to govern his growing institution: no Brother of the Christian Schools should be ordained a priest, and no priest should be a teacher; classes were

Above The interior of Saint-Sulpice in Paris, where John-Baptist de La Salle studied and was ordained.

Below An engraving of John-Baptist de La Salle preaching (H. Jannin and P. Sarrazin, 1845).

to be given in the vernacular, not Latin; pupils were to be silent and taught as a class, not as individuals. By 1700, there were schools across France. Today, there are more than 20,000 members, and Christian Brothers schools can be found across the French- and English-speaking worlds.

Although John-Baptist faced controversy within his brotherhood over rules and teaching methods, his contribution to the training of teachers and educational methods was significant, especially for working-class boys, who previously had been destined for manual labour. His methods of caring for delinquent boys made important advances in the rehabilitation of disturbed youth.

He died in Rheims after a short illness and was canonized in 1900. His relics lie in Rome.

JOHN JOSEPH OF THE CROSS

HIS SOLICITUDE FOR THE UNHAPPY, AND HIS GENTLE MANNERS AS A LEADER, BROUGHT THIS FRANCISCAN PRIEST WIDESPREAD TRUST AND ADMIRATION AMONG THE PEOPLE OF NAPLES.

KEY FACTS
Franciscan minister-provincial
DATES: *1654–1734*
BIRTH PLACE: *Ischia, near Naples*
PATRON OF: *Naples*
FEAST DAY: *5 March*

John Joseph longed to follow the teachings of Franciscan Peter of Alcantara, and to keep rules of simplicity and contemplation. He joined the order when he was 16, but the quality of his character brought him rapid promotion. He was only 21 years old when he was placed in charge of a monastery in Piedimonte di Alife, and despite his longing for seclusion, he was ordained in 1677.

Still devoted to a contemplative life, John Joseph built hermitages where his congregation could take retreats for prayer and penance. He was sensitive in his handling of penitents, guiding them through confession and meditation. However, although he was diligent in following his duties, he begged the Church to release him from his position of authority. After a short period in Naples studying as a novice-master, John Joseph returned to Piedimonte, becoming a menial in 1681. His leadership qualities were such that, in 1684, his fellow friars re-elected him as guardian.

MINISTER-PROVINCIAL

In the latter part of the 17th century, the Spaniards had control of Naples, and with the pope's agreement, they insisted Spanish priests fill all high office in the Neapolitan Church. But when the Spaniards withdrew, John Joseph appealed to the pope to recognize Naples as an Italian province. He also requisitioned two large houses that the Spanish had

Above A view of the island of Ischia, the birthplace of John Joseph of the Cross (English School, 18th century).

claimed for themselves. In recognition of his contribution, the pope made John Joseph minister-provincial of the new province.

John Joseph applied himself to improving the discipline and organization of the monasteries, badly needed after the Spanish era. When satisfied he had done his duty, he obtained exemption from further office. He continued to help sinners and penitents, and offer spiritual counselling. The people of Naples adored him, and would gather round him when he went out in the streets. The more hysterical would try to tear patches from his ragged habit, seeking something of the holy old priest for their own comfort.

After he died, in Naples, a cultus arose, and he was canonized in 1839.

Left This contemporary image of a Franciscan monk shows the austere simplicity of the garments that John Joseph of the Cross would have worn.

JEANNE DELANOUE

JEANNE DELANOUE GAVE UP A BUSY COMMERCIAL LIFE FOR ONE OF PERSONAL SQUALOR, DEVOTING HER LIFE INSTEAD TO CARING FOR THE POOR, PARTICULARLY OUTCAST WOMEN AND REFUGEES.

KEY FACTS
Founder
DATES: *1666–1736*
BIRTH PLACE: *Saumur, France*
FEAST DAY: *17 August*

In her earlier life, Jeanne Delanoue ran the family business, selling drapery and religious items. At the age of 26, she encountered Françoise Suchet, a religious enthusiast who claimed to have experienced visions. Inspired by this eccentric woman, Jeanne turned her home and shop into a guesthouse, transforming the cellars and caves below it into shelters for the homeless.

By 1704, Jeanne had founded an order that came to be called the Sisters of Providence. The order brought solace to homeless women, unmarried mothers, and prostitutes, and during the famine

Right The Castle in Saumur, the city where Jeanne Delanoue was born and founded her religious order.

of 1709 they housed 100 starving people. Each day, having slept in a filthy old shroud, Jeanne would rise at 3 a.m., pray, then tend to the needy women.

Her nickname, "the pig of Jesus", suggests a lack of care for her appearance, but Jeanne was greatly respected for her protection of outcasts, and for her care of refugees during the frequent periods of war and famine. She founded 12 communities before her death in Saumur.

FRANCIS SERRANO

A COURAGEOUS AND FAITHFUL MISSIONARY, FRANCIS SERRANO WAS COMPLIMENTED BY A FELLOW PRIEST FOR WORKING "AS ENERGETICALLY AS A LION FOR THE BENEFIT OF SOULS".

KEY FACTS
Martyr
DATES: *1691–1748*
BIRTH PLACE: *Granada, Spain*
FEAST DAY: *17 February*

Francis Serrano was a Dominican priest who left Spain for the Philippines in 1725. Assigned to the post of Fujian, he showed great virtue as a missionary in a treacherous land.

Serrano was a hardy man, who had an abundance of energy, and was adventurous in spirit. His writings reveal him as a humorous, high-spirited character. He would journey unafraid through the night, crossing rivers and forests, determined to tend to his persecuted flock. He even disguised himself as a local peasant

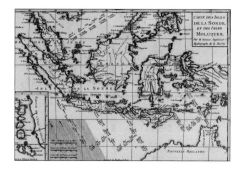

so that he could pass unnoticed into villages to administer the Sacraments in secret.

In 1746, he was imprisoned in Fuzhou and, during 19 months of incarceration, endured violent

Left A map of Indonesia and the Philippines (Charles Marie Rigobert Bonne, 18th century).

beatings that badly damaged his hearing. He and other missionaries were branded on their faces, and Francis wrote, "Our hearts exulted. We were branded as slaves of Jesus Christ…these heads are no longer ours, but the Lord's. He can take them whenever He wishes." Francis, who was finally suffocated to death in his prison cell, is included among the Martyrs of China canonized in 2000.

LEONARD OF PORT MAURICE

LEONARD WISHED FIRST, THAT HE "MIGHT LIVE FOR GOD AND LAST, THAT HE MIGHT LIVE IN GOD". TRAVELLING AROUND ITALY, HE USED THE STATIONS OF THE CROSS TO PREACH THE CHRISTIAN MESSAGE.

KEY FACTS

Franciscan missionary
DATES: *1676–1751*
BIRTH PLACE: *Port Maurice, Italy*
PATRON OF: *Missions in Catholic lands*
FEAST DAY: *26 November*
EMBLEM: *Franciscan habit*

Baptized as Paul Jerome Casanova in Port Maurice, Leonard joined the Franciscan Order, basing his life on the teachings of Christ as he understood them from a close reading of the New Testament, and on the Rules of St Francis of Assissi.

In 1709, Leonard instituted reforms at the friary of San Francesco del Monte in Florence, bringing its practices back into line with the strict austerity demanded by St Francis. He attracted many followers, whom he trained and sent out to preach across Tuscany. He also established a hermitage nearby, with the purpose of enabling the friars to make biannual retreats of silence and fasting. In 1730, he was sent to Rome, where he was appointed Guardian of St Bonaventura. During his time here, he made a point of ministering to soldiers, sailors, convicts and galley slaves.

STATIONS OF THE CROSS

In 1736, Leonard asked to be released from office, and travelled around Italy, often preaching outdoors. As a tool to spread his message, and as a symbol of his devotion, he used the Stations of the Cross, teaching his listeners how to pray before each of the

Left *Leonard of Port Maurice used the Stations of the Cross to teach his listeners about the Christian faith. The Fifth Station recounts how Simon of Cyrene helped Christ carry the cross (Giovanni Domenico Tiepolo, 1749).*

14 incidents that marked Christ's journey to the cross. It is said that he installed about 500 Stations of the Cross throughout Italy.

In 1744, Pope Benedict XIV sent Leonard to Corsica, where he encountered a hostile political atmosphere, and turbulent congregations who brought weapons to church services. The mountainous land was hard for a priest, who had to walk everywhere. Leonard's health suffered, and eventually, a ship had to be sent to bring him home.

Leonard returned to his Italian flock with renewed vigour and, in 1750, set up the Stations of the Cross in the Roman Coliseum, where he preached to a huge, excited crowd.

Soon afterward, he took a mission to the south, but the weather turned against him. Refusing an offer of shelter from some friars at Spoleto, Leonard insisted on continuing to Rome. Here he took to his bed and, exhausted by the journey, he received the last rites and a message from the pope before he died.

Left *The Gulf of Porto in Corsica. Leonard was sent to the island by Pope Benedict XIV in 1744.*

THE MARTYRS OF CHINA

THESE MARTYRS REPRESENT THOUSANDS OF CHRISTIANS WHO WERE TORTURED AND KILLED FOR THEIR CHRISTIAN FAITH IN CHINA OVER A PERIOD OF MORE THAN 400 YEARS.

The history of Christianity in China is a turbulent one that has involved much persecution. The first contact Chinese people had with Christianity was from the Nestorian heresy, which spread East, reaching China by the early 6th century AD.

Later, relative stability, brought by the Mongol expansion in Asia during the 13th and 14th centuries, opened up routes between the East and West and led to direct contact being established between China and Europe. Among those taking advantage of this new connection to the East were missionaries, who were eager to spread the Christian message.

EARLY CHINESE MISSIONS

The first Roman Catholic mission to China was led by Bishop John of Montecorvino (1246–1328), who established friendly relations with the Yuan dynasty.

Unfortunately, later missionaries were not so well received. The Yuan dynasty fell in 1368, and later regimes showed violent hostility to foreigners and foreign religions. Many missionaries to China never returned. Some were defeated by the harsh conditions of travel. One such was Francis Xavier, who died in 1551 soon after being refused entry to the country. Others were deliberately targeted by the ruling powers in China. This was the destiny of Francisco Fernandez de Capillas, a Dominican, who led a mission to Fujian and was beheaded during the early Ching dynasty in 1648.

Above St Jean-Gabriel Perboyre, martyred in China in 1840 (François Constant Petit, 19th century).

THE CHING DYNASTY

The Ching dynasty was particularly anti-Christian, and officials of the regime hounded Christians in China for 400 years. Among the victims were Spanish Dominican missionary Pedro Sanz, who was murdered in 1747, and Francis Regis Clet of St Vincent de Paul, who died in 1820.

Despite the killings of foreign missionaries and thousands of Chinese converts, the faith took root. Early in the 20th century, the Rev. Fang Ho collected the relics of these early Chinese martyrs and translated them to Taipei in Taiwan where they rest in the Chinese Blessed Martyrs Church in Peng Chiao.

Archives from the 19th century record details of some of the martyrs of that period. These names

Left A figure of St Paul inside St Paul's Church in Macau, China.

Above Father Adam Schall von Bell (1591–1666) was a German Jesuit missionary to China (German School, 17th century).

> "ALMIGHTY GOD, WE GIVE YOU THANKS FOR CHOOSING MANY CHINESE FAITHFUL TO WITNESS FOR CHRIST BY GIVING UP THEIR LIVES... WE ALSO PRAY THAT WE MAY FOLLOW THE EXAMPLE OF THESE CHINESE BY REMAINING STRONG IN FAITH, HOPE AND LOVE..."
>
> EXCERPT FROM PRAYER TO THE CHINESE MARTYRS

are included among the 120 Martyrs of China. The latter were chosen to represent the thousands of anonymous victims of religious persecution. First among them is Peter Wu Guosheng, who died in 1814. Another is Agnes Cao Guiying, an account of whose torture and martyrdom in 1856 can be found in Chinese court records. She was kept in a cage so small she could not move her limbs to sit, and died in captivity.

Other known martyrs come from records dated during 1900, at the time of the Boxer Rebellion, when the Chinese rose up against everything perceived as foreign. European and Chinese Christians, nuns and priests, women and children were brutally murdered for their faith. Among them were Mary Guo-Li, who died alongside her four grandchildren and two daughters-in-law. All were beheaded on 7 July 1900. Lang-Yang and her seven-year-old son, Paolo, were stabbed and burnt a few days later. More than 30 men and women were dragged from their cathedral in Taiyuan, Shanxi Province. They were given time to take Mass and pray before they were beheaded in a mass execution on 9 July 1900. They, too, are named among the Martyrs of China.

Above Funeral of St Jean-Louis Bonnard at the seminary of Nam-Dinh (artist unknown, 19th century).

COMMUNISM

The Ching dynasty was toppled in 1907, and after years of war, the Communists took power. Their persecution of Christians was as fierce as that of the previous regime. Churches were burnt, unknown thousands of Christians martyred, and it seemed that the faith had finally been eradicated. Even the ownership of a Bible could lead to imprisonment or execution. However, the faithful did not abandon their beliefs. Instead, they met in secret, risking harsh punishment.

Pope John Paul II proclaimed the 120 Blessed Martyrs of China as saints in 2000. Among them are 33 foreign missionaries and 87 Chinese, including bishops, priests, nuns, friars and 76 lay people. In 2007, the Chinese government gave the Roman Catholic Church permission to build a church, the first in more than 70 years. Christianity is now officially recognized in China and public worship is permitted in churches and cathedrals. No longer persecuted, 22 million Chinese people – Protestants and Catholics – have publicly proclaimed their faith.

HYACINTH CASTANEDA

Hyacinth Castaneda was born in Setaro, Spain, but longed to spread the message of Christianity outside Europe. He travelled across the Atlantic, suffering from infection and seasickness, before walking across Mexico to reach the Pacific coast. From there, he travelled to the Philippines, where he was ordained, then took a boat to China. From his base in Fulcien, he started preaching and converted many people. The Chinese authorities arrested him, imprisoning him in what is now Vietnam. He was held for three years, along with fellow prisoner Vincent Liem. During this time he was branded and tortured, and he was beheaded in 1773. He is listed among the Martyrs of Vietnam.

Below Missionaries to China were martyred in various ways: some were beheaded, others garrotted and some were burnt alive (Indo-Chinese School, 19th century).

GERARD MAJELLA

GERARD MAJELLA, A HUMBLE, SIMPLE LAY BROTHER FROM A MODEST BACKGROUND, HAS BEEN DESCRIBED AS THE "MOST FAMOUS WONDER-WORKER OF THE 18TH CENTURY".

KEY FACTS
Miracle worker
DATES: *1725–55*
BIRTH PLACE: *Muro Lucano, near Naples*
PATRON OF: *Mothers*
FEAST DAY: *16 October*

Gerard Majella's widowed mother said of him that "he was born for heaven", and he demonstrated his religious calling from an early age, spending much of his childhood in prayer.

He initially turned down an apprenticeship as a tailor – his father's profession – to work as a servant in the house of the Bishop of Lacedogna. But the bishop was bad-tempered and unpredictable, and Gerard was neither sly nor subtle enough to withstand such a regime. So he returned home to take up his apprenticeship and worked to support his mother and three sisters.

A SIMPLE LAY BROTHER
In 1752, Gerard fulfilled his long-held dream to join a religious order when he was accepted as a lay brother into the Congregation of the Most Holy Redeemer, or the Redemptorists. St Alphonsus

Above Gerard Majella saving fishermen near Naples (M. Barberis, 19th century).

Below The Market at Naples (Domenico Gargiulo, 17th century). Gerard Majella never travelled beyond the boundaries of the city.

Liguori, the founder of this community, had a particular empathy with peasant and illiterate congregations and Gerard found a role as a gardener, tailor and porter. His fellow priests were puzzled by his frail appearance and shy manners, and decided that he must be "either a fool or a great saint".

MIRACLES AND CHARITY
Claims were soon circulating that Gerard could heal the sick, appear in two places at one time, read minds and tell the future. Perhaps most extraordinary of all, one story tells of his ability to levitate and fly half a mile through the air.

Despite Gerard's lowly position in the Redemptorists, he always found alms and food for the poor, and time and patience for the sick. Because of his purity and sensitivity, he was appointed as the spiritual director of numerous communities of nuns.

He remained unworldly and, when accused of lewd behaviour by a young woman, refused to defend or incriminate himself, believing silence to be the righteous response to dishonesty and injustice. The girl later admitted that the charges were false.

Gerard was only 29 years old when he died of tuberculosis. Although he had never travelled outside the kingdom of Naples, a cultus grew after his death. He is patron saint of unborn children and expectant mothers in particular, and was canonized by Pope Pius X in 1904.

MARGARET D'YOUVILLE

MARGARET D'YOUVILLE IS KNOWN AS THE MOTHER OF UNIVERSAL CHARITY. THE FOUNDER OF THE SISTERS OF CHARITY OF MONTREAL, SHE "LOVED GREATLY JESUS CHRIST AND THE POOR".

KEY FACTS
Founder
DATES: *1701–71*
BIRTH PLACE: *Varennes, Canada*
FEAST DAY: *23 December*

From a very early age, Margaret was faced with responsibility and the rigours of poverty. Born in Varennes, Canada, she was the eldest of six children. Her father died when she was seven years old and, after a brief education from the Ursuline nuns, she helped her mother to bring up her siblings.

From this difficult start in life, she made what appeared to be a good marriage to a fur trader, François Youville. The Governor-General and other grand officials attended the wedding.

Margaret's marriage brought her great unhappiness, during which her faith sustained her. Youville was not only a drunkard and a gambler, but also illicitly traded alcohol with local Indians. The effect of this was so devastating on their community that they begged the governor for protection. Margaret bore four children, of whom only two survived. When her husband died in 1730, she found he had spent her mother's legacy and left her in debt.

DEVOTION TO THE POOR
Margaret opened a shop to support her children and, despite her own hardships, found time to visit others in unfortunate circumstances. She tended to the sick and to criminals and, when her eldest son left home to enter the seminary (both sons became priests), she moved a destitute blind woman into his room. Her female

friends shared her sense of duty and faith and worked as seamstresses to raise money for the poor. But Margaret still struggled to find resources to pay for her good works. She was once forced to beg for funds to pay for the funeral of an executed criminal.

Left The Storming of Quebec *(English School, 18th century). The "Grey Nuns" tended the wounded on both sides of the fighting.*

THE GREY NUNS
In 1737, along with three young companions, Margaret formed a lay order for the service of the poor – the Sisters of Charity of Montreal, known as the "Grey Nuns". They cared for women and prisoners, nursed the sick during a smallpox epidemic, and with an all-embracing policy that made no distinction of race or status, they tended to the wounded of both sides during the war between Quebec and England that ended in 1759. The Grey Nuns' convent was burnt down twice, but the entire community funded the rebuilding.

Margaret died in Montreal, and was canonized in 1990, the first native-born Canadian saint.

Right Montreal on the St Lawrence River in 1760. *Margaret founded her order in the city in 1737.*

VINCENT LIEM

THIS SAINT TOOK THE NAME VINCENT LIEM OF PEACE, YET HE CONFRONTED TERRIBLE, OFFICIALLY-SANCTIONED VIOLENCE, AND EVENTUALLY MARTYRDOM, FOR HIS CHRISTIAN FAITH.

KEY FACTS
Protomartyr
DATES: *1732–73*
BIRTH PLACE: *Tra Lu, Vietnam*
FEAST DAY: *7 November*

In the 16th century, Christian missions from Europe entered the kingdoms of Tonkin, Annam and Cochin, now Vietnam. When Vincent Liem was born in Tra Lu in 1732, his parents were part of a well-established, but furtive Christian community that risked state persecution.

A pious child, Vincent joined the Dominican seminary when he was 12 years old. He was an intelligent and diligent pupil, and in 1753 was sent to the St John Lateran Dominican College in Manila in the Philippines, where he prepared for ordination. In 1759, he returned to his homeland and taught noviciates at the seminary of Trung Linh.

SUFFERING PERSECUTION

The persecution of Christians was remorseless during this period, perhaps as severe as anything the early Christians suffered under the Roman Empire. Documentation of the Vietnamese martyrs is rare, but it is estimated that between the 16th and 18th centuries, more

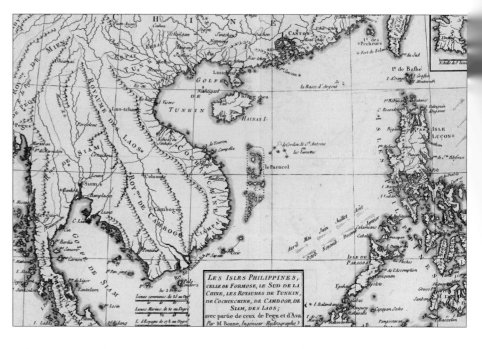

Above A map showing the Kingdom of Tonkin in South Asia (Charles Marie Rigobert Bonne, 1780).

than 100,000 Christians were killed. Torture was common: limbs were cut off, flesh burnt from the living body, and some Christians who escaped death were branded on the face with the words *ta dao*, meaning "false religion".

Faced with religious oppression similar to that endured by the first apostles, Vincent followed their example, undergoing difficult journeys to spread the faith. As Sts Peter and Paul had done, he worked among non-believers, seeking converts despite the fearful dangers he risked.

Vincent was caught and imprisoned in Trung Linh, where he met fellow prisoner Hyacinth Castaneda, a Spanish priest. He was executed in 1773, the first Vietnamese-born martyr. Vincent Liem was canonized in 1988, and is one of the named Martyrs of Vietnam, representing the thousands of anonymous Christians who have been murdered in this part of the world.

Left A coloured engraving showing the forms of torture endured by Catholic missionaries in Tonkin, China (French School, 19th century).

PAUL OF THE CROSS

THE SON OF A NOBLEMAN, PAUL OF THE CROSS REFUSED A RICH
INHERITANCE AND A WEALTHY WIFE BECAUSE OF HIS INNER DESIRE
TO FOLLOW HIS SPIRITUAL VOCATION.

KEY FACTS
Founder
DATES: *1694–1775*
BIRTH PLACE: *Ovada, Italy*
FEAST DAY: *19 October*

Paul Francis Danei refused a considerable inheritance and a promising marriage. Instead, he joined the Venetian army as a volunteer in 1714. This experience affected him profoundly and, within a year, he became a recluse.

In 1720, he emerged with a powerful vocation, determined to share with believers his profound awareness of the Passion of Christ, the suffering Jesus endured as he hung on the cross.

He was ordained as a priest and, with the help of his brother, founded the Passionist Congregation in 1727, with the aim of combining monastic virtue with active missionary work.

Paul wanted his followers to live monastic lives, even as they went forth to spread his message and minister to the sick, but papal authority was granted only after the severe rules of the order were modified. The order expanded throughout Paul's lifetime, and in 1771, an enclosed convent of Passionist nuns was approved.

Right The monastery of the noviciate of the Passionist friars in Italy.

BENEDICT JOSEPH LABRE

PILGRIM AND MENDICANT, BENEDICT JOSEPH LABRE WAS THE
EMBODIMENT OF THOSE RARE, HOLY MEN AND WOMEN WHO ARE
DESCRIBED AS "FOOLS FOR CHRIST'S SAKE".

KEY FACTS
Mendicant
DATES: *1748–83*
BIRTH PLACE: *Boulogne, France*
PATRON OF: *Tramps, the
homeless*
FEAST DAY: *16 April*

All faiths produce exceptional followers, who dedicate their lives to spirituality at the expense of a conventional role in society. Benedict Joseph Labre, the eldest of 15 children of a prosperous shopkeeper, was such a man.

Both the Cistercians and the Carthusians claimed that Benedict was too young and delicate to join them but possibly they sensed his eccentricity. Rejected by these monks, Benedict decided to become a pilgrim, walking from his birthplace of Boulogne to Rome, then visiting, again on foot, the holy sites of Italy, Switzerland and France.

Above Nuns standing in front of the St Labre mission in Ashland, Montana (19th century).

He slept in fields and on street corners, and accepted food when offered, but gave away any money he received. In 1774, Benedict settled in Rome, spending his days praying in the churches, his nights curled up in doorways. Eventually, due to poor health, he moved into a shelter for poor men, where he gave his food to other inmates. He collapsed in church while praying, and was carried to the shop of a friendly butcher, where he died.

The Romans recognized him as a holy man, a cultus developed, and he was canonized in 1881.

ALPHONSUS LIGUORI

ALPHONSUS LIGUORI RECOMMENDED SIMPLICITY IN THE PULPIT AND CHARITY IN THE CONFESSIONAL. A BEGUILING PREACHER, HE WAS LOVED BY HIS CONGREGATION.

KEY FACTS
Founder
DATES: *1696–1787*
BIRTH PLACE: *Naples, Italy*
PATRON OF: *Those who hear confessions, teachers of moral theology*
FEAST DAY: *1 August*

Alphonsus' father was ambitious for his son, propelling him into a legal career in Naples. Alphonsus became a successful barrister, but after eight years a voice prompted him to "Leave the world and give yourself to me". He studied theology privately, and after he was ordained in 1726, proved to be a priest with moderate views, sympathetic to sinners.

As a preacher, he developed a clear, intelligible style, anxious that "even the poorest old woman in the congregation" should understand him. He organized Christian clubs for the unemployed of Naples and, while dining at one, advised a member not to be overzealous in his fasting, but to eat the cutlets God had provided. These comments caused rumours of extravagant goings-on at the "Cutlet Clubs" that abounded in the city. Some members were arrested, but the clubs were allowed to continue and later evolved into the Association of the Chapels.

Above Alphonsus Liguori (artist unknown, 19th century).

THE REDEMPTORISTS
In 1732, aided by his friends Thomas Falcoia and Maria Celeste, Alphonsus founded the Congregation of the Most Holy Redeemer, or the Redemptorists. Unfortunately, the order was stricken by internal dissension.

This, combined with the anti-clericalism of the Italian government and the opposition of the Jansenists, left the Redemptorists in a precarious position. Despite these difficulties, however, the order survived, and Alphonsus received popular acclamation for his religious texts, *Moral Theology* and *The Glories of Mary*.

In 1762, he became Bishop of Sant' Agata dei Goti near Naples, but the congregation was corrupt and lax. Alphonsus was unbending in his reforms. During a famine, he insisted that the wealthy share food with the starving. The subsequent court actions brought against him added to his burdens.

During Alphonsus' career, he faced many professional and personal difficulties, but he never lost the support of ordinary believers. He retired from high office, in 1775, crippled with rheumatism and with his sight and hearing impaired. The Redemptorists still faced fierce opposition and, in 1780, Alphonsus was expelled from his own order when he was tricked into signing a document authorizing reforms favourable to the anti-clerical government.

Alphonsus died believing his congregation had failed, but in 1793, the order was recognized by the Neapolitan state, and it now operates all over the world.

Left Sant' Agatha dei Goti in Campania, Italy, where Alphonsus Liguori became bishop in 1762.

ELIZABETH SETON

ELIZABETH SETON, EXEMPLARY WIFE, MOTHER, WIDOW AND CONSECRATED NUN, WAS THE FIRST AMERICAN TO BE CANONIZED BY THE ROMAN CATHOLIC CHURCH.

KEY FACTS
Founder, first American-born saint
DATES: *1774–1821*
BIRTH PLACE: *New York, USA*
FEAST DAY: *4 January*

Elizabeth Seton was born into a wealthy American family, respected in New York society. Her grandfather had been the Episcopalian Rector of Staten Island, and her father was the first public physician of the city.

When she was 19, Elizabeth married a wealthy trader, William Seton. Theirs was a happy marriage, but at the age of 28 she was left widowed, with five small children, after her husband died while they were on a trip to Italy.

CATHOLIC CONVERSION

Although she had been brought up as an Episcopalian, Elizabeth found spiritual comfort in the Roman Catholic Church. Moved by the charity of the nuns she encountered in Tuscany, she underwent a conversion on her return to New York, and was baptized a Roman Catholic.

Her conversion left her an outcast from her family and her anti-Catholic community. Her religious ardour was regarded as unseemly in her sophisticated circle, and she faced some difficult years of financial trouble during which she repeatedly tried and failed to start a Catholic school in her home city.

THE SISTERS OF CHARITY

In 1808, at the invitation of Reverend William Dubourg, she went to Baltimore to care for poor children. Here, she found her true vocation. She established

Above An engraving showing Elizabeth Seton dressed in the costume of the Sisters of Charity (Maurindel, date unknown).

a small religious community devoted to the relief of the poor, especially children, and to teaching in parish schools. From this grew her congregation, the American Sisters of Charity, based on the rules of St Vincent de Paul.

She took her vows as a nun, and her commitment to Christ was unswerving. Others perceived her dynamic conviction, and were inspired by her to join her cause. The Sisters of Charity is now an influential congregation, active not only in the United States, but also in Latin America, Italy and the developing world. Elizabeth died at Emmitsburg and was canonized in 1975 after prayers for her intercession brought about cures for leukemia and meningitis.

Right The shrine of Elizabeth Seton in Emmitsburg, Maryland.

ANTÔNIO DE SANT'ANNA GALVÃO

MORE THAN A MILLION PEOPLE ATTENDED THE CANONIZATION OF ST ANTÔNIO, A MAN OF PEACE AND CHARITY, AND THE FIRST BRAZILIAN TO BE MADE A SAINT.

KEY FACTS
Founder, miracle worker
DATES: *1739–1822*
BIRTH PLACE: *Guaratingueto,
near São Paulo, Brazil*
FEAST DAY: *11 May*

Antônio de Sant'Anna Galvão was born into a wealthy and deeply religious family, who sent him to a Jesuit seminary at the age of 13. However, because of a strong anti-Jesuit movement in Brazil at the time, his father advised him to join the Alcantrine Franciscans.

Antônio enrolled as a noviciate at St Bonaventure near Rio de Janeiro and was ordained in 1762. In 1768, he became preacher and confessor to the laity at the St Francis Friary in São Paulo. He was also confessor to the women of the Recollects of St Teresa, where he met Sister Helena Maria of the Holy Spirit.

In 1774, inspired by this nun and her religious visions, he founded Our Lady of the Conception of Divine Providence. At this home for girls, young women could receive instruction without being required to take vows. When Sister Helena died, Antônio took sole responsibility for the

Above An altar painting of Antônio de Sant'Anna Galvão in Brazil.

Below Pope Benedict XVI canonized Antônio de Sant'Anna Galvão in front of nearly a million people in São Paulo in May 2007.

Recollects, who were subsequently incorporated into the Order of Immaculate Conception.

Over the following years, Antônio achieved high office. In 1808, he became visitator in general and president of the Franciscan Chapter of São Paulo. When, at one stage, the Church posted him outside the city, the bishop and churchgoers begged for his return.

In his old age, he returned to the St Francis Friary, but it was the sisters from the Recollects da Luz who attended him at his death.

MIRACLE PILLS

Antônio is most famous for his "pills" – scraps of paper inscribed with prayers to Mary, the Blessed Virgin, that the faithful would swallow in hope of a miraculous cure. To this day, the pills are manufactured by the nuns of St Clare, a convent founded by Antônio in Sorocaba near São Paulo.

In 1998, the Archbishop of São Paulo tried to bring an end to what he regarded as a superstition, and ordered the nuns to stop their work. However, at the canonization of St Antônio, Pope Benedict XVI recognized the miraculous power of the saint, acknowledging two healing miracles ascribed to the pills, including a recent case of a four-year-old girl whose hepatitis had been declared incurable by the medical profession. Since the saint's canonization in 2007, the nuns have distributed as many as 10,000 pills in one day.

MAGDALENA OF CANOSSA

MAGDALENA OF CANOSSA HAD "A MOTHER'S HEART AND AN APOSTLE'S ZEAL". HER LIFE WAS DEDICATED TO TEACHING AND EXTENDING SPIRITUAL AWARENESS.

KEY FACTS
*Virgin, founder of the
Daughters of Charity*
DATES: *1774–1835*
BIRTH PLACE: *Verona, Italy*
FEAST DAY: *8 May*

Although Magdalena made a vow to dedicate her life to God at the age of 17, she was compelled to take up a secular life. The third of six siblings left fatherless as children, she found herself in charge of running the family's large estate.

Despite her worldly worries, however, she could not forget her calling, and sought out friends to join her in following Christ with chastity and obedience. In 1808, in spite of family opposition, she moved to the poorest part of town to start her religious life, and built up such a following that, in 1819, she founded the Daughters of Charity. The order was dedicated to establishing charity schools, training teachers for rural areas and supporting women patients in hospital. Later, she founded the Sons of Charity for male followers.

Magdalena died in Verona surrounded by her followers. There are now 4,000 Daughters of Charity all over the world, and the Sons are active in Italy, the Philippines and Latin America.

Above St Mary's College in Hong Kong, founded by the Canossian Daughters of Charity in 1900.

JOSEPH COTTOLENGO

JOSEPH COTTOLENGO WILL ALWAYS BE REMEMBERED AND LOVED AS AN UNSTINTING CHAMPION OF THOSE IN NEED, WHETHER THEY BE ORPHANS, DISABLED, MENTALLY ILL OR FRAIL.

KEY FACTS
Founder
DATES: *1786–1842*
BIRTH PLACE: *Piedmont*
FEAST DAY: *30 April*

Joseph Cottolengo was ordained in 1811 and quickly demonstrated his empathy for the unfortunate. His good works began modestly, with the founding of a hospital of five beds, the "Little House", in a Turin slum.

The hospital expanded quickly, and Joseph and his followers formed the Societies of the Little House of Divine Providence. When the authorities closed the Little House during a cholera epidemic, the brothers nursed the sick in their homes. The Little House then moved to Valdocco, a suburb of Turin, where it was soon

Above The city of Turin, where Joseph Cottolengo did many great works.

surrounded by an assortment of care homes for the deaf and dumb, orphans, elderly people, epileptics and the mentally handicapped.

Joseph also started communities of prayer to bring solace to those in mortal and moral danger. Joseph seemed carefree about finances, believing that the Lord would provide, and so it was with surprise that his successor accepted his perfectly kept account books when he retired.

Although he was only 56 years old, Joseph died of typhoid in his brother's home at Chieri only a week after his retirement.

INCORRUPTIBLES

ALL SAINTS ARE REVERED FOR THE WONDROUS ACTS, AND OFTEN
MIRACLES, THEY PERFORM WHEN THEY ARE LIVING, BUT SOME SHOW
EXTRAORDINARY PHYSICAL QUALITIES EVEN AFTER THEIR DEATH.

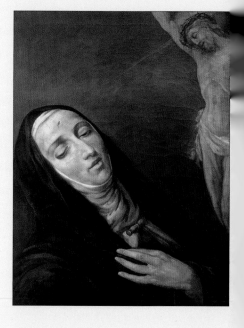

The words "incorrupt" and "incorruptible" are used by the Catholic Church to describe bodies that do not decompose after death. The body is considered incorrupt only if no preservation techniques, such as embalming, have been used, and it is not uncommon for the body's lack of decomposition to be accompanied by a sweet smell. The discovery of an incorrupt corpse is generally made by chance, and when the body of a holy person is found intact, it is traditionally taken as a sign of sainthood.

Alongside other miraculous phenomena associated with saints, including stigmata and the healing of the sick, the survival of a saint's corpse seems to defy any scientific explanation, and many Catholic Christians believe the holiness and piety of an incorruptible saint to be the cause of divine preservation.

Above A portrait of Rita of Cascia in the church of Santa Maria del Giglio, Venice (19th century).

EARLY INCORRUPTIBLES

A very early example of an incorruptible is the 3rd-century saint, Cecilia. When her tomb was opened in 1599, a thousand years after she was buried, her corpse showed no signs of corruption. Sadly, on exposure to the air, it quickly turned to dust.

Left A portrait of Bernadette of Lourdes (19th century).

There was frequent correspondence between Rome and the English clergy after the death of Edward the Confessor in 1066. A cultus grew around this king, and the campaign to have him canonized was strengthened when his body was found to be incorrupt in 1102. Monks from Westminster made enquiries and in 1161, Pope Innocent III finally agreed with their findings and advised that the saint's relics be translated to Westminster Abbey. In 1163, a procession carried the incorrupt body to its final resting place.

THE BLOOD OF ST JANUARIUS

St Januarius, who was martyred in AD 305, is the patron saint of Naples, and his presence is believed to protect the port from harm. Twice every year – on 19 September and on the Saturday before the first Sunday in May – a solemn procession, led by representatives of the Church, progresses through the city displaying a vial of St Januarius's blood, which liquefies and bubbles in just the same way as fresh blood. Believers fear a calamity would hit Naples if the blood failed to liquefy. Other saints whose blood was said to show this quality include Pantaleon, Stephen and John the Baptist.

Right Cardinal Crescenzio Sepe, Archbishop of Naples, looks at the glass vial holding the blood of St Januarius during the Feast of San Gennaro in 2006.

Above The incorrupt body of Catherine Labouré, kept at 140 rue du Bac in Paris, France.

Above The incorrupt body of Jean-Baptiste Vianney is kept in the Basilica at Ars, France.

St Rita of Cascia (1377–1447) is another incorruptible, whose face, hands and feet survive along with much of her skeleton. Her remains are on display in the Basilica of St Rita in Cascia, Italy.

THE LAST 200 YEARS

The body of John-Baptiste Vianney also remained intact after his death in 1859. He won the admiration of his congregation for his faith and goodness. They were amazed, too, by his meagre diet of boiled potatoes, and his habit of sleeping for a mere two or three hours a night. His extraordinary qualities in life were extended in death when his body did not decompose.

Madeleine Sophie Barat was an energetic woman who travelled widely and devoted herself to the Christian education of children. The miraculous preservation of her body, which is kept in Jette in Belgium, reflects the strength and vitality that she always demonstrated in life.

Another holy woman whose body has proved incorrupt is Catherine Labouré. This modest

Right The incorrupt body of St Rita of Cascia is carried around Rome during a celebration on her feast day.

> WE SHOULD SHOW HONOUR TO THE SAINTS OF GOD, AS BEING MEMBERS OF CHRIST, THE CHILDREN AND FRIENDS OF GOD, AND OUR INTERCESSORS. THEREFORE, IN MEMORY OF THEM WE OUGHT TO HONOUR ANY RELICS OF THEIRS IN A FITTING MANNER.
>
> ST THOMAS AQUINAS

nun, who is venerated as a mystic, was canonized in 1947. She died in 1876 and her body rests in the the convent where she lived for nearly half a century, in the chapel at 140 rue du Bac, Paris.

An equally humble woman whose body survives without corruption is Bernadette of Lourdes, who saw visions of the Virgin and lived piously as a nun. After her death in 1879, her corpse was removed three times from its resting place to undergo scientific examination. It now resides in a glass case in the convent at Nevers where visitors can marvel at its preserved state. Doctor Comte who examined St Bernadette's corpse in 1925 wrote, "…the body does not seem to have putrefied, nor has any decomposition of the body set in, although this would be expected and normal after such a long period in a vault hollowed out of the earth".

JEAN-BAPTISTE VIANNEY

JEAN-BAPTISTE FAILED HIS CLERICAL EXAMS, BUT WAS ACCEPTED INTO THE PRIESTHOOD BECAUSE THE CHURCH NEEDED MEN OF SIMPLE GOODNESS AND DEVOTION AS WELL AS MEN OF LEARNING.

KEY FACTS
Founder
DATES: *1786–1859*
BIRTH PLACE: *Dardilly, near Lyons, France*
PATRON OF: *Patriarchal clergy*
FEAST DAY: *4 August*

Jean-Baptiste was a shepherd boy, who, dismayed by the treatment of priests during the Revolution, applied to join the clergy. He was conscripted into the Napoleonic army but, soon after, deserted and resumed his studies for the priesthood. This was a precarious career because anti-clerical forces in control of France remained hostile even after a ban on all monastic orders was lifted in 1810.

VILLAGE PRIEST

Two years after his ordination in 1815, Jean-Baptiste was sent as parish priest to a remote village, Ars-en-Dombes. He had a genuine hatred of immorality, and a recital of sins would often reduce him to tears. This made him intolerant of simple pleasures, such as

Above A contemporary drawing showing Jean-Baptiste Vianney being harassed by a demon.

Below A lithograph portrait of Jean-Baptiste Vianney (1866).

dancing, and minor transgressions, such as lewd language. But villagers forgave Jean-Baptiste's severity because he revealed supernatural talents, producing miraculous supplies of food to feed to orphans, and prophesying the future. He could also read hearts and had knowledge of things happening beyond his sight. He suffered violent assaults from the Devil, who beat him and even burnt his bed.

Jean-Baptiste was so sympathetic to remorseful sinners that confessors queued for his pastoral care, and a special booking office was set up at Arles railway station to handle the 300 visitors travelling every day to visit the wonder worker. He started work at 11 o'clock each morning and spent long hours in the confessional. He wanted to develop his spiritual meditations and tried three times to become a monk, but returned each time to Ars.

Years of listening to the sins of penitents eventually moderated his views on frivolity and pleasure, and he turned his full attention to teaching his flock about the enduring love of God and the significance of Church liturgy.

Jean-Baptiste was a modest man. He never wore the decoration he was given when made a member of the Légion d'Honneur, and to raise money for the poor he sold the luxurious robes of office he received when he was made a canon. He died in Ars, and was canonized in 1925. The cultus for this saint is now worldwide.

GASPAR BERTONI

ALTHOUGH GASPAR BERTONI WAS DRIVEN BY POLITICAL PRESSURE TO TURN FROM MISSION WORK TO EDUCATION, THIS CHANGE OF DIRECTION BROUGHT WISDOM AND FULFILMENT.

KEY FACTS
Founder
DATES: *1777–1853*
BIRTH PLACE: *Verona, Italy*
FEAST DAY: *12 June*

When Gaspar Bertoni was born, revolutionary anti-clericalism held sway in Europe. He came from a legal family in Verona but chose to work as a parish priest after his ordination in 1800. Undeterred when the Napoleonic conquerors held Pope Pius VII prisoner, he abandoned neither his leader nor his faith.

After Napoleon's defeat in 1814, Verona fell under Austrian control and the pope was released. In 1816–17, Gaspar founded a mission that would preach on the Passion of Christ – the suffering of Jesus on the cross. However, the work was jeopardized by hostility from the new regime, and he refocused his attentions on education.

With his brotherhood, Gaspar began teaching in free schools, hoping to inspire boys into a life of service to God. His group became the Congregation of Holy Stigmatics, an educational mission that now works in Europe, Africa, the Americas and Asia. Although he was bedridden for many years Gaspar continued to guide his congregation. He died in Verona and was canonized in 1989.

Above Verona, the city where Gaspar Bertoni was born and died.

CATHERINE LABOURÉ

THE "MIRACULOUS MEDAL" OF CATHERINE LABOURÉ INSPIRED ALPHONSE RATISBONNE, AN ALSATIAN JEW, TO CONVERT AND FOUND THE FATHERS AND SISTERS OF SION.

KEY FACTS
Visionary
DATES: *1806–76*
BIRTH PLACE: *Fain-les-Moutiers,
near Dijon, France*
FEAST DAY: *28 November*

Catherine Labouré was a peasant from Fain-les-Moutiers. She cared for her widowed father, worked in Paris as a waitress and then, in 1830, joined the Sisters of Charity at the rue du Bac.

Her superiors thought little of this plain woman who tended the convent hens, but Catherine had extraordinary visions, the most enduring of which was a picture of the Virgin standing on a globe. The vision was accompanied by the words, "Mary conceived without sin, pray for us who have recourse to thee." On the reverse of the picture was an M with a cross and two hearts.

Above Apparition of the Virgin to St Catherine Labouré 31 July 1830 (Le Cerf, 1835).

THE MIRACULOUS MEDALS
The Archbishop of Paris was persuaded to sanction medals stamped with these images, and in 1832, 1,500 were minted. After the appearance of a pamphlet describing Catherine's vision, 130,000 further medals were sold. The "Miraculous Medal" was authenticated by canonical decree, and is now distributed across the Catholic world.

Catherine's cultus was strengthened by the incorruptibility of her body after her death in the convent she had called home for 46 years. She was canonized in 1947.

MADELEINE SOPHIE BARAT

MADELEINE SOPHIE BARAT DEVOTED HER LIFE TO THE SERVICE OF OTHERS, BRINGING A CATHOLIC EDUCATION TO PUPILS ACROSS THE WORLD THROUGH THE SOCIETY OF THE SACRED HEART.

KEY FACTS
*Virgin, founder,
educational reformer*
DATES: *1779–1865*
BIRTH PLACE: *Joigny, France*
FEAST DAY: *25 May*

From a very early age, Madeleine was placed under the harsh tutelage of her brother, Louis, who was 11 years her senior. She learnt how to deflect his unpleasant manners through patience, charm and diplomacy, traits that were to serve her well throughout her life. Her brother's stubborn, aggressive nature led to his imprisonment for two years when he refused to accept the civil constitution of the clergy.

SCHOOL TEACHER
Madeleine nursed an ambition to become a lay sister with the Carmelites, but was persuaded by l'Abbé Varin to instead join his new community, the Society of the Sacred Heart, dedicated to teaching Christian children, rich and poor alike. In 1800, she was sent to Amiens, to the Society's first convent school. Two years

later, aged just 23, she was made Superior, and soon afterwards travelled to Grenoble and Poitiers to establish other convent schools.

Her youth made her high position precarious, and while she was away from Amiens, a chaplain and another nun tried to displace her. Madeleine responded with char-

Left A portrait of Madeleine Sophie Barat (artist and date unknown).

acteristic tact and patience and, supported by l'Abbé Varin, strengthened her role as Mother Superior, a position she was to hold for 63 years.

EDUCATIONAL REFORMER
During this time she implemented standards of education across every school of the Sacred Heart. Although these guides were uniform, they were not inflexible, with provision made for regular reviews and adjustments to meet changing needs.

The society became truly international under Madeleine's guidance, with communities established in 12 different countries during her lifetime, including foundations in the United States, orchestrated by her friend Rose Philippine Duchesne. Madeleine personally travelled to found new schools and monitor old ones in France, Switzerland and England. The Society of the Sacred Heart has since become one of the most successful institutes in the Roman Catholic educational system.

Still in office at the age of 85, Madeleine died in Paris. Her incorrupt body lies at Jette in Belgium. She was canonized in 1925.

Left The Society of the Sacred Heart operates around the world. Here, Sacred Heart nuns wait to board a ship in May 1949, during the civil war in China.

ANTONY CLARET

ANTONY WAS A PRIEST OF GREAT INTELLECTUAL TALENT, BUT HE WAS ALSO A MIRACLE WORKER AND A GIFTED TEACHER, WHO REACHED OUT TO ALL BELIEVERS IN HIS SERMONS AND WRITINGS.

KEY FACTS
Founder
DATES: *1807–70*
BIRTH PLACE: *Sallent, Spain*
PATRON OF: *Weavers, savings banks*
FEAST DAY: *24 October*

Antony was the son of a Spanish weaver, but decided to enter a seminary and was ordained in 1835. He joined the Jesuits in Rome, but ill health caused his return to Spain. He spread the message of Christianity widely and was a keen speaker and a successful and prolific writer, preaching some 10,000 sermons and writing around 200 texts during his lifetime.

In 1849, Antony founded the Missionary Sons of the Immaculate Heart of Mary (the "Claretians"), an order that still flourishes today. The following year, Queen Isabella II requested he serve as the Archbishop of Santiago in Cuba. Antony's reforms angered many, resulting in an attempt on his life.

After seven years in this post, he was recalled to be Isabella's confessor and used his powerful position to fund educational institutes. In 1868, a revolution drove Queen Isabella into exile, and Antony went with her. He died at the Fontfroide monastery near Narbonne, where he had been placed under house arrest.

Right Antony Claret (artist and date unknown).

CLELIA BARBIERI

CLELIA BARBIERI WAS A PIOUS CHILD AND THE YOUNGEST FOUNDER IN THE HISTORY OF THE ROMAN CATHOLIC CHURCH. ALTHOUGH SHE DIED YOUNG, HER COMMUNITY HAS SPREAD TO 35 COUNTRIES.

KEY FACTS
Founder
DATES: *1847–70*
BIRTH PLACE: *Budrie, near Bologna, Italy*
FEAST DAY: *13 July*

Clelia was born in Budrie, Italy. Her wealthy mother married a servant far below her station and instilled religious values in their children. Their eldest daughter, Clelia, was 11 years old when she was confirmed and had a spiritual experience that made her mourn for her sins and those of all the world.

Clelia joined the Christian Catechism Workers, a mostly male group, and encouraged other girls to follow her example of hard work and religious devotion. In 1868, she founded the Suore Minime dell'Addolorata for her

followers. Though she faced public disdain, she persevered in her mission, nursing sick children and teaching the catechism. Despite her youth, the sisters and the children she cared for called her "Mother".

The conditions in which she lived made her vulnerable to tuberculosis and as she lay dying, she told her followers, "I'm leaving, but I'll never abandon you." She was canonized in 1989.

Left Clelia's order is named after the Mater Dolorosa, *the Virgin of the Sorrows (Albert Bouts, c.1495).*

BERNADETTE OF LOURDES

BERNADETTE HAD VISIONS OF MARY, THE BLESSED VIRGIN, AND HER REMAINS PROVED INCORRUPT, BUT IT WAS HER SINCERITY AND TRUST IN GOD THAT QUALIFIED HER AS A SAINT.

KEY FACTS
Visionary
DATES: *1844–79*
BIRTH PLACE: *Lourdes, France*
FEAST DAY: *16 April (in parts of France 18 February)*

In the tradition of other saints of devout simplicity, such as Jean-Baptiste Vianney and Joseph of Copertino, Bernadette Soubirous was deeply spiritual and blessed by heavenly visions. And, as with those great men, she bore her role with dignity.

Bernadette was a country girl, the eldest of six children born to an impoverished miller in the Basque region of France. As a child, she was thin and stunted from lack of proper nutrition and suffered from asthma.

VISIONS OF MARY

When she was 14 years old, Bernadette experienced her first vision at the rock of Massabielle near Lourdes. Over the next six months, the same apparition of a beautiful young woman appeared

Above Since Bernadette's visions at Lourdes, many ill pilgrims visit the site in the hope that they will be cured.

Below The incorrupt body of Bernadette of Lourdes, kept at the convent in Nevers, where she lived for many years.

to her 18 times. No one else saw or heard the vision, but there were witnesses to her reaction. The vision informed Bernadette that the beautiful woman was Mary of the Immaculate Conception and instructed her to drink from the nearby spring and show penitence.

Church clerics and minor state officials interrogated Bernadette for months. Her answers, simple and unchanging, led some of them to label her stupid, but most were impressed by her sincerity. The resulting publicity frightened Bernadette, but she faced the jokes and cruel jibes, showing no anger. No matter how remorseless the goading became, she never denied her miraculous experience.

In 1866, she joined the Sisters of Notre-Dame of Nevers, and found merciful seclusion from the public. Her health was poor and she spent her remaining years in stoic suffering. Bernadette was canonized in 1933, in recognition of her patience, integrity, simplicity and devout trustfulness.

A PILGRIMAGE CENTRE

Secluded in the convent, Bernadette was unaware that the site where she had met the Blessed Virgin was being transformed into a pilgrimage centre, or that the basilica built there was consecrated in 1876, three years before her death.

Lourdes has become one of the great pilgrimage centres of the Christian faith, drawing to its miraculous waters those seeking spiritual healing.

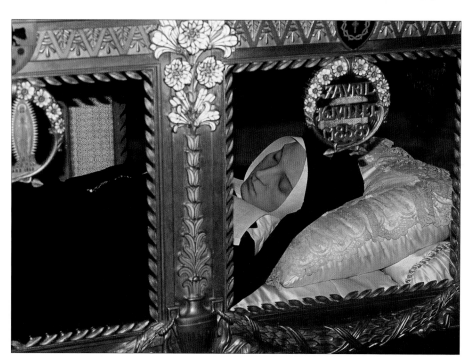

JOSEPH MKASA

JOSEPH MKASA SHOWED GREAT COURAGE AND FAITH WHEN HE DARED TO CONFRONT A TYRANT FEARED FROM ZANZIBAR TO THE CONGO. HE IS NAMED AMONG THE MARTYRS OF UGANDA.

KEY FACTS
Martyr of Uganda
DATES: *c. 1860–85*
BIRTH PLACE: *Uganda*
FEAST DAY: *3 June*

In 1885 Mwanga, the King of Uganda, ordered the killing of the Anglican missionary bishop, James Hannington, and his companions. Joseph Mkasa, a Roman Catholic convert and adviser to the king, was outraged by the killings, and was determined to do something about it, although he was aware that King Mwanga was a dangerous man.

This had not always been the case. As prince, Mwanga had shown no untoward behaviour or aggression toward Christians, but the moment he became king, he turned into a tyrant and a degenerate man, who treated slaves and servants cruelly, and made sexual advances toward the pages in his court. Mwanga was angered by the Christians because their loyalty to God outweighed that shown to himself, and he resolved to rid his country of Christianity.

CONFRONTING THE KING

Fearless for his own safety, Joseph Mkasa decided to make a stand and reproached the king for the murder. The bravery displayed by Joseph is even more impressive in the light of contemporary extracts from the diary of Henry Stanley, an American explorer in Africa. Stanley records the infamous reputation of Mwanga, who was feared by the British Foreign Office, the Arab authorities and merchants in East Africa. Even the infamous slave trader Tippu Tib was wary of him. Anyone travelling through Uganda needed military protection against violence from the king's men.

Above A plaque commemorating some of the Martyrs of Uganda. In 1885 and 1886, a total of 22 Africans were martyred.

Below A stained glass window of the boy martyrs in St Andrews Parish Church, Surrey, England.

On being confronted by Joseph Mkasa, the mad monarch immediately sentenced his adviser to death for being a traitorous convert. Joseph replied simply, "A Christian who gives his life for Christ is not afraid to die." He was publicly beheaded and fierce persecution of both Catholics and Protestants followed.

In time, Mwanga's religious persecution succeeded in uniting Christian and Muslim Ugandans, who put aside their traditional enmity and deposed him in 1889, placing his brother on the throne.

Joseph Mkasa and other named martyrs of Uganda were canonized by Pope Paul VI in 1964.

CHARLES LWANGA

CHARLES LWANGA, ONE OF THE NAMED MARTYRS OF UGANDA, WAS MURDERED BECAUSE HE PROTECTED THE CHILDREN IN HIS CARE AND REFUSED TO DENY HIS FAITH.

KEY FACTS
Martyr of Uganda
DATES: *1865–86*
BIRTH PLACE: *Uganda*
FEAST DAY: *3 June*

The tyrant of Uganda, King Mwanga, beheaded the bishop missionary James Hannington and the Ugandan convert Joseph Mkasa, but he did not stop there.

When Mwanga killed a page, Denis Sebuggwawo, for teaching the catechism, Charles Lwanga, who supervised the court pages, voiced his rage. That night, fearing the worst, Lwanga baptized four of the boys in his charge.

In the morning, the King called up Charles Lwanga, 15 pages and numerous other Christians captured by his warriors. He told

Above The Martyrs Monument at Namugongo in Uganda, which commemorates the martyrdom of Christians on 3 June 1886.

them to deny their faith but they said they would remain Christians "until death". They were marched to Namugongo, where they were beaten, wrapped in reed mats and burnt alive. Their joyful courage has been likened to that of the early Christians.

Mwanga murdered many more Christians, including Matthias Murumba and Andrew Kagwa. In 1964, 22 of the young men, including Charles Lwanga, were canonized as the Martyrs of Uganda. Their feast day is a public holiday in Uganda.

MARIE ADOLPHINE DIERKS

MARIE ADOLPHINE DIERKS WAS A HUMBLE DUTCH WOMAN WHO FELT CALLED UPON AND COMPELLED BY GOD TO BECOME A NUN. SHE SAID, "I WANT TO SUFFER FOR THE LORD".

KEY FACTS
Martyr of China
DATES: *1866–1900*
BIRTH PLACE: *Ossendrecht, Holland*
FEAST DAY: *17 February*

Marie was born in Holland, one of six siblings who lost their mother at an early age and were taken in by poor but kindly neighbours. Marie was dedicated to her studies and her prayers, but soon realized that her adoptive family needed financial help. She worked as a factory hand and as a domestic servant, giving part of her earnings to her family.

However, she felt a strong call to serve God, and in 1893 she joined the Franciscan Missionaries of Mary in Antwerp. With six other nuns, she was sent to the

Left A colour lithograph depicting the murder of a nun during the Boxer Rebellion in China.

Shanxi diocese in China. Work at the hospital and orphanage in Shanxi was hard, but Marie served with patience.

She was beheaded, along with her six Christian colleagues, in a crackdown on foreign missionaries during the Boxer Rebellion of 1900. Her name is included in the list of the 120 Blessed Martyrs of China, canonized by Pope John Paul II in 2000.

JOHN BOSCO

JOHN BOSCO WAS A GREAT TEACHER WHO NEVER PUNISHED HIS PUPILS BUT, INSTEAD, GUIDED BY A CHILDHOOD VISION, USED THE "PREVENTIVE" MEASURES OF LOVE, PATIENCE AND FIRMNESS.

KEY FACTS
Founder
DATES: *1815–88*
BIRTH PLACE: *Piedmont, Italy*
PATRON OF: *Editors, young people, young workers, apprentices and youth of Mexico*
FEAST DAY: *31 January*

John Bosco's life was given direction by a dream he had when he was very young. In this dream, he saw a group of young boys who were playing and swearing. To stop their blaspheming he punched them with his fists, but a man intervened, saying "You will have to win these friends of yours not by blows, but by gentleness and love."

A LIFE OF POVERTY

John was born into a peasant family from Piedmont, Italy, but lost his father when he was only two years old. He was brought up by his mother, and such was their poverty that, when he decided to enter a seminary in 1831, his clothes and shoes were donated by neighbours.

After he was ordained priest in 1841, John became chaplain of a girl's school in Turin. On Sundays, a group of boys who lived on the city streets would come to the school to play and learn their catechism. John quickly realized, with the help of his guide and teacher, Joseph Cafasso, that his life's work lay with these boys.

LED BY HIS DREAM

Bosco left the school and went to live in shabby rooms in the Valdocco area of Turin, where, with his mother as housekeeper, he housed and educated the abandoned boys of the city. He set up shoemaking, tailoring and printing workshops, where the boys could learn a trade, and gave them lessons in Latin and grammar. Never forgetting his dream, Bosco

Above A mosaic tile depiction of St John Bosco in Seville, Spain.

fostered a good relationship with his pupils through recreation, and encouraged picnics, outdoor play and a love of nature and music.

By 1856, he was housing 150 boys and he began to train like-minded people to help him in his work. He called these teachers "Salesians", after St Francis of Sales. They were approved as a religious order in 1874.

Bosco founded a similar order for women – the Daughters of Our Lady, Help of Christians – in 1872. These orders are now established across the globe, and run seminaries and technical and agricultural colleges.

John Bosco died in 1888, shortly after the completion of his church dedicated to the Sacred Heart in Rome, where he had been able to offer only one mass. About 40,000 mourners visited his body and the people of Turin lined the streets to watch the cortège. He was canonized by Pope Pius XI in 1934.

Below Part of an engraving from an Italian newspaper showing the canonization of John Bosco in St Peter's in 1934.

HOUSES OF GOD

MEDIEVAL CHURCHES WERE DESIGNED TO CAST THE MIND TOWARD
HEAVEN AND INSPIRE AWE. MODERN CHURCHES TEND TO BE MORE
SIMPLE AND INTIMATE TO HELP THE VISITOR FEEL CLOSER TO GOD.

As Christianity spread across the Middle East and Europe, so churches were built to provide places of worship for believers. In small towns and villages, these buildings became the centre of community life.

The church was the house of God, and as such, money, time and talent came to be lavished on great cathedrals and grand churches. The faithful entered these wondrous buildings and were filled with awe and reverence. Statues and paintings inside confirmed the reality of the saints, and Christians were convinced that, in these surroundings, their prayers would fly to heaven, where the saints were listening.

THE GOTHIC STYLE

The medieval period saw the building of churches throughout the Christian world on an unprecedented scale. In the West, the predominant architectural style was Gothic.

The Gothic architects erected structures of great grandeur to express the majesty of God and emphasize man's insignificance. These cathedrals featured huge flying buttresses, pointed arches, rib vaults, and large windows. Enormous doors opened into interiors lit by the mysterious glow of stained glass.

> "I AM THE ETERNAL DOOR: PASS THROUGH ME, FAITHFUL ONES. I AM THE FOUNTAIN OF LIFE: THIRST FOR ME MORE THAN WINE."
>
> ON THE PORTAL OF THE CHURCH OF SANTA CRUZ DE LA SERÓS, SPAIN

Façades were laced with decoration and statues of saints, and to remind the faithful of hell, small devilish gargoyles flew from the buttresses or were carved into pews. One of the finest examples of the Gothic style is the 12th-century Notre-Dame Cathedral in Chartres, France.

The construction of Gothic cathedrals often took centuries to complete, so these buildings frequently incorporate a range of architectural and artistic styles.

Left The front façade of the Cathedral of St Michel and St Gudule in Brussels, Belgium.

Above The royal portal on the west front of Notre-Dame Cathedral in Chartres, France (c.1145).

Construction of the Cathedral of St Michel and St Gudule in Brussels, for example, commenced in the early 13th century but the work was not completed for another 300 years. Cologne Cathedral, which has the largest façade of any church in the world, was begun in 1248 and finished 600 years later. Much of the stained glass in the cathedral is from the 19th century.

A NEW DIRECTION

When Martin Luther criticized the power and practices of the Roman Catholic Church in 1517, he began a new era for the church in northern Europe, known as the Reformation.

During the Reformation and in its aftermath, exterior carvings and statues, and the splendid interiors, walls hung with paintings, reliquaries gleaming with precious metals and jewels, and even the shrines so carefully constructed for relics were destroyed by Luther's Protestant supporters.

A new and austere style emerged, and this mood prevails in much modern northern European church architecture. Architects of Protestant churches

Left The dome of the Hagia Sophia in Istanbul, Turkey. This magnificent Byzantine building was the mother church of the Eastern Christians for 916 years before it was turned into a mosque by the Ottomans in 1453. It is now a museum.

no longer seek to replicate heaven; neither do they wish to inspire awe in visitors. Churches are usually designed to be informal, and space is meant to promote fellowship among believers and stress a sense of community. Altar tables and light fittings are simple, and roof levels may be flattened or given low curves more in sympathy with an earthly landscape.

SURVIVAL OF DECORATION

Despite the efforts of the reformers, most medieval churches survived the Reformation. Even after the destructive Civil War in England, hundreds of examples are still relatively intact.

Where the Roman Catholic Church survived, or was unaffected by, the Reformation – in Italy, Spain, Poland, and parts of France and Germany – church architecture remained centred upon the glorification of God with beauty.

In the Balkans, Greece and the Middle East, where the Eastern Orthodox Church prevails, many ancient religious buildings can still be found, although some of these became mosques after the Islamic conquest of the East and the rule of the Ottoman Empire from Istanbul (once Constantinople).

Below The interior of Cologne Cathedral in Germany.

STAINED GLASS WINDOWS

The origin of the stained glass window is unknown, but artists were working in this medium by 1100. Coloured sections of glass, cut to shape and held together by black lead strips, formed elaborate designs that depicted biblical stories and lives of the saints. By the 16th century, artists preferred to paint the glass, and by the 18th century, many windows had been removed. Superb examples of medieval glass can still be seen in their original setting, for example at Notre-Dame Cathedral in Chartres, France, and York Minster in England. Many stained glass windows are preserved in the world's great museums.

Above A stained glass window at Chartres Cathedral showing St Lubin, Bishop of Chartres in the 6th century (c.1200–10).

THERESA OF LISIEUX

THERESA, THE "LITTLE FLOWER", WROTE OF HER RELATIONSHIP WITH GOD WITH AN ARTLESS SIMPLICITY THAT CONVEYED A DEEP SPIRITUALITY, QUALIFYING HER AS A DOCTOR OF THE CHURCH.

KEY FACTS
Virgin, mystic, Doctor of the Church
DATES: *1873–1897*
BIRTH PLACE: *Alençon, France*
PATRON OF: *France, missions, florists and flower growers*
FEAST DAY: *1 October*
EMBLEM: *Flowers*

Theresa of Lisieux lived a very ordinary life. She did not perform great works, found a religious order or convert thousands to Christianity. And yet this young girl, who lived for such a brief time, left a rich spiritual legacy.

AN EARLY VOCATION

Although she was only four years old when her mother died, Theresa had four older sisters to look after her. The eldest, Pauline, became her surrogate mother, but by the time Theresa was ten, her two eldest sisters had left home to enter the local Carmelite convent in Lisieux.

Theresa begged constantly to join the convent, but she was too young to take such vows. On a pilgrimage to Rome with her father, she knelt for a blessing

Above Theresa of Lisieux (artist and date unknown). Aware she was dying, Theresa wrote that, after her death, she would "let fall a shower of roses", meaning that in heaven she would intercede for her friends.

from Pope Leo XIII. Knowing that she was forbidden to speak to him, she broke all protocol and begged him to let her be a nun. He supported the decision of the Carmelites, but when Theresa reached the age of 15, the Bishop of Bayeux, impressed by her piety and determination, allowed the prioress to admit her.

In April 1888, the young girl began her life in the enclosed Carmelite convent, where she began to develop her spirituality by reading the Carmelite mystics and following the austere rules of the order. The abbess forbade

Left A photograph of Theresa of Lisieux in the garden of the Carmelite convent in Lisieux in France (c.1890).

Theresa to fast because she was not physically robust, but she sensed that the young girl was an intuitive thinker, and encouraged her to write. This wise advice allowed Theresa the time and space to produce *The Story of a Soul*, and her many other texts, which include 54 poems, 20 prayers, eight plays and more than 200 letters. In a simple poetic style, these writings describe how every "little life" can be enhanced by faith and reveal her extraordinary relationship with God.

THE "LITTLE WAY"

The young nun longed to be a saint, but aware that, as a Carmelite, she would not be able to achieve great works, she looked for a new path that would lead her to sanctity. "I knew I was a very little soul who could offer only little things to the good God", she wrote. From this thought grew her "little way" of "the doing of the least actions for love".

A year after she had joined the Carmelites, Theresa's father suffered two strokes that left him weak and dependent. Emotionally disturbed and unhappy, he had a nervous breakdown, and in 1894, died in a lunatic asylum. Her fourth sister, Celine, who had spent her life caring for their father, joined Theresa at the Carmelite convent.

Theresa wanted to follow the example of the apostles and

Above The Basilica of St Theresa in Lisieux, France, is the saint's major shrine.

longed for the opportunity to spread the love of Christ in foreign lands. She had always prayed for missionaries – it was a Carmelite discipline to pray for Christian missions abroad – but she also corresponded with the Carmelite nuns in Hanoi, Indo-China (now Vietnam), and they wanted her to join them.

QUIET SUFFERING
Then, in 1895, Theresa had a curious experience. During the night between Maundy Thursday and Good Friday, she heard "as it were, a far-off murmur announcing the coming of the Bridegroom". She seemed unaware that she was bleeding from her mouth – a symptom of tuberculosis. With her health broken, her dream of becoming a missionary would never be realized.

For 18 months, Theresa suffered pain and difficulty in breathing. She was eventually confined to the convent infirmary, where she was so ill that she was unable to receive Holy Communion. She died at the age of 24.

Pilgrims still flock to Lisieux to venerate St Theresa, who is known as the "little flower of Jesus" and Theresa-of-the-Child-Jesus, names that reflect her simple, childlike faith. Her book has been translated into 50 languages and has brought inspiration to millions of people. Theresa of Lisieux was canonized in 1925.

Below St Theresa, from a cycle of Carmelite Life made from mosaic in the Basilica of St Theresa in Lisieux, France (Pierre Gaudin, 1958).

"I DESIRE TO BE A SAINT, BUT I KNOW MY WEAKNESS AND SO I ASK YOU, MY GOD, THAT YOU YOURSELF WILL BE MY HOLINESS."

THERESA OF LISIEUX

GEMMA GALGANI
Born in 1878, Gemma was an orphan, terribly afflicted by tuberculosis of the spine. She resembled Theresa of Lisieux in other ways, too. Hers was a "little life" without office, wealth or public recognition. Faith guided all her actions, only ill health preventing her from entering a convent. Her mysticism was expressed in ecstasies, during which she gave spiritual messages. She had visions of Jesus and stigmata appeared on her body. Heroic in enduring illness and poverty, Gemma died in 1903 and was canonized in 1941.

Above Lucca in Tuscany, Italy. St Gemma Galgani's relics are housed at the Passionist monastery in the city.

RAPHAEL KALINOWSKI

IN HIS ROLE AS A PRIEST, RAPHAEL KALINOWSKI FOSTERED HOPES OF UNITING CHRISTIANS, THROUGH SPIRITUAL GUIDANCE, TO COMBAT THE GROWING POWER OF THE SECULAR STATE.

KEY FACTS
Carmelite
DATES: *1835–1907*
BIRTH PLACE: *Vilnius, Poland
(now Lithuania)*
FEAST DAY: *15 November*

The 19th century in Europe is a story of industrialization, nationalism and secular politics. The life of Raphael Kalinowski reflects the period. Raised a devout Catholic, he became an engineer, working on the new Russian railways. While running a Sunday school at the fortress in Brest-Litovsk where he was a captain, he became increasingly aware of the state persecution of the Church, and of his native Poles.

When the Poles rose against the Russians in 1863, Raphael joined them and was soon taken prisoner. Few survived the forced

march to slave labour in Siberia, but Raphael was sustained by his faith and became spiritual leader to the prisoners. He was released ten years later.

Left Polish Insurrectionists of the 1863 Rebellion *(Stanislaus von Chlebowski, 19th century)*.

Profoundly changed by his experiences in Siberia, Kalinowski joined the Carmelites, and in 1882, he was ordained priest at the monastery at Czerna, near Cracow, the last Carmelite brotherhood allowed in Poland.

Raphael strove to revive the Carmelites in Poland and to bring religious freedom to his oppressed countrymen. He died in Wadowice and was canonized in 1991.

MIGUEL CORDERO

MIGUEL CORDERO OF ECUADOR WAS A GIFTED TEACHER, WHO, THROUGH HIS TEACHING AND WRITINGS, SPREAD THE WORD OF JESUS ACROSS HIS COUNTRY.

KEY FACTS
de la Sallist
DATES: *1854–1910*
BIRTH PLACE: *Cuenca, Ecuador*
FEAST DAY: *9 February*

Miguel Cordero was physically disabled but intellectually precocious. In his thinking, he was a precise theologian, but his actions showed a man concerned with the welfare of his students and fellow priests.

The de la Salle Brothers (the international teaching order founded by St John-Baptist de la Salle) accepted Cordero when he was only 14, and a year later, sent him to Quito in Ecuador. He proved to be an outstanding teacher. At the age of 20, he published a Spanish grammar that became adopted nationwide, and later

Above Cuenca in Ecuador, birth place of Miguel Cordero. Cordero was the first Ecuadorian to be accepted into the de la Salle teaching order.

wrote other acclaimed textbooks, and translated a life of John-Baptist de La Salle.

The Ecuadorian government despised the Church, but in spite of the state's efforts to suppress religion, Cordero's fame as a holy teacher and writer spread.

In 1907, he was called to work in Belgium. However, the Belgian climate did not suit him and he was moved to Barcelona. When an anti-clerical revolution erupted in the city, Cordero had to be rescued by gunboat. He died in Premia del Mar, Spain, in 1910, and was canonized in 1984.

FRANCES CABRINI

A MISSIONARY AMONG ITALIAN IMMIGRANTS IN AMERICA, FRANCES IS KNOWN AS THE "MOTHER OF EMIGRANTS" FOR HER WORK TO KEEP THE FAITH ALIVE AMONG CHRISTIANS FAR FROM HOME.

KEY FACTS
Founder
DATES: *1850–1917*
BIRTH PLACE: *Sant' Angelo Lodigiano, near Pavia, Italy*
PATRON OF: *Migrants and emigrants*
FEAST DAY: *22 December*

Frances Cabrini was a missionary in the New World, but she did not work among the indigenous people. Instead, she was sent to revive the faith of Italian immigrants in America. Initially, she thought the mission unnecessary, believing all Italians to be as devout as her relatives.

Frances was the youngest of 13 children of northern Italian parents. After qualifying as a teacher, she tried to become a nun but was refused by two orders for health reasons. She was a tiny woman, barely 164cm/5ft tall, but a friendly priest, guessing at her

Above The body of Frances Cabrini lies in state in the chapel at the Mother Cabrini High School in New York City.

Left A statue of St Frances Cabrini in the National Shrine of the Immaculate Conception in Washington, DC.

inner strength, appealed to his bishop, who invited her to manage a small orphanage in Codogno, Lombardy. She remained there until the house closed.

THE MISSIONARY SISTERS

The bishop encouraged Frances to start her own missionary congregation. She gathered seven women who had worked with her at Codogno and founded the Missionary Sisters of the Sacred Heart, dedicated to the education of Christian girls.

Frances had always wanted to work in China, but the Archbishop of New York had

invited her to set up schools and orphanages for Italian immigrants. When, in 1889, she and six sisters crossed the Atlantic, they found no one had prepared for their arrival, and they had to live in poverty with the immigrants until Frances was able to find a building and open the orphanage.

SPREAD OF THE MISSION

Success followed, and Frances opened more orphanages and schools in New York. She also founded schools in Managua, the capital of Nicaragua, and in New Orleans. Over the following years, her mission spread to Italy, Costa Rica, Panama, Chile, Brazil, France and England. Her profound faith drove her, and her proudest achievement was in opening the Columbus Hospital in New York.

Before moving to the United States, Frances had never met a Protestant and had difficulty in accepting that they, too, could be Christian. Her views were stern on subjects such as illegitimacy, but her deep love of God and a sense of justice tempered her thinking and ideas.

When her Missionary Sisters of the Sacred Heart were approved in 1907, there were 1,000 members in eight countries, and they served orphans, schools, prisons and hospitals.

Frances died in Chicago in 1917 and, in 1946, was the first American to be canonized.

TERESA OF LOS ANDES

TERESA WANTED TO DEVOTE HER LIFE COMPLETELY TO JESUS AND "TO LOVE AND SUFFER FOR THE SALVATION OF SOULS". THE SIMPLE FAITH OF THIS YOUNG WOMAN HAS BECOME AN EXAMPLE TO MANY.

KEY FACTS
Virgin, Carmelite
DATES: *1900–20*
BIRTH PLACE: *Santiago, Chile*
FEAST DAY: *12 April*

The shrine of St Teresa of Los Andes at La Riconda attracts 100,000 pilgrims every year. She is among those pious young women, such as Theresa of Lisieux, whose every thought and action was directed toward God.

CALLED TO SUFFER

One of six children born in Santiago, Chile, to wealthy, unassuming Christian parents, Teresa was well educated in the sciences, music and the arts. Her parents, who named her Juanita, were pleased by the religious faith of their daughter and the happiness it seemed to bring her.

When she was 14 years old, and suffering a painful bout of appendicitis, Teresa heard the voice of Jesus telling her that her pain was in imitation of his suffering. She had been lively and athletic until then, nicknamed "the Amazon" by her brothers, but after hearing

Above A statue of St Teresa of Los Andes in Chile. A cultus developed after her death and she remains popular, especially with young women.

Jesus speak, she made an inner vow of chastity, took to teaching the catechism to deprived children, and read the biographies of Theresa of Avila and of Blessed Elizabeth of the Trinity.

DEVOTION TO CHRIST

Teresa considered joining the Sacred Heart Sisters, who were an educational order, but was overwhelmed by the need to devote her life to Christ. Her father was reluctant to give his permission when she told him she preferred to join an enclosed order, but he and the family did support her when, at 19, she became a noviciate with the Carmelite nuns.

The Carmelite convent in Los Andes was a rough building that lacked electricity and plumbing. Here, she took the vow of Victimhood, which meant that she was prepared to suffer for the Church and for sinners. Teresa's hours were spent deep in prayer, fasting, learning methods of contemplation, and recording and sharing her spiritual experiences in letters and a diary.

She was not quite 20 years old when she died of typhus at the convent, but her piety was regarded with great respect, and slowly, the power of her "hidden life" of devotion was revealed. A cultus grew around her memory and she was canonized by Pope John Paul II in 1993.

Left Personal messages for St Teresa of Los Andes cover a wall outside the church dedicated to her in Los Andes, Chile.

BERTILLA BOSCARDIN

KEY FACTS
Nun, nurse
DATES: *1888–1922*
BIRTH PLACE: *near Vicenza, Italy*
FEAST DAY: *20 October*

BERTILLA WAS A SIMPLE PEASANT WOMAN WHO HAD BEEN BADLY TREATED AS A CHILD, BUT HER PATIENCE AND STAUNCH RELIGIOUS FAITH MADE HER A WONDERFUL NURSE.

This saint lived a humble life, but those whom she cared for loved her, and miracles have been attributed to her intercession.

Maria Bertilla Boscardin was a peasant girl who joined the Sisters of St Dorothy in Vicenza in 1904. The other nuns, considering her dim-witted, used her as a kitchen and laundry maid until her profession in 1907, when she was sent to care for children with diphtheria at the hospital in Treviso.

During World War I, Vicenza was bombed, but Bertilla remained calm, intent only on saving her patients. When the hospital was moved away from the front line to Como, the military authorities praised her work. But again, her simplicity was misinterpreted, and she was put to work in the laundry. Bertilla never complained, but in 1919, the Superior-General of the order rescued her and placed her in charge of the children's isolation ward back at Treviso, where she nursed with compassion.

Bertilla died while undergoing surgery. Her family and some of her former patients were present at her canonization in 1961.

Above Bertilla Boscardin worked as a nurse in Treviso, where she cared for the sick with patience and sympathy.

GIUSEPPE MOSCATI

KEY FACTS
Doctor of medicine
DATES: *1860–1927*
BIRTH PLACE: *Benevento, Italy*
FEAST DAY: *16 November*

GIUSEPPE MOSCATI BELIEVED HIS SCIENTIFIC KNOWLEDGE AND CARE OF THE SICK WERE A WAY TO REVEAL THE GLORY OF GOD AND CONSIDERED HIS MEDICAL WORK TO BE A "SUBLIME MISSION".

Giuseppe Moscati came from a family brave in their faith. His father was a magistrate who had risked his livelihood, when he refused to deny Christianity during the anti-clerical control of Italy during the mid-19th century.

Giuseppe was a top medical student at the University of Naples, where he specialized in biochemistry. After qualifying, he began working with patients afflicted with syphilis at the Hospital for Incurables, Santa Maria del Populo.

Parallel to his hospital duties, Giuseppe conducted medical research and gave free care to the poor. This entailed visiting the swarming slums of Naples, often at night, to tend the sick. His scientific learning was underpinned by his faith, and he treated patients for spiritual as well as medical problems.

In 1911, he was appointed Chair of Physiology at Naples University, but success did not turn him from his prayers or his veneration of Mary, the Blessed Virgin. Neither did he neglect his charity work. Patients, priests and laymen appreciated the spiritual dimension he brought to medicine. He died peacefully in his home and was canonized in 1987.

Above Pilgrims touch the hand of the Giuseppe Moscati statue at Gesù Nuovo Church in Naples, Italy.

THE CULT OF MARY

MARY, THE BLESSED VIRGIN, IS HONOURED WORLDWIDE BY MILLIONS OF FAITHFUL FOR HER PURITY AS WELL AS FOR HER EXTRAORDINARY ROLE AS THE MOTHER OF GOD.

Devotion to Mary can be traced as far back as the 4th or 5th centuries AD, but the full doctrine has developed gradually. In the earliest days of the Church, Mary, the Blessed Virgin, was called Christokos, "Mother of Christ", but this caused some wrangling among theologians because it implied that Jesus was not divine. In the 6th century AD, they agreed on Theotokos, "Mother of God", and this more emphatic description of Mary confirmed her strong position in the faith as the mother of Jesus, the Son of God. Even the Protestant Church accepted her unique role as the virgin mother of Christ, but some Protestant sects have recently questioned this.

AN EXCEPTIONAL WOMAN
Christians who venerate Mary often call her the Immaculate Conception. This refers to the belief that her spirit was conceived free from original sin, untainted by the sins of Adam and Eve in the Garden of Eden. This has led some theologians to refer to her as the "new Eve".

Not only is Mary believed to be immune from original sin, but she was also a virgin when Jesus was born, hence the title given to her, the Blessed Virgin. Because she embodies

Above A statue of the crowned Virgin and Child in Siena, Italy.

> "GRANT WE BESEECH THEE, O LORD GOD, UNTO US THY SERVANTS, THAT WE MAY REJOICE IN CONTINUAL HEALTH OF MIND AND BODY; AND, BY THE GLORIOUS INTERCESSION OF BLESSED MARY EVER VIRGIN, MAY BE DELIVERED FROM PRESENT SADNESS, AND ENTER INTO THE JOY OF THINE ETERNAL GLADNESS. THROUGH CHRIST OUR LORD. AMEN."
>
> FINAL WORDS OF THE LITANY OF LORETO

purity and perfect motherly love, she has always held a special place in the heart of believers. Augustine of Hippo, when discussing the nature of Mary, said, "After all, how do we know what abundance of grace was granted to her who had the merit to conceive and bring forth him who was unquestionably without sin?"

When Mary had completed her life on earth, it is believed that she was received into heaven as a complete being – body and soul together. This special event is key to both Roman Catholic and Eastern Orthodox belief, but the Anglican Church also includes it

in its calendar. The day of the Assumption, 15 August, occasions great celebration as it is considered to be Mary's heavenly birthday.

THE GREATEST SAINT
Mary has long been perceived as chief among all the saints, mediating with Jesus on behalf of the world. For this reason, the faithful turn to her to resolve their most difficult problems.

In 1587, Pope Sixtus V sealed this view of Mary's role when he approved the Litany of Loreto. In

Left A West African wood carving of Madonna and child (20th century).

Right Catholics seek blessings for their child from a statue of Mary in Hyderabad, India.

Left An Ethiopian icon triptych depicting the Virgin and child (18th–19th century).

Catholic homes, schools and institutions display the image of the Blessed Virgin and often create small shrine-like altars in veneration of her. No Catholic church is without a statue to Mary, the Blessed Virgin and the infant Jesus.

In modern times, Mary is firmly lodged in the Christian culture. She is a central figure in literature and popular idiom, and she is patron saint to a number of countries.

The principal Marian shrines attract huge numbers of pilgrims, millions visiting every year the sites of Lourdes in France, Guadalupe in Mexico, Fatima in Portugal, Walsingham in England and the House of Loreto in Italy.

SOME TITLES OF MARY

There are numerous titles for Mary, many used in the long prayer, the Litany of Loreto. Here are a few examples:
Advocate of Grace
Champion of God's People
Chosen Daughter of the Father
Gracious Lady
Handmaid of the Lord
Holy Mary
Holy Mother of God
Joy of Israel
Most Honoured of Virgins
Mother of Christ
Mother Mary
Our Lady
Perfect Disciple of Christ
Queen of All Saints
Queen of Apostles and Martyrs
Queen of Confessors and Virgins
Queen of Mercy
Queen of Peace
Splendour of the Church
The Blessed Virgin
The Immaculate Conception

this long prayer, believers call upon God to heed Mary, and the text uses her many titles.

WORLDWIDE INFLUENCE

The Eastern Orthodox Church has been untouched by debate about Mary's role. There, she has always had a profound significance and many Orthodox icons are devoted to the image of Mary as Mother with her Holy Infant.

In the Western Church, theologians have long debated her role, but since the 15th century, popular religion has developed a deep devotion to Mary. She represents motherhood and family life, one who understands the universal experiences of joy and pain. Those believers suffering tragedy

Right The famous La Pietà *in St Peter's, Rome (Michelangelo, 1496).*

meditate on the image of Mary with her dying son. The rosary is a set of prayers often recited by Christians who venerate Mary, the Blessed Virgin. A string of beads, also called a rosary, is used as an aide-mémoire for the correct order of the prayers.

MARIA FAUSTINA KOWALSKA

MARIA FAUSTINA KOWALSKA WAS A HUMBLE LAY SISTER, BUT HER HEAVENLY VISIONS, HER OBEDIENCE AND HER DEEP DEVOTION TO GOD, RECORDED IN HER DIARIES, BROUGHT HER SAINTHOOD.

KEY FACTS
*Visionary
and Polish mystic*
DATES: *1905–38*
BIRTH PLACE: *Glogowiec, Poland*
FEAST DAY: *25 August*

Maria Faustina Kowalska offered her own suffering to God to make amends for her sins and the sins of others. Her inspiration came from a miracle described in John's Gospel: after Jesus had healed a man who had been an invalid for 38 years, he said to him, "Sin no more, lest a worse thing come unto thee." The man went away and told others that Jesus had made him well. Maria believed that with faith and virtue, sins would be forgiven, just as the faith of the invalid had banished his disability.

A LIFE GUIDED BY VISIONS

Born in Glogowiec, Poland, Maria was the third of ten children. She was certain that she had a vocation to the religious life, and in 1923,

Above Cracow, Poland, where Maria Faustina Kowalska spent the last few years of her life in contemplation and prayer while she fought off illness.

she had a vision of Christ that strengthened her conviction. In 1925, she joined the Congregation of Our Lady of Mercy in Warsaw as a lay sister.

She did not aim for high office, and nursed no ambition but, in humility and obedience, worked in the garden, the kitchen and as a porter. The compassion and patience she showed toward the poor who visited the convent impressed her fellow nuns.

DIVINE MERCY

Visions of Jesus were a frequent part of Maria's experience, and in one of these Christ is said to have asked her to keep a diary. In this, she began to record the spiritual guidance the visions brought her, primarily the message of the "Divine Mercy of God". Her diary was later published with the title *Divine Mercy in My Soul: The Diary of St Faustina.*

Her health was delicate, and in 1936 she was moved to a sanatorium in Cracow with suspected tuberculosis. Here, she was given her own cell, and in this privacy she was able to surrender herself to prayer and contemplation. Her last years were spent fighting for breath and in constant pain. She died in Cracow, still a young woman, in 1938, and was canonized by Pope John Paul II in 2000.

Left The canonization of Maria Faustina Kowalska by Pope John Paul II took place in front of 100,000 pilgrims in 2000.

MAXIMILIAN KOLBE

MAXIMILIAN KOLBE MADE THE ULTIMATE SACRIFICE, GIVING UP HIS LIFE FOR THE SAKE OF ANOTHER IN A GERMAN CONCENTRATION CAMP. HE IS KNOWN AS THE "MARTYR OF CHARITY".

KEY FACTS
Martyr
DATES: *1894–1941*
BIRTH PLACE: *near Lodz, Poland*
FEAST DAY: *14 August*

Maximilian Kolbe was the son of devout, patriotic Polish parents. After Maximilian entered the Franciscan Order in 1910, his parents separated and began living religious lives. His father was hanged by the Russian government in 1914, because he was fighting with the Polish Legion for Polish independence.

In 1912, Maximilian was sent to Cracow, then to Rome, where he studied philosophy, theology, physics and mathematics. After his ordination in Rome in 1919, he founded Franciscan communities dedicated to prayer and serving the poor at Niepokalanow, near Warsaw, and at Nagasaki in Japan. He was keen to revive the faith and started various religious publications in both Poland and Japan to accomplish this. He also took advantage of modern technology by installing a radio station at Niepokalanow.

HOUSING REFUGEES

When the Germans invaded Poland in 1939, Maximilian closed the Niepokalanow community and sent the priests home, anxious that they should not endanger themselves by joining the resistance. Heedless of his own safety, he and the remaining brothers housed 4,500 Polish refugees, of whom 1,500 were Jewish. Maximilian's various publications continued and included articles critical of the German invaders. In 1941, he and four brothers were arrested and taken to the Nazi concentration camp at Auschwitz in Poland.

Above An undated photograph of Maximilian Kolbe, the Franciscan priest who served, then gave up his life for fellow Poles in World War II.

GIVING HIS LIFE

Maximilian had suffered tuberculosis most of his life, so he found his duties at the camp – carrying logs and moving the bodies of dead inmates – particularly hard. He applied himself to giving his fellow sufferers religious comfort, and somehow even managed to smuggle bread and wine inside the walls so that he could offer the Holy Eucharist.

One day, the inmates from Maximilian's hut were lined up and the wardens selected several men to die. This was a reprisal for a successful escape attempt. One of the chosen, a Polish sergeant named Francis Gajowniczek, cried out, "My poor wife! My poor children! What will they do?" Maximilian stepped forward and announced, "I wish to die for that man. I am old; he has a wife and children."

The swap was approved and the condemned men were locked into Cell 18 and left to starve. Maximilian comforted them, sang psalms and prayed in preparation for their deaths. After two weeks, he was the only man still conscious. He was killed by lethal injection in August 1941.

Sergeant Gajowniczek – who himself died at the age of 94 in 1995 – attended the canonization of St Maximilian Kolbe in 1982.

Below Francis Gajowniczek, the man saved by Maximilian Kolbe in 1941, is embraced by Pope John Paul II in St Peter's Square in 1982.

EDITH STEIN

EDITH STEIN, A JEWISH CONVERT AND PHILOSOPHER, BECAME A CARMELITE NUN, BELIEVING THAT IT WAS HER VOCATION "TO INTERCEDE TO GOD FOR EVERYONE".

KEY FACTS
Martyr
DATES: *1891–1942*
BIRTH PLACE: *Breslau, Germany (now Wroclaw, Poland)*
PATRON OF: *France*
FEAST DAY: *9 August*

Edith Stein was brought up in the Jewish faith and studied philosophy at the German universities of Göttingen and Freiburg. During this time, she was profoundly affected by the writings of St Theresa of Ávila. She converted to Catholicism and was baptized in 1922. Edith did not regard her Christianity as a denial of her family's faith but as an expansion of their Jewish beliefs. She continued to attend synagogue with her mother in order to soften the impact that her conversion would have on her devout Jewish family.

TEACHING AND STUDYING

Although Edith was not at ease in front of a class, she became a German language and literature teacher at a Dominican girls' school. As a woman, academic work in a university was closed to her. She joined the Educational Institute but privately continued her philosophical studies, including a work on the role of women

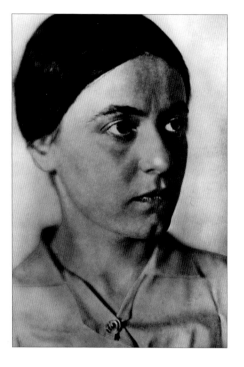

Left The Jewish philosopher, photographed aged 39, became a Carmelite nun in 1934. Reading the autobiography of St Theresa of Ávila inspired her to convert.

in the Christian Church. In 1932, Hitler initiated his anti-Jewish propaganda and Edith wrote, "Christ's Cross is being laid upon the Jewish people…"

In 1933, Edith entered the Carmelite order, where a sympathetic abbess allowed her to continue writing on religious and scholarly topics. Edith prepared philosophical texts on prayer and the Eternal Being, and began a study of St John of the Cross.

By 1937, those of Jewish origin were no longer safe in Germany and the Carmelites sent her to Holland. The Dutch Church campaigned against Nazi anti-Semitic policies but to no avail.

AUSCHWITZ

Edith refused to stay hidden in her convent, fearing her presence would harm the other nuns, and said on learning that she would be sent to Auschwitz in 1939, "I am going for my people."

Edith's faith brought her comfort and strength, and she ministered to her fellow prisoners. An insight into how she regarded her fate can be drawn from her own words: "Sufferings endured with the Lord are his sufferings, and bear great fruit in the context of his great work of redemption." Edith Stein was killed, with her sister Rose, in Auschwitz in 1942, and was canonized in 1998.

Left Edith Stein was captured in the Netherlands during a persecution of Jewish converts. She was sent to Auschwitz death camp, where she was gassed in 1942.

JOSEPHINE BAKHITA

JOSEPHINE WAS SO TRAUMATIZED WHEN CAPTURED AND ILL-TREATED BY SLAVE TRADERS THAT SHE FORGOT HER NAME. PROPHETICALLY, HER KIDNAPPERS NAMED HER BAKHITA – "THE FORTUNATE ONE".

KEY FACTS
Convert, nun
DATES: *1869–1947*
BIRTH PLACE: *Olgossa, Darfur, Sudan*
PATRON OF: *the Sudan*
FEAST DAY: *8 February*

Josephine represents all victims of oppression, and is venerated for her message of forgiveness. For many years a slave, Josephine claimed that, if she were to meet the men who enslaved her, she "would kneel to them to kiss their hands", because without them, she would never have met Jesus.

Born in Darfur, Sudan, Josephine was only nine years old when Arab traders abducted and sold her in Khartoum. She was traded from one unpleasant owner to another until, in 1882,

Right A convoy of slaves in the Sudan, where Josephine Bakhita herself was traded as a slave while still a child.

an Italian named Callisto Legnani bought her. He in turn gave her to his friend Augusto Michieli, who took her to Italy.

While he was away on business, Bakhita, as Josephine had been named, and Michieli's daughter stayed at the Canossian

convent in Venice, where Josephine became a Christian. On her master's return, she requested permission to stay at the convent, and took her vows there in 1896.

Josephine was moved to the Canossian convent at Schio, Vicenza, where she remained for the rest of her life, apart from three years in Milan spent teaching young sisters to work in Africa. She was known and loved for her gentleness, calming voice, and ever-present smile. She died in Schio, murmuring, "Madonna, Madonna!" Pope John Paul II canonized her in 2000.

JOHN CALABRIA

ON THE TOMB OF JOHN CALABRIA ARE THE WORDS: "HE SHONE LIKE A LIGHTHOUSE IN THE CHURCH OF GOD HIS MISSION WAS 'TO PROVE TO THE WORLD THAT DIVINE PROVIDENCE EXISTS'."

KEY FACTS
Founder
DATES: *1873–1954*
BIRTH PLACE: *Verona, Italy*
FEAST DAY: *4 December*

John Calabria's holiness was recognized beyond the Roman Catholic community. During World War II, he protected persecuted Jews, disguising one woman as a nun to save her. He practised charity to everyone, regardless of faith or creed.

John was born in poverty in Verona, and was educated at the Institute for Poor Children. In 1897, he began to work with orphaned and abandoned boys, starting a "Charitable Institution for assistance to poor, sick people",

which became the Congregation of the Poor Servants, and its sister house, the Poor Women Servants of Divine Providences.

John assured his followers that faith would help them in difficult situations "where there is nothing humanely possible", and he sent them to open hospitals and care homes in Italy and India. His writings and sermons encouraged people to follow God's love without prejudice. John died in San Zeno, Verona in 1954 and was canonized in 1988.

Left The San Zeno Basilica, the best-known church in Verona, where John Calabria spent his life.

KATHARINE DREXEL

KATHARINE DREXEL, MOTIVATED BY A PROFOUND FAITH, USED HER INHERITANCE TO IMPROVE THE SOCIAL AND RELIGIOUS WELFARE OF RACIAL MINORITIES AND DEPRIVED PEOPLES.

KEY FACTS
Founder
DATES: *1858–1955*
BIRTH PLACE: *Philadelphia,
USA*
FEAST DAY: *3 March*

Katharine Marie Drexel learnt the Christian virtue of charity from her stepmother, Emma Bouvier, who donated $20,000 a year to the welfare of the poor in Philadelphia. Another influence was Dr James O'Connor, a priest and family friend who campaigned for the just administration of Native Americans.

In 1878, Katharine "came out" in society, but she remained unmoved by the lavish circuit of balls and parties enjoyed by many of her peers. During a trip to Europe, she made a pilgrimage to the home of St Catherine of

Below A statue of Katharine Drexel in the National Shrine of the Immaculate Conception in Washington, D.C.

Above A painting of Katharine Drexel (artist and date unknown) shows her with some of the children she gave her life to serve.

Siena, and later confided to Dr O'Connor that she wished to become a nun.

By 1885, O'Connor, who had recently been appointed Bishop of Omaha, called on Katharine to help him resolve disputes between white and Native Americans in Dakota. On her return, she and her sisters, all wealthy women, founded the Drexel Chair of Moral Theology at Washington University (D.C.).

At an audience with Pope Leo XIII in 1887, she was encouraged by the pope to become a missionary. Taking his advice, and fulfilling her dream of a life dedicated to God, Katharine joined the Sisters of Mary in Pittsburgh.

AIDING MINORITIES

Katharine was determined to start a community devoted to helping ethnic minorities, and, in 1891, founded the Sisters of the Blessed

Sacrament. In 1894, the order's first school for Native American children, St Catherine Indian School, was built in Santa Fe, New Mexico.

She established schools, missions and hospitals in Boston, Chicago, New Orleans, New York, Texas and Tennessee, and her congregation trained nearly 200 teaching sisters and 80 lay teachers. She also founded the first university for African American students, Xavier University in New Orleans.

Katharine worked until she was disabled by illness (she suffered a severe heart attack in 1935). Thereafter, she continued to pray for, and advise her communities, who all knew her as "First Sister". She died in Philadelphia in 1955 at the age of 97. At her funeral, the pallbearers represented the groups she had helped – Native Americans, African Americans and European Americans.

Although Katharine focused on the welfare of racial minorities, her work extended to all the underprivileged. From the time she founded her order at the age of 33 until the end of her life, Katherine gave away a personal fortune of 20 million US dollars to the work of the Sisters of the Blessed Sacrament.

She also funded many convents, monasteries and chapels. Her congregation, which remains rooted in the welfare and education programmes she instituted, still has an important role within the Church. Katharine Drexel was canonized by Pope John Paul II in 2000.

FATHER GEORGE PRECA

FATHER GEORGE PRECA LOVED THE GOSPELS, WHICH HE CALLED "THE VOICE OF THE BELOVED". A HUMBLE MAN, HE DEVOTED HIS LIFE TO TEACHING THE DEPRIVED AND UNEDUCATED.

KEY FACTS
Founder
DATES: *1880–1962*
BIRTH PLACE: *Valletta, Malta*
FEAST DAY: *9 May*

The young George Preca was cured of an illness after prayers of intercession to St Joseph. Throughout his life, George heard heavenly voices and had visions, and these spiritual experiences gave him a powerful sense of his mission on earth. He was inspired, too, by the words of Jesus, "Blessed are the meek, for they shall inherit the earth" (Matthew 5:5).

MALTESE MISSION

After he was ordained in 1906, George began to seek out ordinary working people, and he set up a mission on the waterfront of Valletta, Malta. In 1907, he founded a community that came to be called the Society of Christian Doctrine. This order of laymen and women pursued mission work throughout Malta, and Father George sent them forth with the hope that "the world would follow the gospel". These missions organized daily sessions of prayer and discussion, and taught children the Catechism.

However, the Church in Malta was displeased with George's inclusion of lay people in the Church hierarchy and his use of female missionaries. They tried to shut down the order, but encountered such uproar from believers and other priests that Father George was eventually reinstated, and the Society of Christian Doctrine was given approval in 1932. During the controversy, Father George cautioned his followers to quell their anger and forgive those who taunted them.

Above Pope John Paul II prays at the tomb of Father George Preca in Hamrun, Malta, in 2001.

Below The cityscape of Valletta, Malta, the birthplace of Father George Preca.

A HOLY, HUMBLE MAN

The Maltese admired Father George as a gentle, sympathetic confessor, and as a priest who welcomed the laity into the rituals of the Church. He was regarded as a holy man and saw a vision of the boy Jesus, which, he reported, brought him a sense of great spiritual sweetness. Others claimed he had cured their physical ailments.

The society's reputation spread, and it now has missions in Albania, Australia, Kenya, Peru and Sudan. Pope Pius XII made Father George a Monsignor of the Church, but the honour embarrassed him, and he dropped the title after the pope's death.

Father George Preca died at Santa Venera, Malta, in 1962, and his relics lie in Blata I-Badja. Prayers for his intercession have been known to cure the sick. He was canonized in 2007 by Pope Benedict XVI.

PADRE PIO

THE HUMBLE CAPUCHIN MONK, NOW BEST KNOWN AS PADRE PIO, MODESTLY TRIED TO HIDE THE MARKS OF HIS STIGMATA, SAYING, "I ONLY WANT TO BE A POOR FRIAR WHO PRAYS".

KEY FACTS
Stigmatist
DATES: *1887–1968*
BIRTH PLACE: *near Naples, Italy*
FEAST DAY: *23 September*

St Pius of Pietrelcina, better known as Padre Pio, first knew he belonged to God at the age of five. Throughout his childhood, he experienced visions and spoke with Jesus and Mary. He joined the Capuchin Order and was ordained at the friary of San Giovanni Rotondo, Pietrelcina in 1910.

RECEIVING THE STIGMATA

In 1918, he became "aware that my hands, feet and side were pierced and were dripping with blood". He had received stigmata, but he covered the wounds and tried unsuccessfully to hide them.

Padre Pio may have been awed, even frightened, by this gift of holy marks, but he could not have anticipated the antagonism he met within the Church. When his secret was revealed, other church-men claimed he was a fake and accused him of sexual licence, but

Above Padre Pio as depicted on the front of Italian magazine La Domenica del Corriere *in 1956.*

Below A friar bends over the coffin of Padre Pio. During his lifetime Pio was both revered and reviled. The controversy continued after his death in 1968.

believers crowded the friary, seeking blessings and forgiveness from him. In 1923, the Church placed increasingly severe restrictions on Padre Pio until he was virtually locked away and only allowed to take Mass in private. After Pope Pius XII lifted all these restrictions in 1933, life became easier for Padre Pio, but spiteful attacks from other clergy continued. True to Christ's teachings, Padre Pio remained meek and dedicated, despite slander and injustice.

MAN OF PRAYER

The Capuchins had built, in the friary grounds, a House for the Relief of Suffering, a place that was a hospital, hospice and retreat directed toward families in need. Pius XII encouraged Padre Pio to pray for the hospital. The saint spent long hours praying and meditating on the Way of the Cross, saying, "In books we seek God, in prayer we meet him."

In 1959, he began regular broadcasts on national radio, his sermons reinforcing his belief that "Prayer is the best weapon we possess, the key that opens the heart of God." His example inspired prayer groups across the world and these continue today.

Padre Pio wore mittens to hide the stigmata on his hands, and remained a humble friar, who spent all his life in his friary and died there, yet more than 100,000 people attended his funeral. A mother claimed a miracle cure of her child's meningitis after prayers to Padre Pio, who was canonized in 2002.

JOSEMARÍA ESCRIVÁ

THE FOUNDER OF OPUS DEI, JOSEMARÍA ESCRIVÁ, LIVED CHRISTIAN VIRTUES TO THE HIGHEST DEGREE AND HAD A MISSION TO FILL EVERYDAY LIVES WITH FAITH AND HOPE.

KEY FACTS
Founder
DATES: *1902–75*
BIRTH PLACE: *Barbastro, Spain*
FEAST DAY: *26 June*

As a youth, Josemaría Escrivá saw the footprints of a monk in the snow. He took this as a sign to follow the path to God and was ordained in 1925, soon after his father's death. He began a graduate law course in Madrid and supported his mother and siblings by tutoring other students. His personal experiences taught him that there was a path to God through family life, work and social duty.

OPUS DEI

In 1928, inspired by a religious experience on a retreat, Escrivá founded Opus Dei. This order of laymen lived communally, but their only rule was obedience to their founder. Josemaría taught them how to "sanctify their lives in the midst of the world", and to show how an everyday life can be enriched if it is dedicated to God.

When Spain erupted into civil war, thousands of religious were killed and, despite support from the pro-Church side, Josemaría was forced to flee across the Pyrenees. Some of those martyred have been canonized as individuals, while others are honoured as the Martyrs of the Spanish Civil War.

After the war ended in 1939, Opus Dei grew rapidly, working largely in the world of education, establishing houses in Europe and Latin America. In 1943, Pope Pius XII gave approval for members of Opus Dei to become priests. The order now has 80,000 members, many of whom are lay men and women, in 80 different countries. It owns radio stations and newspapers, which it uses to promote traditional faith and liturgy, to integrate faith into work and social responsibility, and to encourage religious domestic life.

Above Chapel of St Josemaría Escrivá at the Catedral de la Almudena, Madrid.

Alongside providing guidance for his order, Josemaría continued to study and to support his mother. When she died, he went to Rome to further his studies, and was made an honorary prelate of the Pontifical Academy of Theology.

Secularists have criticized Opus Dei for blurring the line between religion and politics. Others accuse the order of being secretive and exclusive, but few deny the goodness and spirituality of Josemaría, who died in his office in Rome, and was canonized in 2002 by John Paul II.

Left Josemaría Escrivá with a group of his followers in Rome in 1971.

GAZETTEER OF OTHER SAINTS

ON THE FOLLOWING PAGES ARE BRIEF ACCOUNTS OF SAINTS WHO HAVE NOT BEEN INCLUDED IN THE MAIN SECTION OF THIS BOOK BUT WHO NEVERTHELESS DESERVE MENTION.

CORENTIN
dates unknown

Cornish hermit who later became a bishop in Brittany, where his cultus revived in the 1600s after he appeared to a believer in a vision.
Feast Day: 1 May

JULIAN THE HOSPITALLER
dates unknown

According to legend, he killed his parents in a case of mistaken identity, then fled and built a house for poor people. He revived a dying man who disappeared into a bright cloud, which was seen as a sign that Jesus had forgiven Julian's sins.
Feast Day: 29 January

URITH OF CHITTLEHAMPTON
dates unknown

Legend has it that her pagan stepmother arranged her death – by harvesters wielding scythes – but that as she fell to the ground, a spring burst from the earth.
Feast Day: 8 July

ALBAN
3rd century AD

Protomartyr of Britain, this Roman citizen was converted by a priest whom he hid from persecution and helped escape. After disguising himself as the priest, he was arrested and later beheaded.
Feast Day: 2 August

CALLISTUS I
died AD 222

Born a slave and served time as a criminal before his conversion. He became Bishop of Rome and a pope, respected for his kind treatment of sinners. It is thought he died a martyr.
Feast Day: 14 October

PONTIAN AND HIPPOLYTUS
died c.AD 236

Hippolytus criticized bishops of Rome, Zephyrinus and Callistus I. He was banished to the Sardinian quarries, where he met Pontian, a former pope. Both died as prisoners and were later hailed as martyrs. Hippolytus' text, *Apostolic Tradition,* is a record of Christian worship during the Roman era.
Feast Day: 13 August

APOLLONIA
died c.AD 249

This aged deaconess of Alexandria was persecuted by an anti-Christian mob, who knocked out all her teeth. She chose to walk into the flames rather than deny her faith. Patron of toothache.
Feast Day: 9 February

BABYLAS
died c.AD 250

Antioch's most famous early bishop was martyred along with three boys whom he had converted. He is the first martyr whose relics are recorded as having been translated.
Feast Day: 24 January

LAURENCE
died AD 258

Legend claims he was a deacon of Rome and that he was roasted on a gridiron. Fra Angelico painted his life cycle in the Vatican.
Feast Day: 10 August

Above The Martyrdom of St Laurence *(altar from Waldburg, c.1520).*

CRISPIN AND CRISPINIAN
died c.AD 285

It would seem these men were of Roman origin and fled the city to avoid persecution. Their relics were moved to Soissons, France, which became the centre for their cultus from the 6th century.
Feast Day: 25 October

SEBASTIAN
died c.AD 300

Roman martyr sentenced to be shot to death by arrows. Popular subject for Renaissance painters. Patron of archers; one of the Fourteen Holy Helpers.
Feast Day: 20 January

ERASMUS (ELMO)
died c.AD 300

According to legend, this bishop fled persecution in Syria to hide as a hermit in Lebanon, but was discovered, rolled in pitch and set alight. An angel rescued him.
Feast Day: 2 June

MEN(N)AS
died c.AD 300

This Roman soldier was converted and martyred in Egypt, where he is still highly venerated. Miracles were attributed to him, and the water inside clay bottles made at his grave was believed to have curative powers.

Feast Day: 11 November

FLORIAN
died AD 304

A converted Roman army officer, Florian joined persecuted Christians and was tortured, then drowned in the River Enns. His body was recovered and his relics enshrined in St Florian Abbey, Linz.

Feast Day: 4 May

NINO
died c.AD 340

A slave girl credited with bringing Christianity to Georgia. She was taken to the royal court, where her powers of curing illness in Jesus' name caused the king to ask her to teach his people about Christianity.

Feast Day: 15 December

PAULA
died AD 404

A young widow of noble Roman birth, Paula settled in Bethlehem, where she built a convent and monastery, helped Jerome with his studies, and gave away her wealth.

Feast Day: 26 January

MOSES THE BLACK
c.AD 330–c.AD 405

An Ethiopian servant in Egypt who became a criminal. After his conversion, he joined a community of desert monks and was ordained. He was killed by raiding Berbers.

Feast Day: 28 August

HONORATUS OF ARLES
died AD 429

Born and converted in Rome, he founded a monastic community in Greece with his brother. After the latter's death, he moved to southern France and built another monastery. He died two years after becoming Bishop of Arles.

Feast Day: 16 January

PAULINUS OF NOLA
died AD 431

Born in Bordeaux, Paulinus trained as a lawyer and poet in Italy. After their baby died, he and his wife found faith, began to give away their wealth, and moved to a large house in Nola, Spain, where they provided shelter for pilgrims and fugitives. Paulinus was ordained Bishop of Nola c.AD 409.

Feast Day: 22 June

CASSIAN
(JOHN CASSIAN)
c.AD 360–433

Probably born in Romania, Cassian became a disciple of John Chrysostom in Constantinople. When the latter was exiled, Cassian went to Rome to plead his cause with the pope. He later founded two monasteries in Marseille.

Feast Day: 23 July

DANIEL THE STYLITE
AD 409–93

Joined an abbey when he was only 12. An admirer of Simeon Stylites, he locked himself in an abandoned temple for nine years, and when Simeon died in AD 459, he built a pillar and lived on it until his death.

Feast Day: 11 December

FLORENCE OF MONT GLONNE
5th century

Ordained by Martin of Tours, he lived as a hermit before founding a monastery in Saumur. His cultus lasted for centuries.

Feast Day: 22 September

CLOTILDE
c.AD 474–545

Married to Frankish King Clovis, a pagan who converted after he asked "Clothilde's God" for victory in battle and his prayer was granted. She later retired to a monastery, but through her northern Europe took its first steps toward Christianity.

Feast Day: 3 June

Above The martyrdom of Crispin and Crispinian *(French glass painting, 15th century).*

Above Clovis and Clotilde *(French stained glass, 19th century).*

MARCOUL

died c.AD 558

Born into a rich family, Marcoul preached in Normandy before becoming a hermit. He had many disciples and founded a monastery. Kings of France used to pray before his shrine.

Feast Day: 1 May

PETROC

6th century AD

This Celtic missionary trekked Cornwall, Devon and Brittany, made pilgrimage to Jerusalem and Rome, and was briefly a hermit.

Feast Day: 4 June

VENANTIUS FORTUNATUS

c.AD 530–610

An Italian who settled in Poitiers (elected its bishop in AD 600), he became chaplain to a convent. He wrote hymns, verse to the Blessed Virgin, and biographies of saints.

Feast Day: 14 December

FINBAR

c.AD 560–610

Irish saint who made a pilgrimage to Rome with Welsh St David. Venerated in Cork as founder of its monastery and for mission work.

Feast Day: 25 September

KENTIGERN

died AD 612

Celtic monk and Bishop of Glasgow and Cumbria. Legends abound: one tells that his mother was thrown into the sea and he (her illegitimate son) was born in a coracle.

Feast Day: 13 January

THEODORE OF SYKEON

died AD 613

Child of a prostitute mother and circus-artist father, Theodore was ordained a priest at 18. He took a pilgrimage to Jerusalem, then returned to Galatia, where he was an influential preacher. For a while, he was Bishop of Anastasiopolis, near Ankara, but returned to live as a monk at Sykeon.

Feast Day: 22 April

BRAULIO OF SARAGOSSA

died AD 650

Braulio became a monk and joined St Isidore in Seville before returning to his hometown of Saragossa, where he became the city's bishop. He defended converted Jews and fought against Arianism.

Feast Day: 26 March

ELOI

c.AD 588–660

His artistry in metalwork made Eloi famous throughout western Europe. He was Bishop of Noyen and counsellor to the queen-regent, Bathilde, a freed slave. Together they forbade the export of slaves from the kingdom.

Feast Day: 1 December

FIACRE

died c.AD 670

Irish by birth, Fiacre lived as a hermit most of his life in France. He was known as a gardener and cared for those suffering from venereal diseases. His cultus flourished in France until the 1700s.

Feast Day: 30 August

Below Eloi miraculously replaces the foreleg of a horse in this French tapestry (16th century).

AMAND

c.AD 584–675

French-born bishop who travelled as a missionary to Flanders and Carinthia, and founded monasteries near Ghent and a convent at Nivelles. His cultus spread through Flanders, Picardy and England.

Feast Day: 6 February

EBBE

died AD 683

Ebbe, the daughter of the King of Northumbria, was the first abbess of Coldingham. Despite the convent's lax reputation, she was holy and wise, and was instrumental in releasing St Wilfred from prison.

Feast Day: 25 August

THEODORE OF CANTERBURY

AD 602–90

Born a Greek, yet became Archbishop of Canterbury, England. His devout and scholarly leadership brought much-needed unity. His canonization was supported by the Venerable Bede's writings.

Feast Day: 10 September

LAMBERT

c.AD 635–c.AD 705

A leading churchman in the Low Countries, where pagans predominated. As Bishop of Liège, he was forced into exile for a time and later died as a martyr in the city.

Feast Day: 17 September

244

GILES
died c.AD 710

Born in Athens, he became a hermit near Nîmes, France. A strong cultus developed after his death, penitents believing his intercession would bring forgiveness.
Feast Day: 7 September

ODILE
AD 660–720

Daughter of the Duke of Alsace, Odile was born blind, but her sight was restored at baptism. She became an abbess and founded a nunnery. Her relics were spread across Europe to give those with weak sight access to her power.
Feast Day: 14 December

JOHN OF BEVERLEY
died AD 721

A monk in Whitby, then Bishop of Hexham and later of York, he showed patience and kindness to the mentally handicapped. A cultus grew quickly after his death.
Feast Day: 7 May

FRIDESWIDE
c.AD 680–727

Fleeing from a seducer, this virgin sought refuge in Oxford, where she became abbess of a monastery. Her shrine in Christ Church, Oxford, still attracts pilgrims.
Feast Day: 19 October

HUBERT
died AD 727

A missionary in the Ardennes, he became Bishop of Liège, where he built the cathedral. Many miracles were attributed to him.
Feast Day: 30 May

WILLIBRORD
AD 658–739

A Yorkshireman sent by the pope to organize a diocese in Utrecht. He seemed successful in establishing the faith, despite persecution.
Feast Day: 7 November

JOHN DAMASCENE
c.AD 657–749

A monk, then a priest, he spent his whole life under Muslim rule, first in Damascus, later at an abbey near Jerusalem. He was declared a Doctor of the Church in 1890.
Feast Day: 4 December

PIRMIN
died AD 753

Probably a Spaniard who fled Moorish rulers. He went first to Switzerland, where he rebuilt a monastery at Dissentis and later, as abbot of Riechenau monastery, built up a library. Political unrest forced him to flee to Alsace, where he founded more monasteries.
Feast Day: 3 November

ANDREW OF CRETE
died AD 766

Eighth-century Constantinople saw fierce arguments over icons, with Emperor Constantine V torturing and killing his opponents. Andrew (from Crete), who was visiting the city, criticized the emperor for his cruelty and was beaten, scourged, then stabbed to death in the streets.
Feast Day: 20 October

Above The Miracle of St Walburga *(Peter Paul Rubens, c.1610–11).*

WALBURGA
died AD 779

English-born missionary who became abbess of the monastery in Heidenheim. After her death, it is said that her shrine exuded oil believed to cure ailments. But her name became associated with witchcraft: on Walpurgisnacht in Germany, people dress as spooks, bats and witches.
Feast Day: 25 February

LIOBA
died AD 782

Educated in England, she went to Germany as a nun. As abbess of Tauberbischofsheim, she was known for being calm, cheerful and wise.
Feast Day: 28 September

ANSKAR
AD 801–65

Born near Amiens, France, Anskar devoted his life to taking the Christian message to pagans from Denmark to Sweden. Christianity was established in Scandinavia 200 years after his death.
Feast Day: 3 February

LUDMILLA
died AD 921
Martyr saint and grandmother of Prince (King) Wenceslas.
Feast Day: 16 September

ADALBERT OF PRAGUE
AD 956–97
A pioneer in taking Christianity to north-eastern Europe. After being exiled twice, he became a missionary in Poland, Prussia and the Baltics, and was martyred near Königsberg. His relics lie in Prague.
Feast Day: 23 April

ABBO OF FLEURY
died 1004
A Benedictine monk, scholar and martyr saint, he visited England, where he wrote a biography of St Edmund and reformed the monastic movement.
Feast Day: 13 November

WILLIGIS
died 1011
Priest, politician and missionary in Germany and Scandinavia.
Feast Day: 23 February

VLADIMIR
AD 955–1015
Forced to convert on marrying Princess Anne of Constantinople, he is venerated for introducing Christianity to Russia.
Feast Day: 15 July

WILLIAM OF ROSKILDE
died 1070
Set up a mission in Denmark, where he became a preacher and Bishop of Roskilde, Zeeland.
Feast Day: 2 September

DOMINIC OF SILOS
c.1000–73
A peasant from Navarre, Spain, whose piety, miracles, and liberation of captives taken by the Moors made him a much-loved priest.
Feast Day: 20 December

Above Vladimir the Saint
(Ivan Yakovlevich Bilibin, 1925).

BERNARD OF MONTJOUX
c.AD 996–c.1081
As archdeacon of Aosta Cathedral in the Alps, he cleared mountain passes of robbers and established resthouses for travellers.
Feast Day: 28 May

ROSALIA OF PALERMO
12th century
Born into a noble Sicilian family, she chose to live in a cave. Pilgrimages are still made to the church built over her hermitage.
Feast Day: 4 September

BRUNO
c.1032–1101
His Carthusian Order set a benign but influential example of spirituality throughout Europe.
Feast Day: 6 October

IVES
died c.1107
In 1100, in the village of Slepe, four bodies were found: someone dreamt their unusal insignia belonged to a Persian bishop (Ives), who had lived in England as a hermit. The bodies were translated to Ramsey Abbey, and miracles occurred.
Feast Day: 24 April

ALBERIC
died 1109
Co-founder of Cistercian Order, which insisted on poverty and labour for God. By the time of his death, there were nearly 400 Cistercian houses in Europe.
Feast Day: 26 January

ROBERT OF MOLESME
1027–1110
Spent most of his life as abbot at Molesme. Co-founder of the Cistercian Order at Citeaux, based on the rule of St Benedict, which grew into an influential worldwide organization.
Feast Day: 29 April

LEOPOLD III
1075–1136
Reigned for 40 years as the third Duke of Austria. He reformed existing monasteries and founded new ones, strengthened Austria as a nation and promoted Christianity.
Feast Day: 15 November

WILLIAM OF NORWICH
died 1144
When the 12-year-old's body was found in a wood near Norwich, his uncle claimed Jews had tortured and murdered him. A cultus developed, but papal letters directed Norwich to stop the ghastly story, and his shrine was abandoned.
Feast Day: 26 March

MALACHY
1094–1148
Archbishop of Armagh who introduced the Cistercian Order into Ireland and was a pioneer in Ireland's early religious reform.
Feast Day: 3 November

UBALDO
died 1160

As dean (later bishop) of Gubbio Cathedral in Umbria, he persuaded clerics to live a communal life. Patron against rabies.
Feast Day: 16 May

GODRIC
c.1069–1170

He walked barefoot to Rome before becoming a hermit. His poems set to music are the earliest known in the English language.
Feast Day: 21 May

GILBERT OF SEMPRINGHAM
c.1083–1189

An English pastor who organized women, then men, into Benedictine communities, where they nursed orphans and lepers.
Feast Day: 4 February

BARTHOLOMEW OF FARNE
died 1193

A priest and monk until his vision of Christ, after which he went to Farne Island as a hermit. Miracles were attributed to him by visitors.
Feast Day: 24 June

THORLAC OF SKALHOLT
1133–93

As bishop of Skalholt, Iceland, Thorlac reformed the priesthood and founded a community. His miracles are recorded, and a cultus flourished until the Reformation.
Feast Day: 23 December

HOMOBONUS
c.1120–97

Neither priest, king nor martyr, this "good man" of Cremona, Italy, was a tailor and merchant, who cared for the sick, fed the poor and buried the dead. Patron of tailors and clothworkers.
Feast Day: 13 November

WILLIAM OF ROCHESTER
died 1201

This Scottish fisherman vowed to visit Jerusalem, but was murdered by his travelling companion near Rochester. Miracles are said to have occurred at his burial site.
Feast Day: 8 June

SAVA (SABAS) OF SERBIA
c.1173–1236

Born a prince, he became a monk. He founded a monastery on Mount Athos, Greece.
Feast Day: 14 January

RAYMUND NONNATUS
1204–40

Ordained priest who became a slave in Algiers, hoping to rescue others from this dreadful fate.
Feast Day: 31 August

LUTGARDIS
1182–1246

Cistercian nun whose contemplative life caused many to turn to her for spiritual counselling.
Feast Day: 16 June

FERDINAND III
1199–1252

Revered King of Castile and Leon who wrested Andalusia from the occupying Moors, bringing it into the Christian world.
Feast Day: 30 May

ROSE OF VITERBO
c.1235–52

The 12-year-old Rose, dressed as a Franciscan, preached in the streets and loudly supported the pope, despite hostile opposition.
Feast Day: 4 September

ZITA
1218–72

A lifelong servant, venerated for her devotion and for her care of the poor and condemned convicts.
Feast Day: 27 April

RAYMUND OF PENNAFORT
c.1180–1275

He worked in Barcelona and Bologna before becoming confessor to Pope Gregory IX. He codified laws and wrote many texts. In his old age, he tried to convert the Moors who occupied Spain.
Feast Day: 7 January

CELESTINE V
1210–96

A devout hermit, he founded the Celestine Order in 1274. He was appointed Pope Celestine V in 1294, but abdicated five months later, the only pope ever to do so.
Feast Day: 19 May

LOUIS OF TOULOUSE
1274–97

Held for seven years as hostage after the King of Aragon captured his father, Charles II of Naples. Released in 1295 and ordained a Franciscan in 1297, he was immediately promoted to Bishop of Toulouse, but rejected the trappings of office, living in poverty.
Feast Day: 19 August

Above Louis of Toulouse *(panel, Simone Martini, 1317).*

MARGARET OF CORTONA
c.1247–97

Mistreated by her stepmother, she ran off with a knight and bore him a son. When her lover died, she was destitute and became a Franciscan tertiary, famous for public acts of penance. Miracles were attributed to her, and sinners sought her help.
Feast Day: 22 February

ALEXIS FALCONIERI
died 1310

Joined a community of hermits as a lay brother. The group (the Seven Founders) funded a mendicant order, the Servants of Mary (Servites). He also helped establish a Servite community in Siena.
Feast Day: 7 February

PEREGRINE LAZIOSI
died 1345

A Servite, recognized for his piety and dedication to the poor.
Feast Day: 1 May

CATHERINE OF SWEDEN
1331–81

Daughter of Bridget of Sweden. After nursing her husband until his death, she joined her mother in the convent of Vadstena, later becoming abbess. She worked hard to obtain approval of the Brigittines (her mother's order), and for the latter's canonization.
Feast Day: 24 March

SERGIUS OF RADONEZH
1315–92

From a noble family who fled the Tartars and settled in Radonezh, near Moscow. He and his brother restored the monastery there and Sergius became an important figure in religious and state life.
Feast Day: 25 September

Right Gospel Folios of St Sergius of Radonezh (Russian School, 14th century).

HEDWIG
1374–99

Daughter of the King of Hungary and Poland, she was used as a political pawn, but eventually married Jagiello, Grand Duke of Lithuania and Ruthenia, and together they set about converting their subjects.
Feast Day: 17 July

VINCENT FERRER
1350–1419

Dynamic preacher who converted Jews and Muslims in his native Spain and gained a reputation for miracle cures.
Feast Day: 5 April

FRANCES OF ROME
1384–1440

A powerful, religious presence in Rome, she experienced visions and cared for plague victims and war-wounded. Other women joined her and she founded the Oblates of Tor de' Specchi, which still exists.
Feast Day: 9 March

BERNARDINO OF SIENA
1380–1444

After nursing plague victims, he became a Franciscan evangelist, attacking greed and the warmongering of Italy's city-states.
Feast Day: 20 May

COLETTE
1381–1447

The antipope Bernard XIII made her a Poor Clare in charge of France's Franciscan nuns. She founded 17 new convents.
Feast Day: 6 March

JOHN OF CAPISTRANO
1386–1456

A married man and governor of Perugio, he became a Franciscan. A fierce believer, keen to reform, he was appointed inquisitor-general to Vienna in 1451.
Feast Day: 23 October

ANTONINUS OF FLORENCE
1389–1459

Dominican friar who founded the convent at San Marco. As archbishop of Florence, he lived in poverty, nursed plague victims and fed the hungry. He wrote important texts and advised papal reforms.
Feast Day: 10 May

CATHERINE DE'VIGRI OF BOLOGNA
1413–63

Well-born and highly educated, she refused marriage and joined the Augustinian tertiaries.
Feast Day: 9 March

Above Stanislaus Kostka
(artist unknown, 17th century).

JOHN OF SAHAGUN
c.1430–79

He reconciled fighting factions in Salamanca, a town riven by feuds. In 1463, he joined the Austin Friars. Miracles followed his death.
Feast Day: 12 June

CATHERINE OF GENOA
1447–1510

After she helped win her husband back to faith, they ran a hospital together in Pammatone. In later life, she wrote about spirituality and experienced visions.
Feast Day: 15 September

JEROME EMILIANI
1481–1537

A priest, Jerome founded a small community (the Somaschi), where he built hospitals, orphanages and homes for reformed prostitutes.
Feast Day: 8 February

JUAN DIEGO
died 1548

Born near Mexico City, he was baptized at age 50. Allegedly received an image of the Blessed Virgin miraculously printed on his cloak, signifying Jesus' rebirth.
Feast Day: 12 December

STANISLAUS KOSTKA
1550–68

Refused by local Jesuits, he walked more than 300 miles to Rome. A devout young man who experienced mystical visions.
Feast Day: 13 November

PHILIP OF MOSCOW
1507–69

As metropolitan of the Russian Church, he upbraided Ivan the Terrible for his bloodshed and cruelty. He was arrested, held in chains, and eventually martyred.
Feast Day: 9 January

EDMUND CAMPION
1540–81

An Anglican, scholar and founder of Trinity College in Ireland, he became a Jesuit in Rome. Arrested and executed on a false conspiracy charge, he is one of the Forty Martyrs of England and Wales.
Feast Day: 25 October

ALEXANDER BRIANT
c.1556–81

When Catholicism was banned in England, he refused to reveal the hiding place of a family he had persuaded to convert. For this he was cruelly tortured, then executed. He is one of the Forty Martyrs of England and Wales.
Feast Day: 25 October

CHARLES BORROMEO
1538–84

Archbishop of Milan and favoured nephew of Pope Pius IV. He instituted Sunday schools and opened seminaries to train priests.
Feast Day: 4 November

MARGARET CLITHEROW
1556–86

With her Protestant husband, she hid Catholic priests during a time of persecution. One of the Forty Martyrs of England and Wales.
Feast Day: 25 October

Above St Charles Borromeo *Fasting (19th-century copy, after Daniele Crespi from 1620).*

CATHERINE DE'RICCI
1522–90

Became a Dominican nun in 1535, later promoted to prioress.
Feast Day: 2 February

ALOYSIUS GONZAGA
1568–91

Despite his family's military ambitions for him, he became a Jesuit.
Feast Day: 21 June

Above St Aloysius Gonzaga in Glory *(Giovanni Battista Tiepolo, c.1726).*

Above Philip Howard imprisoned in the Tower of London (Henry Barraud, 19th century).

PHILIP HOWARD
1557–95
Converted to Catholicism from Anglicanism. He would not deny his faith and spent the rest of his life in the Tower. One of the Forty Martyrs of England and Wales.
Feast Day: 19 October

MARY MAGDALENE DE' PAZZI
1566–1607
She entered the Carmelite convent in Florence at the age of 17. Her writings reveal a love of the local landscape, as well as her devotion to God.
Feast Day: 25 May

ANDREW AVELLINO
1521–1608
After failing in a mission to reform a riotous house of nuns, he joined the Theatines, a new order, revealing his talent as a preacher and sensitivity toward confessors.
Feast Day: 10 November

CAMILLUS OF LELLIS
1550–1614
Founded the Servants of the Sick for priests and laymen, opened hospitals around Italy and was the first to send ambulances to a battlefront.
Feast Day: 14 July

JOHN BERCHMANS
1599–1621
His youthful piety and theological understanding encouraged a cultus.
Feast Day: 13 August

JOSAPHAT
1580–1623
Archbishop of Polotsk in Belarus, and martyr saint. A brisk reformer who sought unity with Rome.
Feast Day: 12 November

JOHN FRANCIS REGIS
1597–1640
Jesuit priest who worked exhaustively, preaching, serving the poor and nursing plague victims.
Feast Day: 2 July

JANE FRANCES DE CHANTAL
1572–1641
Founded the Visitation Order. By the time she died, 86 convents had been established in Europe.
Feast Day: 12 December

JOSEPH CALASANZ
1550–1648
He gave up his office of vicar-general of Andorra to teach slum children in Rome. After his death, his congregation was revived as the Piarists.
Feast Day: 25 August

ANDREW BOBOLA
1591–1657
Polish nobleman who devoted his life to God, cared for the suffering and died for his faith.
Feast Day: 21 May

JOHN KEMBLE
1599–1679
Jesuit priest and one of the Forty Martyrs of England and Wales.
Feast Day: 25 October

OLIVER PLUNKET
1625–81
Jesuit archbishop of Armagh. His charm won the grudging admiration of Irish Protestants, but English overlords dragged him to Newgate, London, tried him for high treason, and executed him.
Feast Day: 1 July

CLAUDE DE LA COLOMBIÈRE
1641–82
French Jesuit imprisoned in England as a Catholic. He was saved by Louis XIV of France, but he died soon after.
Feast Day: 15 February

MARGARET MARY ALACOQUE
1647–90
Entered the Visitation convent at Paray-le-Monial, where she revived the medieval cult of devotion to the Sacred Heart of Jesus.
Feast Day: 17 October

GREGORIO BARBARIGO
1625–97
Priest who founded a seminary, set up printing presses and tried to reconcile Eastern Orthodox and Roman Catholic Churches.
Feast Day: 18 June

JOSEPH ORIOL
1650–1702
A popular ascetic priest. It is said he saw the Virgin as he lay dying.
Feast Day: 23 March

JOSEPH TOMASI
1649–1713
Much-loved scholar and teacher, known as "the prince of liturgists".
Feast Day: 1 January

FRANCIS DE GIROLAMO
1642–1716
A Jesuit who preached in the docks and slums of Naples.
Feast Day: 11 May

JOHN BAPTIST ROSSI
1698–1764
Preached to and cared for beggars, prisoners and prostitutes in Rome.
Feast Day: 23 May

JULIE BILLIART
1751–1816
Co-founder of the Institute of the Sisters of Notre Dame, dedicated to teaching children.
Feast Day: 8 April

VINCENT STRAMBI
1745–1824
Bishop who improved education of priests. Exiled for refusing to take an oath of allegiance to Napoleon.
Feast Day: 25 September

MARCELLIN CHAMPAGNAT
died 1840
Born a peasant, he was known for his zeal for education and schools.
Feast Day: 6 June

Above Many missionaries, including Theophane Vénard, were martyred in Vietnam in the 19th century (Indo-Chinese School, 1838).

PETER CHANEL
1803–41
An early member of the Society of Mary, he was sent as a missionary to the French territory of Futuna, where he was martyred.
Feast Day: 28 April

VINCENT PALLOTTI
1795–1850
Founded the Society of Catholic Apostolate and later the Pallotine Missionary Sisters, which encouraged membership of lay men and women. His mission is now found throughout the Catholic world.
Feast Day: 22 January

PHILIPPINE DUCHESNE
1769–1852
Born in Grenoble, she established schools for Native American children in Louisiana and Missouri.
Feast Day: 17 November

JOSEPH CAFASSO
1811–60
Ministered to young priests, prisoners and condemned men, and established an institute for boys.
Feast Day: 23 June

JOHN NEUMANN
1811–60
Bishop of Philadelphia. Supervised the building of 100 churches and 80 schools and wrote several texts.
Feast Day: 5 January

THEOPHANE VÉNARD
1829–61
One of the named Martyrs of Vietnam, he was held in a bamboo cage before being beheaded.
Feast Day: 2 February

MARY ROSE MOLAS Y VALLVE
1815–76
Founded the Sisters of Our Lady of Consolation to serve the needs of deprived children.
Feast Day: 11 June

Above A woman prays in the Maronite church of St Sharbel in Lebanon.

TERESA OF JESUS JORNET Y IBARS
1843–97
Founded the Little Sisters of the Poor in 1872. She showed particular sympathy for the elderly.
Feast Day: 26 August

SHARBEL THE MARONITE
1828–98
A Lebanese, he joined Our Lady of Mayfug monastery before becoming a hermit. Miracles occurred after his death.
Feast Day: 24 December

MARIA GORETTI
1890–1902
A youth tried to rape the 12-year-old Maria. When she fought back, he stabbed her. She died the next day, having forgiven her attacker.
Feast Day: 6 July

LEOPOLD MANDIC
1866–1942
Born in Croatia, he was ordained a Capuchin Franciscan and ministered in Padua for 40 years. He showed great compassion as a spiritual adviser and confessor.
Feast Day: 12 May

FG

Above St Hugo of Grenoble in the Refectory of the Carthusians.

HI

JK

Above St Cuthbert.

Above St Vincent de Paul.

Created for Hermes House by Toucan Books Limited.

Publisher: Joanna Lorenz
Editorial Director: Helen Sudell
Managing Director: Ellen Dupont
Editors: Malcolm Day, Anne McDowall
Project Manager: Hannah Bowen
Project Assistant: Amy Smith
Designer: Elizabeth Healey
Picture Researcher: Debra Weatherley
Proofreaders: Marion Dent and Catherine Best
Indexer: Michael Dent

ETHICAL TRADING POLICY
Because of our ongoing ecological investment programme, you, as our customer, can have the pleasure and reassurance of knowing that a tree is being cultivated on your behalf to naturally replace the materials used to make the book you are holding.
For further information about this scheme, go to www.annesspublishing.com/trees

A CIP catalogue record for this book is available from the British Library.

PUBLISHER'S NOTE
Although the advice and information in this book are believed to be accurate and true at the time of going to press, neither the authors nor the publisher can accept any legal responsibility or liability for any errors or omissions that may be made.

PICTURE CREDITS: akg-images front cover tl, back cover bl, 15b, 27t, 28b, 30b, 31t, 32b, 51b, 66t, 71b, 88t and b, 91b, 92t and b, 97m, 106t, 117b, 129b, 133t, 140t and b, 149, 165bm, 170b, 171t, 183t, 184l, 185tr, 216b, 225bl, 226t, 235t, 236t, 245, /Amelot 251b, /Orsi Battaglini 134b, /British Library 11b, 49t, 83l, 90r, 100t, 142t, 143b, 185b, /Cameraphoto 34b, 36t, 37, 50bl, 56l, 61t, 102t, 105, 107t, 161b, 203t, /Church S Maria, Mater Domini/Cameraphoto front cover ml, /Hervé Champollion 220b, 227t, /Gérard Degeorge 6b, /Stefan Diller 19, /Jean-Paul Dumontier 59t, 84b, 243l and r, /Electa front cover tml, back cover bml, 51t, 62b, 64b, 91tl, 109t, 249tr, /Galleria Franchetti, Venice/Cameraphoto front cover tmr, back cover bmr, /Hilbich 24t, 86t, /Andrea Jemolo 36b, 138b, /Kunstsammlung Böttcherstraße 67t, /Tristan Lafranchis 173l, /Erich Lessing front flap, 3t and b, 7, 9t, 12t, 23tl and b, 28t, 46b, 47t, 57b, 59b, 61b, 65t, 68b, 74b, 76t, 78t, 82b, 84t, 101b, 172l, 181bl, 224t, 225br, 242, 244, /Paul M.R. Maeyaert 23tr, /Joseph Martin 112r, /Gilles Mermet 249tl, /James Morris 69t, 183b, /Musee du Louvre, Paris front cover tm, back cover bm, /Nimatallah 155tr, 187t, 247, /Pirozzi 97t, 130b, 164b, 179, /Rabatti-Domingie 21, 44t, 57tl, 65br, 89b, 137br, 256, /Jürgen Raible 185tl, /Gerhard Ruf 90m, /Sambraus 29, /Sotheby's 246, /Michael Teller 128t, /Ullstein Bild 214t, /Yvan Travert 95b, **Alamy** /Peter Adams Photography 227br, /Arkreligion.com 192b, /Cubo Images Sri 210b, 231t, /Julio Etchart 190t, /Eye35.com 224b, /Eddie Gerald 204b, /Barbara Gonget/G&B Images 221t, /Image & Stories 225t, /Images of Africa Photobank 222t, /Interfoto Pressebildagentur 210t, /Andre Jenny 211b, /William S Kuta 229b, 238b, /Mary Evans Picture Library 216t, 237t, 240t, /Northwind Picture Archives 207b, **ArkReligion.com** 188t, /Agence Ciric back flap, 215tl, tr and b, /Tibor Bognar 217t, 234t, 239b, /Richard Powers 228b, /John Randall 223t, /Helene Rogers 221b, **The Art Archive/Gianni Dagli Orti** 80bl, 227bl, 233b, /Armenian Museum Isfahan 17, /Chapelle de la Colombiere 192t, /Collection Antonovich 233t, /Domenica del Corriere 223b, /Eglise Saint Laurent Paris 195m, /Missions Etrangeres Paris 30t, 205t, /Museo della Civilta Romana, Rome 87t, /Museo Nacional Bogota 31bl, /Santuario San Gerardo Maiella Materdomini 206t, /St Julian Cathedral Le Mans 80t, **The Bridgeman Art Library** spine b, 13r, 16b, 33b, 41r, 70b, 78b, 79t, 82t, 118t, 137tr, 142b, 148t, 161t, 167bl, 168l and r, 182, 188b, 199t, 204t, 209b, 217b, 222b, 232bl, /Agnew's, London 189t, /Alte Pinakothek, Munich 125t, /Archivo Capitular, Spain 159br, /Art Museum of Estonia, Tallinn 79b, /Ashmolean Museum, University of Oxford back cover tl, 94t, /The Barnes Foundation, Pennsylvania 153t, /Biblioteca Nazionale, Turin 13l, /Bibliotheque Mazarine, Paris t,

/Bibliotheque Municipale, Avranches 122r, /Bibliotheque Nationale, Paris 101t, 200b, /Bibliotheque de L'Arsenal, Paris 12b, /Bibliotheque de L'Institut de France, Paris 190b, /Bibliotheque Les Fontaines, Chantilly 204m, /Bibliotheque Royale de Belgique, Brussels 155b, /Bonhams, London 26t, 172t, 228t, /British Library Board 24b, 116t, /British Library, London 122l, 127t, 159t, 254, /Cheltenham Art Gallery and Museums, Gloucestershire 118b, /Christie's Images 38b, /Church of Notre-Dame-de-Bonne-Nouvelle, Paris 115b, /Collection of the New York Historical Society 207t, /Duomo, Sicily 95t, 103t, /Eglise Saint-Louis-en-L'Ile, Paris 189b, /Fitzwilliam Museum, University of Cambridge 180b, /Werner Foreman back cover tr, /Galleria degli Uffizi, Florence 144b, /Galleria Nazionale delle Marche, Urbino 153b, /Groeningemuseum, Bruges 113t, /Guildhall Library, London 87b, /Hamburger Kunsthalle, Hamburg 45br, /Held Collection 196t, /Hermitage, St. Petersburg 5b, 146t, 156b, /His Grace the Duke of Norfolk, Arundel Castle 163t, 250, /Kremlin Museums, Moscow 72t, /Kunsthistorisches Museum, Vienna 53bl, /Lambeth Palace Library, London 201 t, /Lobkowicz Palace, Prague Castle, Czech Republic 131t, /Louvre, Paris 94br, 104t, 196b, /Magyar Nemzeti Galeria, Budapest 134t, /Missions Estrangeres, Paris 205b, /Musee Bonnat, Bayonne 194t, 255, /Musee des Beaux-Arts, Caen 172s, /Musee des Beaux-Arts, Marseille 50br, 154, 155tl, /Musee des Beaux-Arts, Orleans 167t, /Musee Conde, Chantilly 77t, 123b, 126b, 139b, /Musee de la Ville de Paris 208b, /Musee de l'Oeuvre de Notre Dame, Strasbourg 48, /Musee Guimet, Paris 178b, /Musee Jacquemart-Andre, Paris front cover bl, 81b, /Museo Catedralicio, Castellon 86b, /Museo de Santa Cruz, Toledo 191t, /Museum of History, Moscow 248, /Museumslandschaft Hessen Kassel 112l, /Nationalgalerie, SMPK, Berlin 129t, /National Museum of Ancient Art, Lisbon 15t, /Orihuela Cathedral Museum, Spain 158, /Palazzo Ducale, Venice 75b, /Palazzo Pitti, Florence 170t, 201b, /Piccolomini Library, Siena 18t, /Regional Art Museum, Kaluga 156t, /Richard and Kailas Icons, London 6tl and tr, 16tl, /Roy Miles Fine Paintings 110b, /Samuel Courtauld Trust, Courtauld Institute of Art Gallery 159bl, 249b, /San Diago Museum of Artback cover tm, 150l, /Sant'Apollinare Nuovo, Ravenna 67b, /Sir Geoffrey Keynes Collection, Cambridgeshire 55, /South West Museum, California 31br, /Staatliche Kunstsammlungen, Dresden 160t, /Universitatsbibliothek, Heidelberg 119, /Ken Welsh 77b, 202b, 208t, **Corbis** 34t, 72b, 198t, /Alinari Archives 53t, 73b, 104b, /Araldo de Luca 125b, 176b, 193t, /Archivo Iconografico, S.A. back cover tmr, 52, 70t, 96tl, 102b, 114, 117m, 124t, 136b, 141, 157, 167br,

181t, 197bl, 253, /The Art Archive 49b, 69b, 76b, 94bc, 120t, 135t, 206b, /Arte & Immagini srl 4, 136t, 150r, 169b, /Atlantide Phototravel 186t, /Austrian Archives 128b, /Bettmann 91tr, 146m, 171b, 211t, 214m, 229t, 235b, 236b, 240b, /Jonathan Blair 99t and b, /Brooklyn Museum 175t, /Burstein Collection 151, /Fablan Cevallos front cover tr, back cover br, /Christie's Images 60b, 68t, 219b, /Elio Ciol spine t, 14b, 56r, 60t, 71t, 89t, 96tr, 106b, 146b, 148b, 152t, /Geoffrey Clements 162b, /Richard A Cooke 35bl, /Pablo Corral V 230t and b, /Richard Cummins 187b, /Gianni Dagli Orti 74t, 113b, 195b, /Araldo de Luca 110t, /Leonard de Selva 75t, /EPA 38t, /Fine Art Photographic Library 5t, 127b, /Werner Forman 115t, /The Gallery Collection 40, 42b, 57t, 147r, 165br, 173r, 177b, 194b, /Gianni Giansanti 100b, /Christian Guy/Hemis 202t, /Lars Halbauer/dpa 231b, /Jon Hicks 16tr, /Historical Picture Archive 85b, 109b, /Hulton-Deutsch Collection 199b, /Andrea Jemolo 145t, /Krause Johansen 174, /Mimmo Jodice 62t, 103b, /David Lees 8, 123t, /Danny Lehman 39, /Massimo Listri 1, 98b, 180t, /Francis G Mayer 111bl, /The National Gallery Collection; by kind permission of the Trustees of the National Gallery, London 2, 42t, 50t, 54t and b, 63, 108b, 121t, 147bl, /Michael Nicholson 25, 115rm, /Fred de Noyelle /Godong 232t, /Hamish Park 131b, /José F. Poblete 130r, /Gérard Rancinan/Sygma 220r, /Vittoriano Rastelli 121b, /Reuters 18b, 234b, 239t, /New York Historical Society 35t, /Joel W Rogers 107b, /Bob Sacha 213b /Marcelo Sayao/epa 212t, /Sean Sexton Collection 237b, /Stapleton Collection 138t, /Summerfield Press 10b, 43, 145b, /Sygma 35br, /Sandro Vannini 65bl, 169r, /Nik Wheeler 33t, /Roger Wood 111m, **Getty** 26b, 124b, 132, 144t, 178t, 238t, 241b, /AFP 32t, 214b, 218b, 232br, 251t, /Oliver Benn 27bl, /Bridgeman Art Library 11t, 20b, 108t, 137tl, 143t, /Byzantine 165bl, /Matthias Grunewald back cover tml, 164t, /Hulton Archive 47b, 83r, 93, 162t, 175b, 176t, 181br, 197br, 226b, /Francisco Jose de Goya y Lucientes 177t, /Yannick Le Gal 203b, /Lorenzo Lotto 152b, /Petr Mikhailovich Shamshin 165t, /Jim Richardson 116b, /Dante Gabriel Rossetti front cover br, 166, /Time & Life Pictures 85t, /Travel Ink 163b, /Paolo Uccello 160b, /Vatican Museums and Galleries/Pietro Perugino 120b, **Andrew Leaney** 133b, **Mary Evans Picture Library** /Interfoto 219t, **Demetrius Matthiosi** 6tm, **Photo12.com** 195t, /Hachédé 193b, 198b, /Oronoz 191b, 241t, **SCALA, Florence** 209t, **Shutterstock** 186b, 200t, **Sonia Halliday Photographs** 10t, 20t, 44b, 45t and bl, 46t, 53br, 58t and b, 64t, 66b, 73t, 80br, 81t, 97b, 98t, 117t, 135b, 137bl, 139t, 184r, /Bibliotheque Nationale, Paris 126t, 197t, /F.H.C. Birch 22t, /Polly Buston 22b, **Topfoto.co.uk** 218t.